Rhetoric:

A Tradition in Transition

Donald C. Bryant

RHETORIC:

A TRADITION

IN TRANSITION

In Honor of
DONALD C. BRYANT
with a reprinting of his "Rhetoric:
Its Functions and Scope" and " 'Rhetoric
Its Functions and Scope' Rediviva"

EDITED BY
WALTER R. FISHER

MICHIGAN STATE UNIVERSITY PRESS
1974

★
★
★
★
★

Contents

About the Contributors

John P. Bakke, Ph.D. 1966, University of Iowa
Professor of Rhetoric and Communication Arts
Memphis State University

Samuel L. Becker, Ph.D. 1953, University of Iowa
Professor of Speech and Dramatic Art
University of Iowa

Lloyd F. Bitzer, Ph.D. 1962, University of Iowa
Professor of Communication Arts
University of Wisconsin

John Waite Bowers, Ph.D. 1962, University of Iowa
Professor and Director of Communication Research Laboratory
Department of Speech and Dramatic Art
University of Iowa

Oscar Brownstein, Ph.D. 1963, University of Iowa
Professor of Speech and Dramatic Art
University of Iowa

Donald C. Bryant, Ph.D. 1937, Cornell University
Emeritus Professor of Speech and Dramatic Art
University of Iowa

Gary L. Cronkhite, Ph.D. 1965, University of Iowa
Visiting Professor of Speech Communication
California State University, San José

Walter R. Fisher, Ph.D. 1960, University of Iowa
Professor of Speech Communication
University of Southern California

Bruce E. Gronbeck, Ph.D. 1970, University of Iowa
Associate Professor of Speech and Dramatic Art
University of Iowa

About the Contributors

Michael C. McGee, Ph.D. 1974, University of Iowa
Assistant Professor of Rhetoric and Communication Arts
Memphis State University

James Richard McNally, Ph.D. 1966, University of Iowa
Associate Professor of Rhetoric and Communication
State University of New York, Albany

Gerald R. Miller, Ph.D. 1961, University of Iowa
Professor of Communication
Michigan State University

Marie Hochmuth Nichols, Ph.D. 1945, University of Wisconsin
Professor of Speech
University of Illinois

Donovan J. Ochs, Ph.D. 1966, University of Iowa
Associate Professor of Speech and Rhetoric
University of Iowa

Robert E. Sanders, Ph.D. 1971, University of Iowa
Assistant Professor of Speech Communication
State University of New York, Albany

Karl R. Wallace, Ph.D. 1933, Cornell University
Late Professor of Speech (1968–73)
University of Massachusetts

Foreword

The resurgence of rhetorical studies in the twentieth century has had many causes. Chief among them has been the contribution of Cornell University in producing a distinguished succession of scholars committed to the highest standards of humane learning. Exemplary of these men is Donald C. Bryant, Carver Professor, Department of Speech and Dramatic Art, University of Iowa. In his teaching, research, publication, professional work, and involvement in public affairs, he has demonstrated erudition, a compelling regard for the best that men have thought, said, and done, and a compassionate concern for the welfare of all men. This collection of essays is meant to honor his presence and influence on all of us.

Between degrees—A.B. (1927), A.M. (1930), and Ph.D. (1937), at Cornell University—Professor Bryant taught high school history and mathematics in Ardsley, New York, and was instructor in English at New York State College for Teachers, Albany. After earning his Ph.D. degree, he moved to Washington University where he became Professor of English and, later, Department Chairman. In 1958, he began his brilliant career in the Department of Speech and Dramatic Art at the University of Iowa, where he served until his retirement in the spring of 1973.

Professor Bryant, a leader in his field in publication and professional achievement, has specialized in the historical and critical study of the late eighteenth century British Parliament with special attention to the speaking and writing of Edmund Burke. He has written at least eight books or monographs, numerous scholarly articles, and over two hundred reviews. Prominent among his works are: *Edmund Burke and His Literary Friends, The Rhetorical Idiom, Select British Speeches, Rhetorical Dimensions in Criticism,* and "Rhetoric: Its Functions and Scope," perhaps the most frequently reprinted essay in the field of speech communication in the last three decades. Professor Bryant's original essay is featured in this volume along with his "revisitation" of it; both were solicited without his knowledge of our editorial intent.

Professor Bryant served as editor of *The Quarterly Journal of Speech* from 1957–60, and as President of the Speech Communication Association in 1970. He has been a significant force in the National Council of Teachers of English and the newly formed Rhetoric Society. He also was President of the United Nations Association of Iowa City, 1969–70.

Along with the recorded accomplishment of Donald Bryant and the prior recognition he has won for distinguished scholarship and service, this collection of studies in his honor is further testimony to the major impact he has made on his field and upon his colleagues, students, and friends.

This project was initiated in conversations with Professor John Bakke in December 1967. It was decided that I would take principal responsibility for putting the collection together and that he and Professors Lloyd F. Bitzer and Gerald R. Miller would serve as editorial advisors. We solicited papers from Professor Bryant's close colleagues and students whose work he guided or strongly influenced. By the time the final essays were selected, a clear pattern, a theme, seemed to emerge—*a tradition in transition.*

Rhetorical study may be defined not only by the methodologies that it employs but also by the phenomenon it observes. That phenomenon is the suasory function of symbols. The tradition of rhetorical scholarship records an abiding interest in how and in what ways man uses and is used by symbols of inducement, how man's symbol-using affects personal and social decision-making, and shapes the hierarchy of values by which man guides his conduct.

Although rhetorical inquiry has been devoted to the examination of the various persuasive forms of discourse which have been dominant in different ages and cultures, rhetorical study has been fostered by an underlying regard for the dynamics by which symbols become inducing and for the personal, social, political, and cultural implications of inducement. Because symbolic inducement is one of man's most fundamental behaviors, its study has been as diverse as there are ways of studying man. Because the process involves men in particular and men in general, its study has philosophical, psychological, historical, social, and cultural dimensions. Because it involves symbols influencing behavior, the study has humanistic and behavioral aspects. And because men prize the art and sometimes fear its power, rhetorical study has had a prominent place in education and rhetorical practice has been a constant object of social and political criticism.

Rhetorical study should not be confused with those disciplines from which it has derived concepts or methodologies or with other forms of communication with which it is closely associated. Rhetorical study does not encompass all kinds and forms of communication. Its focus is a *function,* the suasory function of verbal and nonverbal symbols. The rhetorician's interest is not just the "linking" of sources with audiences by way of messages; it is not synonymous with the psycholinguists' interests in the grammar or mental processes of encoding and decoding; it is not the same as the literary or dramatic critic's concern for the aesthetic functions of symbols; it is not involved with animal or machine communication. The rhetorician's interest is knowledge and theory relating to human symbolic interactions that influence behavior.

It is important to recognize the relationship of rhetorical knowledge and rhetorical theory. Biographical, critical, literary-linguistic, and some philosophical inquiry leads to knowledge but not to theory. To a considerable extent rhetorical scholarship is productive of, and finds its end in, erudition. Such inquiry may presume or imply theory, but rhetorical study need not immediately contribute to theory building for it to have value. Such inquiry is necessary and desirable; it represents the work of rhetoricians in the mainstream of humane study. Rhetorical theory is a subspecies of rhetorical knowledge. It seeks rules which account for the generation, formulation, functions, and effects of symbolic inducement.

That the essays in this collection illustrate a transition in the tradition of rhetorical study raises the question: transition from what to what? The answer requires consideration of the major conceptions that have governed rhetorical theory and practice in critical historical periods. Although rhetoric is not, nor can it become, a science, at least in the way of the natural sciences, its evolution as an art can be paralleled with that of science. Just as the history of science marks revolutions based on investigations stemming from the paradigms of Ptolemy, Newton, and Einstein, so is the history of rhetorical art marked by theory, teaching, and criticism based on the thinking of Aristotle, Bacon, and Chaim Perelman or Kenneth Burke. Where the revolutions in science derive from different conceptions of the universe, the innovations in rhetoric are derived from radical changes in the conception of man or his society.

P. Albert Duhamel identified the specific factors that shape the development of rhetoric (in "The Function of Rhetoric as Effective Expression," *Journal of the History of Ideas,* June 1949). He wrote, "The content of the idea of 'rhetoric' . . . is dependent upon the epistemology, psychology, and the metaphysic of the system in which it occurs." The political nature of the "system" is also a vital factor. Thus, one may consider Aristotle's *Rhetoric* being the master statement on inducement based on the epistemology of deductive logic, "rationalist" psychology, and a (limited) democracy. His presuppositions were the foundation of Ciceronian and

Quintilian views of rhetoric. Aristotle's ideas *evolved* into a form and content adapted to Roman needs and demands.

After the so-called "Christianization" of rhetoric was concluded, the next master statement was that of Bacon, reflecting the epistemology of inductive logic, faculty psychology, and middle class influence on parliamentary power. Bacon's views evolved into the scientific rhetoric of Thomas Sprat on the one hand and the associational theory of George Campbell on the other.

Whether Chaim Perelman or Kenneth Burke has constructed a new "master statement" is an open question at this date. One can, however, perceive similarities in their presuppositions and perhaps a "new" model of man. Both reject formal logic as being adequate to account for rhetorical communication; both are influenced by contemporary psychology—Burke, especially by Freudian thinking; and both are concerned that communication be improved to preserve world order and humane values.

When we talk of transition, then, we refer to evidence of Renaissance and Reformation. The "chaos" discussed by Professor Becker in the lead essay of this collection points to such evidence. It is not the mere broadening of perspective, but the interaction of new perspectives that is the key. The use of behavioral methods of research is not in itself revolutionary; on the other hand, the underlying mechanistic, thermostatic model of man that it often presupposes is. Behavioral models used in communication study will always be subject to criticism and revision and even rejection as long as they do not fully accord with a conception that represents the fullness of man. These models need to recognize the biographical history of the subject, plus the constraints of situation. They should also require the assessment of messages according to what the best thinking—psychological, philosophical, rhetorical—indicates they must be in form, content, and presentation.

It is often argued that a need exists for a set of precise terms and specific questions to ask in the pursuit of rhetorical knowledge and theory. This is a reasonable contention up to the point where this demand would try to make rhetoric a science and up to the point where this would stifle rather than stimulate the creative thinking of young scholars. And it should also be noted that with the transition and adoption of new paradigms (underlying models of man), there naturally emerges an attempt to create a new grammar of rhetoric; and we are still in the process of codifying and labeling the reformed concepts of the twentieth century.

These general views, then, have led to the grouping of the essays in this book. All the essays are traditional in subject matter, because all of them are ultimately concerned with the question—how and in what ways man uses and is used by symbols of inducement. The essays, from Brownstein to Nichols, are also traditional forms of rhetorical scholarship, contributing mainly to rhetorical knowledge.

Clear evidence of transition is to be found in the studies of Becker, Bryant, Bitzer, Cronkhite, Miller, and Bowers and Sanders. In each of these essays, there are indications of broadening, refining, new methods of investigation, and a move toward a conception of man underlying rhetorical scholarship that departs from the dominance of the thinking of Aristotle and Bacon, a conception based on contemporary philosophy, psychology, and social science. These essays especially contribute to the reformation of rhetorical scholarship and, with the other essays, reflect the vitality of the tradition and the promise of its future significance and contribution.

I wish to thank my colleagues for their cooperation in producing this collection, and especially Professors Bakke, Bitzer, Miller, Becker, Gronbeck, and Douglas Ehninger for special editorial assistance. I would also like to express my appreciation to Mrs. Aileen Brothers, editorial consultant for the Michigan State University Press, for her many competent, helpful corrections and suggestions.

WALTER R. FISHER

INTRODUCTION

Rhetorical Scholarship in the Seventies

Samuel L. Becker

The state of rhetorical scholarship in the 1970s might be described most accurately as chaotic. In a sense, though, it is a productive chaos. The field is vacillating between humanism and behaviorism; it may be in a transitional state from one to the other; though, if so, it is not clear which is the initial and which the terminal state or whether the field is moving toward some fresh amalgam of the two modes of thought. This chaotic state creates discomfort among many in the field, but it may account for the wealth of exciting rhetorical research increasingly appearing in journals and monographs. It clearly accounts for the large amount of questioning and self-examination which manifest themselves in publications such as *Conceptual Frontiers in Speech-Communication*[1] and *The Prospect of Rhetoric.*[2]

This paper isolates and discusses what I see as the key issues in the debate about the future of rhetorical studies, especially as these issues are reflected in the papers in the present volume.

One Paradigm or Many?

In *The Structure of Scientific Revolutions,* Thomas S. Kuhn's major thesis is that any science needs a paradigm, "some accepted examples of actual scientific practice—examples which include law, theory, application, and instrumentation together—[which] provide models from which spring particular coherent traditions of scientific research."[3] Kuhn believes that a scientific community must agree upon a single paradigm so that it can be free from the need to constantly re-examine its first principles, hence free to concentrate upon the solution of the problems which are its goal. A major question facing the rhetorical scholar is whether Kuhn's generalizations are valid and, more to the point, whether they are valid for rhetoric. Kuhn notes, for example, that none of the social sciences yet has probably acquired a paradigm of the sort that he defines and that nonscientific fields, at least after a certain point, progress in a way different than science. He suggests that we need to study communities of scholars in these other fields in order to discover the way in which they progress.[4]

Even if we define paradigm differently than Kuhn does, deleting the notion of law and instrumentation in the scientific sense, there is clearly no single paradigm which dominates this field today, nor has it ever; our history has been marked by an alternation between periods of dominant and competing paradigms. Competing paradigms characterize contemporary rhetoric, as the essays in this volume demonstrate.

Though the scientific study of communication has played a role in rhetoric from its earliest days, that role has been a subordinate one. The observations and experiments of the communication scholar have answered questions, tested hypotheses, and explored theories which grew out of the paradigms of the humanistic rhetorician. William James, John Watson, Clark Hull, Kurt Lewin, Edward Tolman, and other behavioral scientists influenced the rhetorician, but their influence was relatively trivial until recent times. They contributed to the answers which the rhetorician sought and the methods by which he sought the answers; they did not contribute to the fundamental questions which the rhetorician perceived and posed. To put this in Kuhn's terms, they did not alter the paradigm which dominated rhetorical studies; until recently, they served almost exclusively a "prerhetorical function" for our field.[5] Now, though behavioral scientists continue to play this role, we also find the beginnings of a new function, the creation of new paradigms from which different questions flow. This difference is seen if one compares the Bowers and Sanders' study in this book with that of Miller. The question posed by the former scholars grew out of the practice and theory of the humanistic rhetorical scholar. The effects of paradox have been a source of speculation among critics for a long time; Bowers and Sanders designed a study to test some of those effects. Miller, on the other hand, has asked a question which had little probability of occurring to the humanistic rhetorical scholar. The rhetorician has traditionally been concerned with the ways in which man influences and is influenced by others; Miller, approaching persuasion with a new paradigm, has focused on a different kind of question, how man persuades himself.

This ambivalence between rhetoric as humanistic study and rhetoric as social science raises many questions. A major one is whether rhetoric is to be a cumulative or an evolutionary (perhaps even revolutionary) discipline. Nichols notes this distinction when she contrasts science's destruction of its past with the "humane tradition in rhetoric [which] destroys neither its past theory nor its past critical practices. Aristotle lives on at the same time as does Donald Bryant."[6] Is this to be a discipline which accumulates theories so that its progress is marked by a continual expansion of the theoretical statements perceived as valid and available for use as Nichols suggests? Or is it to be a discipline which seeks, whether successfully or not, a rhetorical theory which supersedes and, hence, makes unnecessary those theoretical statements which preceded it? In developing theory, are we to search for ways to explain a wider range of communication phenomena *more* adequately, or are we to search for ways to explain them *differently* or in ways that provide different *kinds* of insight?

We see these fundamentally different positions represented in this volume by those who are concerned largely with *reinterpreting* existing theory on the one hand and by those who are concerned largely with *revising* or *replacing* existing theory on the other. This difference is analogous to the difference in methods that we have for keeping the United States Constitution viable for the present. We can change the Constitution through reinterpretation by the Supreme Court (deciding that "separate but equal" is unconstitutional, even though an earlier Court had decided that it was constitutional) or through Constitutional amendment (granting suffrage to eighteen-year-olds). Wallace, Ochs, and McNally in this volume are representative of the former approach, though their primary purpose is clarification or illumination of the theoretical statements considered. Brownstein, on the other hand, is moving toward the latter approach in that he not only reinterprets but also creates what he terms a "sympathetic extrapolation" or an addition to the theory.

To a very large extent, though not universally, this division between reinterpreting and revising is between those who study descriptive or prescriptive theories and those who study explanatory theories. There is also an historical dimension to this distinction: it is the rare rhetorician who would talk of revising or even refining Quintilian; it is common, on the other hand, even expected, for rhetoricians to talk about refining or replacing Osgood. To some degree, this difference between interpretation and revision or replacement is a function of the specificity of the theories involved. The more specific a theory, the more it demands revision or replacement with time and knowledge. The more general a theory, the more it demands interpretation. Leon Festinger's theory of cognitive dissonance, for example, is more general than Charles Osgood's congruity hypothesis, but less general than Aristotle's rhetorical theory. Thus, Festinger needs both revision and interpretation, whereas one does not think of revising or replacing Aristotle or of interpreting or reinterpreting Osgood.[7]

There is another sign that the field of rhetoric may be in a transitional state. The trend toward greater specialization within all disciplines, including ours, has been recognized for some time, and strongly attacked and defended. Almost beneath the cover of this crossfire, there has been a contrary trend going on virtually unobserved, one which will probably have a greater impact on rhetorical studies in the seventies than the trend toward specialization has or will have. This is the trend toward the virtual elimination of distinctions among disciplines within the humanities and among disciplines within the social sciences. The problems being agitated, the methods for attacking them, and the paradigm and theories which guide thought are decreasingly distinguishable among the humanistic disciplines, including the historical and critical study of rhetoric. The same can be said for the various behavioral science disciplines, including the behavioral study of rhetoric. This trend has been accelerated, if not initiated, by scholars such as Donald Bryant who moves as easily among historians, literary scholars, and philosophers as he does among rhetoricians. The result is that the papers by Wallace, Brownstein, Bakke, Nichols, Gronbeck, Ochs, and McNally may have more in common with some of the work of philosophers, historians, and classicists than they do with that of Cronkhite, Miller, Bowers, and Sanders, while the latter may be more closely allied to the scholarly work being carried on by social psychologists, sociologists, and political scientists.

This apparent divergence of the humanists and behavioral scientists among us, this conflict between a scientific and an historical/critical paradigm, is occurring at the same time as another type of divergence. One of the characteristics by which one may distinguish between some of the paradigms for rhetorical study is what the scholars following a particular paradigm perceive as "figure" and what as "ground." For some, the focus is upon the discourse—analysis of it in terms of the situation, the source or sources of the discourse, the receivers, and their responses. Hence, the discourse is the figure and all the rest is ground. For other scholars, the responses of receivers (attitudes, actions, and so on) comprise the figure to be explained and all the remainder is the ground, including the discourse. In a sense, Bitzer is suggesting that the situation be the figure, with both discourse and responses the ground. Bryant, in *Rhetorical Dimensions in Criticism,* makes a distinction according to function "between the treatment of artifacts as significant primarily for what they *are* and the treatment of them as primarily significant for what they *do.*[8] For Bryant, the figure in both cases is the discourse; the external effects are of only tangential interest. Such is not the case for all rhetorical critics and theorists of the seventies; hence, the figure/ground ambivalence that can be observed in much of contemporary rhetorical criticism.

Context

That rhetoric and rhetoricans must consider the context in which discourse occurs has been consistently recognized by scholars. The interesting debate of the past decade—and one which will undoubtedly continue through the seventies—is that concerning the conception of context which is most relevant and fruitful. The increased focus on the context of communication events has been signaled most clearly by Bitzer's paper in this volume, "The Rhetorical Situation." Bitzer conceives of context as the "complex of persons, events, objects, and relations presenting an actual or potential exigency which can be completely or partially removed if discourse, introduced into the situation, can so constrain human decisions or action as to bring about the significant modification of the exigency." He sees three constituents of any rhetorical situation which must exist prior to the creation and presentation of discourse: the *exigency,* "the *audience* to be constrained in decision and action, and the *constraints* which influence the rhetor and can be brought to bear upon the audience."[9] Brownstein, on the other hand, sees the context of rhetoric as debate: "the individual speech is but a fragment of a dialogue and cannot be understood apart from the dialogue."[10] I have taken the position elsewhere that the relevant context, if we are to understand rhetorical processes, includes all the elements of information in an individual's environment which interact with the elements in the message on which the scholar is focusing.[11]

What rhetoricians concerned seriously with context seem to be moving toward is a view closely akin to that of the systems theorist. That is to say, there appears to be not only a decreasing concern with examining speeches or other messages in isolation (even assuming such to be possible), but correspondingly an increasing interest in how the system (whether a small group, a legislative body, a community, or some other larger social system) maintains itself and especially the role of communication in that maintenance. The result is that some rhetoricians are beginning to focus upon the structure of the system and the functions which communication serves within that structure, rather than focusing upon discrete messages or sets of messages and the effects which they have.[12]

Though all rhetoricians who are thus analyzing context may appear to be moving in parallel or even converging paths, in fact they are not. The key difference provides another example of the figure and ground distinction: it is whether the context is to be used as an aid or basis for understanding and judging the discourse, or whether it is to be viewed as an inseparable part of the cloth in which discourse forms but part of the thread.

In this volume, the Bakke and McGee papers best exemplify the Bitzer conception. McGee, concerned with the effect of context on the way in which discourse functions, demonstrates that a closed society of the sort found in England in the eighteenth century creates different rhetorical exigencies and constraints than found in an open society such as England or the United States today. Bakke, focusing on a more limited problem, analyzes the rhetorical exigency that demanded that someone support the dismissal of officials of the West Indian Company and the establishment of a company accountable to Parliament. Even more important, Bakke demonstrates, at least indirectly, that Burke's discourse on this matter itself became part of the context which created a rhetorical exigency for Pitt and smoothed the way for parliamentary passage of Pitt's bill.

Gronbeck's paper, on the other hand, is based upon a conception of context more closely aligned to that of Aristotle via Brownstein than to that of Bitzer. He is less concerned with rhetorical exigencies than with explicating the debate in order to better understand Burke's role.

Though rhetoricians have not yet developed methods for full-blown systems analyses, or what I term mosaic analyses, there have been elements of such analyses in the best rhetorical studies for a number of decades, including the Bakke and Gronbeck studies in this volume. This trend toward analyzing discourse in terms of *function*, rather than *effect*, will undoubtedly accelerate in the seventies.

Scope

One of the important points of dispute in this period of competing paradigms is the kind and scope of the phenomena which we study or about which we theorize. What are the critical objects? Traditionally, of course, they have been informative and persuasive discourse. The past decade has witnessed an increasing press for expansion of what are considered legitimate objects for rhetorical analysis. This press is occurring along various dimensions. One of the less-heralded of these involves the kinds of discourse which fall within the purview of the rhetorician. Some critics suggest that we include communication which has ends other than information or persuasion, such as "socialization, self-discovery, and the maintenance of a group, or the promotion of a movement."[13] Rhetorical analyses of such discourse are not new, but it appears now that they will become increasingly accepted during the seventies as legitimate responsibilities of our field.

We also seem reasonably agreed today that rhetorical studies must cope with questions involving more than single speeches if we are to understand complex communication processes. However, we are not agreed on how far beyond the single speech we can go or should go before we are outside the realm of rhetorical studies. A decade or two ago some of us might have been concerned about whether written as well as oral discourse was properly within the domain of rhetorical studies; today we are concerned about whether nondiscursive events, events which only metaphorically can be labeled discourse, can fruitfully be considered rhetorical. We are uncertain whether to agree with Douglas Ehninger that rhetoric is "that discipline which studies all of the ways in which men may influence each other's thinking and behavior through the strategic use of symbols."[14] We are even more uncertain about whether to agree with those who advocate the inclusion not only of instances of influence through *symbols*, but also instances of influence through any event or object with symbolic *value*. The extremes of these positions are probably best stated by John Waite Bowers and Donovan Ochs in *The Rhetoric of Agitation and Control* and by Newton

Garver in his review of that work and Marie Nichols in this volume. Bowers and Ochs define rhetoric as "the rationale of instrumental, symbolic behavior," and make the focus of their rhetorical analysis of agitational situations the "instrumental, symbolic events that are largely nonverbal, or extraverbal."[15] Nichols refuses to accept this enlargement of the scope of rhetoric: "Rhetoric is a verbal art; . . . it does not include extra-linguistic symbols."[16] Garver says "We expect a book on rhetoric to be a book about language." He criticizes the Bowers and Ochs' work because the authors divorce it "from the study of patterns and forms and uses of language as such." He concludes that, "while it is true that the science of rhetoric could use dramatic revitalization, that goal will not be achieved by simply confusing it with sociology."[17] In his second paper in the present collection, Donald Bryant also questions the fruitfulness of enlarging the scope of rhetoric beyond the confines of what might reasonably be termed discourse. He labels as "reckless" the statement of the Rhetorical Criticism Committee of the 1970 National Conference on Rhetoric that the focus of rhetorical study be "any human act, process, product, or artifact which, in the critic's view, may formulate, sustain, or modify attention, perceptions, attitudes, or behavior." Like Nichols, Bryant is concerned that we not join together such diverse phenomena as "pelting policemen with feces, lying down in front of army buses, editorializing in the *Chicago Tribune,* and toasting the Chinese hosts in the Great Hall of the People." He fears that the principles needed for covering them will "need to be stated so broadly and vaguely as to be unserviceable for the illumination or generation of constructive distinctions."[18] On the other hand, Robert L. Scott and Donald K. Smith justify the inclusion of these various phenomena, such as confrontations, with the argument that the "confrontation, . . . as diverse as its manifestations may be, is inherently symbolic. The act carries a message. It dissolves the lines between marches, sit-ins, demonstrations, acts of physical violence, and aggressive discourse. In this way it informs us of the essential nature of discourse itself as human action."[19]

Though the views of Garver and Nichols are undoubtedly irreconcilable with those of Bowers and Ochs, the bulk of rhetoricians are probably much closer together on this issue than their statements might indicate. Bryant and other serious scholars who question the current press for extensive enlargement of the critical object for rhetorical analysis are not saying that such phenomena as sit-ins, the slashing of tires, and the burning of flags should not be considered by the rhetorician. They are saying rather that these should be considered as part of the context rather than the focus of rhetorical study· these phenomena are ground and not figure. This particular figure-ground issue is certain to continue to be debated throughout the seventies. More important in its resolution than the debate, though, will be our observation of the usefulness of the research produced by those proposing this enlargement of the concept of the rhetorical object. As James Andrews has noted, "as the scope of criticism expands, one engaged in such a pursuit begins to feel a kinship with Aladdin as he uncorked the magic lamp; how does one cope with such an enormous and perhaps unfathomable phenomenon as a jinni or a communication event?"[20] Whether we will find *fruitful* ways to cope with it is still an open question.

If we accept some broader scope for rhetorical studies, we will also make even more important than it already is the question of whether we should expect the different forms or functions of communication to operate by a fundamentally common set of principles. That is to say, can we assume that a reasonable end of our studies is *a* rhetorical theory—or is our end a *set* of theories: a rhetoric of confrontations, a rhetoric of the bar, a rhetoric of sex, a rhetoric of instruction?[21] The assumption that we make here will shape our approach to communication and the criticism and theory which emerge.

Method

Another observable trend in much of the rhetorical study of the seventies, which should accelerate as the decade passes, is an increase in the self-consciousness with which the rhetorician carries out his research. It is especially noticeable in this collection of papers in McGee's focus on the dependent variables or potential effects whose assumption guides studies of different types of rhetorical situations. It is also evident in Bowers and Sanders' detailed analysis of the social judgment test which they devised, and Miller's sensitivity to the critical difference between his study's underlying paradigm and that of most rhetorical studies.

This trend toward self-consciousness manifested itself in the last decade in a debate about the "best" or "most appropriate" or "most fruitful" research methods for the scholar of rhetoric. With the possible exception of Nichols' paper, the present volume and other signs indicate that that general question is decreasingly at issue, that the development of rhetorical theory demands a variety of methods. This conclusion is well stated by Carroll C. Arnold:

> Virtually every question [about human communication] demands many different kinds of methods of study to do the work. On virtually *no* question of importance about communication will any *one* research style suffice to answer the basic issues. To differentiate ourselves by research styles is to emphasize *form* over content and to put *means* above theory in research. In the world of communication, the rhetorical is a territory; and *it* cannot be understood by a single method of probing.[22]

Relevance

Yet another issue that agitated rhetoricians during the past decade is that of relevance. This issue has carried over into the seventies, but is being dealt with in more sophisticated ways. In the sixties, the question was whether to carry on with one's scholarship or get into the streets and act. If one's answer was the former, there was pressure to make the focus of one's study those who were acting or, at the minimum, other contemporary communication so that, presumably, the results would be "relevant." In the seventies, the press for relevance continues, but there appears to be increasing recognition—or, perhaps, rerecognition—of the fact that nothing is more relevant or useful than a good theory and that a theory that is valid for contemporary communication does not necessarily develop solely from study of contemporary communication. As a result of this press, the seventies should be witness to a spurt in the development of fresh theoretical statements about rhetorical processes and in the refinement of existing statements.

Conclusion

For rhetoricians, this is clearly a time to test new paradigms, but there is little or no sign of our relinquishing the old ones. We appear to be testing and comparing, searching for common ground, which seems to point to the conclusion that the seventies comprise a transitional period for rhetoric that will eventuate in the acceptance of a common paradigm. On the other hand, an examination of our history indicates that rhetoric has harbored these competing paradigms virtually from the inception of the field. With the exception of those periods such as the Renaissance when rhetoric went wholly over to the humanities, we have been both a humanistic discipline and a behavioral science. Even within each of these modes of inquiry rhetoricians have followed, and continue to follow, multiple paradigms. This "transitional" state appears not to be very transitory.

The absence of a common paradigm has created and will continue to create problems for our field. The questions that we select for study and, hence, the information that we gather are too much dependent upon chance. Without a common paradigm we have no good basis for determining that one question is more important than another or that one fact is more relevant than others. As we argue about the scope of rhetoric, the lack of a common paradigm leaves us without a criterion to use in resolving the disagreement. Hence, the argument seems to revolve solely about the question of what we *choose* to include within the definition of rhetoric, rather than what *must* be included for the kinds of explanations or the kinds of generalizations which we seek. Without a common paradigm, we have no basis for agreement on the answers to questions about rhetorical study such as those raised in this volume by Bryant, Bitzer, Miller, Cronkhite, and Nichols.

The arguments for agreement on a paradigm appear overwhelming—until one considers the nature and nurture of scholars and the complexity of the phenomena which must fall within the province of rhetorical study. It is inconceivable in the 1970s that a single paradigm can serve to generate questions and define the constraints within which questions will be answered well for all of the rhetorical problems with which we must cope. Even more important, at this point in time—and perhaps for all time—the press for a common paradigm will probably inhibit rather than free the creative scholars upon whom growth in knowledge depends. To the extent that we decrease the diversity created by Wallace and Miller, Ochs and McGee, and the other imaginative scholars represented in this collection and in our field, we lessen the contribution to knowledge of rhetorical studies. Thus, I believe it is well that the seventies will see the continuing attempt to join the solid foundation of past thought to contemporary ideas without undermining either, to marry the humanistic approaches of history and criticism to the scientific discipline of communication research, in order to perceive rhetoric in richer ways and to discover ever better means for coping with communication in all of its manifestations.

Whether rhetorical scholarship is or should ultimately be moving toward more diverse paradigms or toward a single one has no immediately visible answer. What is visible in the seventies, though, is the trend of our society and, hence, our communication environment to grow increasingly complex, so that the need for "adjusting ideas to people and people to ideas"[23] is more critical now than it has ever been.

NOTES AND REFERENCES

1. Robert J. Kibler and Larry L. Barker (eds.), *Conceptual Frontiers in Speech-Communication* (New York: Speech Association of America, 1969).

2. Lloyd F. Bitzer and Edwin Black (eds.), *The Prospect of Rhetoric* (Englewood Cliffs, N.J.: Prentice-Hall, 1971).

3. Thomas S. Kuhn, *The Structure of Scientific Revolutions,* 2nd ed. (Chicago: University of Chicago Press, 1970), p. 10.

4. *Ibid.,* p. 209. There have been attempts to define a single paradigm for rhetorical studies. One of the most notable of these is Wayne E. Brockriede, "Toward a Contemporary Theory of Rhetoric," *Quarterly Journal of Speech* 52 (1966): 33–40. On the other hand, one of the most cogent arguments for multiple paradigms in rhetorical studies can be found in Douglas Ehninger, "On Systems of Rhetoric," *Philosophy and Rhetoric* 1 (1968): 131–44.

5. This is the reverse of what John Waite Bowers proposes in "The Pre-Scientific Function of Rhetorical Criticism" (*Essays on Rhetorical Criticism,* edited by Thomas R. Nilsen. New York: Random House, 1968). Bowers suggests in this work that the noblest end of rhetorical criticism "is to produce testable hypotheses which, when verified, will have the status of scientific laws."

6. Marie H. Nichols, "Rhetoric and the Humane Tradition," p. 186.

7. Though unequivocal evidence does not exist, I do not believe that even the most ardent neo-Aristotelian today seeks to *replace* Aristotle's theory; he wants rather to supplement it, to provide a companion work for use with problems or situations not covered in the classic. He probably believes that every young scholar of rhetoric will always need to know Aristotle. The scholar who revises Festinger or Osgood, though, is attempting to make knowledge of the original unnecessary.

8. Donald C. Bryant, *Rhetorical Dimensions in Criticism* (Baton Rouge: Louisiana State University Press, 1973), p. 27.

9. Lloyd F. Bitzer, "The Rhetorical Situation," p. 252.

10. Oscar L. Brownstein, "Aristotle and the Rhetorical Process," p. 26.

11. Samuel L. Becker, "Rhetorical Studies for the Contemporary World," in Bitzer and Black, *The Prospect of Rhetoric,* pp. 21–43.

12. See, for example, Bruce E. Gronbeck, "The Rhetoric of Social-Institutional Change: Black Action at Michigan," in *Explorations in Rhetorical Criticism,* Charles J. Stewart, Donovan J. Ochs, and Gerald P. Mohrmann (University Park: Pennsylvania State University Press, 1973), pp. 96–123. The systems approach is treated even more fully in Bernard L. Brock, James W. Chesebro, John F. Cragan, and James F. Klumpp, *Public Policy Decision-Making: Systems Analysis and Comparative Advantages Debate* (New York: Harper & Row, 1973).

13. Examples cited by Douglas Ehninger, *Contemporary Rhetoric* (Glenview, Ill.: Scott, Foresman, 1972), p. 3. Another and quite different type of effort to define the phenomena which might comprise the focus of rhetorical studies is that by Richard L. Corliss in "A Theory of Contextual Implication," *Philosophy and Rhetoric* 5 (1972): 215–30.

14. Ehninger, *Contemporary Rhetoric,* p. 3.

15. John Waite Bowers and Donovan Ochs, *The Rhetoric of Agitation and Control* (Reading, Mass.: Addison-Wesley, 1971), pp. 2, 6.

16. Nichols, "Rhetoric and the Humane Tradition," p. 180.

17. Newton Garver, review of *The Rhetoric of Agitation and Control,* in *Philosophy and Rhetoric,* 5 (1972): 194–95.

18. Donald C. Bryant, "Rhetoric: Its Function and Its Scope 'Rediviva,' " p. 240.

19. Robert L. Scott and Donald K. Smith, "The Rhetoric of Confrontation," *Quarterly Journal of Speech* 55 (1969): 7.

20. James A. Andrews, "Disintegration and Liberation in Rhetorical Studies," *Today's Speech* 20 (Summer 1972): 41.

21. As Bryant has indicated, some scholars may not accept all of these kinds of theories as rhetorics. However, "prevailing and developing uses of discourse [and, some would add, other instrumental symbolic events] invite the discovery or formulation of adequate rationales appropriate to them. If for reasons of tradition those rationales may not be conceived as rhetorics, they must be developed nevertheless." Bryant, p. 238.

22. Carroll C. Arnold, "Rhetorical and Communication Studies: Two Worlds or One?" *Western Speech* 36 (1972): 80.

23. Donald C. Bryant, "Rhetoric: Its Functions and Its Scope," p. 211.

STUDIES IN THE CONTINUING TRADITION

Aristotle and the
Rhetorical Process

Oscar L. Brownstein

Aristotle begins *The Rhetoric* with the astonishing, and subsequently troublesome, assertion that "Rhetoric is the counterpart *(antistrophe)* of Dialectic." His master, Plato, had shown dialectic and rhetoric to be rivals —not similar in some significant ways, certainly not coequal sovereigns in distinct spheres of activity. To Plato, rhetoric was a vastly inferior claimant to the throne of philosophy. At its most effective, rhetoric was a dangerous instrument of personal power; having no inherent connection with truth or morality, its equal usefulness to any side of a controversy (and only one side could be *true*) gave it the amoral utility of a knife, but with a far greater potential for harm. Only the perfected philosopher, therefore, should be allowed to practice this art. In contrast with rhetoric, as he understood it, Plato conceived of dialectics as the method by which imperfect men could *discover* the Good and the True; indeed, dialectic was the methodological aspect of philosophy. Unlike rhetoric, it needed no claim to prior knowledge to set it in operation, and it made no claim to insinuate into minds something that was not already there; when dialectical agreement was reached, Truth had been found in the minds truly participating in the dialogue.[1]

Aristotle's conceptions of dialectic and rhetoric were vastly different. Having analyzed Plato's dialectical method into logical elements (represented in the works of the Organum), he retained the term dialectics for only that kind of logical discourse which takes probabilistic premises (*Top.* 100a, 30).[2] Dialectics remains a method of cross-examination in search of theoretically probable absolutes or universals: dialectics is one of the theoretical methodologies, and

The end of theoretical knowledge is truth, while that of practical knowledge is action (for if they consider how things are, practical men do not study the eternal, but in some relation and at some time). [*Meta. a*, 993b, 20–22]

Theoretical knowledge is produced by the application of formal logic to given premises (Aristotle describes the purpose of the study—rather than the use—of dialectics as the purification of logic, the discovery of real and apparent syllogisms; this is the counterpart to his description of the purpose of the study of rhetoric as the discovery of all the available means of persuasion); but practical wisdom is not the product of reasoning alone, for it contains elements which are both "irrational" and existentially unique. Therefore, dialectics cannot produce practical wisdom.

Aristotle's conception of dialectics as part of his general philosophy seems sufficiently clear; my purpose here is to interpret Aristotle's general conception of rhetoric. As I understand it, and will argue, that conception might be summarized as follows. Rhetoric is the counterpart to dialectics in an important sense because both are processes or systems that require progressive *speech interactions:* the rhetorical process is conceived as a dialectic of public speeches. Dialectic and rhetoric are also alike in being methods for solving problems, but dialectic is to rhetoric as theoretical is to practical. Theoretical knowledge does not exist theoretically or generally but in specific propositions; practical wisdom *(phronesis)* is likewise a capacity of the mind having no objective existence except in wise action *(prakton agathon).* Just as nature provides man with the capacity for practical wisdom in order that he may survive as an individual, man's social nature required that his communal organizations have survivability and therefore a parallel capacity to take wise action. In my view, *rhetoric* is conceived by Aristotle as the social *phronesis,* deriving its force and capacities not simply from the capacity for practical wisdom in individuals and producing solutions more likely to be appropriate, more often, than is in the capacity of any individual.

If this is indeed Aristotle's implicit view of the nature and function of rhetoric, then the neo-Aristotelean tradition has been non-Aristotelean in some fundamental ways. This is a rhetoric the ultimate aim of which is to produce solutions and not merely persuasion; it deals with matters not resolvable by logic alone and therefore its means cannot be reduced to formal logic; it is impelled and guided by self-interest rather than by an impersonal desire for the Good and the True; its model is an assembly of men deliberating together instead of an orator declaiming to a mob or a teacher lecturing to students; and the smallest rhetorically (as against, e.g., esthetically or pedagogically) significant unit will be the exchange rather than the speech. It is worth noting, I think, that the second element in each of these clauses is a Platonic concept, either of rhetoric itself or of an acceptable means or end.

Rhetoric as the Social *Phronesis*

If, as Burnet says, the Ethics is "part of Aristotle's system of Politics and has no special reference to the individual considered apart from the community,"[3] no less can be said of rhetoric; one might say, in fact, that rhetoric is the methodological aspect of his politics and social ethics. Though the ethical, political, or rhetorical aspects of this interdependent triumvirate may be abstracted for contemplation, in the real world a public act is simultaneously all of these. The ethical and political dimensions of a public act are produced by a particular rhetorical process, and therefore they are contingent and relative, not having the character of absolutes. (One implication of this is that to suggest that the function of Aristotle's rhetoric is to translate ethical or political ideas into practice is a Platonizing error, for such a view assumes that the particular appropriate public act, the expedient, is in some "essential" way deducible from rules or that theoretical knowledge is practical in all regards except for a particular public's willingness to apply it.)

Men seek happiness (*Nich. Ethics,* 1095a, 15–20), for which purpose it is rational to live in society (*Nich. Ethics,* 1097b, 7–12); thus, "it is evident that the state is a creation of nature and that man is by nature a political animal" (*Pol.,* 1253a, 1–2). The state is the natural vehicle by which man may achieve the good life: "if all communities aim at some good, the state, which is the highest of all, and which embraces the rest, aims at good in a greater degree than any other, and at the highest good" (*Pol.,* 1252a, 2–7). The highest good for the individual man is "the good life" (*Pol.,* 1252b, 30), and in the state it is justice ("Good in the sphere of politics is justice": *Pol.,* 1282b, 1). But the good life and justice are only separable in thought, because justice is "equality according to proportion and for every man to enjoy his own" (*Pol.,* 1310a). Therefore, constitutions which consider the common interest are right constitutions (*Pol.,* 1279a, 11). The health of a state depends on justice in law and administration (*Pol.,* 1307a), and so the whole welfare of a state depends on its laws (*Rhet.,* 1360a, 19–30). An unjust state defeats its final purpose and is internally weak, while a just state serves its end and is strong (*Pol.,* 1295b, 81; 1307a; 1307b).

Plato's conception of the ideal state in *The Republic* makes it autonomous (self-sufficient and isolated even from the rest of the world of men), authoritarian (purpose moves from the minds of the philosophers through the will of the soldiers to the control of the appetites of the masses), and it is ultimately at the service of philosophy and its pursuit of truth: his state is a secular monastery. Plato conceives of absolute and unchangeable laws, just as Truth and Goodness are objective absolutes for him. In contrast, Aristotle's conception requires that the state be flexible and responsive; if it ceases to respond to ever-changing conditions, problems, and challenges from within or without, it dies. His state exists in the world of contingency, where, as he says repeatedly, there are neither absolutes nor scientific guidance (e.g., *Nich. Ethics,* 1142a, 22–25). Plato's state is modeled on his tripartite notion of the eternal human soul; at bottom, Aristotle's state seems to be conceived as a mortal living organism, but a higher organism than man and not strictly analogous to him. This social organism can "learn" from experience (its own history and that of others) but it must create and re-create its own laws and institutions in the moving present; crucial, therefore, is its ability to absorb and process information, again from within and without, which may affect its well-being.

In Plato, the Good, the ultimately true and moral, is a tangible reality whose shadow of a shadow we see in the phenomenal world. Therefore, moral knowledge is the knowledge of Forms; and, though difficult, it is finally possible for philosophers to achieve that knowledge by abstraction and logic—that is, by Plato's dialectics. Jaeger says that "when the theory of Forms was abandoned [by Aristotle] being and value fell apart, and dialectic thereby lost its direct significance for human life, which to Plato was an essential feature of it." For Aristotle, moral knowledge is essentially problematic because it finally exists only in the world of contingencies, neither wholly accessible to reason nor subject to permanent capture and not separable from real acts in the real world of flesh and sinew.[5]

Scientific truth has no evaluative component (*Nich. Ethics,* 1139a, 27) and philosophic truth has no active component (*Nich. Ethics,* 1143b, 20);

so neither is an adequate guide to human choices, which exist in the phenomenal world and must simultaneously contain in them particular fact and value, reason and virtue (*Nich. Ethics,* 1139a, 33). A dialectical inquiry into that part of politics concerned with virtuous acts, such as the *Nichomachean Ethics,* is not itself a virtuous act—it is an exercise in theoretical, not practical wisdom (*Nich. Ethics,* 1179a, 35—1179b, 3); the virtues, which are "modes of choice" (*Nich. Ethics,* 1106a, 4), are the product of *phronesis,* which is "common sense," prudence, practical wisdom (*Nich. Ethics,* 1145a, 1).

> Intellect itself . . . moves nothing, but only the intellect which aims at an end and is practical. [*Nich. Ethics,* 1139a, 35–36]
>
> ＊ ＊ ＊
>
> Nor is practical wisdom concerned with universals only—it must also recognize the particulars; for it is practical, and practice is concerned with particulars. This is why some who do not know, and especially those who have experience, are more practical than others who know; for if a man knew that light meats are digestible and wholesome, but did not know which sorts of meat are light, he would not produce health, but the man who knows that chicken is wholesome is more likely to produce health. [*Nich. Ethics,* 1141b, 14–20]

The objective of choice is the *prakton agathon,* which is the best for man attainable through action (*Nich. Ethics,* 1141b, 14), a concrete act of enlightened expediency, for which only *phronesis* is a sufficient operational guide through the imponderables of the world of contingency.

There is a remarkable, but largely unremarked, affinity between *phronesis* and rhetoric. They have the same ultimate objective, the *prakton agathon;* for both, this is a product of their first objective, judgment or choice; both deal with the contingent; in both, reasoning starts from probabalistic premises, but each is "more than a reasoned state"; and both produce their ends by means of deliberation. It is clear that rhetoric externalizes, and makes public and social, the internal and personal characteristics of *phronesis;* by means of communalized and institutionalized dialectic—the deliberative process in assemblies and courts—rhetoric harnesses and projects *phronesis* on a scale necessary to the well-being of the state.

Phronesis "enables man to come to a wise decision in regard to good and evil things" (*Rhet.*, 1366b), just as "the object of rhetoric is judgment" (*Rhet.*, 1377b); *phronesis* is the general decision-making faculty of the individual, as the rhetorical process is the general decision-making faculty of the social organism. The man of practical wisdom is said "to be able to deliberate well about what is good and expedient for himself" (*Nich. Ethics*, 1140a, 25–6); deliberation is an essential quality of practical wisdom (*Nich. Ethics*, 1139a, 13–14) and even its equivalent: "the man who is capable of deliberating has practical wisdom" (*Nich. Ethics*, 1140a, 31). Deliberation is necessary because the starting point of practical wisdom is the contingent and its end is action:

> Now no one deliberates about things that are invariable, nor about things that it is impossible for him to do. Therefore, since scientific knowledge involves demonstration, but there is no demonstration of things whose first principles are variable (for all such things might actually be otherwise), and since it is impossible to deliberate about things that are of necessity, practical wisdom cannot be scientific knowledge or art; not science because that which can be done is capable of being otherwise, not art because action and making are different kinds of things. [*Nich. Ethics*, 1140a, 31; 1140b, 3]

The three forms of "proof" which Aristotle discusses in *The Rhetoric* (reason, emotion, and character) are apparently derived from phronesis, for at the first level of analysis practical wisdom has two aspects, "true reasoning and right desire" (*Nich. Ethics*, 1139a, 24–25, 29–30), and practical wisdom itself is the equivalent of character ("with the presence of the one quality, practical wisdom, will be given all the virtues," [*Nich. Ethics*, 1145a, 1]; "the virtues are . . . *states of character*," [1106a, 10]; this is summarized at 1139a, 21–27).

Both in the broad sense of the term (concerning all that is good for man attainable by action) and in the restricted sense (concerning all that is good for man attainable by action in public assemblies and courts), politics is merely another term for applied *phronesis* (see *Nich. Ethics*, 1141a, 21 for the first, and *Nich. Ethics*, 1140b, 10–11, and 1177b, 7 for the second). Aristotle distinguishes the four kinds of *phronesis* as: individual ("concerned with a man himself"), household management, legislation, and politics, "and of the latter one part is called deliberative and the other judicial" (*Nich. Ethics*, 1141b, 29–32). By the third kind, translated as "legislation," Aristotle seems to mean the establishment of general guidelines and policies, such as a prime minister or a constitutional monarch might provide (presumably from deliberations with his "cabinet," councilors, personal advisers), rather than the generation of particular laws (see *Nich. Ethics,* 1141b, 24–26). In any case, it is clear that in the *Nichomachean Ethics* Aristotle makes the identical distinction between the two kinds of political *phronesis,* deliberative and judicial, as he does between the two kinds of political oratory in *The Rhetoric.*

Rhetoric as a Dialectical Process

According to Aristotle, rhetoric, like ethics and politics, is natural to man and, as he usually does, Aristotle claims merely to understand and systematize nature (see *Rhet.,* 1354a, 3–12; 1355b, 3); in fact, to say that man is innately political and language-using is to say that he is a rhetorical animal. In his role as public legislator, man operates in modes which are at once most ethical, political, and rhetorical; for the legislator in the assembly, significant action is inescapable, since even his efforts at avoidance are ethical and political actions, and all his actions are words or in response to words: the legislator both speaks and decides, debates and judges the debate, deliberates and acts upon his deliberation. Deliberation is necessary because it is clear that the good of the state (the truly expedient) requires that choices be made, that the choices be drawn from among the alternatives available, and that a proper choice at one time does not settle all matters or settle them permanently; deliberation ends only with the extinction of the deliberative body. "Rhetoric deals with such matters as we deliberate upon without certain knowledge and such as seem to present us with alternate possibilities" (*Rhet.,* 1377b, 21). Each speaker advocates a possible course of action, and each hearer is to judge the better course.[6]

> Most of the things about which we make decisions, and into which therefore we inquire, present us with alternative possibilities. For it is about our actions that we deliberate and inquire, and all our actions have a contingent character. [*Rhet.,* 1357a, 24–26]

Since the contingent is that for which the conditions are not ascertainable, strictly speaking our deliberations will be *necessarily* inadequate (in evidence and logic) to our decisions. Yet—though beyond the reach of science

or logic—the contingent *must* be dealt with by effective actions (in addition
to prayers and propitiation, of course).

In its social function, rhetoric is an instrument with which human societies—the social organism in contrast with individuals—confronts contingent reality as it is made accessible within the perspectives provided by
different speakers and hearers and through which decisions for appropriate
actions are taken. The purpose of rhetoric itself is not the demonstration
of the "truth"—no science or faculty can determine the noble, the just, or
the expedient in particular (i.e., real) circumstances. The rhetorical process
cannot discover the better course of action except insofar as, and in the sense
that, the alternatives having been urged by the best arguments available, the
judges decide which is the most compelling view of reality. Aristotle does
not ask that the rhetorician speak the "truth," for only God could meet the
demand; he assumes that the speaker is the advocate of an alternative. Since
the true or the good is in this system the most probable or the most
expedient, operationally it lies within the perspectives available and is relative to them. Therefore, in whatever sense truth may be said to exist in the
rhetorical process, it cannot be isolated from that process nor be adjudged
in the single speech-act taken as autonomous. The greater the number of
alternative proposals and the greater the skill with which the most persuasive arguments are found for them, the more likely it is that the "better"
options—the more appropriate responses to a more adequately perceived
reality—will be acted upon.

From Aristotle's statement that rhetoric deals only with those things
which seem to present alternate possibilities, it is clear that in his view where
there are no alternative possibilities there is no rhetoric; from his statement
that rhetoric exists to produce decisions, it is clear that oral discourses not
directed toward decision making do not fall within the scope of his conception of rhetoric; from his statements that the speaker supports *one* proposition, it follows necessarily that two or more speakers must present the
alternatives—and therefore Aristotle is assuming what I have called here
the rhetorical process. It is clear that just as Aristotle considers man in the
context of society, he considers rhetoric in the context of debate; the individual speech is but a fragment of a dialogue and cannot be understood apart
from the dialogue.

Aristotle says that "Rhetoric is a combination of the sciences of logic and
the ethical branch of politics; and it is partly like dialectic, partly like

sophistical reasoning" (*Rhet.*, 1359b, 9–11). In what way is rhetoric like sophistry if it also is like dialectics? Aristotle has earlier compared dialectics and rhetoric as the only arts which draw opposite conclusions impartially (*Rhet.*, 1355a, 34–36). It would seem that he has overlooked sophistical reasoning, or lumped it with dialectics, for he says that sophistics, too, may be used to draw opposite conclusions (*Soph. Elen.*, 1656, 6–7). Obviously, the operative word is *impartially.* Aristotle distinguishes dialectics from sophistics on grounds of the dialectician's faculty and the sophist's "moral purpose" (*Rhet.*, 13556b, 19–22), a distinction which shifts categories from means to ends. The fully developed contrast seems to be one between the faculty by which the dialectic method is used impartially (i.e., for the discovery of theoretical knowledge) and the faculty by which the dialectic method is used for the expression of moral purpose (i.e., to make one's own view prevail). Thus, rhetoric is partly like dialectics because both represent dialogues or debates of two or more speakers from which the conclusions drawn are not predetermined (otherwise, there would not truly be alternative possibilities within the process itself); but rhetoric is like sophistics because both the rhetor and the sophist use the techniques of their arts tendentiously, to achieve victory over an opponent. There is no counterpart in rhetoric for the distinction between sophistics and dialectics because rhetoric combines the relevant features of each: it is like sophistics in the single speech, dialectics in the debate. In effect, Aristotle allows Plato's claim that orators are sophists but disallows the inference that therefore rhetoric is sophistry; no matter how sophistical, how full of tricks and specious reasonings may be the arguments of the orator, he does not control the debate or the judgment produced.[8]

It is obvious that Aristotle believed advocacy to be essential to the working of the rhetorical process, but he does not explain how it functions; what follows is an attempt at sympathetic extrapolation. If I understand him, Aristotle's conception of the rhetorical process can be likened to a kind of natural and extraordinarily subtle computer for effectively dealing with the contingent. The components of this computer are human minds self-programed to perform a variety of specialized functions. This apparently clumsy yet ingeniously simple system uses human conflict to exploit the virtues of its highly complex but delicate and erratic subsystems. It gets its original energy, its focus, its creativity, and its functional objectivity not from rules but from the self-interested competitiveness of its components;

it is a paradoxical system that harnesses private interests and perceptions to serve the common interest and impersonal decision making. The conflict of interests energizes the search for the most convincing alternatives and arguments; the conflict of interests produces focus on the issues, driving them more deeply as the scope of interests represented is enlarged; and conflict and judgment provide the connecting links among the components of the system. Though it is not yet the exclusive form, rhetoric is the uniquely human form of combat.

If it is accompanied by any degree of coercive power, of course, advocacy may threaten the ultimate disinterestedness of the system; yet advocacy plays the most important role in keeping the system honest. Many "neo-Aristotelean" rhetorics reveal their debt to Platonism by defining the true rhetorician as a good man skilled in speech.[9] These rhetorics share with Plato the assumption of moral dualism, that goodness is a quality distinguishable from truth in the phenomenal world, for without "goodness" the skillful speaker might use even truth for "bad" purposes. They share with Plato a concept of rhetoric that assumes the centrality of the individual orator as the moral guide. Most of all, they share with Plato a fundamental distrust of the rhetorical process that Aristotle did not have. The Good Teacher, who uses rhetorical skills in order to make his wisdom prevail over those without the capacity to participate in it, is an image wholly alien to Aristotle, but it would suit Plato in *The Republic* very nicely. Though Aristotle makes clear that the apparent virtues of the speaker are important instruments of advocacy, he specifically rejects morality as a defining characteristic of the rhetorician and he provides an ample account of the sophistries rhetoricians use to sway judgments. At issue, finally, is whether rhetoric, as a total process, is a neutral instrument without inherent connection with knowledge or virtue, as Plato believed, and therefore requiring the importation of standards (*via* the nonrhetorical facets of the character of the rhetorician), or whether, on the other hand, it is a self-regulating mechanism in some way. Aristotle says that there is a "natural tendency" for the truth to prevail; though he does not spell out how nature accomplishes this, given his assumptions about the human mind as part of nature and rhetoric as likewise a natural process, and his assertion that rhetoric is not "partial," the trend of his thought is not difficult to understand. That "natural tendency" is systemic because the rhetorical process possesses functional objectivity (that which belongs to the object independent of any individual's perception of it). The system is not wholly dependent on the morals, truthful intent, or truthful capacity of an individual speaker; it can only operate, however, if it is dealing with real issues that concern the community and if each participant desires his own well-being.[10]

The rhetorical process operationalizes objectivity through two of its essential features; to use Aristotle's own terms these are *alternatives* and *judgment,* but to unlock the principles from too narrow constraints I will call them multiplicity and adaptation (*synthesis* and *analysis,* the English approximates of the terms Plato used to characterize dialectics, are obviously involved here, but to use them would be too abstract, too suggestive of formal logic, and too easily misunderstood as activities in which individual minds might autonomously engage). The first of these is a product of the whole system; the second, of its component parts. The process as a whole is nonpersonal because it is multipersonal and must embrace multiple perspectives, those of the advocates and the judges.[11] Scope is insured for useful insights from a minimum of three sources. For the second, though theory may define absolutely the participant's positions and roles, in fact these human components are not rigid—nor can they be if they are to be rhetorically effective. In actual deliberations the views even of the advocates undergo alteration as they accept, reject, clarify, and pursue the implications of arguments offered.[12] In the rhetorical process it is not only the judges who make judgments and act on them. Moreover, the study of rhetoric, as a preparation for debate, enhances the truth-value of the system by increasing its tendency to multiply sources and to adapt to the issues that emerge. The effort to discover all the available means of persuasion helps to insure that every scrap of advantage will be exploited, however apparently irrational. The trained orator's enhanced ability to anticipate possible alternatives or counterarguments helps to insure that he will consider those alternatives seriously and search through his own arguments for weaknesses relative to them; the propositional statements which finally evolve will be more precise, more sophisticated, and, insofar as there is a positive relationship between method and reality, more accurate.

Indeed, the system needs all the help it can get because its task—to forge the *prakton agathon* out of opinion and information which is, all of it, either biased or false or incomplete or irrelevant or irrational and always inadequate—is not, on rational grounds, possible at all. Only an assumption such as Aristotle's, that each human mind has insight into reality-as-it-is, however much that insight in any individual may be fragmentary and distorted relative to the problem at hand, can explain what it is that the rhetorical process multiples and filters.[13]

NOTES AND REFERENCES

1. R. Robinson, *Plato's Earlier Dialectic* (Oxford: The Clarendon Press, 1953), p. 70; O. L. Brownstein, "Plato's *Phaedrus:* Dialectic as the Genuine Art of Speaking," *Quarterly Journal of Speech,* 51 (Dec. 1965), 392–98. C. Perelman quotes Descartes at his most Platonic when he proclaims that "Every time two men make a contrary judgment about the same matter it is certain that one of them is mistaken. What is more, neither of them possesses the truth, for if one of them had a clear and precise view of the truth, he would be able to expound it to his opponent in such a fashion that it would force the latter's conviction" (*The Idea of Justice and the Problem of Argument* [New York: The Humanities Press, 1963], pp. 135–36).

2. All citations to Aristotle's writings are from W. D. Ross, *The Works of Aristotle,* 12 vols. (Oxford: The Clarendon Press, 1908–52).

3. John Burnet, *The Ethics of Aristotle* (London: Methuen, 1900), p. xxvii.

4. Werner Jaeger, *Aristotle* (Oxford: The Clarendon Press, 1934), p. 83.

5. In Plato, being and value are identical only "at the top," where the Forms merge into the purest Form, the Good, which is also True Being. Monan argues that Jaeger has mistaken Aristotle's intellectual evolution away from Platonism and that his final view, especially as embodied in the *Eudemian Ethics,* reintegrates being and value existentially in the *prakton agathon* (J. D. Monan, *Moral Knowledge and its Methodology in Aristotle* [Oxford: The Clarendon Press, 1968], p. 144). Monan is certainly correct because, as Aristotle points out repeatedly, being and value are one only "at the bottom": not in abstractions, where one thing is split, mentally, into many things, but in particular actions. Jaeger fails to recognize the *prakton agathon* as the only unity of being and value in Aristotle because he (like Plato and most of the rest of us) is seeking a *concept,* an abstract absolute.

6. Since epideictic oratory is ceremonial or contest oratory, the judgment rendered upon it is isolative and esthetic, like the judgment of a single poem or painting. The judgments made of deliberative and forensic oratory, on the other hand, are not properly critical at all—neither esthetic, logical, nor even "rhetorical" in the usual sense—because the judgments are not rendered on the speeches

themselves but on the alternative choices which have been made more or less persuasive by the speeches (*Rhet.*, 1377b, 21–22). Judgment is directed toward the *real* probable past in the court and to the *real* probable future in the assembly. Judgment is an independent component in the rhetorical process; no less than does oratory, judgment brings *phronesis* into the process (see *Nich. Ethics,* 1143a, 19–35). Otherwise, for example, it would not be possible to admire one speech most and yet choose an action advocated by another.

7. In my view, Aristotle makes deliberative debate the model rhetorical process. In the first chapter of Book I of *The Rhetoric* he claims to be the first to give consideration to deliberative oratory, though, he says, it is nobler and more worthy of the statesman than is forensic oratory; he also says that it is more self-sufficient, less likely to deal in nonessentials, and more likely to produce true judgments. Significantly, only in deliberative debates are the parts of the speech-act which Aristotle distinguishes (speaker, subject, judge) invested in *all* of the participants: all may speak, all have a personal stake in the subject (*Rhet.*, 1354B, 30–32), all must judge.

8. Whitney Oates asserts that "Aristotle apparently is disturbed by the fact that no such term as 'sophist' is available to him in the field of oratory" (*Aristotle and the Problem of Value* [Princeton, N.J.: Princeton University Press, 1963], p. 338). The emotion is a projection by Oates; had such a term been necessary —and there is no sign anywhere that Aristotle wished to classify orators according to their desire for victory—there is no reason to believe that Aristotle's genius for creating technical terms would have failed at what would be, were it needed, a point of great significance.

9. In this volume see Bryant, "Rhetoric: Its Functions and Its Scope," p. 203: "The resolving of such problems [as rhetoric addresses] is the province of the 'Good man skilled in speaking.' It has always been, and it is still. Of that there can be little question."

10. If the purpose of rhetoric is not that the community *know* evanescent reality— an impossible goal—but deal with it adequately, then it cannot function without the application of the regulative force of reality at every point in the process. Thus, deliberations in which the participants have no power of decision (e.g., competitive college debates) are not instances of the rhetorical process, for their goal is not action. Rhetoric exists only where practical alternatives are deliberated, and alternatives are practical (as against theoretical) only where those who deliberate them can effect them. Of course, any human activity may be performed as a game or as an art form, but it would be a grave error to apply principles or definitions evolved for the game or the art form to the practical human activity from which they originally derived. Aristotle avoided this error only by, in effect, reversing it; he stretched his rhetorical concepts to make them apply to epideictic oratory, which has become a cause for error in others.

11. Aristotle refers often to the unique value of multiple perspectives in his works: The investigation of the truth is in one way hard, in another easy. An indication of this is found in the fact that no one is able to attain the truth adequately, while on the other hand we do not collectively fail, but everyone says something true about the nature of things, and while individually we contribute little or nothing to the truth, by the union of all a considerable amount is amassed [*Meta. a*, 993a, 30 ff.]

12. Aristotle's descriptions of how ideas have evolved, as in *Meta. A*, illustrates the principles of this adaptive process.

13. *Phronesis* is not only crucial to the rhetorical process (providing those insights), once again it seems to serve as the model. In Aristotle's theory of knowledge, the primary function of *phronesis* is to be that common sense which integrates the data of the sense organs; Aristotle believes that only through the collaboration of the several physical senses and the common sense can the actual qualities of experience be isolated (C. Perelman, *An Historical Introduction to Philosophical Thinking* [New York: Random House, 1965], p. 60).

Melanchthon's Earliest Rhetoric

J. R. McNally

Philipp Melanchthon (1497–1560), the *Praeceptor Germaniae,* was a figure of considerable importance in the intellectual history of modern Europe. In theology, his collaboration with Martin Luther guided the early stirrings of religious impatience in northern Europe along the path to a reformed Christianity.[1] In education, his leadership was instrumental in leavening the dry scholasticism of the still-medieval university with the yeast of "biblical humanism."[2] And in the history of man's speculations about communication, Melanchthon's influence upon Englishmen such as Cox and Wilson in rhetoric and the "systematics" in logic assures him a place in every history of those subjects.[3]

For all his historical importance, however, relatively little attention has been paid directly to Melanchthon. Published scholarship on Melanchthon's rhetoric, in particular, is so rare as to be very briefly enumerated. A published edition of his 1542 *Elementorum Rhetoricae Libri Duo* by Bretschneider; a study of the sources for Book One of this edition by Buellemer; several interpretive articles by Breen; and a dissertation devoted to the 1542 edition are all that command consideration.[4] There are, of course, brief discussions of Melanchthon's rhetoric included as parts of biographical studies, as well as in histories of education, logic, rhetoric, and theology.[5]

As a result of the paucity of scholarship on Melanchthon's rhetoric, many are perhaps unaware that the German humanist's name appears upon at least three very different rhetorics: a *De Rhetorica Libri Tres* (1519); the *Institutiones Rhetoricae* upon which Leonard Cox based his *Arte or Crafte of Rhethoryke,* and the *Elementorum* whose 1542 edition Bretschneider printed.[6] Fewer still, perhaps, know the extent to which the three rhetorics differ, or the biographical and historical explanations for those differences. It is not my purpose here to supply such vast amounts of information and analysis as would satisfactorily answer these questions. Instead, my more modest aim is to describe the contents and emphases of Melanchthon's earliest (1519) rhetoric in an introductory way; to discuss a philosophically important innovation embodied in that rhetoric—his conception of the relative roles of rhetoric and dialectic as modified by a new theory of the epideictic genre; and to provide a translation of several important portions of the work.

Content and Emphases of the 1519 Rhetoric

Melanchthon's earliest rhetoric is a work of some seventy pages, written in a rather dense and rough style, quite different from the more elegant Renaissance Latin of his later years.[7] Its first and longest book—comprising fifty-four of the book's seventy pages, or over three-fourths of its entirety —is devoted to *inventio,* a fact which deserves remembering in view of the common presumption that Renaissance rhetorics deal chiefly with style. The treatment of invention in Book One includes most of the subjects covered in Book One of Cicero's *De Inventione,* discussing: (1) the *duties* of the orator (invention, arrangement, style, memory, delivery); (2) the *kinds* of rhetoric (epideictic, deliberative, forensic); and (3) the *parts* of each sort of oration (exordium, narrative, argument, refutation, peroration). Such similarities of subject, however, belie the fact that Melanchthon's viewpoints on these familiar subjects are often distinctive. A foretaste of Melanchthon's distinctiveness can be gained from observing that in Book Two, on *dispositio,* Melanchthon refuses to repeat the "parts of the oration" doctrine previously presented—a piece of redundancy frequently observed in traditional rhetorics. Instead, we are presented, in capsule form together with illustrations from *Pro Milone* and several hypothetical speeches, with a recommendation to deductive reasoning: in the *argumentatio*-portion of the speech the major premise (the *krinomenon*) is first to be presented and developed; the minor premise *(aition)* and its development follows; after which the conclusion, titled and identical with the *status caussae* or "point of contention," is presented. This four-page treatment of *dispositio* is only slightly briefer than the discussion in Book Three of *elocutio:* in just over eight pages a digested treatment of the three stylistic "characters" or levels (low, middle, grand), and the four Quintilianic modes of amplification (increment, comparison, reasoning, enumeration) are presented, followed by a discussion of the nature and major kinds of tropes, schemes, and figures of thought.

So much for the general outline of contents in this early sixteenth century rhetoric, whose popularity is attested by the fact that Bretschneider was able years ago to discover at least five editions. Before moving to a more specific consideration of the philosophically significant features of the work, we might note several characteristics which make the 1519 *De Rhetorica* historically interesting. The first is the writer's frequent expressions of irritation with the scholastic culture still dominant in the schools of northern Europe. As examples, we might note two statements from the opening chapter of the book:

> Rhetoric, the theory of speaking, was undoubtedly of considerable utility to the ancients, not merely in imparting an education by means of academic exercise, but also and above all in the conduct of the state, its courts and assemblies. . . . For this reason, it held first place in elementary instruction, and children were taught rhetoric, partly that they might have some sort of method by which to understand other disciplines, and partly that they might come to correct decisions on political issues: Aristotle indeed calls it a political skill. It had its own professors, the rhetoricians and sophists; but, as the schools surrendered to the philosophers, dialectic gradually assumed all of rhetoric's functions—so much so that in our times the very name of rhetoric, to say nothing of its practice, is scarcely known. After its demise, certain barbarous and unlettered grammarians taught a dialectic so weak and sickly that it has wandered off into senile nonsense and a set of absurdly childish puzzles, and its general value, which consists wholly in matters of invention and judgment, has been lost. [f. A 3 r°]

* * *

> I seek a reader who refuses to believe that any advantage at all is to be found in those commentaries on dialectic which the schools of our times tenaciously cling to. [Ibid.]

A second historically interesting characteristic of this work is its use of illustrations drawn from the contemporary scene. In addition to numerous references to Roman and earlier Renaissance authors (although Melanchthon clearly reads and writes Greek, he seems much more familiar with the

Roman than the Greek writers on rhetoric), Melanchthon relies upon
Agricola, Trebizond, Mosellanus, and especially Erasmus. More than that,
he is wont to illustrate theory, not only from the speeches of Cicero, but,
almost as often, from St. Paul's epistles and from hypothetical speeches on
such current questions as freedom of the will, the efficacy of grace, and
modes for coping with the Turkish threat.

A third characteristic worthy of mention in the work is Melanchthon's
awareness of a broader field for the application of rhetoric than that of
speech giving. Although we shall see more about this later, in considering
Melanchthon's particular conception of rhetoric, we may note here fairly
extensive treatments of such minor or limited rhetorical forms as the paraphrase, textual exegesis or commentary writing, historical and allegorical
narration, the letter, and the sermon. Melanchthon, it seems, is attempting
to restore to rhetoric both the curricular completeness and the social relevance which he had found in the *artificium dicendi* of antiquity.

Innovations in the 1519 Rhetoric

In addition to the characteristics listed earlier, which to a great extent
merely identify the work as a northern European Renaissance rhetoric, one
major innovation in rhetorical theory is discernible.

This innovation has to do with Melanchthon's conception of rhetoric as
it relates to other academic disciplines. It may be recalled that a centuries-
old struggle for supremacy in preprofessional education had been waged
among grammarians, logicians, and rhetoricians. An historical dialectic, in
fact, may be seen operating on several levels in this dispute, which continues
into our own times.[8] Writing in a period and region in which the contest
had been renewed with particular acerbity, logic's claims being maintained
by the entrenched scholastics but being vigorously challenged by the new,
revolutionary apostles of "rhetorical humanism,"[9] Melanchthon is very
conscious of the dispute and its issues. Another statement from the opening
chapter illustrates this awareness:

> We are devoting ourselves to this end, that young men may understand in
> what ways rhetoric is related to dialectic and in what ways it is not. We shall
> prescribe a function for each art, and shall advise as to the manner in which
> the rhetoric and dialectic of the ancients are to be understood. [Ibid.]

What is Melanchthon's position on the grammar-rhetoric-logic contest for supremacy? Did he, like the Italians and Germans who preceded him in the early days of the Renaissance—Petrarch, Valla, Barbaro, Agricola, and others—champion the "revolutionary" cause? Did he side with the intellectual "establishment" of his own and later days—Ramus, for example—who subordinated the claims of rhetoric to those of dialectic? Or did he presage the eighteenth century "solution," still holding on in most quarters in our own days, according to which literary studies of the sort pursued by the ancient *grammaticus* were accorded supremacy? Later on in his life, it would seem from the contents of his subsequent rhetorics, Melanchthon was content with the "modern" solution, a corollary of which is that rhetoric is relegated to the status of advanced grammar or stylistics. But—and hence the philosophical significance of this early work—at this moment in his development Melanchthon inclined to the revolutionary, humanistic, rhetorical side in the dispute. It is true that Melanchthon does say:

> I am writing [on the subject of] rhetoric for this reason chiefly, that you may pursue the places of invention, judgment, and arrangement somewhat more easily than [in the manner] they are commonly taught. For these matters are all but ignored by the great rhetoricians and, *although they are properly the concern of dialecticians alone* [italics mine], the rhetoricians also claim them as their own. [f. A iv. v°]

One might wonder what "great rhetoricians" Melanchthon is thinking of who "all but ignored" invention, judgment, and arrangement, especially since he had already, on their authority, identified invention and arrangement among the "five duties of the orator." Nonetheless, it does seem clear that Melanchthon considers, from that point in time at least when "the schools surrendered to the philosophers," that propositional analysis, invention, or "method" has been "the capstone and head, so to speak, of dialectic."

> Just as rhetorical considerations have to do with practical matters, so the entire study of the dialecticians embraces demonstration or apodeixis—that is, a readily intelligible method of instruction. [f. A iv. r°]

* * *

For in all the volumes of the dialecticians, nothing else is treated of but the places of invention and judgment. [f. B i r°]

From such remarks it would seem that, even in 1519, Melanchthon is siding with "the establishment" of scholastic logicians and theologians against the Renaissance "revolutionaries" of rhetorical humanism. What tends to set the record straight, however, is the realization of two other facts. First, despite such lip service to dialectic's claims, the concessions are made in the course of Melanchthon's attempt to present a theory of specifically *rhetorical* invention. Secondly, and more significantly, in order to effect this integration of "the theory of method, demonstration, or apodeixis" within rhetorical invention, Melanchthon has decided to reorder, and reassign functions to, the traditional genres of rhetoric—deliberative, forensic, and epideictic. He first of all makes epideictic—traditionally the genre of praise and blame addressed to mere spectators and concerned with the present[9]—into the *basic* genre of rhetoric:

Quintilian indicates that at one time young men used to be exercised first in causes of the epideictic kind, either because of its frequent employment in other genres—since it often furnished places and arguments for forensic and deliberative speaking—or because it seemed the easiest of the kinds to teach. We begin with the epideictic kind for this reason principally, that *here all the places of invention and the whole theory of judgment arise* [italics mine], and pave the way for the other kinds. One who precisely and carefully has treated this genre will have much assistance in properly teaching letters, particularly regarding public matters. [f. A. iv. v°]

Secondly, Melanchthon alters the central concern of epideictic—that of treating praise and blame—by making its chief concern the theory of communicating information, instruction, or explanation.

For the epideictic kind is concerned primarily with instruction, and only secondarily with praise and blame. The rhetoricians [have written] at sufficient length about the latter; the former has been cultivated [only] in part, for the reason that, having been lured into the classrooms by the dialecticians, it has [there] lain hidden. [Ibid.]

Finally, to this reconstituted epideictic genre Melanchthon assigns the whole of "method," "apodeixis," "epistemesis," or proof, which had heretofore been "properly the concern of dialecticians alone."

The epideictic genre, or theory of teaching, is that which sets down by means of established places, and thereby discloses, the nature and character of each subject in such a manner that, if the thing in its own right is at all capable of being understood, it cannot elude the inquirer. There are two functions to this genre: having immediately at hand by means of the proper places all that can be said about a given subject; and that of meting out those places in the order which will most effectively insinuate knowledge into the hearer's mind. The latter is what some call "method," others "apodeixis," or "epistemesis." [f. A iv. r°]

* * *

Essentially, the epideictic genre of things is that with which method is concerned, which offers the capability of setting forth the meaning of any thesis in a comprehensive, artful, and compendious manner—an ability without which you can teach nothing properly, nor stir the efforts of even a willing reader. [Ibid.]

The details of the way Melanchthon develops this new species of epideictic and integrates it within his "dialectical rhetoric" we may leave the reader to observe in the translation which accompanies this study. But of obviously greater importance than the details is the fact of Melanchthon's effort, which was in essence an attempt to remake rhetoric into what it had been for Cicero and Quintilian: *the* art or theory of public communication, concerned with and responsible for every aspect of its subject, from preliminary "situational" analysis, through research, strategic arrangement, and artistic expression to final presentation to and evaluation by an audience. In this effort Melanchthon resembles an earlier writer, Rudolph Agricola, whose *De Inventione Dialectica* had been an effort to refurbish dialectic with the help of rhetoric so as to create a comprehensive theory of public communication.[10] Furthermore, by means of this restructuring of rhetoric, Melanchthon was anticipating two supposedly "modern" developments: the creation of a "rationale of informative discourse" aimed at "enlightening the understanding," and the rescuing of epideictic from a status of inferiority and tangentiality.[11] But, most importantly, Melanchthon's effort, had it been accepted, might have provided an alternative to Ramus's own application of the "law of justice," and rhetoric, rather than dialectic, might have been conceived, as it is for McKeon and others, as the architectonic account of public communication.[12] What if, one is tempted to ask, Ramus had heeded, not superseded, Melanchthon? Would subsequent intellectual history have avoided the path down which it trod, one consequence of which was the need to rediscover, in early twentieth century America, the original and heuristic meanings we currently associate with rhetoric?

A Translation of Illustrative Portions
of Book One, *Philippi Melanchthonis*
De Rhetorica Libri Tres (1519)

Rhetoric, the theory of speaking, was undoubtedly of considerable utility to the ancients, not merely in imparting an education by means of academic exercise, but also and above all in the conduct of the state, its courts and assemblies—proposing laws, discouraging wrongdoing, sanctioning the oaths of war and peace, and, in a word, assisting in all the functions of a well-ordered state. For this reason, it held first place in elementary instruction, and children were taught rhetoric, partly that they might have some sort of method by which to comprehend other disciplines, and partly that they might come to correct decisions on political issues: Aristotle indeed calls it a political skill. It had its own professors, the rhetoricians and sophists; but, as the schools surrendered to the philosophers, dialectic gradually assumed all of rhetoric's functions—so much so that in our times the very name of rhetoric, to say nothing of its practice, is scarcely known. After its demise, certain barbarous and unlettered grammarians taught a dialectic so weak and sickly that it has wandered off into senile nonsense and a set of absurd childish puzzles, and its general value, which consists wholly in matters of invention and judgment, has been lost. Those who regard dialectic as the proper preparation for worthy studies have in fact imposed upon young students an introduction whereby before a boy may be sent to the poets, he must first have learned only to make loud and barbarous noises.

We are devoting ourselves to this end, that young men may understand in what respects rhetoric resembles dialectic, and in what ways it does not. We shall prescribe a function for each art, and shall advise as to the manner in which the rhetoric and dialectic of the ancients are to be understood. I seek a reader who refuses to believe that any advantage at all is to be found in those commentaries on dialectic which the schools of our times tenaciously cling to.

The Kinds of Causes

The kinds of speeches vary with the differences among arguments, and there are as many kinds of speeches as there are types of things or causes about which one deals. Now things are either future or past: and about future things we advise, whereas things past are either called into court, or become matters of instruction, praise, and censure outside the court-room. From these distinctions there arise three kinds of speeches, the kinds of causes being threefold: the *deliberative,* which pertains to advising—for instance, whether or not to marry; the *forensic,* (which) deals with litigation—for instance, Milo killed Clodius, and killed him legitimately; and the *epideictic,* (which is) suited to teaching, reporting past events, praising, and blaming. Each of these I shall explain in separate chapters.

The Duties of the Speaker

The speaker will address causes, once he has *discovered* the nature, function, parts, attributes, correlates and contraries of the subject of his speech; has *arranged* them according as the character of the subject or his own strategy requires; and has *adorned* them with language and thought.

INVENTION consists of reducing the argument proposed to the places of invention. For instance, if you are to speak about justice, you will consult the places of invention: what justice is, what its parts are, what are its effects, what things accord with justice, what things conflict with justice. About the places more (will be said) later.

DISPOSITION is the artful arrangement of materials discovered.

EXPRESSION (is) ornament and beauty of speech, humble and sublime causes requiring differences (in treatment).

Nature supplies MEMORY AND DELIVERY, and on these matters you must learn from other authors what art has to say. I myself am writing on rhetoric for this reason chiefly, that you may pursue the places of invention, judgment, and arrangement somewhat more easily than they are commonly taught. For these matters are all but ignored by the great rhetoricians and, although they are properly the concern of dialecticians alone, the rhetoricians consider them as their own.

Parts of the Speech

A speech consists of these parts as a rule: an Exordium, whereby we prepare the auditor; a NARRATIVE, which is the setting forth of the subject; a CONTENTION, in which we support our position and refute its opposite; and a PERORATION, which is the colophon of the speech.

The Epideictic Genre

Quintilian indicates that at one time young men used to be exercised first in causes of the epideictic genre, either because of its frequent employment in other genres—since it often furnishes topics and arguments for forensic and deliberative speeches—or because it seemed the easiest of the kinds to teach.

We begin with the epideictic genre for this reason principally, that here all the places of invention and the whole theory of judgment arise, and pave the way for the other genres. He who has precisely and carefully studied this genre will have great assistance in properly mastering letters, particularly in matters of public concern. For the epideictic genre is concerned primarily with instruction, and only secondarily with praise and blame. The rhetoricians (have written) at sufficient length about the latter; the former has been cultivated hardly at all because, having been lured into the classroom by the dialecticians, it has (there) lain hidden. For though there are three kinds of causes, the rhetoricians have kept for themselves (only) those which occur frequently in the courts and assemblies; the one kind in which the most artistry is (found) and upon which the others depend is left for the schools. But unless the studious ponder this kind, they will effect little in the others.

The epideictic genre, then, is twofold: one part is concerned with teaching, the other with praising and censuring. We will speak later of the laudatory kind, and will treat first of the species concerned with teaching. For it takes many forms, and is especially necessary for those learning properly; yet in these matters there is almost complete ignorance.

On the First Species of the Epideictic Genre

The epideictic genre, or theory of teaching, is that which sets forth precisely by means of established places the nature and character of each subject in such a manner that, if the thing in its own right is at all capable of being understood, it cannot elude the inquirer. There are two functional aspects to this species: that of having immediately at hand by means of the proper places all that can be said about a given subject; and that of meting out those places in the order which will most effectively insinuate knowledge into the hearer's mind. The latter is what some call "method," others "apodeixis," and still others "didaxis" or "epistemesis." And it is this function which Aristotle made as it were the chief part and head of dialectic. Thus, just as rhetorical considerations have to do with practical matters, so the entire study of the dialectician embraces demonstration or apodeixis—*scil.,* a certain readily intelligible system of teaching, which ought to have been learned before political causes are approached. For though expression may be properly treated without recourse to the study of political causes, it cannot be suitably treated apart from the epideictic genre, since all intellectual pursuits are measured by the demonstrative genus as if by a ruler. Moreover, providing a system of proof (which is to say, an order for speaking) is the essence of the dialectician's profession. And one who is not a master of this—a common state among professors—recognizes neither the function of dialectic nor any use at all for demonstration; yet those who ought to be especially proficient are the very ones who enmesh themselves in nets and becloud themselves as if in Cimmerian mists, clearly resembling the man who is said to have had a cloud in his mouth.

Essentially, the demonstrative genus of things is that with which method is concerned, which offers the capability of setting forth the meaning of any thesis advanced in a comprehensive, artful and compendious manner—an ability without which you can teach nothing properly, nor stir the efforts of even a willing reader. For if one spews out everything which, so to speak, comes into his head, such a confused and inefficacious discourse will collapse of its own weight. To say nothing for the moment of those who have not become accustomed to method, such is surely the mark of jaded and sterile minds, and they must be inept in all the tasks of letters, since they are on their own account altogether unable to create, and cannot rightly judge of the writings of others. On the contrary, those who have become accustomed to method, themselves create much, judge wisely, and teach clearly. So far is a man who does not know the use of dialectic from being thought learned, that it would even be more profitable not to have tasted letters than to have learned them in such shameful impurity.

A speech of this genus does not really require an exordium, its narrative is continuous, and, depending upon the subject, certain considerations are supported while others again are refuted, as I shall be advising along the way at the appropriate places.

The whole speech revolves about certain questions, which will serve us in this context as substitutes for the "states." For they are the tools of invention.

DOES IT EXIST?

WHAT IS IT?

OF WHAT CAUSES OR PARTS DOES IT CONSIST, ONE OR MANY?

WHAT ARE ITS PARTS?

WHAT IS THE RELATIONSHIP AMONG THE PARTS?

WHAT ARE ITS FUNCTIONS?

WHAT ARE ITS CORRELATES?

WHAT ARE ITS OPPOSITES?

Just as the discovery of those matters which were hidden is easy once the (proper) place has been pointed out and recognized, so when we wish to explore we ought to have the places in readiness. Otherwise, what is regarded as of first importance becomes impossible, that the hearer be led from things in which he has all but certain faith to things he does not yet admit. He therefore who would wish to draw forth some subject from its very sources ought to pursue the thread leading to such things as his "pathmaker."

Now there are certain questions which Aristotle (whom in this regard we follow chiefly for this end, that use of the things which are taught in the schools may be understood) discusses in the *Posterior Analytics,* where he clearly delineates the theory of invention, arrangement, and instruction. But there he hands down only four questions—the reason being that, having hunted down only considerations pertaining to substance, he did not embark upon external relations, accidents, functions, and contraries. Yet in the *Topics* the same subject is pursued more extensively: there he appends to considerations intrinsic to the nature of the thing the notions of sameness and difference, to "accident" notions of greater and less degree, and so forth. It has seemed to me preferable to gather all the questions together, both in order to make them available for the instruction of the young, and to enable them to understand that in all the volumes of the dialecticians nothing else is treated but the places of invention or of judgment.

[*There follow six brief chapters explaining the meanings attached to each of the eight places or questions identified. The content of these chapters—ca. 180 lines of text—is suggested by the example and summary statement which follow.*]

EXAMPLE

I.   *What* is justice? The virtue whereby what is owing to each person is given him.

II.   What are its *causes?* The will acting in consonance with laws and customs.

III.   What are its *species?* Commutative and distributive, in a twofold manner. For we share with fellow citizens either by exchanging goods or by means of human and civil custom.

IV.   What is commutative justice? Justice in contractual matters.

V.   What is distributive justice? Justice in political life.

VI.   What are the kinds of distributive justice? Public and private. Public distributive justice is "piety," for it is as it were the crown of all the virtues, maintaining the civil customs of men as regards one another, as well as the customs of magistrates regarding the citizenry and of the citizenry in turn with regard to the magistrates. Private distributive justice is the honorable and tranquil commerce of citizens with each other.

VII.   Its *functions* are to render to the citizen, the magistrate, the country, children, wives, and friends what is owing to them.

VIII.   *The relationship among the parts.* Distributive justice includes commutative, as is proved by the fact that arguments regarding both are drawn from the same (definition). But the end of distributive is more noble, hence it is a higher form than commutative, as is proved by causal argument.

IX.   *Related* are courage, generosity, and temperance.

X.   *Opposed* are fear, avarice, and luxuriance.

This, unless I am mistaken, is the whole inventional system as set forth by dialectic, and he who desires to use it to the full ought to take in hand Cicero's *De Officiis*—which was written after the fashion called "didactic" as its author himself attests when he says he is following the manner of address, so appropriate for the schoolroom, in which all philosophical writings are found to have been written.

. In addition, this method, which I have briefly set forth, is the font, so to speak, whence the other modes of speech are derived. For this reason, I should wish it zealously commended to young scholars. For it is of great assistance in teaching, and one who is ignorant of its ways cannot himself properly learn, much less teach correctly. This, however, is to be prudently avoided, not to so weaken one's speech as to think he has at last achieved an artistic expression when cultivation of style is lacking—a position I see adopted by certain dialecticians. For one must always reach for the best and most beautiful, and one's talents must be exerted to the point at which fecundity spontaneously appears. It is the first indication of coming achievement, just as the robust bodies of infants are a promise of mature strength. Let me not even mention those who have grown into a kind of spare and nerveless style, and who thereafter are wont to express everything harshly and downright barbarously, even if capable of something better.

But you have far and away the best of all models for employing this method in the *De Officiis* of Marcus Cicero and in almost all of Plato's works. And it will prove extremely useful for young men from their very first introduction to greater studies to develop commonplaces by this method—namely, by investigating fully and deeply their nature and function, so that each one properly understands their usefulness in common questions. The commonplaces are the virtues, the vices, fortune, life, death, wealth, talent, youth, age, and in a word all the subjects which occur in public affairs. These, as I have cautioned above, it will behoove the young man setting forth to have noted and have in readiness.

[*Melanchthon next discusses several applications of "didactic method," among them the textual exegesis, the commentary, history writing and allegorical tales. He then discusses what must be called propositional, as opposed to topical, analysis. That is, he teaches a method for discovering and establishing the truth or falsity of a statement such as "Piety is Justice," "Death is Life." This done, Melanchthon moves to a consideration of the deliberative and forensic genres, after which he concludes Book One.*]

NOTES AND REFERENCES

1. See Clyde L. Manschreck, *Melanchthon, The Quiet Reformer* (New York: Abingdon Press, 1958); Vilmos Vajta (ed.), *Luther and Melanchthon.* Papers of the Second International Congress on Luther Research (Münster: Muhlenberg Press, 1961).

2. Ernest G. Schwiebert, "New Groups and Ideas at the University of Wittenberg," *Archiv für Reformationsgeschichte* 49 (1958): 60–78; Manschreck, *op. cit.*, pp. 131–57.

3. See for example Wilbur S. Howell, *Logic and Rhetoric in England, 1500–1700* (New York: Russell and Russell, Inc., 1961), pp. 92, 94–95.

4. *Corpus Reformatorum,* Carolus G. Bretschneider (ed.), 28 vols. (Halis Saxonum: Schwitschke, 1834–60), v. 13, pp. 220 ff.; K. Buellemer, *Quellenkritische Untersuchungen zum I. Bucke der Rhetorik Melanchthons,* dissertation, Friedrich Alexanders Universität (Wurzburg: Becker, 1902); Q. Breen, "Melanchthon's Reply to Pico Della Mirandola," *Journal of the History of Ideas* 13 (1952):413–26; Q. Breen, "The Subordination of Philosophy to Rhetoric in Melanchthon," *Archiv für Reformationsgeschichte* 43 (1952):13–28; La Fontaine, Sister M. J., "A Critical Translation of Philipp Melanchthon's *Elementorum Rhetorices Libri Duo*" doctoral dissertation, University of Michigan, Ann Arbor, 1968.

5. A relatively recent bibliography of Melanchthon research in English is provided in Robert Stupperich, *Melanchthon,* translated by R. H. Fisher (Philadelphia: Westminster Press, 1965), pp. 151–66.

6. For information as to editions of Melanchthon's various dialectics and rhetorics see Bretschneider, *loc. cit.*

7. The edition I am using is *Philippi Melanchthonis de rhetorica libri tres* (Wittenbergae in Saxonibus: n.p., 1519).

8. On this dialectic, see for example H. I. Marrou, *A History of Education in Antiquity,* translated by G. Lamb (New York: Sheed & Ward, 1964), pp. 121–36.

9. J. R. McNally, "*Rector et Dux Populi:* Italian Humanists and the Relationship between Rhetoric and Logic," *Modern Philology* 67 (1969):168–76.

10. J. R. McNally, "*Dux Illa Directrixque Artium:* Rudolph Agricola's Dialectical System," *Quarterly Journal of Speech* 52 (1966):337–47; J. R. McNally, "Rudolph Agricola's *De Inventione Dialectica Libri Tres:* A Translation of Selected Chapters," *Speech Monographs* 34 (1967):393–422.

11. Professor Bryant a number of years ago remarked on the peculiar status of the epideictic genre in traditional rhetoric. He suggested that, by making epideictic a "miscellaneous" category, Aristotle had "given an opening for . . . the primarily informative and instructional." "Rhetoric: Its Function and Scope," reprinted in this volume pp. 201. More recently, Chaim Perlman, perceiving the same ambiguity in the conception of epideictic, has attempted to provide the genre with a more central role (*The New Rhetoric,* translated by J. Wilkinson and P. Weaver [Notre Dame: Notre Dame University Press, 1971], pp. 47–51), and Professor Bryant has come to prefer "the rationale of the informatory and suasory *in* discourse" as a definition of rhetoric: "Rhetoric: Its Function and Scope, *Rediviva,*" reprinted in this volume, pp. 239.

12. See Richard McKeon, "The Uses of Rhetoric in a Technological Age: Architectonic Productive Arts," in *The Prospect of Rhetoric,* edited by L.F. Bitzer and E. Black (Englewood Cliffs, N.J.: Prentice-Hall, 1971), pp. 44–64.

Bacon, Rhetoric, and Ornament of Words

Karl R. Wallace

In understanding Bacon's view of rhetoric, certain locutions have presented difficulties. Among them are "ornament of words" and "ornament of speech." They have puzzled scholars because in the few instances in which Bacon uses the phrases they appear to associate him with a rhetoric of style rather than with a rhetoric of substance. The basic, and perhaps most critical, linking of rhetoric with ornament occurs when Bacon offers a concise evaluation of logic and rhetoric:

> these two, rightly taken, are the gravest of sciences; being the arts of arts, the one for judgment, the other for ornament; and they be the rules and directions how to set forth and dispose matter.[1]

The communication of scientific observations, discoveries, and principles, said Bacon, must be done in aphorisms, bereft of ornament and adornment. In particular, in the presentation of the data of natural history, which constitutes the proper subject matter for scientists to contemplate, "all that concerns ornaments of speech, similitudes, treasury of eloquence, and such like emptinesses" should be "utterly dismissed."[2] In counseling King James on the union of Scotland with England, Bacon was aware of his mode of address, and remarked: ". . . the length and ornament of speech are to be used for persuasion of multitudes, and not for the information of kings . . ."[3] Another passage links speech with adornment. It occurs when Bacon, concerned with the moral problem in communication, declares that rhetoric, like other arts, naturally favors good rather than evil.

We see that speech is much more conversant in adorning that which is good
than in colouring that which is evil; for there is no man but speaketh more
honestly than he can do or think.[4]

In fact and by function, rhetoric is in the service of virtue:

> it is the business of rhetoric to make pictures of virtue and goodness, so that
> they may be seen. For since they cannot be showed to the sense in corporeal
> shape, the next degree is to show them to the imagination in as lively represen-
> tation as possible, by ornament of words.[5]

In his classification of the intellectual arts, Bacon sees rhetoric as part of
the art of communication, its particular function being "the Illustration or
adornment of discourse."[6]

Passages such as these, taken singly or together, do not commit Bacon
to a rhetoric whose emphasis is on style. All are consistent with a rhetoric
whose emphasis is on content and subject matter. This, I hope, will become
evident later. But such passages fit almost equally well into a Ramean
rhetoric; and Ramus, as historians of rhetoric know, sponsored a view that
limited rhetoric to style *(elocutio)* and delivery *(pronuntiatio)* and gave to
dialectic the operations of invention *(inventio)* and judgment *(dispositio)*.
Ramus's *Institutiones Dialecticae* (1544) and Talaeus's *Institutiones Oratoriae* (1544) had great influence on the theory of logic and rhetoric on the
continent and in England as well. Bacon doubtless knew these works or
later books in the same tradition. *The Advancement of Learning* (1605) and
its expanded version, *De augmentis scientarum* (1623) both approve and
disapprove of Ramean theory and its application. The number and character of references to Ramus suggest that Bacon derived his information from
his own reading or from his teachers at Cambridge, and did not glean the
materials from commonplace books. Some scholars think that the Ramean
influence is to be seen most notably when Bacon discusses "the uses and
objects of the faculties of the human soul."[7] The notion of use and practice
provides the basis, in the *Advancement,* for the Intellectual Arts, whose
parts are four: the art of invention, the art of judgment, the art of memory,
and the art of transmission (or communication). The art of transmission is
subdivided three ways: the organ of discourse, the method of discourse, and
the illustration of discourse, or rhetoric. The Rameans assigned inventing,
judging, and remembering exclusively to logic and held that rhetoric as a

discipline must not consider them. Classical rhetoric, on the other hand, held that both arts and logic and rhetoric, each from its own point of view, treated of invention and disposition (judgment and method), and memory. So if Bacon were under the influence of the Ramean tradition when he looked at the logical and rhetorical arts, it would be easy and natural for him to think of rhetoric as the Rameans did and give it a stylistic cast. But he did not so think, as I hope to make clear.

In undertaking a close analysis of the locutions, ornament of words, and ornament of speech, I want to center attention on these matters: the grammatical function of the prepositional phrases; the meanings Bacon attaches to the notions of *words* and *ornaments;* and the substantive character of Bacon's conception of rhetoric. If the analysis is convincing, it should not only throw light on Bacon's rhetorical theory and practice, but also invite further probing into the so-called stylists among rhetoricians of the English Renaissance who talked of rhetoric as the art of ornamenting, adorning, or garnishing of speech. Their categories and presuppositions are implicit and more hidden than Bacon's. Because Bacon had to classify knowledge in his desire to reform learning and show the way to discovering new knowledge, his categories and basic concepts are sometimes explicit. When they are not named, they usually emerge clearly from his language because of his deep respect for method, i.e., for the order and arrangement of ideas.

The language of the locutions cannot mean that words and speech in themselves are being ornamented and adorned. The phrases, "of words" and "of speech," are, of course, adjectival in the obvious sense. If one were to read "word ornament" and "speech ornament," it would mean that there is a class of ornaments, of things ornamental, and that words and speech are members of the class, other members being dress, jewelry, and the like. Words, then, may be considered ornaments. If so, words are ornamenting something; they are not ornamenting themselves—except, perhaps in that class of stylistic things labeled "schemes." This interpretation leads to another meaning. It becomes evident that "ornament" is a verbal noun, and is perceived as an active noun in its most abstract form, ornamentation. So something is being ornamented, and it may be ornamented *by means of* or *through* words, speech, dress, etc. A means-end relationship is implied. So when Bacon talked of ornament of words, he was thinking of the kind of ornamentation that was accomplished through words. There also may be implied a cause-effect relationship. This is often evident in other similar linguistic constructions of Bacon's. ". . . there belongeth to kings . . . both tribute of duty and presents of affection."[8] Clearly it is one's consciousness of duty that prompts tribute, and it is affection that produces presents. ". . . the observant eye of duty and admiration . . ." And ". . . the poverty of learning . . ."[9] Similarly, in the expression, "juggleries of words," it is not that words are juggled (except figuratively) but that a speaker may accomplish jugglery, may be tricky, through his use of words. I conclude, then, that Bacon did not mean that the material basis of ornamentation is words and speech; it is not language itself that is adorned. Or, coming closer to Bacon's English: language is not the subject of rhetoric; rather, the "subject of Rhetoric" is "imaginative or insinuative reason."[10]

If something is ornamented or adorned, the implication is that there is something that is not unadorned. What is it? There is something other than language which language reflects. What is reflected, so Bacon declares at one time, is matter. ". . . words are but images of matter . . ." and this relationship he had in mind when he identified the first "distemper" of learning. The disease became evident, he declared, "when men study words and not matter . . ." Schoolmen often fell victims of the distemper, and when they did it was falling in love with words, the same as falling in love with a picture. To regard words as images only, as objects only, was to miss what they represent, namely, the "life of reason and invention."[11] In another place, as he continues his criticism of scholastic learning, Bacon remarks: ". . . substance of matter is better than beauty of words . . ."[12] Here too it is clear that words are different from the matter and substance of communication. There is, then, something behind words, language, and speech.

Although we may never know absolutely what Bacon meant by the notions of matter and substance, we can arrive at plausible interpretations. He probably took matter in the classical sense as that which was undetermined and undifferentiated and which required form to render it determinate. Furthermore, when form and matter combined to "cause" something that could be grasped by the senses, the product was said to be substantial. Any individual thing revealed aspects of matter, form, and substance. Each natural object did, including man. So did each artistic object made by man. Man made his language; hence, each word and each utterance revealed matter, form, and substance. When words were considered as objects (and indeed all speech and language behavior), their substantial nature was evident in speech and writing. This, I think, is part of Bacon's meaning when he is mindful of linguistic behavior. Or, to use more modern terms, he was thinking of the distinction between human experience and the physical manifestation of human experience. In part, he was thinking also that the objectification of what has been learned and stored away as experience is the work of imagination. He concisely described imagination as the "representation of an individual thought."[13] The reference to representation here was probably to the power of the imagination to reproduce experience, both the experience man acquired through the activity of his sense organs and the experience he learned through the exercise of all his faculties. Without the reproductive function of the imagination, experience could not become palpable, nor could it become public and communicable.

"Word" and "speech" in his vocabulary meant more to Bacon than the physical objects employed in communication. Speech and writing were of course the "medium" or the "vehicle" of communication.[14] But they also were signs of thought and thinking; they were signs of meaning. This fact is evident in *The Advancement of Learning* at one of the few places where Bacon commends Aristotle. "Words are the images of cogitations, and letters are the images of words." Bacon reiterated the point when he revised and expanded the *Advancement: "Cogitationum tesserae verba, verborum literae,"* which Spedding renders in Bacon's English taken from the *Advancement.*[15] So the imagination, in representing thoughts, produced both objects and signs. As signs, words reflected man's experience. Words, furthermore, as they appeared in arguments, were "the current tokens or marks of Popular Notions of Things."[16] That is: words reflected man's *civic* experience—what man held in common of ethical and political behavior.

In explaining what Bacon meant by ornamenting and adorning, especially when these processes involved speech and language behavior, one must understand that Bacon recognized a distinction between bodily and mental processes on the one hand and their manifestation outside body and mind on the other. The distinction is evident in our discussion of "word" above. One must understand, further, that linguistic events, as external to a receiver, were communicative in nature. Man could think without signs, but he could not communicate without them. Bacon saw clearly that linguistic communication depended upon men's abilities to interpret language signs as these were heard and read. He saw, too, that persuasion was concerned with more than the instruction of men's minds; it must also move them to accept the position or belief or conduct proposed. These convictions, widely shared by men of his age, help to account for Bacon's abiding interest in what he called the art of tradition or art of transmission, and indeed in any subject matter or art that required something to be "delivered over" from one man to another.

Bacon's interest in communication helps to account, too, for his interest in method. His concern for method in discourse led him to describe a number of methods, each dependent upon the purpose and subject matter of the composition. Scholars have remarked upon this point, but what has been overlooked is the idea implicit in his treatment of methods. That idea is adaptation, especially adaptation to audience. A speech, an essay, a bit of scientific discourse comes into being and is shaped by its audience as well as by its purpose and content. This idea, I think, is implied in Bacon's conception of ornament, for ornamentation and adornment are never, for Bacon, sanctioned for their own sakes. A communicator dresses his thought as he dresses his person. His thought is conceived in terms of its being appropriate and acceptable. Clothes do more than render the body presentable; they make the whole person fitting and acceptable.[17] Speech and language do more than present thought, for to both creator and respondent linguistic objects are more than a sequence of neutral, naked objects; they are appropriate or inappropriate things, acceptable or unacceptable things. There is a difference between ornamenting language and the ornamental *function* that the imagination performs when joined with reason in producing communications. It is the activities of reason, then, prompted by the needs of communicating with popular audiences, which receive ornamentation. Dr. Tenison found among Bacon's papers certain collections "of divers sayings, aptly and smartly expressed, and containing in them much good sense in little room." These Bacon himself had entitled, *"Ornamenta Rationalia,"* which may be rendered the rational or the reasonable ornamented or, perhaps, plausible ideas ornamented.[18] The sayings are lost, but examples may be found, so Spedding thinks, in one of Bacon's commonplace books, *The Promus of Formularies and Elegancies.* In these sayings, two faculties, reason and imagination, are jointly at work.

Bacon's care with method and his respect for the fitting and appropriate in discourse, however, did not lead him to produce a formal classification of audiences. A classification is probably implicit in his writings, but it is not to our purpose now. He did, however, recognize two large groups of respondents to language communications. The groupings reflect his fundamental reliance upon the notions permeating his faculty psychology; they serve to differentiate two basic arts, logic and rhetoric; and they illuminate the general nature of ornament by linking adornment with rhetoric and not with logic.

Bacon's broadest division of audiences was twofold: those who could follow the course of logical discussion and those who could not. Some men could grasp and use the abstractions and formal relationships evident in dialectic, in disputation, criticism, and examination. The faculties which Bacon held responsible for abstract analysis and synthesis were two: understanding and reason. The former, abstracting from sensory data and experience, produced concepts; the latter, combining and dividing concepts, built statements, syllogisms, and inductions. The materials with which these faculties worked were abstractions precisely because they were as remote and withdrawn from concrete experiences as it was possible for the mind to conceive. On the other hand, the materials of everyday living, the materials to which all men were privy, were anchored in sensory experience, either directly or in memory. These materials were always colored with feeling and passion. The faculties Bacon held most responsible for conducting concrete discourse and argument were imagination, appetite, and will. The power of reason was always at work, of course, and for Bacon, as for any rationalist of his day, the best decisions and the most praiseworthy conduct were those reflecting rational processes.

The distinction between audiences who find abstractions congenial and those who do not is seen most clearly when Bacon talks of logic and rhetoric. Logic is not suited to most minds:

> That part of human philosophy which regards Logic is less delightful to the taste and palate of most minds, and seems but a net of subtlety and spinosity. For as it is truly said that "knowledge is the food of the mind," so in their choice and appetite for this food most men are of the taste and stomach of the Israelites in the desert, that would fain have returned to the flesh-pots, and were weary of manna; which though it were celestial, yet seemed less nutritive and comfortable. And in a like manner those sciences are (for the most part) best liked which have some infusion of flesh and blood; such as civil history, morality, policy, about which men's affections, praises, fortunes, turn and are occupied. But his same "dry light" parches and offends most men's soft and watery natures.[19]

Bacon repeats the common distinction between logic and rhetoric: the former is like the fist, the latter like the open hand. By the simile he may have meant that in logical discourse reasoning is tight, strict, and compelling, and that in rhetorical discourse reasoning is less strict, less evident and demanding. He may have meant, too, that in practice the materials of dialectical discourse are presented concisely, without development, whereas the materials of rhetorical discourse are amplified and open. ". . . the length and ornament of speech," we remember, "are to be used for persuasion of multitudes, and not for the information of kings . . ." The two arts at work, then, are in part distinguished by two different kinds of audiences. Furthermore, the two arts have their psychological underpinning in two distinct faculties. Logic—or perhaps we should say, dialectic—is "subservient" to the understanding, and "Rhetoric is subservient to the imagination."[20] Quite in keeping with the closed fist-open hand figure, Bacon is indicating, I think, general features of the two arts, the one being abstract and formal, the other concrete and substantive. This is not to imply, however, that rhetoric is nonlogical, for in his most exact characterizations of rhetoric Bacon specifically associates the art with the faculty of reason. "The duty and office of Rhetoric, if it be deeply looked into," he asserts, "is no other than to apply and recommend the dictates of reason to imagination, in order to excite the appetite and will."[21] In the *Advancement,* he declares that the "subject" of rhetoric is "imaginative or insinuative reason."

Returning now to ornament, it is evident that Bacon saw two broad kinds of discourse: logical and rhetorical. The medium or vehicle of both kinds was words, i.e., speech and writing. What, then, was the special concern of rhetoric as an art of communication? It is not to ornament the language of logic or of dialectical disputation. Bacon describes no such language, and we would have to guess what it would consist of. (His deep interest in scientific communication lies in axioms and the axiomatic method.) Yet, in saying this, one must recognize that Bacon saw a difference between a "bare" statement and a statement less bare. There are, he said, "naked and simple propositions and proofs."[22] These are the products of dialectical thought and invention. So what is being ornamented by means of the language of rhetoric? The products of rhetorical thought and inventiveness, however, reflect matters close to the flesh and blood of social, political, and moral living. Hence, rhetorical verbalizations reflect matters closer to men's imagination and common experience than to their intellects. Bacon's own language makes the essential point:

Aristotle doth wisely place Rhetoric as between Logic on the one side and moral and civil knowledge on the other, as participating of both: for the proofs and demonstrations of Logic are toward all men indifferent and the same; but the proofs and persuasions of Rhetoric ought to differ according to the auditors . . . [which] in perfection of idea, ought to extend so far, that if a man should speak of the same thing to several persons, he should speak to them all respectively and several ways . . .[23]

To employ discourse that is "ornamental," I conclude, is to speak imaginatively and appropriately on matters that *affect* men at large, that directly touch men as political and moral creatures. Rhetoric is the art, said Bacon, that handles reason "as it is planted in popular opinions and manners."[24]

Bacon's rhetoric, I believe, can hardly be said to emphasize style. Rather, it is a substantive rhetoric, and it is an art complete in itself, not dependent upon logic. Although these two points overlap, they may gain in clarity and emphasis through separate treatment. The second shall be first.

In his cyclopedia of knowledge, *The Advancement of Learning*, and the longer, later *De augmentis scientarum*, Bacon discusses the arts and sciences more fully and analytically than anywhere else in his works. Since he was pointing out new directions for the discovery of knowledge, he had to indicate the deficiencies in the old, the received knowledge, as well as suggest new paths of study. His observations and judgments on rhetoric are grouped, generally speaking, into the old and the new. In a sweeping reference to classical rhetoricians and speakers, his judgment of the old is unmistakable:

> as to the labouring of it [i.e., development of the art of rhetoric], the emulation of Aristotle with the rhetoricians of his time, and the experience of Cicero, hath made them in their works of Rhetorics exceed themselves. Again, the excellency of examples of eloquence in the orations of Demosthenes and Cicero, added to the perfection of the precepts of eloquence, hath doubled the progression in this art; and therefore the deficiencies which I shall note will rather be in some collections which may as handmaids attend the art, than in the rules or use of the art itself.[25]

In generally approving of classical rhetoric, Bacon is approving of a complete rhetoric, a rhetoric understood in its broadest scope, whose parts or divisions were invention, disposition, elocution, memory, and delivery. Although such a rhetoric gains by being mindful of its kin, logic and dialectic, politics and ethics, it embraces the full rationale for instruction in, and criticism of, nonspecialized discourse. It had, furthermore, the dignity of a knowledge, or in Bacon's language, it was a "science," a science not only "excellently well laboured," but also "a science excellent."[26]

The new cast that Bacon gave to the art of rhetoric is due to two circumstances. His cyclopedia of knowledge was based on psychological functions. So when he approached rhetoric, "to stir the earth a little about the roots of this science," he associated it with imaginative reason, i.e., with the imagination behaving rationally, within the bounds of possibility and probability. The other circumstance is the location of rhetoric in his cyclopedia. It is placed among the intellectual or rational arts, as we have said before. These arts are four: invention, judgment, memory, and transmission or communication. Each is identified from the point of view of its "uses and objects." The art of invention is for inquiry and discovery, of judgment for examination and criticism, of memory for custody, of communications for wording (speaking and writing) and delivery to others. These are activities or operations engaged in by any individual; they involve the faculties of understanding, reason, memory, and imagination. The art of transmission "includes all the arts which relate to words and discourse."[27] Discourse needs an organ, i.e., physical elements, such as the sounds of speech, that function alone or in combination, to reveal thought and thinking. Abstractly considered, the organ of discourse is grammar; concretely considered, it is speech and writing. Discourse needs method; hence, there is an art of organizing ideas and materials. Discourse requires, finally, an art that illustrates and illuminates the speaker's or writer's ideas. This is the art, Bacon avers, that is commonly understood as Rhetoric or Oratory.

By thus giving rhetoric a new cast, he did not intend to restrict its bounds to word play, vocal behavior, and gesture. He viewed the intellectual arts as he did for the purpose of emphasizing the psychological operations involved in them, and thus set the stage for later describing the proper behavior of the understanding in scientific discovery and communication. Bacon did not like strict dichotomizing, for it squeezed things into unnatural compartments. After discussing the problems of discovering new knowledge, he recognized the problems in using received knowledge, of finding arguments and the ways in which they had been met by both logic and rhetoric. General topics have been "sufficiently handled in logic, so that there is no need to dwell on [them]."[28] In rhetoric, the aids to finding and "prompting" of arguments, though they have been well labored, show deficiency. Nevertheless, he will defer "the fuller discussion of [them] to rhetoric."[29] Similar awareness that different verbal arts legitimately treat some of the same matters is explicitly revealed when Bacon starts his discussion of the Method of Discourse. "This has been commonly handled as a part of Logic; and it also finds a place in Rhetoric, under the name of *Disposition.*"[30] In brief, each science knows best what subject matter and special topics are.[31]

The one passage noted earlier which seems to exclude invention from rhetoric is incomplete and certainly is confusing. Logic and rhetoric are declared to be "the arts of arts, the one for judgment, the other for ornament; and they be the rules and directions how to set forth and dispose matter . . ." The province of logic was never limited to judgment by any logician, least of all by Ramus, who made much of invention. Are we to understand from the passage that the disposition of matter is assigned to logic and the setting forth of matter to rhetoric? Or, despite the ambiguity of "they," does each art set forth and dispose matter? The context of the passage reduces its ambiguity only a little. Bacon was criticizing the universities for allowing "unripe" scholars to undertake disputation and oratory before they had acquired adequate subject matter—"that which Cicero calleth *sylva* and *suppellex,* stuff and variety . . ."[32] Even the "place" of the art of private negotiation or conference did not disturb Bacon. It could be handled in either politics or rhetoric.[33]

But if the passage does not adequately characterize either logic or rhetoric, it offers some evidence that Bacon considered rhetoric to be an art of substance rather than an art of style merely. Rhetoric, as well as logic, had something to do with matter, presumably with the materials and subject matter of discourse. Elsewhere Bacon broadly identifies the materials much as Aristotle did. They are located in the opinions that men in general hold, as distinct from the Truths held by men of science; they are opinions about political and social life, about morality and ethics as these were reflected in public life:

Logic handleth reason exact and in truth, and Rhetoric handleth it as it is planted in popular opinions and manners. And therefore Aristotle doth wisely place Rhetoric as between Logic on the one side and moral or civil knowledge on the other, as participating of both.[34]

Despite his sometimes puzzling use of "logic," "Logic," "dialectic," and "Dialectica," Bacon in general is here reflecting the Aristotelian tradition. Working with the materials of discourse, both learned and popular, reason produced conclusions or "truths" that constituted degrees of probability. When the audience or "judges" were learned, discourse was labeled dialectic; when the audience was popular, rhetoric or poetic. It is important for the modern interpreter to understand that an art or a science in Bacon's time, if not always today, was distinguished by its materials and subject matter as well as by its ends and methods.

There are other evidences that Bacon recognized the substantial basis of rhetoric and rhetorical discourse. Consider his additions to the art, by which he believed he was removing some of the deficiencies of the old rhetoric. He isolated and analyzed some of the recurring "sophisms" of popular discourse. He presented, too, a list of "antitheta," a collection of contrasting ideas expressed as statements. He offered both as aids to invention, to help the communicator to find materials, issues, and arguments. Consider, too, his discussion of the first distemper of learning, when men were content with limited knowledge. The schoolmen, shut up "in the cells of monasteries and colleges," knew little of history or of nature. They substituted quick wits for breadth of knowledge. Hence, their writings showed "no soundness of matter or goodness of quality."[35] Such men, like spiders weaving their intricate webs, brought forth "cobwebs of learning, admirable for the fineness of thread and work, but of no substance or profit."[36] The quantity and quality of man's creative endeavors depend upon the scope and variety of his study and experience. "For the wit and mind of man, if it work upon matter . . . worketh according to the stuff, and is limited thereby . . ."[37] The schoolmen, too, were wrong in their method. They defended their positions by barking objections and wrangling over little particulars when they should have depended upon "evidence of truth proved by arguments, authorities, similitudes, examples . . ."[38] Here is Bacon's plain suggestion that sound rhetorical methods are in their nature closer to the substance than the form of discourse. Indeed, Bacon seems to have assumed that much of rhetorical "ornamentation" by means of speech has a referential function, at times pointing to concrete situations, at times to ideas and opinions. At the trial of Oliver St. John, for example, he asked his audience to take heed of St. John's speaking "seditious matter in parables, or by tropes and examples."[39] At another time he is concerned over the detection of popular errors of fact. It is difficult to recognize such errors because they become embedded in fables. Then, too, men's opinions, whether they be true or mistaken, are ever occurring "in similitudes and ornaments of speech."[40]

It would appear, finally, that in characterizing his "new" rhetoric Bacon understood an art that is fully rounded and substantial. The imagination was the key faculty. In rhetorical utterances, it was linked with reason in a special way. It illustrated or illuminated the work of reason. This it did by giving discursive thought more body than less, for imagination by nature was nearer the sensory world than the intellectual world. In working with reason in communicative situations, imagination and reason seemed to fuse and become one in function. That something of the kind was held to occur is implied in Bacon's coinage, imaginative reason. The melding of the two faculties is most readily seen in the symbol, for always involved in a symbol is a fusion of idea and image, of meaning and vehicle. For Bacon the image must be unmistakably rational, for in its rhetorical activity the imagination must obey reason. It must meet the requirements of possibility and probability that communicator and audience find in the subject, occasion, and materials at hand. The imagination is not to raise itself above reason, as it does when spirit speaks directly to spirit, as in revelation and divine inspiration. Nor is it free to indulge in improbable images, as it sometimes does in the myth and in poesy.

Imaginative reason is always at work in communicative situations. But when it is called into play by a specific occasion that invites or demands action, it is insinuative in effect. The symbols invented *fit* the occasion; they meet the requirements for action desired by the speaker and acceptable to the audience. In other words, the symbols are persuasive. They are insinuative in the sense that reason is "bent" to satisfy man's will and affections. This rhetorical fitness—the appropriateness of argument, idea, and language—is like the fit of a key to the ward of a lock. When speaker or writer is dominated by his sense of the fitting and appropriate, he produces utterances that are characteristically persuasive. A rhetorical utterance, to Bacon, was evidence of man's inventive powers when constrained or challenged to say something and at once be saying it aptly.

The notion of fitness or appropriateness is inherent in Bacon's view of rhetoric. Once this is perceived, one understands how reason and imagination constitute a partnership in discharging the duty and office of rhetoric.

Neither partner works independently. Each partner does what it best can, reason engaging in analytical and judgmental operations with appropriateness as guide, and imagination finding corresponding images with appropriateness as the goal. As partners, heedful of each other, they do whatever is necessary for the invention, disposition, and linguistic realization of discourse that in kind ranges from formal speeches to private conference. Reason makes the product plausible; it gives to utterance the fact of truth. Imagination renders the product sensible and appealing; it gives to utterance the face of goodness. In rhetorical activity, imagination becomes more than a messenger between reason and will; it becomes an ally of reason.[41]

We conclude by pointing to Bacon's own illustrations of imaginative reason at work. First are the sophisms, the popular signs of good and evil, that Bacon offered as intellectual stimulants to rhetorical invention. They illustrate what happens with statements when reason and imagination are operating with one faculty dominant. Here are Bacon's statements:

This will be evil for you.
Your enemies will be glad of this.

For the first statement, reason is primarily responsible; for the second, imagination. The use of utterances like the second one, said Bacon, "is not more for probation than for affecting and moving."[42]

In the sophisms, also, Bacon illustrates what is meant by reason working analytically. Each sophism is weighed, probed for its plausibility, and its exceptions or "answers" carefully noted. Illustrated is the kind of thinking that a persuasive speaker undertakes when in preparation he considers possible arguments, accepting some, rejecting others.

As illustrations of what occurs when imaginative reason produces whole discourses Bacon points to "great examples in Xenophon, Cicero, Seneca, Plutarch, and of Plato also in some degree . . ." These men demonstrate what it is "to clothe and adorn the obscurity of philosophy itself with sensible and plausible elocution." Hence, "if a man be to have any use of such knowledge in civil occasions, of conference, counsel, persuasion, discourse, or the like; then shall he find it prepared to his hands in those authors which write in that manner."[43]

NOTES AND REFERENCES

1. *The Works of Francis Bacon, Baron of Verulam, Viscount of St. Alban, and Lord High Chancellor of England,* collected and edited by James Spedding, Robert Leslie Ellis, and Douglas Denton Heath, 7 vols. (London: Longmans and Company. . . . Virtue and Company, 1879), vol. 3, p. 326. All references to Bacon's works are to this edition.

2. Aphorisms on the Composition of the Primary History, *Works,* 4:254.

3. *The Letters and Life of Francis Bacon Including All of His Occasional Works,* collected by James Spedding, 7 vols. (London: Longman, Green, Longman, and Roberts, 1861–74), vol. 3, p. 219.

4. *Works,* 3:410.

5. *Works,* 4:456.

6. *De dignitate et augmentis scientarum,* VI, 1; *Works,* 4:439. Compare the Latin counterpart: "Sermonis Illustrationem sive Ornatum," *Works,* 1:651.

7. *De augmentis,* V, 1; *Works,* 4:405.

8. *Works,* 3:261.

9. Ibid., p. 175.

10. *Advancement of Learning,* II; *Works,* 3:383.

11. The three quotations are from *The Advancement of Learning,* I; *Works,* 3:284.

12. Ibid., p. 285.

13. *Sylva Sylvarum,* 945; *Works,* 2:654.

14. *Advancement of Learning,* II; *Works,* 3:399; *De augmentis,* VI; *Works,* 4:439.

15. *Advancement of Learning,* II; *Works,* 3:399; *De augmentis,* VI; *Works,* 1:651; 4:439. Compare Aristotle, *De Interpretation* 16 a 1–4: "Spoken words are the symbols of mental experience and written words are the symbols of spoken words." (Trans. E. M. Edghill.)

16. *Advancement of Learning,* II; *Works,* 3:388.

17. George Puttenham, for example, took notice of dress as something appropriate to the effect intended. *The Art of English Poesie* (London, 1589), Book III, 1. A recent edition is that by Gladys Doidge Willcock and Alice Walker (Cambridge, 1936).

18. *Works,* 7:189.

19. *De augmentis*, V, 1; *Works*, 4:407.

20. *De augmentis*, VI, 3; *Works*, 4:455.

21. Ibid.

22. Ibid., p. 456.

23. *Advancement of Learning*, II; *Works*, 4:411.

24. Ibid.

25. *Advancement of Learning*, II; *Works*, 3:409. Cf. *De augmentis*, VI, 3; *Works*, 4:455.

26. *Advancement of Learning*, II; *Works*, 3:409.

27. *De augmentis*, VI, 1; *Works*, 4:439.

28. *De augmentis*, V, 3; *Works*, 4:423.

29. Ibid.

30. *De augmentis*, VI, 2; *Works*, 4:448.

31. Bacon makes the point in the *De augmentis*, V, 3; *Works*, 4:424.

32. *Advancement of Learning*, II; *Works*, 3:326.

33. Ibid., p. 411.

34. *Advancement of Learning*, II; *Works*, 3:411. Compare the Latin of the *De augmentis*, *Works*, 1:673.

35. *Advancement of Learning*, I; *Works*, 3:285.

36. Ibid, pp. 285–86.

37. Ibid., p. 285.

38. Ibid., p. 286.

39. *Letters and Life*, vol. 5, p. 145.

40. *Advancement of Learning*, II; *Works*, 3:331.

41. Bacon's metaphor of the imagination as an instrument and messenger of both reason and will occurs in *De augmentis*, V, 1; *Works*, 4:406.

42. *De augmentis*, VI, 3; *Works*, 4:458. It should be recognized that the imagination is more or less at work in the production of both statements. The response to the first statement may involve a vague self-image at least. The response to the second statement is intended to evoke a more or less definite image of a personal enemy or perhaps a national enemy, such as the French. In any event, "Your

enemies will be glad of this" evokes more imagery than "This will be evil for you." Bacon thought of the two statements as "meaning the same," as he said, but as *affecting* differently. A modern rhetorician would go further and hold that though the two sentences carry the same general sense they are unique in meaning. The creative activity of the imagination has made the difference. When Hamlet muses, "the native hue of resolution is sicklied o'er with the pale cast of thought . . . and enterprises lose the name of action," he is saying something more than the commonplace, "reflection hinders action." This point is made by W. H. Clemen in "The Image of Hamlet," *Shakespeare: Modern Essays in Criticism,* edited by Leonard F. Dean, rev. ed. (New York: Oxford University Press, 1967), pp. 231–32.

43. The entire passage occurs in *Advancement of Learning,* I; *Works,* 3:284.

Charles Butler on Methods of
Persuasion: A Translation

Donovan J. Ochs

English grammar schools in the sixteenth and seventeenth centuries occupied themselves with the task of preparing their students for the universities. Taught through such devices as the theme and the oration, rhetoric
came to occupy the position of first importance in the curriculum of the
grammar schools, especially in the higher forms. As Foster Watson noted:

> Indeed, if there is one school subject which seems to have pre-eminently
> influenced the writers, statesmen and gentlemen of the sixteenth and seven-
> teenth centuries, in their intellectual outfit in after life, probably the claim for
> this leading position may justly be made for Rhetoric and the Oration.[1]

The chief textbooks used to teach rhetoric in the grammar schools were
those of Audomarus Talaeus and Charles Butler. Talaeus's *Rhetoric,* published in 1547, was based upon Ramistic doctrine. Traditionally, rhetoric
was taught in the classical manner of Aristotle, Cicero, and Quintilian, and
encompassed the five arts of invention, disposition, style, delivery, and
memory. Ramus reformed scholastic logic and traditional rhetoric by advocating one system of logic for both science and opinion and one theory
of invention and disposition for both logic and rhetoric. Applying his so-
called "law of justice" to the corpus of material contained in the scholastic
rhetoric, he removed "the findings of suitable arguments" and "the proper
arrangement of arguments in a discourse" from rhetoric and assigned these
tasks to logic. As a result, rhetoric was left only with style and delivery.[2]
Ramism found its first interpreter in England in the person of Gabriel

Harvey. In 1577 Harvey published his *Ciceronianus* and *Rhetor* which promulgated Ramus's theory that discourse draws upon logic for its subject matter and rhetoric for its expression.

The popularity of Ramism continued through the latter half of the sixteenth century and carried over into the first half of the seventeenth. In 1625, however, there appeared a work which began to give it serious competition. This was Thomas Farnaby's *Index Rhetoricus* (1625).

Farnaby, a schoolmaster and sound classical scholar, produced a textbook containing a popular discussion of the classical or Ciceronian rhetoric. To Farnaby, rhetoric was the faculty of speaking well, its purpose being to delight, teach, and move the auditors. All rhetorical theory came under the headings of invention, arrangement, style, and delivery. Traces of the Ramistic reform were not, however, completely absent; memory as one of the five classical arts, was excluded. Furthermore, Farnaby treated the six parts of an oration under the heading of arrangement, whereas the Hellenistic rhetoricians considered these under invention.

By way of further promulgating the doctrines of Ramism, Charles Butler published, *Rameae Rhetoricae Libri Duo* in 1597. This, his first rhetorical work, was limited to style and delivery, one book being devoted to each.

Relatively little is known about Charles Butler the man. We do know that he was "born at one of the Wycombes in Buckinghamshire."[3] He entered St. Mary Magdalen College, one of the older colleges at Oxford, in 1579 and later became a Bible clerk. His Bachelor of Arts degree was granted on February 6, 1583; his Master's degree, on June 28, 1587. Upon leaving Oxford, Butler became master of a free school in Basingstoke, Hampshire. Concurrently with this appointment, he also served as curate of a small church at Skewres. These positions he held for seven years before being moved to a larger parish. Says Wood:

[Butler was] promoted to the vicaridge of Lawrence-Wotton, three miles distant thence (a poor preferment, God wot, for such a worthy scholar), where, being settled, he wrote and published these books following which showed him to have been an ingenious man, and well skilled in various sorts of learning.[4]

Butler served at Lawrence-Wotten for forty-eight years. He died on March 29, 1647, and was buried in the chancel of Lawrence-Wotten Church.

In addition to his rhetorics, Butler wrote a book on bees, *The Feminine*

Monarchie (4th ed., 1609), *Affinity in Marriage* (1625), *English Grammar* (1633), and *Principles of Music* (2nd ed., 1636). Concerning his rhetorics, the *Catalogue of the British Museum* gives the following information: *Rameae Rhetoricae Libri Duo* (1597); an edition at Oxford, 1600, entitled, *Rhetoricae Libri Duo,* and another in 1618. The 1629 edition of the *Rhetoricae* is listed as including the *Oratoriae Libri Duo,* and this combined work was reprinted three times in 1642, and again in 1655.[5] Watt has recorded other editions of the *Oratoriae Libri Duo* as 1633, 1635, and 1645.[6]

One year after Butler published his first rhetorical treatise, *Rameae Rhetoricae Libri Duo,* he wrote the revised and considerably expanded *Rhetoricae Libri Duo,* which became the most famous textbook in the history of Ramistic rhetoric in England.[7] Although Ramus's name no longer appeared in the title, the treatment of the subject follows closely the pattern designed by Ramus. For example, in the preface, Butler compares Ramus to Virgil as a tribute to his brief methods and clear examples. Rhetoric, as we would expect, is the art of speaking well and consists of two parts, style and delivery. The *Rhetoricae* includes a two-stanza quotation from Edmund Spenser, which is of some significance as a departure from the customary practice of using only Latin examples in textbooks on rhetoric. Watson claims: "English literature was not taught in the schools of the first half of the seventeenth century, but Butler in his *Rhetoric* takes us very near to the suggestion of it."[8]

At the age of sixty-eight Butler added two books to his already popular *Rhetoricae.* These four books, two on rhetoric and two on oratory, were published as a single work under the title, *Rhetoricae Libri Duo . . . Quibus Recens Accesserunt De Oratoria Libri Duo.*

Butler begins the *Oratoriae Libri Duo* by defining oratory as "the faculty of forming an oration about some question."[9] After some initial remarks on punctuation, he devotes sixteen pages to the methods of persuasion. Then, although style was treated in the *Rhetoricae,* Butler adds five pages on this subject, which he terms as, "both character and a type of speaking, that is, rising from certain forms of orations, certain vocabulary phrases, sentiments, and ornaments."[10]

Seven pages are devoted to the exordium as the first part of an oration, the classical division into direct and the indirect being observed.

He treats the narration, proposition, confirmation, and confutation in the traditional manner, while the peroration is said to consist of two parts, the enumeration and an amplification.[11]

Book I concludes with an exposition of the nature and *status* of questions. Not only the subject of the *status,* but the topics and arguments for the three kinds of orations, demonstrative, deliverative, and judicial, are explained in full. At its conclusion Butler says:

Now that the first book is completed, the partition follows. There are five parts of an oration: invention and disposition, elocution and pronunciation, and memory. From which the first parts refer to dialectic, the next to rhetoric, the last is gained not from art but from nature, since before other arts, memory assumes a necessary and somewhat peculiar role and brings to completion its own precepts.[12]

In Book II Butler devotes twenty-nine pages to invention, twenty-one pages to disposition. Disposition to Butler is the ideal placing of the arguments in the oration. The speaker should gain favor in the introduction by using the middle style; teach in the argumentative part of the oration by using the low style; and arouse the emotions in the conclusion with the sublime style.

Elocution and pronunciation each receive only a portion of a page and the reader is referred to the *Rhetoricae* for a more complete treatment of these subjects.

The fifth canon of classical oratory, memory, occupies ten pages and has been translated completely by Hultzēn.[13]

Concluding the last book, Butler states:

A perfect faculty of speaking is acquired in three ways: by nature, art, and exercise. Nature is first and gives skill, memory, form, and voice. Art, a more certain leader, corrects the gifts of nature. Exercise completes and conquers both of these. Exercise consists in genesis and analysis. Genesis is that by which we form our speech from the precepts of art and in imitating the examples of the orators. Analysis is that by which we resolve a different speech, observing in it both those things which art prescribes and by imitation of the worthy virtues of the authors. Imitation is that by which we copy the rules of another's speech. There are two precepts of imitation, that we imitate those who excell and those things which excell in these men, especially gifts of nature which are apt in them, by which the more easily we ourselves excell.[14]

With the contents of the *Oratoriae* thus summarized, it remains to point out the conflicting opinions held by scholars concerning the importance and

the classification of Butler's book. Howell argues that this textbook is
Ramistic despite the problem that memory, arrangement, and invention
have been addéd to style and delivery. He explains:

> The answer is that in the earlier work, he [Butler] was writing on rhetoric,
> which as a Ramist he had to limit to style and delivery, while in his later work
> he was in reality writing on logic, and as a Ramist he had to develop this
> subject under the headings of invention and arrangement.[15]

Terming the *Oratoriae* a book on logic, Howell does note several qualifications to his position. Ramus, he says, would not have approved of treating
memory as a part of logic, and would not have discussed "the positions of
an argument" and "the kinds of oratory" in a treatise on logic since this
would be a violation of the law of justice and the law of truth.[16]

Howell's statements are in direct opposition to those of William P. Sandford:

> Butler's shift in terminology from *rhetoricae* (1598) to *oratoriae* (1629) should
> not mislead the reader. It was made apparently for the sake of maintaining
> a surface consistency between his two works, separated by approximately
> thirty years. Thus he explains in the forward to the *Oratoriae Libri Duo* that
> whereas rhetoric is concerned with the ornamentation of speech, oratory has
> to do with persuasion; that the parts of the former are *elocutio* and *pronun-
> tiatio*, whereas, those of the latter are *inventio, dispositio,* and *memoria.* But
> in *Oratoriae Libri Duo* he lists *elocutio* and *pronuntiatio* as parts of the
> subject, referring the reader to his rhetoric for their treatment. Moreover, in
> the earlier work he deals throughout with style and delivery as if they con-
> stituted the whole of the speaker's art.[17]

Briefly, then, these are the two sides of the issue. Howell maintains, with
certain reservations, that the *Oratoriae* was a book on logic; Sandford, that
Butler had returned to the classical five-part rhetoric.

It is my opinion that Butler was introducing a classical rhetoric rather
than a logic, and that he did this surreptitiously because at the time Ramistic rhetoric was still in vogue. I believe that this position is supported by
an examination of the contents of the *Oratoriae*. The terms and principles
that are used are those of the classical rhetoricians. Furthermore, Butler
called his book *Oratoriae* and not *Logicae,* even though the latter would
have been more acceptable to a Ramistic audience. Howell may well be

correct in contending that Book II can be interpreted as Ramistic. I would stipulate that Book I is classical in content, as an examination of the translation given below indicates.

For this translation I have used a microfilm copy of the 1629 edition of the *Oratoriae,* the original of which is at the Huntington Library. This text was chosen not only because of its accessibility, but also because this was the first combined edition of the *Oratoriae* and *Rhetoricae.* Book I, Chapter 2, Section 2 of the *Oratoriae,* entitled "On Methods of Persuasion," was selected for translation for these reasons: (1) Butler devotes sixteen of the sixty-seven pages of the first book to this topic; more than to any other. Hence, he evidently wishes to emphasize this material. (2) This section fairly illustrates how Butler uses authority to support his statements. (3) The section is a detailed account of what the classical writers had said about persuasion, although the arrangement and presentation are primarily Butler's. (4) With this translation available, students of the period may be able to arrive at a more accurate interpretation of the *Oratoriae.*

Concerning the format of the book, Hultzēn states:

> The plan of the text and commentary, widely used at this time, had been directly borrowed by Butler from *Audomari Talaei Rhetoricae . . . e P. Rami . . . Praelectionibus Observata,* which he had edited in 1597 as *Rameae Rhetoricae Libri Duo.*[18]

Following this pattern, Butler begins the section on persuasion with forty-two lines of large type for the heading material and at certain key words in this heading material, inserts the letters, (a), (b), etc., to serve as guides for the amplification and substantiation which follows in the next fifteen pages. The remainder of the material is set in smaller type with forty-six lines to the page. The guide letters are repeated throughout this amplification. Sometimes Butler uses italics for quoted passages; sometimes he uses quotation marks. Italics are likewise used to mark references to words in his own chapter headings. I have avoided italics in my translation, but have enclosed all italicized matter in quotation marks.

Butler's references are taken, in many cases, from older manuscripts than those which we now have. For these seemingly incorrect reference citations, I have given the complete citations from the Loeb Library translations. It also became necessary to translate portions of the Greek authors cited, since modern translations are generally taken from the original Greek texts, whereas Butler appears to have used a Latin translation of the Greek original. Since Butler was using earlier editions of several of the classical sources, some variations occur in the quoted passages. In these cases, I have inserted the material in the translation of Butler's text and noted such insertions.

Chapter 2. Section 2.
ON METHODS OF PERSUASION

The end of an oration is (a) to persuade: that is, to draw over the listeners to our feeling; which is done in (b) three ways: (by gaining favor, by arousing, and by teaching).

Gaining favor is a method for persuasion by which (c) we win over the love and good will of the listeners for ourselves, and this (d) usually precedes the handling of the subject for discourse.

Arousing is that by which (e) we excite more vigorous emotions, and this usually (f) concludes the handling of the theme.

The arousing of feeling with reference to the subject treated is done by (g) declaring good or evil things. The declaration is of the same sort either equal or unequal.

That is equal which says neither more nor less than the bare truth of the matter demands.

The unequal is an exaggeration whether it is (h) amplification or an extenuation or a diminution.

(i) Exaggeration is that which increases the nature and quality of some matter or deed whether good or evil and makes it greater. Extenuation, on the other hand, is that which lessens.

(k) That is instruction by which we teach the hearers a matter set before them and usually it is contained in the very (1) handling of the theme; of this there are three parts: explication, proof, and amplification.

(m) Explication is instruction which clears up an obscure (n) word or (o) matter in the theme.

Proof is that which brings credence to a doubtful matter by argumentation. (p) Argumentation, however, which consists properly of three forms of premises: (q) (the major, the minor, and the conclusion) by which is set forth sometimes more, sometimes less, is explained.

Less, (r) if either the major premise ends without the minor or the minor premise ends without the major; or the major and minor once expressed, the conclusion which necessarily follows thence is understood.

More, (s) when its own proof is joined closely to the major or minor or both of these.

(t) Amplification is that which makes the proposed matter greater, and it is either extension or digression.

(u) Extension is that which, for the sake of illustration, enlarges the proposed matter with (v) suitable arguments or says the same things in varying ways.

(x) Digression is that which amplifies some special argument with reference to the matter set forth for the (y) sake of pleasing with its own (z) arguments.

For Chapter 2. Section 2.

(a) to persuade: *De Inventione* i. v. 6. "The [19] function of eloquence seems to be to speak in a manner suited to persuade an audience, the end is to persuade by speech. For example, we may say that the function of the physician is to treat the patient in a manner suited to heal him, the end is to heal by treatment.[20] So in the case of an orator we may understand what is meant by function and end when we call what he ought to do the function, and the purpose for which he ought to do it, the end."

(b) in three ways: *De Oratore* ii. xxvii. 115, thus under the person of Antony, Cicero says, "for purposes of persuasion the art of speaking relies wholly upon three things: (1) that we teach[21] what we maintain to be true, (2) the winning of our hearer's favor, and (3) the rousing of their feelings to whatever impulse our case may require." Which idea he repeats twice in differing ways in the same place: and again in ii. lxxvii. 310. See (k) in the notes. He gives the rule in ii. xxix. 129: "For, of necessity the arbitrator who is to decide in our favor must either lean to our side by natural inclination, or be won over by the arguments for the defence or constrained by stirring his feelings." Cicero sets forth all these things and places them in the best type of orator, "The supreme orator then is the one whose speech instructs, delights and moves the minds of his audience. The orator is in duty bound to instruct; giving pleasure is a free gift to the audience, to move them indispensable."[22] Which things he also requires in famous orators, *De Oratore* ii. lxxvii. 310, "Three things ought to be brought about in speaking: that he to whom it is addressed is taught, that he is delighted, that he is moved more vehemently."[23]

(c) Love. In which manner this love and benevolence of the listeners may be conciliated, Antony teaches, *De Oratore* ii. xliii. 182, "Now feelings are won over by a man's merit, achievements, or reputable life, qualifications easier to embellish if only they are real, than to fabricate where nonexistent. It is very helpful to display the tokens of good nature, kindness, calmness, loyalty, and a disposition that is pleasing and not grasping or covetous, and all the qualities belonging to men who are upright, unassuming and not given to haste, stubbornness, strife or harshness, are powerful in winning good will.[24] But attributes useful in an advocate are a mild tone, a countenance expressive of modesty, gentle language, and the faculty of seeming to be dealing reluctantly and under compulsion with something you are really anxious to prove." And in *De Oratore* ii. li. 206, "We observe that love is won if you are thought to be upholding the interests of your audience, or to be working for good men, or at any rate for such as that audience deems good and useful.[25] For this last impression more readily wins love and the protection of the righteous esteem; and the holding-out of a hope of advantage to come is more effective than the recital of past benefit. And to make it plain that the man, for whom you are to win this love, in no respect consulted his own interests and did nothing at all from personal motives. For men's private gains breed jealousy while their zeal for other's service is applauded." *De Oratore* ii. xliii. 183, "But all this kind of advocacy will be best in those cases wherein the arbitrator's feelings are not likely to be kindled by what I may call the ardent and impassioned onset. For vigorous language is not always wanted, but often such as is calm, gentle, mild: this is the kind that most commends the parties.[26] And so to paint their characters in words, as being upright, stainless, conscientious, modest and long-suffering under injustice, has a really wonderful effect; and this topic, whether in opening, or in stating the case, or in winding-up, is so compelling, when agreeably and feelingly handled, as often to be worth more than the merits of the case." (See also Ch. 3, Sec. 1, and (d) in the notes.

(d) (e) *De Oratore* ii. lxxix. 322, "The most proper place for gaining favor and arousing is in the exordium and the peroration."[27]

(f) concludes. *Institutio Oratoria* vi. i. 13, "The peroration also provides freer opportunities for exciting the passions of jealousy, hatred, or anger. As regards the circumstances likely to excite such feelings in the judge, jealousy will be produced by the influence of the accused, hatred by the disgraceful nature of his conduct, and anger by his disrespectful attitude to the court." *De Oratore* ii. lxxxi. 332, "But all these arguments must as a rule be rounded off either by enlarging on your points or by arousing the feelings of the judge or calming them down." And *De Partitione Oratoria*, "Enlargement has a special place here in the peroration, and if somehow in the course of the oration exaggeration occurs, it seems to be out of place in the disposition."[28]

(g) Emotions. *Arist. Rhet. ad Theodecten*, i. ii. 1,[29] "Emotion is that by which men who are aroused (from an apparent good or an apparent evil) judge when they are friendly and when they are hostile, not when they are angry and when they are in a gentle mood; for the person on trial seems to one who loves him to have done either no wrong or a small wrong. Moreover, to one who desires and hopes for something, it seems that something will happen and will happen for the good, but the opposite seems to be the case to one who is adverse and he gives up home."[30] So also Cicero, "There is nothing more necessary in speaking than that the one who hears favors the orator; and thus he himself is so moved that he is governed more by the impetus and confusion of the mind than by judgment and counsel. Men judge much more by hate or love or desire, or wrath or sorrow or job or hope or fear or error or some other attitude of the mind than by truth or prescription or some rule of a law or form of a judgment or by laws."[31] For this reason among the Areopagites and others, it was prohibited by the laws, so that nothing could be said "outside the fact of the case." [ἔξωτοῦ πραλματος .][32] And Caesar in the works of Sallust says, "It is fitting that all men who confer upon difficult questions ought to be free from hatred and friendship, anger and pity."[33] Although if an orator should be such as he ought to be, to that extent he ought to be recognized as [a good man]. Good men would not arouse emotions from something simulated but from something truly good or bad, and they will have a great and laudable power for promoting true and good things and thus the speech of these men is emotional.

Cicero enumerates fewer "emotions" than does Aristotle, but he does not list those by which judges should be moved. He grants the first place to pity, and in the inspiring of pity for himself, "it was of so great a force and efficacy that in a pitiable case[34] he filled the forum with groans and wails." (He said) that it appears in the perorations, although books lack that breath of life which usually makes such passages seem more impressive when spoken than when read. Then he adds, "Nor is the appeal for sympathy the only way of arousing the emotions of the jury, but the juror must be made to be angry or appeased, to feel ill will or to be well-disposed, he must be made to feel scorn or admiration, hatred or love, desire or loathing, hope or fear, joy or sorrow. The sterner of these various emotions may be exemplified from the Accusation of Verres, the milder from my speeches for the defense."

In this listing, the word "well-disposed" means the same as "to favor" just as "to wilfully choose" signifies "love." Moreover, Aristotle contrasts indignation to pity, if anyone should desire this.[35] Cicero contrasts pity to "ill-will," just as Aristotle contrasts pity to indignation. See (g) in notes.

Types of emotions

Emotion is				
	simple			1 Pleasure
				2 Pain
	for a future	good, 4 Hope		5 Desire
		evil, 3 Fear		6 Aversion
				7 Love
		primarily	gentle,	9 Anger
			harsh,	10 Mildness
	for the present and past			11 Admiration
				13 Benevolence
		arising	from love	14 Emulation
				16 Pity
	composed* of an object		from anger	8 Hate
				12 Contempt
				15 Envy
				17 Indignation
	of the present, past, and future			18 Modesty
				19 Immodesty

*A compound emotion is one in which a simple emotion, either pain or pleasure, is mixed. From whence Aristotle defines through pain those which are partakers of pain.

Pleasure is an emotion from a good thing which has been acquired; pain, on the other hand, from an evil.

For all men rejoice if a thing happens as they wish; if things are otherwise, they grieve.[36]

To which Cicero said, "Everything that causes gratification is a pleasure just as everything that causes annoyance is a pain."[37]

"Fear is a certain disturbance, or a pain, from the imagination of a future destructive evil or of one bringing pain. Why it is necessary that those things should be terrible and frightful, whatsoever seem to have a great power of destroying or of so harming is that the harm spreads out to a great pain."[38]

Trust or "Hope, the contrary of fear, is caused by the imagination of safe things which may be nearby: in the case of things to be feared, however, the cause seems to be either because they are nonexistent or because they are far away."[39]

Desire is the wanting of a future thing and arises from the imagination, what is likely to come. For there is also a wish for the impossible, but that is not hope.

Aversion is the contrary of desire.

Love is an emotion by which we want what seems good for someone, not for our own sake, but for his. And, therefore, we rejoice in things favorable to him, while we grieve at the opposites. Friendship is, moreover, reciprocal love. "To love is to wish for someone what he thinks good, for his, not one's own sake. A friend, however, is one who loves and is posited, one who both congratulates in good affairs and sympathizes in sorrow, from no other cause except, the one loved, should be considered a friend."[40]

Hate is opposed to love; it is desiring the greatest evil for someone. "Concerning enmity, however, and hate, it is apparent that they must be considered contraries. One who is angry will be pitied in many ways: one who hates, in no fashion. The former wishes the one against whom he is angry to grieve in turn: but the latter wishes the one whom he hates not to exist. The former wishes to be understood: the latter does not care."[41]

"Anger seeks revenge involving pain, on account of an undeservedly acquired slight, either against oneself or against those near to one's self."[42]

"Anger is the contrary of mildness. Mildness is, therefore, a quelling and a reduction of anger. If, therefore, they are angered by those slighting them, and the slight is willingly done, it is apparent that for those who do none of these things, or do them involuntarily, are mild and meek."[43]

Admiration is an emotion by which we greatly esteem and revere a man on account of some outstanding good. "However, they admire those who have good qualities worthy of honor, or those who are masters of those affairs which they themselves ardently undertake. Truly, they hold in high regard the prudent just as they do the truthful, just as they do the elders and the learned."

Contempt is the contrary emotion by which we may scorn especially the weakness, ignorance, baseness, and cheapness of anyone who is arrogant. "Contempt is an act of the mind toward that state which is considered not at all worthy. However, they despise unworthy things."[44]

"Benevolence is that through which those are said to do some favor without hope of reward for one who asks for it. That is, not for something in return, nor that those who do it may attain something for themselves, but they do it as a favor for someone. The favor will be great either because the one seeking aid needs it very much, or because his needs are great and difficult or because he requires them in circumstances of this sort, either because he was the only one doing the favor, or the first, or he did it in a great way; on the other hand, the favor will be slight if either they do it for their own sake, or they did that which is hardly benevolent, or it happened by chance that they did the favor or they were forced to do it, or they returned a good deed or did not actually do anything."[45]

"Emulation is a certain pain about good and worthwhile objects, which someone perceives from similarities in nature, not because they adhere in others, but because we do not also possess them."[46]

"Envy is a certain pain because certain goods seem to have been acquired by others. This causes envy in us not that we do not have any for ourselves, but because they have them."[47] Moreover, it is opposed to both benevolence and jealousy; to benevolence, because the one filled with benevolence rejoices when it is well with another; an envious person grieves in the same circumstances; to jealousy, because the jealous one does not rejoice that it is well for another, an envious person grieves in the same circumstances; to jealousy, because the jealous one does not rejoice that it is well for another, but sorrows that it is not well even for himself, but he sorrows that it is well for another. "Therefore, emulation is something good and is characteristic of good men. Envy, on the other hand, is something wicked and is characteristic of wicked men."[48]

"Pity is a certain pain arising from an apparent evil circumstance toward one not deserving to suffer it, because he will think that he himself or some of his friends might also suffer it."[49]

"That which they term 'to be indignant' is greatly opposed to pity. For grieving on account of adversity which undeservedly befalls them, is opposed in some fashion to pity because it is grieving at the fortunate circumstances of another person undeservedly gained. And both these are passions of men of good character."[50]

"Modesty is a certain pain and a passion from either present or past or future evils which may bring infamy. Wherefore, it is necessary to be ashamed of these evils, which are things which seem to be disgraceful either for ourself or for those persons who matter to us."[52]

From these, that light and placid emotion of love, "to gain favor," is properly termed; the more vehement (which $\pi\acute{a}\theta\eta$ $\kappa\alpha\tau$' $\epsilon\xi o\chi\grave{\eta}\nu$ [53] and from which the rule for pathetic proof is derived) can be used for arousing. The rule for gaining favor has been set forth above: See (c) in the notes: the rule for arousing follows.

(f) concludes. See (d).

(g) good or evil. Which good or evil things are useful to arouse each emotion, Aristotle shows abundantly in the chapters noted. And in *De Oratore* ii. li. 208, where Cicero teaches that hate is aroused in ways opposite to which the ways in which love is gained. "If you glorify the doing of something ruinous or unprofitable to your particular audience, hate is engendered: while if it be something done against good men in general, or those to whom the particular doer should never have done it, or against the State, no such bitter hate is excited, but a disgust closely resembling ill-will or hate."

But on pity and jealousy, as I have stated, he insists especially, "But I rather think (he said) the emotion of jealousy is by far the fiercest of all, and needs as much energy for its repression as for its stimulation. Now people are especially jealous of their equals or of those ones beneath them when they feel themselves left behind and fret at the others upward flight; but jealousy of their betters also is often furious, and all the more so if these conduct themselves insufferably, and overstep their rightful claims on the strength of pre-eminent rank or prosperity; if these advantages are to be made fuel for jealousy, it should before all be pointed out that they were not the fruit of merit; next, that they even came by vice and wrongdoing; finally that the man's deserts, though creditable and impressive enough, are still exceeded by his arrogance and disdain. To quench jealousy, on the other hand, it is proper to emphasize the points that those advantages were the fruits of great exertion and great risks, and were not turned to his own profit but to that of other people; and that, as for any renown he himself may seem to have won, through no unfair recompense for his risk, he nevertheless finds no pleasure therein, but casts it aside and disclaims it altogether: and we must by all means make sure (since most people are jealous and this failing is remarkably general and widespread, while jealousy is attracted by surpassingly brilliant prosperity) that the belief in such prosperity shall be weakened, and that what was supposed to be outstanding prosperity shall be seen to be thoroughly blended with labor and sorrow. Lastly, pity is awakened if the hearer can be brought to apply to his own adversities whether endured or only apprehended, the lamentations uttered over someone else, or if, in his contemplation of another's case, he many times goes back to his own experience. Thus, while particular occasions of human distress are deeply felt, if described in moving terms, the dejection and ruin of the righteous are especially lamentable."[54]

It is especially helpful, however, to effect pleasure in speaking and to delight the listeners, and this not only by delightful digressions, adorned with elegance and brilliance of style, by the marked concinnity of thoughts disposed properly, and a variety of pleasing things connected attractively, but occasionally by appropriate wit and charm.

Concerning Wit

"Jesting, too, (Antony said) and shafts of wit are agreeable and often highly effective: but these, even if all else can be taught by art, are assuredly the endowment of nature and in no need of art." Caesar soon confirms this thought of his about the parts which are to be discussed in this section.[55] Concerning usefulness he said, "I have very often seen much done in court by humor and flashes of wit: either because that very gaiety procures their benevolence through which it is aroused or because everyone often admires a shrewd position in one word, especially of the one replying, sometimes even of the one attacking; or because it breaks the opponent, who is impeded, made light of, slowed down, refuted; or because it denotes that the orator is an accomplished man of learning, wit, and most of all that he eases and relaxes gloominess and harshness; and he often dissolves a hateful affair, which is not easy to dilute with reasoning, by a jest or a pun. And since it is derived from nature, nor is it able to be taught by art, there are (he said) two types of witticisms, one running with equal flow all through a speech while the other, though incisive, is intermittent. But while art is not wanted in that continuous sort of jocularity (since nature moulds mankind, and produces mimics and witty storytellers, helped by their features, intonation, and individual style of speaking) what reason, pray, is there for art in raillery, which is that other sort, wherein the shaft of wit has to be sped and hit its mark, with no palpable pause for thought? For what help could my brother here have got from art, when Phillippus inquired of him, 'What are you barking at, Master Puppy?' and he answered, 'I see a thief.' "[56] In this place he recounts two outstanding types of wit that Crassus used against Brutus: one of the latter, one of the former kind.

And yet Caesar warns at the same time that an art of wit was impossible, nevertheless, lest any part of speaking seem to be passed over here, he sets forth the sort of things which he has discovered in nature, zeal and exercise, bringing forth another division of wit and certain precepts which had been acquired in each type.

2. Division of Wit

"There are (he said) two types of wit: one employed on the facts, the other on words. Which when you speak certain words and they are witty, it is contained in the fact, yet should you change the words it loses its flavor; it has every pleasantness in the words. On facts, wherever any tale is told, some anecdote for instance, or that type which is taken from imitation. As regards words, however, the laughter is awakened by something pointed in a phrase or reflection. Ambiguity depends on language not on facts, and it wins really vast applause on its own merits, as I said before, for the power to divert the force of a word into a sense quite different from that in which other folk understand it, seems to indicate a man of talent; yet the jest arouses wonder rather than laughter. Another category which uses a slight change in spelling, the Greeks call $\pi\alpha\rho\alpha\nu o\mu\alpha\sigma\acute{\iota}o\nu$.[57] There is a point also in the explanation of a name, when you make fun of the reason."[58] He reviews many and varied examples of these types.

"Precepts to be observed in joking"[59]

1. "As in that type above, either of narration or of imitation, any similarity to the stage mimics should be avoided, so orators ought greatly to avoid ribald jests.

2. "Too much imitation is for the mimics as is also obscenity: the orator should steal the imitation he needs, as the one who listens knows more than he sees: let him show a like ingenuity and his color by the cut of his words not by the obscenity of the affair.

3. "A rule of timing, a moderation of his raillery, and a novelty of words distinguish an orator from a jester: and as we speak with a reason, not that we seem ridiculous, but that we advance something, not just talk for a whole day without a reason.

4. "With jesting and ribald men it is most difficult to establish a rule for men and for timing; and it is equally difficult for a person to contain those things which may occur since they are able to be said most humorously. Ennius said that a flame could be squeezed from a wise, glowing mouth more easily than it could hold in humorous sayings.

5. "Neither an unproven aspect nor a pitiful aspect should be laughed at. Most people wish to be branded as criminal for their strength rather than for their ridiculousness; they do not wish unfortunate circumstances of others, lest by chance they should fall themselves.

6. "The good deeds of men ought to be spared most of all, lest you speak rashly against those things which they hold dearest; not against anyone except when there is need; as against an adversary, and greatly so if his foolishness is able to be rankled; against foolish, desirous, or light testimony if men seem to be going to be heard easily.

7. "Those things we say when provoked are much more acceptable than those we work out beforehand; for both the swiftness of the skill is greater when it appears in a response and it is the reply of humanity; for we seem to have been going to be still, except that we were provoked.

8. "Those things that are thought to be purposeful, should be laughed at least of all.

9. "Men are greatly delighted if some laughter is brought about by joining the fact and the word.

10. "The more severe and harsh the countenance the more witty the saying seems. As Crassus, although he was the most witty and comely of

all, both was and seemed the most grave and severe of all and won the envy of Antony."

In addition, many witty authors are cited by Caesar, men famous and solemn, Socrates, Fabricius, Africanus, Maximus, Cato, Lepidus. "I regard Cicero as being (says Quintilian) the professor of a remarkable turn of wit." That man's agreeable orations attest to this: "Pro Ligaria" (where, except for the word about the mercy of Caesar, the entire exordium is filled with humor), "Pro Quinctio (where he censured the rapacity and cruelty of a powerful adversary pleasantly), "Pro Muraena" where the exceedingly severe paradoxes of the Stoics were violently attacked by wit and raillery against Cato himself.

For agitiating the emotions usefully, however, it is highly profitable to distinguish the proper manner which is appropriate to each one's age and fortune; which Aristotle, indeed, graphically depicted. See *Theod.*, 1. 2. from chapter 12 to chapter 18.[60]

Furthermore, because the more successful go out to find benevolent listeners in order to move their emotions, "Another desirable thing for the advocate is that the members of the tribunal, of their own accord should carry within them to court some mental emotion that is in harmony with what the advocate's interest will suggest. For, as the saying goes, it is easier to spur the willing horse than to start the lazy one. But if no such emotion be present, or recognizable, he will be like a careful physician who, before he attempts to administer a remedy to his patient, must investigate not only the malady of the man he wishes to cure, but also his habits when in health, and his physical constitution. This indeed is the reason why, when setting about a hazardous and important case, in order to explore the feelings of the tribunal, I engage wholeheartedly in a consideration so careful, that I scent out with all possible keenness their thoughts, judgments, anticipations, and wishes, and the direction in which they seem likely to be led away most easily by eloquence. If they surrender to me, and as I said before, of their own accord, lean toward and are prone to take the course in which I am urging them on, I accept their bounty and set sail for that quarter which promises something of a breeze. If, however, an arbitrator is neutral and free from predisposition, my task is harder, since everything has to be called forth by my speech, with no help from the listener's character. But so potent is that eloquence, rightly styled by an excellent poet 'soulbending sovereign of all things,' that she cannot only support the sinking and bend the upstanding, but like a good and brave commander can even make prisoner a resisting antagonist, especially if the orator speaks with feeling to excite the judge, he himself should seem on fire first. Moreover, it is impossible for the listener to feel indignation, hatred, or ill-will, to be terrified of anything, or reduced to tears of compassion, unless all those emotions, which the advocate would inspire in the arbitrator, are visibly stamped or rather branded on the advocate himself."[61]

"If you would have me weep, you must first feel grief yourself."[62] But, on the other hand, if the chance for moving them to laughter occurs and the person either smiles or laughs himself, he will merit derision not laughter. See above (10).

Just as emotions can be useful either in our behalf or to arouse ill-feeling against our adversary, so too, it is useful for the adversary to assuage ill-feeling that has been aroused against us. An aroused emotion is calmed by arousing its contrary. "When either a lesser case of gaining favor, or a stronger case of exciting the emotions are given, they should be rendered neutral by the contrary emotions as hate with kindness, or as mercy with jealousy."[63] So also, serious arguments are made sport of with jesting; a joke can be shaken apart by a serious handling.

(h) Amplification. That which is properly termed exaggeration, is called amplification by Quintilian in viii. iv., where he uses the word "amplification" in different places, but only once the word "exaggeration".[64] However, among speakers, each word denotes separate things. See (g) in Ch. 3. Sec. 6.

(i) Crassus interprets exaggeration and diminution as the exaggeration of the truth for the sake of adding or diminishing.[65] Aristotle defines these as follows, "Exaggeration and diminution are enthymemes for showing a thing to be great or small."[66] Both are found in "that famous balance of Critolaus who claims that if in one scale he puts the good that belongs to the body and good things which come from outside man, the first scale sinks so far as to outweigh the second with all the land and seas thrown in as well." Whence Cicero infers as follows: "What then prevents either this thinker or the famous Xenocrates as well, that most influential of philosophers, who exalts virtue as earnestly and depreciates and rejects everything else from making not merely happy life depend on virtue but supremely happy life as well?"[67]

"Αυξήσις [Exaggeration] is especially noteworthy in the 'commonplaces,' so called because they seem to be the same in many cases."[68] Of prime importance among these "places" are cause, effect, subject, adjunct, parts, equals, greater, or lesser.

From the object, exaggeration occurs when the audience or noteworthy persons are shown to be exceptionally in error, as *De Oratore* ii. 1i. 208, "For if you glorify the doing of something ruinous or unprofitable to your particular audience, hate is engendered: while, if it be something done against good men in general, or those to whom the particular doer should never have done it, or against the State, no such bitter hate is excited, but a disgust closely resembling ill-will or hate."

From the lesser, *Institutio Oratoria* vii. iv. 11, "At times, again, we may advance a parallel to make something which we desire to exaggerate seem greater then ever, as Cicero does in the 'Pro Cluentio' where, after telling a story of a woman of Miletus who took a bribe from the reversionary heirs to prevent the birth of her expected child, he cries, 'How must greater is the punishment deserved by Oppisnicus for the same offence. For that woman by doing violence to her own body did but torture herself, whereas he procured the same result by applying violence and torture to the body of another.' "[69] A similar example is *In Catalinam* i. i. 3. "Did that illustrious citizen, the Pontifex Maximus, Publius Scipio, acting merely in his private capacity, kill Tiberius Cracchus when he introduced but slight changes for the worse that did not seriously impair the constitution of the state, and shall we as consuls suffer Cataline to live, whose aim was to lay waste the whole world with fire and sword?" Here Gracchus is compared with "Cataline," the constitution of the state to the "whole world," a slight change for the worse to "fire and sword and desolation," and a private citizen to "the consuls," all comparisons as being lesser, and to be used for further individual expansion, if anyone should desire to do so.

Exaggeration growing in rather great leaps is termed augmentation. "It can be made more striking by pointing the comparison between words of stronger meaning and those for which we propose to substitute them as Cicero does in denouncing Verres: 'I have brought before you, judges, not a thief, but a plunderer, not an adulterer, but a ravisher; not a mere committer of sacrilege, but the enemy of all religious observance and all holy things; not an assassin, but a bloodthirsty butcher who has slain our fellow-citizens and our allies!' Even those things which are the lesser seem to be most powerful when placed with the great as, 'It is a sin to bind a Roman Citizen, a crime to scourge him, little short of the most unnatural murder to put him to death, what then shall I call his crucifixion?' "[70]

Diminution comes from the same arguments as exaggeration, except that in equals the greater should be placed before the lesser because as in exaggeration the ascent was from the lesser to the greater, so here the descent should be from the greater. And diminution "is effected by the same method as augmentation since there are as many degrees of descent as ascent."[71]

Cicero teaches that the strength of exaggeration and diminution is very great, "there is no limit to the power of an oration to exalt a subject or render it contemptible. This must be done in the midst of arguments, whenever an opening is offered to amplify or disparage; and there is almost unlimited opportunity for it in the peroration."[72] See (f).

(k) Instruction. The direct manner alone here (which, not as in the other two, persuades by affecting the mind with troubles but by informing the intellect with argumentation) does not want to be deceitful or hasty. "And because as I have repeatedly said already there are three methods of bringing people to hold our opinion, instruction or persuasion or appeal to their emotions, one of these three methods we must openly display, so as to appear to wish solely to impart instruction, whereas the two remaining methods should be interfused throughout the whole structure of our speeches like the blood in our bodies."[73]

(1) Management belongs in the changeable[74] parts [the proposition, confirmation, and confutation] of the oration. For, in these parts, explication, proof, and amplification (except delaying and digression) have their place. *De Oratore* iii. xxvi. 104. "Amplification is desired in all those places which are used to make a speech convincing." *De Oratore* ii. lxxvii. 312. "And accordingly very often either a place is given to a digression devoted to exciting emotion after we have related the facts and stated our case, or this can rightly be done after we have established our own argument or refuted those of our opponents, or in both places, or in all the parts of the speech, if the case is one of this importance and extent."

(m) The use of explication is in obscure parts, so that what is being disputed is understood.

(n) Word. An obscure word is explained by interpretation or by etymology, periphrase, or paraphrase; and (if the obscurity should arise from ambiguity), it is explained by distinguishing.

(o) Fact. An obscure fact is explicated by logical arguments, for example, by definition, description, by causes and effects, by subjects and adjuncts, likenesses, cognates, contraries, etc.

(p) The four types of argumentation are commonly enumerated: syllogism, enthymeme, analogy,[75] and example. From which Tully admits only two[76] [the syllogism which he terms deduction and analogy.] The former he defines as, "Deduction or syllogistic reasoning is a form of argument which draws a probable conclusion from the fact under consideration itself; when this probable conclusion is set forth and recognized by itself by its own import and reasoning."[77] The other as, "analogy is a form of argument which leads the person with whom one is arguing to give assent to certain undisputed facts; through this assent it wins his approval of a doubtful proposition because this resembles the facts to which he has assented. For instance, in a dialogue Aeschines Socraticus,[78] etc." Peter Ramus includes everything in one syllogism. For, an enthymeme is an imperfect syllogism that is mutilated in some member; it occurs when either the major or the minor is omitted as being obvious. An analogy is an enthymeme in which one fact is inferred from many because of a likeness; it is good and conclusive if it should enumerate every example or species, or best of all if a little statement of this sort can be attached, "No example to the contrary can be found." And, example is also an enthymeme or an imperfect analogy, the arguments for which, when it is an outstanding example, adds an ornament to the question rather than anything substantial, from which comes the statement, "An example illustrates but does not prove." See Peter Ramus *Dialecticae Libri Duo* ii. 9; and Piscator on the same subject,[79] where Ramus defines, "A syllogism is a deduction on a given question when the argument is so disposed that by reason of what has been placed first it concludes necessarily." This is not too different from Aristotle, *De Sophisticis Elenchis* Ch. 1., "Deduction is based on certain statements made in such a way as necessarily to cause the assertion of things other than those statements and as a result of those statements." And in the *Topics* i. i. "Deduction is a discussion in which, certain things having been laid down, something other than these things necessarily results through them."

(q) These parts, Peter Ramus defines as, "The major is the first part of the antecedent, from which, at least, the consequent of the major is arranged with proof. The minor is the second part of the antecedent which is assumed from the major. The conclusion is the final part of the syllogism which ties together the parts of the question and brings it to a conclusion."

(r) Less. *Dialecticae Libri Duo* ii. 9. "If any part of the syllogism should be lacking, it is termed an enthymeme." Moreover, an enthymeme is termed παρὰ τὸν ενθυμεῖσθαι [80] [to turn over in one's mind, to think]. For, since it is a syllogism, of which some one part is not expressed in words, that enthymeme ought to be supplied by cogitation, moveover, an enthymeme is so familiar in orations, that as a result it is called an oratorical syllogism. See (p).

(s) More. Certain people enumerate the proofs of the parts in the works of Cicero in sections. And so they make argumentation not only threefold as consisting of the major premise, the minor, and the conclusion, but also fourfold when one part of the antecedent section has a proof attached, and fivefold when both premises have a proof attached. "Those who have thought this form of argument worthy of a very careful consideration have said that it has five parts and others have thought that it could be divided into not more than three parts. Those who think that the syllogism ought to be divided into five parts say that the first one should state the basis of the argument in this way: 'Things that are done by design are managed better than those which are governed without design.' This they count as the first part. Then they think it should be supported by a variety of reasons and the greatest possible fullness of expression in the following manner, 'The house that is managed in accordance with a reasoned plan is in every respect better equipped and furnished than one which is governed in a haphazard way with total lack of design. The army that is commanded by a wise and shrewd general is guided in all ways more advantageously than one which is governed by someone's folly and rashness. The same line of reasoning is applicable to navigation, for a ship which has the services of the most expert pilot makes the most successful voyage.' When the major premise has been proved in this fashion and two parts of the syllogism have been completed, in the third part they say you should state as a minor premise what you wish to show, this being in line with the thought of the major premise; the following will be an example, 'Of all things nothing is better governed than the universe.' And then in the fourth place they introduce another proof, that is, of the minor premise, in this way, 'For the risings and the settings of the constellations keep a fixed order, and the changes of the seasons not only proceed in the same way by a fixed law but are also adapted to the advantage of all nature, and the alternations of night and day have never through any variations done any harm.' All these points are proof that the nature of the world is governed by no ordinary intelligence. In the fifth place they put the conclusion, which either merely states the necessary deduction from all the parts, as follows, 'Therefore the universe is administered by design,' or after bringing the major premise and the minor premise together in one brief statement adds what follows from them, after this fashion, 'Therefore if those things are administered better which are governed by design than those which are administered without design, and nothing is governed better than the universe, then the universe is governed by design.' This is the way in which they think the argument is expressed in five parts. An argument consists of four parts when we state a premise, either major or minor, without giving the proof. This should be done either when the major premise is self-intelligible or when the minor premise is an obvious statement needing no proof. Those, however, who think that it is threefold, [the major premise and proof], which the other group count as two parts, seem to them to be one, namely, [the major premise]. Likewise, what is called by the other group, minor premise and proof, seems to them merely the minor premise."[81] But truly proof is neither a principal part of the syllogism as those say, nor a part of the sections as they think are to be counted, but separate from that part to which it adds substance, which may be changed into a prosyllogism in this manner, "If a home, an army, a ship and things of this same sort are governed better by design than without design: but the antecedent is assumed true, therefore the consequent is also true." Likewise, the proof of a minor premise in a prosyllogism concludes the proof itself.

A prosyllogism is a proving syllogism added to the main syllogism, for the purpose of proving its doubtful parts: even though what is now written with a simple "σ" nevertheless, the word seems to be composed of πρὸς not just πρὸ. See *Prior Analytics*. i. 26. With reference to arguments [in the matter of argumentation] and their types, see invention; concerning the order of arguments and the varied order of its parts, see arrangement.

(t) Amplification. *De Oratore* iii. xxxvi. 104. The importance of amplification is noted, "But the highest distinction of eloquence consists in amplification by means of ornament." And in the *De Partitione Oratoria* xv. 52. its proper place, "In the actual course of the speech opportunities occur, when something has been proved or refuted, for turning aside to amplify."

(v) Extension is. *De Partitione Oratoria* vii. 23. "When a speech is contracted from a word and the word is led into many words: or when the statement has been made once in a direct form as prompted by mere instinct the order is inverted and the same things is said as it were upside down or the other way round, and then the same thing in a piecemeal and mixed-up form."

(u) With arguments. The places of contraction are especially the cause and effect, subject and adjunct, species, testimony, example: concerning the common importance of the places, Cicero says, "Amplification is especially noteworthy in the commonplaces: so called because they seem to be the same in many cases."[82] Although elsewhere the same factor seems to restrict contraction to the place of genus either entirely or principally, "There was no one who understood how to amplify his case and, from a question restricted to a particular person and time, transfer it to universals."[83] And *De Oratore* iii. xxx. 120. "Well, then, the most ornate speeches are those which take the widest range and which turn aside from the particular matter in dispute, to engage in an explanation of the meaning of the general issue, so as to enable the audience to base their verdict in regard to the particular parties and charges and actions in question on a knowledge of the nature and character of the matter as a whole."

An example of extension from the effects is that which Seneca uses, describing one who is angry, "But you have only to behold the aspect of those possessed by anger to know that they are insane. For the marks of a madman are unmistakable—a bold and threatening mien, a gloomy brow, a fierce expression, a hurried step, restless hands, an altered colour, a quick and more violent breathing."[84]

(x) Digression. *Institutio Oratoria* iv. iii. 14. "Παρέκβασις may, I think, be defined as the handling of some theme, which must, however, have some bearing on the case, in a passage that involves digression from the logical order of our speech.

(y) Enjoyment. *De Oratore* iii. liii. 203, "for a great impression is made from digression from the matter at issue; and after a thing has supplied enjoyment, the return to the subject will have to be neatly and tactfully effected," as Cicero says, "But one should go back to the place from which the digression started." Digression, moreover, entertains in extolling and cursing a man or regions, in the description of regions recording historical or even legendary occurrences, exhorting, dissuading, warning, asking. As examples of this type, I may cite the praise of Sicily and the rape of

Proserpine in the orations against Verres, and the famous recital of the virtues of Gnaius Pompeius in the "Pro L. Cornelio."[85]

(z) Argument. The principal places of digression are cause, effect, subject, adjunct, genus, species, but digression from a species to a genus is excellent as in extension. Such is the "Pro Archia Poeta" where Cicero, after confirming the proposition that, "Archias must not be dropped from the roll of the Romas Citizens," digression from Archias' learning into the praise of studies and literature, "You will no doubt ask me, Gracchus, etc."[86] but not until he had first begged pardon, "I crave your indulgence, speaking as I am on behalf of a distinguished poet and a consummate scholar, before a cultivated audience, an enlightened jury, to enlarge somewhat upon enlightenment and cultivated pursuits." Finally, an elegant regression is used, "How often, gentlemen, have I seen my friend Archias, etc."

Prominent Examples of Amplification in the "Pro Muraena"[87]

Since there are three headings of the prosecution, 1. the accusation's against Murena's way of life, 2. a comparison of the merits of the contestants, 3. the charge of bribery. On the accusations of Murena's way of life, Cicero proves to Cato, who had brought up the dancing of Murena, that this could not be brought against him truthfully because the vices which are the cause of dancing were not found, "(drunkenness, insanity, an indecorous and evil banquet, places of enjoyment, many delightful amusements, love, debauch, lust, extravagance). When these are taken away, (he says) this vice is not able to exist at all." Which extension is an expansion of extravagance which he presently lists singly as though treating the entire grouping. "Do you think you can find the shadow of extravagance in that man in whom you cannot find extravagance itself?" In the comparison of merits of the contestants, there are three famous comparisons. The first is of the old and new nobility, which from the causes [virtues, and the rewards of virtues] he does not amplify with examples of the most noble of men, especially of Pompeius and Aemilius. "Nor have I ever thought there was less worth in Quintus Pompeius, who was a new man and a brave hero, than in that high-born man, Marcus Aemilius Scaurus. For it requires the same quality of mind and character to hand down to his posterity (as Pompeius did) a distinction of rank which he had not inherited, and as for Scaurus it requires the same qualities to revive by his own genius the almost extinct memory of his family." The second point is a comparison of his life as a lawyer and his wartime valor, in which he digresses on a certain objection of Sulpicius to which when he had replied, he returns in this regression to the comparison he had begun, "but drop this subject and return to a comparison of pursuits and professions. How can you doubt, etc." When this comparison was finished (in which he maintained that Murena was more worthy of the consulship on account of his wartime valor than was Sulpicius for his legal background), he digresses into the third comparison, namely, the knowledge and ability to speak, "Weighty indeed and full of dignity, etc." Moreover, this final comparison is to be called not extension, but a digression by saying for what reasons, on account of what facts, for the sake of entertainment, it is used. He does not touch the point of bribery on the part of the candidates, as he does the two earlier points. In the same place, he replies at length in a little oration against Cato to whom he responds separately about the crimes of bribery, immediately from the exordium in which he gains favor of the judges, by not diminishing either the authority or dignity of Cato, he commences the case for Lucius Murena, digressing into a brief commendation of Cato himself. And then he makes a new digression into a longer, but good-natured, rebuke for his eloquence and his philosophy (which he had imbibed from the exceedingly difficult and austere school of the Stoics). Finally he returns thus, "Therefore, to return to the point at which I began—take Cato's name, please, out of the case, forget his enthusiasm, disregard his influence. In a trial, contending with me in the crimes themselves, this should either have no force at all or should count for acquittal." And then he comes to the very point, knowledge of the crime, namely, bribery, which when he had done away with it, he digresses into the sharp invective against the conspirators, then into a serious and weighty exhortation against Cato himself that he should look after himself and the republic, finally he gives his peroration by means of an emotional complaint, a prayer, and a counterpromise. Let that prudent practice of Antony conclude these precepts about the three means of persuasion—instruction, gaining favor, and arousing the emotions. "For my part when I am launched on a case and have to the best of my ability passed all the facts under consideration, having discerned and ascertained the arguments that belong to the case and also the topics calculated to win the favor of the court and those adapted to arouse its emotions, I then decide what are the good and what the bad points in the case of each of the parties; to take the good points of my case and elaborate these, embellishing and enlarging and lingering and dwelling on and sticking to them, while any bad part or weakness in my case I leave to one side, not in such a manner as to give the appearance of running away from it but so as to disguise it and entirely cover it up by embellishing and amplifying the good point referred to. And if the case is one that turns on arguments, I maintain all the strongest among them in full measure, whether they are several or only one, or if it is a matter of winning favor of arousing feeling, I concentrate particularly on the part of the case that is most capable of influencing men's minds."[88]

NOTES AND REFERENCES

1. Foster Watson, *The Old Grammar Schools* (New York: G. P. Putnam's Sons, 1916), p. 440. See also, J. Howard Brown, *Elizabethan Schooldays: An Account of the English Grammar Schools in The Second Half of the Sixteenth Century* (Oxford: Basil Blackwell, 1933); Arthur F. Leach, *English Schools at the Reformation 1546–48* (London: Archibald Constable & Co., 1896); J. Bass Mullinger, "English Grammar Schools," *The Cambridge History of English Literature,* edited by A. W. Ward and A. R. Waller (New York: Macmillan Co., 1939), vol. 8, p. 368; S. J. Curtis, *History of Education in Great Britain* (London: University Tutorial Press Ltd., 1957); A. Monroe Stowe, *English Grammar Schools in the Reign of Queen Elizabeth* (New York: Columbia University Press, 1908), and Henry Peacham, *The Compleat Gentleman,* edited by G. B. Gordon, (Oxford: At the University Press, 1906).

2. Foster Watson, *The English Grammar Schools to 1660: Their Curriculum and Practice* (Cambridge: At the University Press, 1908), p. 441. Wilbur Samuel Howell, *Logic and Rhetoric in England, 1500–1700* (New York: Russell & Russell, 1961), p. 155. William P. Sandford, "English Rhetoric Reverts to Classicism 1600–1650," *Quarterly Journal of Speech* 15 (1929): 506–07.

3. A. H. Bullen, "Charles Butler," *DNB,* 8: 44.

4. Anthony A. Wood, *Athenae Oxonienses,* edited by Philip Bliss (London: Printed for F. C. & J. Rivington, 1813), vol. 3, p. 209.

5. British Museum Department of Printed Books, *The British Museum Catalogue of Printed Books, 1881–1900* (Ann Arbor: J. W. Edwards, 1946), 29: 577.

6. Robert Watt, *Bibliotheca Britannica* (Edinburgh: Printed for Archibald Constable & Co. and Longman Hurst, Rees, Orme, Brown, and Green, 1824), 1: 117k.

7. Cf. Howell, *Logic and Rhetoric,* pp. 262–63.

8. Watson, *English Grammar Schools,* p. 442.

9. Charles Butler, *Oratoriae Libri Duo* (Oxford: Printed for William Turner, 1629), A1. (Translations mine.)

10. Ibid., D1.

11. Ibid., F2.

12. Ibid., K4.

13. Lee S. Hultzēn, "Charles Butler on Memory," *Speech Monographs* 6 (1939): 44–62.

14. Butler, *Oratoriae,* Q3.

15. Howell, *Logic and Rhetoric,* p. 268.

16. Ibid., pp. 268–69.

17. Sandford, "English Rhetoric Reverts to Classicism," p. 503. Also consult his *English Theories of Public Address 1530–1828* (Columbus, Ohio: H. L. Hedrick, 1931), pp. 104 ff. for an elaboration of his argument.

18. Hultzēn, "Charles Butler on Memory," p. 44.

19. Cicero, *De Inventione,* translated by H. M. Hubbell (Cambridge, Mass.: Harvard University Press, 1949), i. v. 6. Butler cites the spot reference as *"Invent* I. 1. 8″ which, of course, does not agree with Hubbell, cited above. In all probability, Butler used or had access to the editions of Cicero's *De Inventione* by Manutius (1540) or Lambinus (1566), both of which are now lost.

20. Butler's Latin agrees substantially with that of Hubbell's text; however, omits the following sentence at this point, "There is a difference between function and end: in the case of function we consider what should be done, in the case of the end what result is to be produced."

21. The only variants here are the reference, and the substitution of the verb *probandum* (proving) for Butler's *doceamus,* which is translated as "we teach."

22. Cicero, *De Optimo Genere Oratorum,* translated by H. M. Hubbell (Cambridge, Mass.: Harvard University Press, 1949), i. 3.

23. Butler's words do not correspond to *De Oratore* ii. lxxvii. 310. which reads, "There are three methods of bringing people to hold our opinion, instruction or persuasion, or appeal to their emotions."

24. These words are omitted: "while the want of them estranges it from such as do not possess them, accordingly the very opposites of these qualities must be ascribed to our opponents."

25. Sutton and Rackham add, "You must struggle to reveal the presence in the cause you are upholding of some merit or usefulness."

26. This sentence is omitted: "By 'parties' I mean not only persons impeached, but all whose interests are being determined, for that was how people used the term in the old days."

27. Butler's quotation is, at best, a paraphrase. Section 322 reads, "Conciliation of the audience must indeed permeate the whole of the speech, and especially the peroration, but nevertheless this class of consideration does supply a great many modes of opening."

28. Cicero, *De Partitione Oratoria*, translated by H. Rackham (Cambridge, Mass.: Harvard University Press, 1942), xv. 52.

29. Butler either confused the *Theodectea* with the *Rhetorica* or considered them synonymous, since with only two exceptions his references to the *Theodectea* can be located in the *Rhetorica*, in precisely the chapters cited. Cf. E. M. Cope, *An Introduction to Aristotle's Rhetoric* (London and Cambridge: Macmillan and Co., 1867), pp. 55 ff.

30. Cf. Aristotle, *Rhetorica*, translated by Lane Cooper (New York: Appleton-Century Co., 1932), 1377^b. The first sentence does not appear.

31. Butler may be paraphrasing *De Oratore* ii. xliv. 185.

32. Cf. *Rhetorica* 1354^a. "For by common consent the laws should forbid irrelevant speaking and some courts, as that of the Areopagus actually do forbid it." Also see Athenaeus, *Deipnosophistae* xiii. vi. 590.

33. Sallust, *Bellum Catilinae*, translated by J. C. Rolfe (New York: G. P. Putnam's Sons, 1921), li. 1.

34. Butler is here paraphrasing *Orator* xxxvii. 130.

35. Cf. *Rhetorica* 1386^b.

36. Cf. *Rhetorica* 1381^a.

37. *De Finibus* i.xi. 37.

38. Cf. *Rhetorica* 1382^a.

39. Cf. *Rhetorica* 1383^a.

40. Cf. *Rhetorica* 1380^b.

41. Cf. *Rhetorica* 1382ᵃ.

42. Cf. *Rhetorica* 1378ᵃ.

43. Cf. *Rhetorica* 1380ᵃ.

44. Cf. *Rhetorica* 1378ᵇ.

45. Cf. *Rhetorica* 1385ᵃ.

46. Cf. *Rhetorica* 1388ᵃ.

47. Cf. *Rhetorica* 1387ᵇ.

48. Cf. *Rhetorica* 1388ᵃ.

49. Cf. *Rhetorica* 1385ᵇ.

50. Cf. *Rhetorica* 1386ᵇ.

51. Cf. *Rhetorica* 1383ᵇ.

52. Cf. *Rhetorica* 1383ᵇ.

53. The term means "from unexpected emotions."

54. *De Oratore* ii. lii. 209–211.

55. Butler, in this sentence, is paraphrasing from ii. liv. 216–219.

56. Caesar's brother was named "Catulus," which means "a little dog" or a "puppy." The joke is the play on his name and his unexpected response. Phillipus was, at the time, thought to be guilty of theft.

57. The term means "assonance."

58. Cf. *De Oratore* ii. lix. 239; ii. lxiii. 257.

59. *Institutio Oratoria* vi. iii. 29. These ten rules which Butler advances are brief paraphrases of vi. iii. and vi. iv. The wording and arrangement are Butler's, the ideas seem to be those of Quintilian's.

60. Cf. *Rhetorica* 1389ᵃ. This section treats of the types of character, i.e., the young, the old, the prime of life, etc.

61. *De Oratore* ii. xiiv. 185 ff.

62. Horace, *Ars Poetica,* 102.

63. *De Oratore* ii. li. 205.

64. *Institutio Oratoria* viii. iv. 11.

65. *De Oratore* iii. liv. 206.

66. Cf. *Rhetorica* 1403[a].

67. *Tusculanarum Disputationes* v. xvii. 51.

68. *Orator* xxxvi. 126.

69. Cicero, *Pro Cluentio,* trans. H. Grose Hodge (Cambridge, Mass.: Harvard University Press, 1943), xi. 32.

70. *Institutio Oratoria* viii. iv. 2–4.

71. *Institutio Oratoria* viii. iv. 28.

72. *Orator* xxxvi. 127.

73. *De Oratore* ii. lxxvii. 310.

74. Butler distinguishes between the changeable and the fixed parts of an oration. The word *insitio* carries the meaning "inherent."

75. I have here and hereafter translated *inductio* as "analogy," since this seems to be what the classic writers meant by the term. To render the word as "induction" seems to include more than was originally intended. Analogy here should be understood as argument from parallel examples.

76. *De Inventione* i. xxxi. 51: "All argumentation, then, is to be carried on either by induction or deduction" are the words used by Hubbell; however, he foot-notes this translation by saying, "The process which he [Cicero] calls induction might more accurately be described as analogy . . ."

77. *De Inventione* i. xxxiv. 57.

78. *De Inventione* i. xxxi. 51. The passage continues with Socrates questioning Xenophon's wife and Xenophon himself over a quarrel which they had.

79. John Piscator, *Epistolae de P. Rami Dialectica* (1602).

80. "Reflective thinking" is a close English approximation.

81. *De Inventione* i. xxiv. 57ff.

82. *Orator* xxxvi. 126.

83. *Brutus* xciii. 322.

84. Seneca, "De Ira," in L. *Annaei Senecae Dialogorum,* translated by John W. Basore (New York: G. P. Putnam's Sons, 1928), i. i. 3.

85. This speech is lost.

86. Cicero, "Pro Archia Poeta," in *Orationes,* translated by N. H. Watts (Cambridge, Mass.: Harvard University Press, 1935), vi. 12. Butler is here selecting the major divisions of the speech.

87. Cicero, "Pro Murena," in *Orationes,* trans, Louis E. Lord (Cambridge, Mass.: Harvard University Press, 1937), v. 11.

88. *De Oratore* ii. lxxii. 291.

The Rhetorical Process in Eighteenth Century England

Michael C. McGee

There has been a tendency among rhetoricians to think of "broad" rhetorical principles operating in much the same way regardless of intellectual or political climate.[1] This tendency has made students of British and American public address more prone than most to what Herbert Butterfield calls the "Whig fallacy" in our understanding of the history of Anglo-America. We tend to accept a discounted portrayal of the history of Anglo-America as a God-driven progression from the absolute evils of autocracy, aristocracy, and monarchy to the absolute goods of democracy, representative government, and free speech.[2] Because rhetorical principles were conceived in a democracy of sorts, and because they currently operate most visibly in western democracies, it is assumed that rhetoric functioned in the past as it does today. We take fashionable prejudices about communication and persuasion in "free societies" as a touchstone and proceed to trace the "origins" of these prejudices. This bias, though at times illuminating, is counterproductive first because it tautologically reinforces a monistic view of rhetoric—but more than that, the bias undercuts an opportunity to see rhetoric functioning in relatively "closed" societies. We who work in ages when democracy was heresy defeat ourselves when we look for the effects of public argument in election results, votes in national assemblies which are only apparently "deliberative," or in legislated "reforms" which "anticipate" democracy.[3]

The Whig fallacy—in rhetoric as in history—is essentially a psychological one.[4] If we assume the rhetorical process in a free society to be perfect, our past can only be imperfect, as a child is an imperfect adult. We take it to be right that the people are employers of ministers. And when we look back to Swift's *Observor* or Burke's *Reflections on the Revolution in France,* we note the tremendous popular response to them—but we characterize their importance as a link in a chain of causation from past to present, hardly looking at all for the *intrinsic* significance of popular will in the eighteenth century. Think, for example, how it would change our notion of rhetoric if, instead of thinking of the eighteenth century as a period of imperfect democracy, we think of it as a period of perfect monarchy. It was, of course, neither; but the supposition allows us to see how thoroughly a psychological set can mislead us in understanding the rhetorical process.

The purpose of this paper is to isolate the rhetorical process in a predominantly closed society—England in the eighteenth century. It is an unusual undertaking because, in an attempt to avoid a Whiggish bias, scant attention is paid the usual theme of British public address. Though there is some evidence of social "movement" from a predominantly "closed" society in 1688 to a predominantly "open" society in 1832, I believe such a theme to be misleading. If only because of the intrusion of the French Revolution and the near-pathogenic reaction to it, English society remained nearly as closed in 1800 as it was in 1700.[5] Rather than think of the eighteenth century rhetorical process as an imperfect form of the one we enjoy today, I would reinforce the notion that rhetoric functions differently in different political systems.

The Structure of Power

Without constructing speculative myths about the origins of government, one may safely suggest that politics is the art of giving form to that power which inherently resides in the state. Through the medium of law, precedent, or perhaps a written constitution, power is distributed in societies and "rules" established for its exercise. Men who are made arbiters of power are governed to a great extent by the form of power itself, what might be called the "political structure." But, because they are men, each has the opportunity to choose whether that portion of the state's power he manipulates should be used, how it should be used, when and where it should be used. This capacity to choose gives rise to public argument in two ways. First, and most obviously, there are men who can assume power that they are not entitled to by persuading the officers of state to use their powers in certain ways. Secondly, public officials who are entitled to power use public argument to justify their decisions—as Sir Lewis Namier observes, even "monarchs feel constrained to give reasons."[6] It is obvious that advocates—whether they intend to persuade or to justify—must be governed by the form which persuasion must take if it is to be effective. The form which persuasion must take may be called a "rhetorical process."[7] The rhetorical process parallels the political structure in that the means of persuasion must vary according to the relative power, accessibility, and inclination of the individual official addressed. Rhetoric has no real power in itself. It is entirely dependent on political power and the whims of those who control it. Theoretically, in short, all rhetorical processes are peculiar to the power structure in which they operate.

Though democratic or "open" in appearance, the eighteenth century English political structure was autocratic or "closed" in at least three ways directly affecting the rhetorical process: (1) elections served more to guarantee public service than to affect national policy; (2) deliberative assemblies were more formal than functional; (3) because of deliberative apathy, executive authority was in practice final.

The People

The eighteenth century House of Commons was divided into 558 constituencies: 489 elected in England, 24 named from Wales, and 45 for Scotland. The Commons was composed of representatives "elected" by "the people" every seven years or at the death of a monarch. "The people," however, meant 2.3 percent of the population, those who had the franchise. "Election," too, had an unusual meaning: excluding Scotland (where the Duke of Argyll in effect named all 45 members), a total of 106 borough "patrons" determined or influenced the election for 192 seats in Commons. An additional 32 seats were under the immediate patronage of the Crown. Thus, 234 of the English seats in Commons, some 41.9 percent of the votes in Commons, were determined without what modern men would call an "election."[8]

Most of the remaining 324 seats belonged to the counties, where the influence of what Namier calls "the squirearchy" determined the outcome of elections. The squires owned the land and dictated the votes of the various freeholders in their areas. J. S. Watson writes:

> The village lived very much unto itself. . . . The multitude of small producers
> . . . would find their best patron in the local squire or lord. To offend him
> was desperately bad for business. The squire was the centre of authority and
> of culture.[9]

Though Namier believes that "not more than one in twenty voters at county elections could freely exercise his statutory rights," that fact is misleading for a modern reader.[10] The squires did not permit "free" elections, and that from a modern bias is bad; but the squires did pride themselves on their "independence" from the government and thus constituted the most "democratic" element in the House of Commons.[11]

Elections could be called meaningful in a modern sense only in the twenty-two boroughs with an electorate in excess of one thousand. In commenting on these so-called "open constituencies," Namier agrees with Aristotle that "the many are more incorruptible than the few": quoting an election agent of Newcastle's, he concludes that "it's not in the power of any single person, let his weight be what it will, to determine the mood of sixteen or seventeen hundred English electors."[12] Even here, however, there was nothing approaching "democratic elections" as we understand that term, for though the "large constituencies opened a field for mass movements," it was nonetheless true that "power to exercise decisive influence in problems of national importance . . . was used primarily to satisfy local or even personal needs."[13]

If elections in Michigan counted for no more, we would say that the system there was "corrupt." But that judgment can be passed on the eighteenth century system only if we assume that voters in that period accepted a modern political ethic. This was not the case. Elections in the eighteenth century were not meant to guarantee a voice in government. Voting was a "right" for the freeman, but it was a *property* right in the eighteenth century, not the human right it has become. In an age of limited government, the election system guaranteed governmental services now provided by the vast bureaucracies in Washington, London, or Ottawa. There was no Ministry of Labor or Department of Health, Education, and Welfare—not even an Army Corps of Engineers—but there was a local patron, who, in return for the freeman's vote, provided the public services we have come to expect from legislation.[14]

So the very conception of "people" and "election" in the eighteenth century political system precluded an open rhetorical process. Though in another time substantive political issues would be debated on the hustings and decided at the polls, the elections of the eighteenth century were, in modern terms, meaningless formalities. Persuasion aimed at influencing the outcome of elections could end only in alienating important arbiters of power, the various patrons and squires who determined the membership of the House of Commons.

The Parliament

If elections were mere formalities, deliberations in Parliament were only a little less so. It was true in the eighteenth century, as it is in the twentieth, that no minister could sustain a government without a working majority in the House of Commons. As Commons was anxious to demonstrate to their erring American cousins in the passage of the Declaratory Act of 1766, ultimate effective power rested in Parliament as a result of settlements reached in 1688.[15] That power, however, was exercised so capriciously that parliamentary authority became a technicality, not a matter of fact. Characteristically, Parliament deferred its power to the Cabinet Council. The Council consisted of the king and his most trusted advisers, or of men who, for one reason or another, were deemed essential for the maintenance of a majority in the House of Commons. Only on a whim, or on rare occasions when it appeared that the power or privilege of Parliament was threatened, was there a confrontation between either the Council and the Parliament or the king and the Parliament.

It was a matter of constitutional principle that the king's ministers were "accountable" to "the people." "The people" of course were represented in Parliament. "Accountability" referred to the responsibility of ministers to outline their intended actions, explain them, and offer some justification for them. The justification did not have to be one with which all Members *agreed;* it merely had to be one which all Members could *understand* and think *reasonable.* Strangely enough, John Wilkes, an outspoken and demagogic opponent of the Bute ministry, stated this principle (and then ridiculed it) in one of the *North Briton* essays:

> I have happily taught myself the useful lesson that those who are superior to me in rank, must, of consequence, be superior in understanding also. . . . Till

the contrary appears, it is justice we owe to every administration, to suppose they have some reason for what they do.[16]

So ingrained was this sense of presumption on the part of government that we find Sir Fletcher Norton, the king's Attorney General, perplexed in the debate on General Warrants that speakers could continue arguing against the legality of the General Warrant:

> He should regard a resolution of the Members of the House of Commons no more than the oaths of so many drunken porters in Covent Garden when the Administration found that no justification, no precedents, no usage of office, would avail [to quiet the opposition].[17]

As a consequence of government's presumption, ministers in the eighteenth century were not "forced" from office for lack of a majority in the House of Commons. Several men, under pressure from mob violence and an organized opposition, were "persuaded" to leave their posts, but in each such case there had been a demonstrated majority for the key policies of their administration.[18] This, of course, is not to say that the administration always voted in the majority. The balance of power in the House of Commons was always held by "independents." From time to time, particularly in the last quarter of the century, they were wont to demonstrate their intractability by voting against the government, as in the passage of the Dunning Resolution.[19] Such votes, however, were, according to Brooke and Namier, "whims and caprices" rather than calculated to "force a change of hands." They see as characteristic of antiministry votes the mood detected by an agent of the younger William Pitt in 1785:

> The explanation to all this is neither more nor less than that the House of Commons being at present perhaps *too independent* . . . has many whims and caprices, and will decide against any minister, sometimes without ill-will to him in the main.[20]

And the presumption of government even overrode Commons' "whims and caprices". North, for example, lost four votes of middling significance in 1773, 1774, 1779, and 1780, each unconnected with his American policy. He begged to be allowed to resign in 1778, but the king would not allow it—and, though he lost skirmishes, he held his government and his majority together for four years until *George* decided to give up his American ghost! Parliament balked, hesitated, and complained, but in the end it supported the existing government.[21]

Though "oppositions" arose in moments of crisis, it is also true—paradoxically so—that the government's presumption was strongest in such times. With but few exceptions between 1688 and 1814, momentary threats to ministerial policy were marked by poor attendance in the House of Commons, and votes were cast in preponderance for the established government. In the crucial division over the treaty proposed to end the Seven Years War, for example, a noisy opposition led by the Great Commoner himself, William Pitt, garnered only 65 votes to the ministry's 319—this in spite of the fact that most political observers believed that Pitt and his followers could defeat the peace. Fully 174 Members were not in attendance.[22] In the debate over General Warrants, where an important constitutional liberty was at stake, Commons sustained the Council's opinion that such warrants could be issued by a vote of 234 to 220—this in the face of contrary decisions by two of England's foremost jurists. Lord Chesterfield said that he "never knew a stricter muster and no furloughs allowed," yet 103 Members were not in attendance.[23]

In sum, though the Parliament was an important arbiter of power, it derived that power more from its *de jure* existence than from its actual legislative function. As C. J. Fox observed:

> Suppose . . . a person in a distant country had no other way of judging the temper of this House, and of the motives of their conduct, but from our printed votes; could such a man form any judgment of the reasons why such a line of conduct was approved, and why such a one rejected? Sir, it would be ridiculous in the extreme to suppose it.[24]

A modern man, like the person from a distant country, would look precisely at the votes in the House of Commons to locate the end of the rhetorical process. But, as Fox argues, that would be a mistake. The Commons characteristically approved policies which were explained and which were reasonable, whether or not the majority of Members were in agreement with them. This is not to say that the House of Commons was "corrupt." On the contrary, though "venality" in eighteenth century Parliaments became a popular myth of the reform years of the nineteenth century, Members of the eighteenth century House of Commons deferred their considerable power to the executive because, in terms of *their* political morality, it was their *duty* to do so until they were persuaded that the constitution itself was in danger.[25]

King and Council

Because Parliaments characteristically deferred their considerable power to the Cabinet Council, the executive exercised what was, in effect, final authority. According to Charles Yorke, later the crown's Solicitor General, it was the second "great policy of the Constitution" that in all cases "Whatever the King does should seem to come *ex moro motu;* the result of his own wisdom and deliberate choice."[26] In other words, any governmental policy prepared and debated in the Cabinet Council was made public from the mouth of the sovereign, in his words, expressed as his idea. Theoretically, the Council spoke through the king, with the authority of a king; but as representatives of Parliament, they were supported by "the people," and spoke also with the authority of a nation.

Though it was common practice for policies to be decided in the Council and made public as the wish of the monarch, officials did not think of *themselves* as the possessors of power. Namier makes the point well:

> [Leaders of the political nation] had no conception of a party-government unconnected with the King. . . . For the King was to them a real factor in government, and not a mere figurehead or an abstract idea. . . . The mere conception of a "Sole Minister," a *de facto* ruler, was indignantly disclaimed by them. It was the King's business to see the government of the nation carried on, and for that purpose he had a right to choose his "instruments"; and "support of Government" was considered "a duty, while an honest man could support it." To try to impose oneself on the King by means of a systematic opposition, "to force a change of hands," was considered by them factious and dishonest.[27]

So long as the king accepted the "advice" of the Council, that advice assumed the proportions of a royal edict supported by popular authority. The attitude which this constitutional policy generated is illustrated in a letter of the Bishop of Gloucester:

> Let us private men endeavour to preserve and improve the little we have left
> of *private virtue;* and if one of those infected with the influenza of politics
> should ask me, what then becomes of your *public virtue?* I would answer him
> with an old Spanish proverb; *The King has enough for us all.*[28]

Such an attitude toward executive authority was by no means a matter
of private opinion. The sanctity of ministerial policy was preserved in law.
According to the law as interpreted in 1760, anything written or spoken
"that shall disturb the government, or make a mischief and a stir among
the people, is certainly a slander"[29] What was thought to "disturb government" is specified by Lord Chief Justice Holt:

> If people should not be called to account for possessing the people with an
> ill opinion of the government, no government can subsist. . . . Nothing can
> be worse to any government than to endeavour to procure animosities as to
> the management of it. This has been always looked upon as a crime, and no
> government can be safe without it be punished.[30]

Nor did it matter that a "slander" was in fact true:

> If any person have slandered the government in writing, you are to examine
> the . . . slander which it imports . . . and, be it never so true, yet if slanderous
> to the king or the government, it is a libel and to be punished.[31]

Particularly in the last third of the century, after the explosion attending
Grenville's suppression of John Wilkes' *North Briton,* the libel laws were
rarely enforced. Indeed, the standard mode of opposition throughout the
century involved a scurrilous attack on ministers raising questions as to
parentage, private motives, occasionally even policies. Yet, the ministry had
an omnipresent option of suppressing opposition argument, an option freely
exercised during the Napoleonic Wars.[32]

Law, custom, and the current political ethic thus combined to make the
executive's authority nearly final. This does not mean that either the king
or his ministers could abuse their power by disregarding either "the people"
or their representatives in Parliament. Every administration of the century
had to be "capable" in the eyes of the nation. A ministry's ability, however,
was assumed until *in*ability was demonstrated. Even ignorant and drunken
men such as Francis Dashwood were tolerated in important offices simply

because, though ignorant, they were neither foolish enough to insult Parliament, significant enough to cause riots, nor naive enough to accept responsibility for their actions.[33]

We have seen that direct appeals for voter intervention at the polls were futile, perhaps even counterproductive, because elections had no real bearing on matters of national policy. We have seen that a direct appeal for votes in Parliament held only a remote chance of success (though there was a chance) because the legislature was more formal than functional, inclined in all cases that mattered to leave the business of government in the hands of a Cabinet Council. And we have seen that only a Council composed of devils, democrats, or idiots could fail to exercise authority effectively. It seems clear, then, that the rhetorical process of the eighteenth century could not have been more than barely parallel to that which operates in modern democracies. The elements of autocracy in the "balanced" eighteenth century constitution meant that no executive could be *forced* to abandon policies or office except in the unlikely circumstance of a direct ministerial attack on the principles of the constitution.

The Rhetorical Process

We are accustomed to thinking of a tripartite rhetorical process. We picture as antagonists an "administration" and an "opposition" who argue with one another and are judged by a third party, a "legislature" or "the people." Therefore, we say an administration is *forced* from its office when either the legislature or the people decide against it. But in the eighteenth century there was no third party. The people had not the opportunity to judge, and the Parliament in nearly all cases thought it immoral to judge. Those who disagreed with administration policy and those who wished to be rid of an administration had to *persuade the executive itself,* for there was no one with functional power over the executive:

> The paralyzing atmosphere of hostility, and the Minister's own consciousness of his inability to carry on, would make him withdraw, though still assured of a majority. Revolutions often succeed merely because the men in power despair of themselves, and at the decisive moment dare not order the troops to fire; and it repeatedly happened in the eighteenth century that a Minister, while retaining the full confidence of the Crown and a comfortable majority in Parliament, no longer dared to avail himself of either. It was thus that

Newcastle resigned in 1756, Bute in 1763, and that North, in 1778, begged to be allowed to resign.[34]

The rhetorical process in the eighteenth century thus was more epideictic than deliberative in nature, an exercise in praise and blame designed to seduce the executive into changing policies or resigning office.

Plato made the point that rhetoric deals more with appearances than with fact. Whether or not our vanity allows us to see a truth in that statement, it is nonetheless an accurate description of public argument in the eighteenth century. Though they lived in a relatively closed system, the English had clothed their politics in the rhetoric of a much more open society, and it was that rhetoric which provided a basis for praise and blame in public argument. The supremacy of Parliament established in the previous century had been justified because two kings reduced their subjects to "slavery," abusing their lawful "prerogatives," "usurping" the rights of Parliament, and instituting a "tyranny" in place of monarchy. These actions were said to restrict "social liberty," a thing so precious that to an Englishman "tyranny" was symbolic or spiritual death.[35] To guarantee "social liberty," William and Mary had agreed "That it is the right of the subjects to petition the King, and all commitments and prosecutions for such petitioning are illegal," and "That freedom of speech, and debates or proceedings in Parliament, ought not to be impeached or questioned in any court or place out of Parliament."[36] It was unethical to be "factious" in the eighteenth century, but it was also a "duty" to oppose "tyranny." "Opposition" proceeded normally through exercising the rights of petition and debate, but should such normal exhortations fail to persuade the executive to abandon its "tyranny," Whig writers maintained a right of revolution inherent in the people governed.[37]

There were no bloody revolutions in eighteenth century England. When the latent power of the masses, so central to the rhetoric of Whiggism, threatened on occasion to become active, Parliament and the executive cooperated to control it. Similarly, the Parliament never actively rebelled against the executive. When there was danger of a parliamentary uprising, ministries changed policy or kings changed ministers. The rhetoric of the Glorious Revolution, however, made it possible to blame ministers by associating them with "tyranny" and to threaten them with the possibility of that revolution which tyranny justified. It also made "opposition" possible, for a man is to be praised in dutifully arguing against "tyranny," though his method of argument might be "seditious," "libelous," or "factious" were there no "tyranny."

Two forms of public argument were used to create what Namier calls a "paralyzing atmosphere of hostility" and a "consciousness of inability to carry on" in an administration. The right of petition spawned a genre of public argument which might be called "popular rhetoric," a coordinated series of documents meant to produce action in a mass audience. Petitioning and civil disorder, though all but irrelevant in the functioning political structure, created an atmosphere of hostility and posed a rhetorical threat of revolution. Without "credit" in the House of Commons, a ministry could not exercise authority, so the right of debate generated public argument designed primarily to discredit an administration, associating it with impositions on "social liberty." "Popularity" in the nation and "credit" in the Commons were stick and carrot used to seduce the executive into abandoning policies or office.

Popular Rhetoric

The most common medium for popular rhetoric in the eighteenth century was printed propaganda.[38] Pamphlets, newspapers, and broadsides were used by incendiaries (often hired by politicians intent upon gaining or extending their power) to incite popular unrest. Almost to a man, the incendiaries attacked the character of individual ministers more than administration policies. John Wilkes, for example, compared the Earl of Bute (a Scots minister, George III's "Dear Friend," who concluded the Treaty of Paris ending the Seven Years War) with all the "usurpers" and "Favourites" he could find lying about in English history. He found in the reign of Edward III an Earl Mortimer who had seduced the Queen Mother and, through her offices, persuaded the king to conclude a "dishonourable" peace with Scotland.[39] Bute was rumored to have been the Princess Dowager's lover.[40] Arguing obliquely through historical parallels allowed incendiaries such as Wilkes to circumvent the libel laws and to avoid a burden of proof for their insinuations. Such propaganda was entertaining because it exposed to ridicule the misadventures of the great. But more than that, rumors and innuendo in the eighteenth century were deadly. All ministers claimed the nation's loyalty by proclaiming themselves to be noble and unselfish "servants" of the Crown doing no more than their sworn duty. Incendiaries typically sought, first of all, to undercut that image. They pursued two epideictic topics, arguing that the administration was "ambitious," perhaps even "tyrannical," and asserting that it was the duty of all "honest men" to preserve English "liberty" by opposing abusers of power.

Because incendiaries started fires among the people, administrations in times of crisis hired propagandists of their own to put out the fires. Administration spokesmen "undeceived" the people by writing encomia on their employers. Each ministry's apologist claimed with conviction that England had never had a greater set of ministers. The historical parallel was the primary form for the argument, as it was with the incendiaries, but the men compared to the existing ministers were those of the highest reputation. As the government was praised, the opposition was roundly condemned. Like Tobias Smollett's appraisal of the Pittites in his debate with Wilkes, administration writers based their attack against opposition on a charge of "faction":

> The tools of faction are fairly convicted of the vilest calumny levelled at the present administration, and glanced at the S-------n himself. Deluded in this worst species of detraction, they have shuffled and evaded: they have endeavoured to explain away their own meaning: they have pleaded insanity in excuse of sedition, and floundered from one absurdity into another until they have excited the compassion, even of those who detest their malice.[41]

Administration writers actually had the easier job, for it was widely assumed that "the people" did not "pretend to direct" the government unless "deceived" by those who "practised the black art of faction."[42] The more visible incendiary propaganda became, and the more effective it was, the easier it was for writers such as Smollett to warrant their charges of "faction" and creeping "republicanism."

In fact, despite the administration's propaganda efforts, the more popular elements did tend traditionally to oppose the government.[43] It was thought that mobs did not riot unless paid and that petitions did not appear unless conjured by demagogues—but, apparently on their own, the popular elements in times of crisis petitioned government in behalf of opposition and engaged in riots to make their annoyance with ministerial policy painful for an administration.[44] When the open constituencies petitioned and the mobs rioted, public discontent was taken to Parliament to be used both as a warrant for conducting a formal opposition and as an indication of the current ministry's "incapacity" (meaning their inability to preserve order and enforce the law).

Rhetoric in Parliament

In more normal times, deliberations in Commons (if they can be called that) consisted of formulary approval of ministerial recommendations. The session would begin with the reading of an "Address from the Throne" (composed by a "minister of measures," approved by the Council and the king), which contained an outline of the "duties" the executive expected Parliament to fulfill. The king would be thanked for "his" speech and assured that "his servants" in Parliament would do what they could. Representatives of the government (usually appointed by the ministry's Leader in the House) would then introduce and defend the specific bills the Council wanted. Several speakers would rise in favor of the administration bill, a few to carp about high taxes and "the good old days." The Commons would then approve ministerial legislation as a matter of form.

When there was an opposition and an uproar out-of-doors, however, orators used their right of debate to find out why, to make the ministry justify their policies. "The House of Commons then had little legislation to discuss," remarks Peter Brown. "Concentration on first principles of state resulted." One of those first principles was a guarantee of "social liberty," another was a guarantee of order in the state. When incendiaries were successful in their propaganda, either or both of those guarantees was apparently threatened. Commons' orators had topics to challenge their prowess—and a man made his reputation in Commons primarily with his skill in the art of public speaking: "The evidence of the importance then attached to this art is overwhelming."[45]

As a rule, it was wealthy borough patrons anxious for power—men such as the Marquis of Rockingham and the Duke of Bedford—who came together in various combinations to make a nucleus of "opposition." Neither they nor the ministry commanded an absolute majority in times of crisis; though, because of its presumption, the administration could probably count on the largest single bloc of votes in the Commons. The balance of power was held by "independents" who, on paper, constituted a majority or near majority in the House.[46] Of this group Namier writes:

Their votes being determined by individual convictions, and not by pursuits or manoeuvres of party, on ordinary problems they were, as a rule, so much divided as roughly to cancel out each other. But whenever a strong movement of public opinion produced some degree of unity among them, their weight made itself felt.[47]

Though there was little probability that the squires would try to "force a change of hands," opposition debaters in Commons sought to provide an appearance of unity among them which might seduce a ministry into resignation.

"Independent" members were swayed primarily by a speaker's "weight," of which his skill in public speaking was but a part. Perhaps the most difficult measure Grenville managed, for example, was John Wilkes's expulsion in 1763. He did not himself want to introduce the business, wishing there to be as little connection as possible between the expulsion and the ministry. He cast about for some months looking for the right man to handle the bill, "one whose high rank and unspotted character, and whose experience and knowledge in Parliament, will give it the utmost weight and authority."[48] He settled on James Stanley, Lord Strange. Strange had been connected with Newcastle until, in the wake of the ministry's victory on the Peace Preliminaries in 1762, he switched allegiances to Bute's government. His "high rank" was established by his property and his birth, for he was a wealthy country gentleman from Lancashire and the eldest son of the eleventh Earl of Derby. His "unspotted character" was established by his "independence," his sympathy and friendship with large numbers of the country gentry, and his family's Whig connections dating back at least to 1688. He had been in Parliament since 1741 and had served as Lord Lieutenant of Lancashire since 1757. He spoke often in Commons and was reckoned by Walpole among the foremost speakers in the House.[49] Such were the qualifications of a man considered to have "weight and authority." These men were sought by the ministry as spokesmen for pending legislation and courted by those who would attempt to build an opposition. When such men did find their way into opposition, their considerable "weight" combined with out-of-doors pressure to make a minister's life uneasy.

The very "independence" which gave a parliamentary opposition some slim hope of making a minister feel his "inability to carry on" also prevented any but the barest thread of unity among a government's opponents. There was never a coherent "opposition policy," little for opponents of government to argue *for*. Argument in the House of Commons, therefore, tended to be justificatory on the part of the government and almost purely refutative on the part of opposition spokesmen. Pitt, for example, viciously attacked Grenville's justification of the Cider and Perry Excise in 1763, but he never broached an alternative proposal. When pressed by Grenville for a countersuggestion, the Commoner refused, dismissing the demand with ridicule.[50]

Burke's famous "Speech on Conciliation with the Colonies" is a classic example of opposition argumentative strategy in the House of Commons. Burke urged "conciliation" as a general contrary of "force" in handling civil disorders in America—he did not make *specific* recommendations to the ministry. A tone of refutation pervades the speech. He asserts that colonials were Englishmen and entitled to the same consideration given Britons living at home, thus casting doubt on the administration's picture of a land totally subject to the whims of English government. Burke denies that force can attain its object. He denies that it is the duty of the weaker to make concessions, asserting the contrary, that the superior power can offer peace with honor and safety, while the weaker power can offer peace only as an admission of fear. He finally denies that conciliation would in any way impair the whole authority of England.[51] Even though Burke appears to be arguing for a specific "opposition" policy, the whole chain of argument does little more than attack ministerial justifications for the use of force. In no way is the speech "presumptuous"—it neither recommends an alternative "system" nor casts doubt on the right of the ministry to conclude any plan it wished. The speech is not aimed so much at gaining votes and ousting a ministry as at indirectly persuading the ministry to change policy.

If argument in opposition in the House of Commons were perceived to be weighty enough to negate a ministry's justification, another justification would have to be found. Opposition speakers attacked it in like fashion. When the ministry had exhausted every possible justification for its program, an opposition was said to be "successful." A change of policy—perhaps even a corresponding change of government—was at length effected.

Conclusion

In sum, there were three arbiters of power involved in the eighteenth century rhetorical process: the executive, wherein lay functional power; the

House of Commons, wherein lay a superior but quiescent power; and the popular masses, wherein lay the latent power of numbers. The political structure in effect precluded the tripartite rhetorical process we associate with twentieth century politics, for the executive could not be *forced* to abandon policies or office except in the unlikely circumstance of a direct attack on the principles of the constitution. The ministry had rather to be *persuaded* to abandon or modify its program or to resign from office. Because of the functional power of the executive, only an appearance of rebellion in the Commons or of a popular uprising could warrant an "opposition." Opposition could succeed only when the Council was *demonstrably* unable to rule. So, when an opposition was contemplated, propagandists were hired to generate popular petitions and encourage civil disorder—not to influence elections, but to create the impression that the Council was unable to maintain order and keep subjects content. In this atmosphere of hostility, opposition debaters attacked the "credit" of the administration in the House of Commons—not expressly to secure a majority against government (though that was a bare possibility), but to discredit the king's ministers, thereby seducing them into voluntarily abandoning a policy or an office.

We may conclude that the rhetorical process in eighteenth century England ended much more subtly than in the counting of heads at elections or in deliberative assemblies. Rhetorical principles operated in that time as they do in any time—but, tied as they must be to the political process, rhetorical maneuverings bore only the faintest resemblance to rhetorical processes in more open societies. The eighteenth century experience strongly suggests that those who would deal with rhetorical operations in a closed society do so on the basis of assumptions and hypotheses appropriate to that society, not on the basis of an ideological history or values derived solely from the litany of modern democracies.

NOTES AND REFERENCES

1. See Michael C. McGee, "Thematic Reduplication in Christian Rhetoric," *Quarterly Journal of Speech,* 56 (April 1970): 196.

2. Herbert Butterfield, *The Whig Interpretation of History* (New York: Norton, 1965).

3. The problem lies largely in our language. Consider the term "public opinion" as an example: "The people" (meaning the masses who are governed) are inherently powerful in any political system if only because they are the many. So we can say that public opinion, and the public argument which helps to mold it, is always important. But is it always important for the same reasons and in the same way? Today a government in Anglo-America draws its power periodically from "the people" who "appoint" ministers of state by election. A president or a prime minister governs, not at the pleasure of a monarch, but at the pleasure of the people. Expressions of public opinion are therefore orders from "the boss." In the eighteenth century, however, "the boss" was the king himself. It was at his pleasure, and his alone, that ministers of state were appointed. Public opinion *was* important, but when the people spoke, they spoke as subjects outside the polity, not as employers who possessed a real power. Modern men looking at eighteenth century public argument, thus, are apt to commit two errors of language: we must always make clear our realization that the "public" in "public opinion" then was not the same "public" our readers see today; and we must never assume that political leaders then reacted to "public opinion" for the same reasons or in the same way modern leaders react to it. See A. F. Pollard, *The Evolution of Parliament* (New York: Longmans-Green, 1926), p. 343.

4. See Butterfield, *The Whig Interpretation,* pp. 9–33, 107–32.

5. There can be no doubt that the eighteenth century produced what Archibald Foord called "The Waning of 'the Influence of the Crown.' " (*English Historical Review* 58 [1947]:484–507.) That trend was nonetheless halted by the nation's violent reaction against the revolution in France. Though E. C. Black sees in developing extraparliamentary political associations a "key to the future," he also notes that "the ministry stayed in tune with the temper of the nation" in passing even more severe sedition and libel laws than had been in effect in 1700. What he calls, from his modern democratic writing bias, "repressive legislation" passed between 1793 and 1800, reflected a "public opinion" which "did not want and would not tolerate seditious republicanism." See E. C. Black, *The Association: British Extraparliamentary Political Organization, 1769–1793* (Cambridge, Mass.: Harvard University Press, 1963), pp. 273–74. In the end, "reform" was a nineteenth and not an eighteenth century phenomenon, a product of the emergence of party government. See L. B. Namier, "Monarchy and the Party System," in *Personalities and Powers, Selected Essays* (New York: Harper, 1955), pp. 13–38.

6. L. B. Namier, *England in the Age of the American Revolution* (London: Macmillan, 1930), p. 63.

7. The means of persuasion shift so rapidly with circumstance that they cannot be said to form a "structure." As Bryant argues, "rhetoric *does* rather than *is*," it is a "motion" or "process." Donald C. Bryant, "Rhetoric: Its Function and its Scope," p. 210.

8. All statistics descriptive of the political structure are taken from L. B. Namier, *The Structure of Politics at the Accession of George III*, 2 vols. (London: Macmillan, 1929), vol. 1, *passim*.

9. J. S. Watson, *The Reign of George III* (Oxford: Clarendon Press, 1960), p. 37.

10. Namier, *Structure*, 1: 93.

11. Watson notes (p. 48) that "County gentlemen . . . felt themselves fully capable of running the county without assistance and would indeed brook none." This spirit of self-sufficiency meant that borough barons and governments alike had to bargain for county support. The gentry's "independence" made them a sort of "popular" influence in Commons—though, as Namier underlines, the squirearchy "constituted the purest type of class representation in Great Britain." (*Structure*, 1: 92–93.)

12. Namier, *Structure*, 1: 100.

13. Ibid., pp. 163–64. For an example of such a "mass movement" in the large constituencies, see George Rudé's *Wilkes and Liberty* (Oxford: Clarendon Press, 1965). Dorothy Marshall says of the people's significance in the political structure that "public opinion had only the right to beat its unorganized waves against the Palace at Westminster." In the eighteenth century, "the property-owner . . . dominated the great institution of Parliament." (*The English People in the Eighteenth Century* [London: Longmans-Green, 1956], p. 76.)

14. Namier, *Structure*, 1: 128, 195–98.

15. Parliamentary sovereignty was not a completely settled matter, particularly in regard to America. If George III were in a serious feud with the Commons, or if he had been intent upon extending his "prerogative," he might legitimately have supported the colonial position, claiming direct and independent sovereignty over America. Had he done that, much of the force which led ultimately to American rebellion might have been dissipated, but a potentially more dangerous confrontation with Parliament would have been provoked. A partisan but judicious statement of the dominant feeling in Parliament in 1768 concerning their institutional power is provided by William Knox, a propagandist writing for George Grenville, in his pamphlet *The Present State of the Nation* (London and Dublin: John Almon, 1768), pp. 39–47.

16. *The North Briton* (London), December 4, 1762.

17. [J. Debrett], *Debates of Both Houses of Parliament, 1743–1774* (London: Debrett, 1792), vol 4, p. 173.

18. The only exception to this rule is Shelburne's resignation in 1783. In that period, North, Fox, and Rockingham all kept majorities. For a detailed description of the mood of parliament in this period, see John P. Bakke, "The Debates on the Fox and Pitt East India Bills, 1783, 1784: A Case Study in the Rhetoric of the House of Commons," Ph.D. dissertation, University of Iowa, 1966.

19. In what was taken in the nineteenth century to be a budding democratic spirit, John Dunning proposed, and carried in Commons, a resolution stating that "the influence of the Crown has increased, is increasing, and ought to be diminished." This was in the wake of disenchantment with North's conduct of the American war and, as R. J. White points out, was more in keeping with the attitude consistently displayed by country gentlemen throughout the century than with any sort of embryonic democracy. See R. J. White, *The Age of George III* (New York: Walker, 1968), pp. 32–33.

20. Daniel Pulteney to the Duke of Rutland, March 4, 1785, in L. B. Namier and John Brooke, *The History of Parliament: The House of Commons, 1754–1790,* 3 vols. (London: Her Majesty's Stationer's Office, 1964), 1: 194.

21. Lecky notes that on the American question, a ministerial policy which mattered very much, the North government was representative of the feeling in the Commons until about 1780. He consistently maintained large majorities ranging from 64 to 73 to 186 to 187. (W. E. H. Lecky, *A History of England in the Eighteenth Century* [London: Longmans-Green, 1890], vol. 3, pp. 524–45.) Namier and Brooke conclude that, in the crisis most resembling a contest between the executive and the Commons, "An analysis of the division lists for the last weeks of North's Administration shows that there were 241 Members who supported Government, 237 who voted with the Opposition, and 31 who concurred with the Opposition on the American war yet opposed any censure of North's Administration." Namier and Brooke, *History Commons,* 1: 202.

22. See Denis le Marchant (ed.), *Walpole's Memoirs of the Reign of George III* (London: R. Bentley: 1845), 1: 164; Thomas Birch to Lord Royston, November 13, 1762, in *The Life and Correspondence of the Earl of Hardwicke* (Cambridge: At the University Press, 1913), vol. 3, p. 330; Thomas Ramsden to Charles Jenkinson, November 8, 1762, in John Russell (ed.), *The Bedford Correspondence* (London: Longman, 1846), vol. 3, pp. 159–60.

23. Chesterfield to Lord Stanhope, October 19, 1764, in Namier, *Structure,* 1: 184.

24. *The Speeches of the Right Honourable Charles James Fox in the House of Commons* (London: Longman, Hurst, & Rees, 1815), vol. 1, pp. 105–6.

25. In opposing parliamentary reform in 1781, Viscount Feilding made the point that "The balance of power in the House . . . [is held by] the country gentlemen. . . . By the support of these men, and not as had been asserted, by the low arts of corruption, did the present minister stand." Namier and Brooke, in quoting

Feilding, note that "The country gentlemen as a group were disposed to give any minister appointed a fair trial . . . and yet to watch Administration with a critical eye." (Namier and Brooke, *History Commons,* 1: 146–49.) They voted against government on specific issues, but rarely on motions of confidence. Indeed, as indicated above, only once in the century did a minister so fail his "fair trial" as to lose the support of enough of the gentry to be forced from office. As Roger Newdigate put it, "I like the King and shall be with his ministers as long as I think an honest man ought, and believe it best not to lose the country gentleman in the courtier." Namier and Brooke, *History Commons,* 1: 147.

26. Charles Yorke to Joseph Yorke, February 15, 1745, in Namier, *Age of Revolution,* p. 47.

27. Namier, *Age of Revolution,* p. 51.

28. Bishop of Gloucester to Richard Berenger, July 4, 1762; *Historical MSS Commission Reports* 17 (1892), Fortescue Papers.

29. Case of the Seven Bishops (1688); *Sources of English Constitutional History,* translated and edited by C. Stephenson and F. G. Marcham (New York and London: Harper, 1939), No. 117–E, p. 585 fn. 6.

30. The Queen vs. John Tutchin (1704), ibid., No. 124–E, p. 641.

31. This is the doctrine of *De Libellis Famosis* in Coke's reports as stated by Lord Chief Justice Wright in the Case of the Seven Bishops (1688); ibid., No. 117–E, p. 585 fn. 6.

32. "Seditious libels" were permitted in the House of Commons, where Members were protected from governmental prosecution by their parliamentary "privilege," a "right" debated well into the eighteenth century which originated in the reign of Henry IV. See "Parliamentary Rolls of Henry IV: Parliament of 1399," ibid., No. 66–A, pp. 256–57.

33. Dashwood, later Lord LeDespenser, incredibly proposed a tax on cider produced for *household consumption,* to be levied on every subject over the age of nine years! The tax was an excise, easily the most unpopular form of taxation in England, and Dashwood could not even estimate its produce closer than 100,000 pounds. Yet the tax was approved, and it took two years and a change of ministry to repeal it. See Lecky, *History of England,* 3: 55–56.

34. Namier, *Age of Revolution,* pp. 157–58.

35. See John Locke, *An Essay Concerning the True Original Extent and End of Civil Government,* IV, 21. (In *Great Books of the Western World,* 25: 25–81.)

36. The Bill of Rights (1688) in E. N. Williams, ed., *A Documentary History of England* (Baltimore: Penguin Books, 1965), vol. 2, p. 110.

37. Locke, XIV, 168; XVIII, 206.

38. See R. R. Rea, *The English Press in Politics, 1760–1774* (Lincoln, Neb.: University of Nebraska Press, 1963). Techniques of agitation changed little during the century: The same sort of newspaper, broadside, pamphlet, and book was produced by Locke, Milton, Swift, Arbuthnot, and Bolingbroke in the first quarter of the century as by Burke, Paine, Wyvill, and Reeves in the last quarter. Indeed, with Burke the lone exception, the art of propaganda seems to have deteriorated rather than prospered through the century. The only refinement on techniques of popular agitation seems to have been the brief emergence of the political "association" in 1769–1770 and 1782–1793. The association functioned as a channel for petitions and protest much as the London Common Council had functioned through the entire century. If we are looking for antecedents of modern systems, the association is probably a forerunner of the political party—though it was a short-lived affair with only rhetorical significance, buried by the French wars. See Black, *Association.*

39. *North Briton* (London), July 3, 1762.

40. See Lecky, *History of England,* 3: 12, 49. The lower orders of London were said to have shouted "no petticoat government" in opposition to Bute, and a jackboot tied to a petticoat was the popular symbol of the "Favourite's" ministry.

41. *The Briton* (London), June 26, 1762.

42. "The mob," by edict of Constitutional presumption, was mindless. A standard legal treatise justified the election laws in force in 1768 as ideal: "Only such are excluded, as can have no Will of their own: there is hardly a free Agent to be found, but what is entitled to a Vote in some Place or other in the Kingdom." See "A Gentleman of the Inner Temple", *Laws Concerning Elections* (London: W. Owen, 1768). To George III, everyone who did not actually sit in Commons practiced "faction" simply by exercising their right of petition: "What times do we not live in, when a parcell of low shopkeepers pretend to direct the whole Legislature," he said of a petition from the City of London. George III to Lord Bute, March 30, 1763 in R. Sedgwick (ed.), *The Letters from George III to the Earl of Bute* (London: Macmillan, 1939), pp. 207–8.

43. See L. S. Sutherland, "The City of London in Eighteenth-Century Politics," *Essays Presented to Sir Lewis Namier,* edited by A. J. Pares and A. J. P. Taylor (London: Macmillan, 1956), pp. 57–58.

44. As E. N. Williams notes, there was an undercurrent of economic discontent in mass demonstrations and riots of the eighteenth century: "In 1749 the mob uprooted turnpikes in Bristol; in 1758 they tore down enclosures in Wiltshire. In Norwich in 1740 there was a five-day riot over the price of mackerel." (*Life in Georgian England* [London: B. J. Batsford, 1962], p. 119.) Rudé, however, claims that there was no "close general concordance between high food prices and popular disturbances" in the larger boroughs, where propagandists sought

to pull out the mob. ("The London Mob of the Eighteenth Century," *The Historical Journal* 1 [1959]: 10–11.) Indeed, the mob seemed to be politically conscious—politics was a chief form of entertainment, particularly in London: "All Englishmen are great newsmongers. Workmen habitually begin the day by going to coffee rooms in order to read the daily news." (H. de Misson, *Memoirs and Observations in his Travels over England* [London: D. Browne, 1719], p. 6.) It is a mistake to think of rioters, the audience for propagandists, as uniformly the "unwashed masses." According to Rudé's survey of arrest records in 1768–1769, most were respectable citizens, gainfully employed. See "The Middlesex Electors of 1768–1769," *The Journal of English History* 75 (October 1960): 614.

45. Peter Brown, *The Chathamites* (London: Macmillan, 1967), p. 27.

46. Excluding Scottish and Welsh Members, 267 seats in Commons were free of either crown or patron "influence." See Namier, *Structure,* 1: 180–81.

47. L. B. Namier, "Country Gentlemen in Parliament, 1750–84," *Personalities and Powers,* p. 76.

48. George Grenville to Lord Strange, October 15, 1763, in *The Grenville Papers,* edited by W. J. Smith (London: J. Murray, 1852), vol. 2, pp. 134–36.

49. Namier and Brooke, *History Commons,* 3: 453–55.

50. Grenville claimed that the Cider Excise was a reasonable source of revenue and the only alternative. In debates against Pitt, he repeated "with a strong emphasis two or three times, 'Tell me where you can lay another tax!' Mr. Pitt replied, in a musical tone, 'Gentle shepherd, tell me where.' The whole house burst out in a fit of laughter, which continued for some minutes." The House had a laugh, but Grenville got his tax. (Debrett, *Debates,* 4:132.)

51. Edmund Burke, "Speech on Conciliation with the Colonies", in *The Works of the Right Honourable Edmund Burke* (London: Rivington, 1803), vol. 3, pp. 23–132.

Edmund Burke and the East Indian Reform Movement

John P. Bakke

In his *Reflections* Edmund Burke remarked that he had never seen a plan before the House of Commons which had not been improved by those less capable than the person who took the lead in bringing forth the plan under consideration.[1] Though Burke himself hardly was less capable than his associates, it is true nevertheless that he spent most of his political career in opposition and, thus, his name was associated with few bills which became law. This did not mean, however, that Burke did not have considerable impact on the Commons especially in respect to the effort there to reform the British East India Company.

Whereas Burke's name has been linked with "Indian reform," the major Indian reform bill passed during Burke's political career bore the name of Burke's frequent adversary, William Pitt. The Pitt India Bill, passed on July 26, 1784, was opposed bitterly by Burke who had drafted the ill-fated Fox East India Bill, which had been the focus of a controversy that had allowed King George III to oust Charles James Fox from power and to open the door for young Pitt to reign supreme in Parliament.

Despite the fact that the Indian reform movement resulted in a significant defeat for Burke, Burke played an essential role in the passage of the Pitt bill, for, as L. S. Sutherland has stated, "it was Burke and his associates who made some sweeping reforms inevitable."[2] It is the purpose of this article to sketch the role of Burke in the Indian reform movement and to argue that Burke's essential and perhaps only contribution was a consequence of his rhetoric.[3]

The reform of the East India Company was a significant political undertaking which spanned a period of over eighteen years. The intent of the "reform" was to make the private, powerful, and prestigious company subservient to the government of England, but the company had been protected from such government encroachment upon its commercial freedom by a charter which dated back to the time of Queen Elizabeth.[4]

While there was a prevailing sentiment that the government should not interfere in the company's commercial business, there was also strong feeling that the society of merchants who directed the company had no justification to meddle in Indian politics, especially when company policies triggered wars which forced England to send money, supplies, and troops to protect "company interests" from enraged Indian princes and natives.

Whenever the government made the claim that a private company had no right to govern people, it met the counterclaim that a government had no right to interfere with the business of a private concern granted commercial rights by a government. The counterclaim was answered by the assertion that in reality politics and commerce were inseparable, meaning that the claim to the one meant the possession of the other. As the company had chartered rights to commerce, any claim to reform the company meant that the burden of proof was on the government to show either that politics could be separated from commerce or that the company had no right to what apparently had been guaranteed in the company's charter by the government itself. From 1766 to 1783, reformers had tried to argue the first premise. Burke, on November 1, 1783, operating in an extraordinary political climate, chose to deny the first and press the second.

Prior to 1766 the government's main interest in the India Company was financial. In 1766 Lord Chatham, William Pitt the Elder, together with John Robinson, Charles Jenkinson, and Henry Dundas, planted the seed for what was to become the government's master scheme for controlling the company and tapping the revenue from India. This master scheme, hereafter referred to as the plan of the traditional reformers, was to change the structure of the company from a loosely organized check-and-balance system to a tight authoritarian structure which could be controlled by government through the appointment of the "right men" to positions of power in India.[5] Such a scheme, intended to maximize government's power while minimizing responsibility, had to be advanced when the company came to the government for relief of temporary financial straits and when the Indian issue was more or less removed from the politics of the Commons.

Chatham, in August 1767, challenged the company's exclusive right to Indian profits on the fact that Bengal had been subdued in a war in which the king's forces had taken part. Naturally, the company resisted and found an ally in Edmund Burke who argued unequivocally that any government intervention would violate the company's chartered rights.[6]

The North Regulating Act, passed in 1773, proved to have little effect on the independence of the company. The North Act forced rotation in the Court of Directors and instituted a Governor-General and Council for Bengal to be appointed first by government and then in perpetuity by the company. Result: The Court of Directors changed from a real twenty-four to a virtual thirty who dutifully elected each other after absences caused by the forced rotations.[7] Warren Hastings was appointed Governor General and soon became the center of controversy as he proved uncontrollable by the government.

In 1778 North's Secretary, John Robinson, conceived a further step in Indian reform, but because of the unsettling war with the American colonies he thought it inadvisable to to make his plan public. Like the North Act, the Robinson plan was an attempt to allow the British government to exert new influence within a slightly modified structure. In respect to the old "charter issue," Robinson thought that the politics and commerce of the company were so intertwined that they should be regulated under a single administration, but, he wrote,

> I think that the errors which must be committed in the management of such acquisitions at so great a distance from the seat of Government, had better fall upon the directors of the Company than fall directly upon the Ministers of the King, who in the midst of the difficulties that at present surround them and of the calumnies to which they are necessarily subject, can hardly now retain a sufficient degree of authority and respect for the Government of this country.[8]

Profit and power without responsibility, in short, was still the goal of the man who along with Jenkinson and Dundas had been a part of the reform movement since 1766.

By 1781 it was evident that America would win its independence, and thus it became more psychologically as well as economically important to England that India be secured within the British Commonwealth. In 1781 Jenkinson engineered a successful bill which allowed the government a share in the company's profits, but no real control over the company. The reform progress in 1781, however, resulted from the blunders of Lord North in appointing two committees to study Indian affairs.

North appointed mainly members of his opposition to serve on the Select Committee on Indian Affairs—a supposedly nonpolitical committee designed to study friction between the executive and judiciary systems in India. One of the appointees was Burke, who took his work seriously and began to investigate the whole Indian situation in a way which furthered North's deteriorating political position.

After a new outbreak of the war in the Carnatic, in April 1781, North formed the Secret Committee on Indian Affairs. This time he thought he was appointing the "right people," for Robinson, Jenkinson, and Dundas were given key roles. North, however, did not anticipate the ambitious and independent nature of the sagacious Scot, Chairman Dundas, who soon directed the committee's interest beyond the war. Dundas rejected a cabinet post in the North administration, attached himself to a rising young politician named William Pitt, and used the India question to further his own career. In his committee he used the experience of Robinson and Jenkinson and pushed for reforms regardless of the political consequences to North. Hence, in 1781 two committees led respectively by vigorous and tenacious men in opposition to North and to each other were dedicated to some kind of Indian reform.

Sutherland has observed that in the two years between the fall of North and the rise of Pitt the India question emerged from a question "just below the surface of politics to one of the major controversies and problems which claimed the attention of Parliament and politicians."[9] Conditions in India were growing worse and the government had little choice but to challenge the company openly.

The India problem itself demanded solution, but it was political machinations in England between 1782 and 1784 that enhanced the likelihood of Indian reform. The Marquis of Rockingham followed North as head of the Ministry and died shortly thereafter.[10] After George III appointed the Earl of Shelburne to replace the late Rockingham, the Rockingham remnant led by Fox went willfully into opposition.[11] Finally, Fox formed a coalition with North, whom he had opposed for more than a decade. In such a situation of political change, leaders of both majority and minority had committed themselves to Indian reform. In Lecky's words, "All parties had pledged themselves . . . to the necessity of reforming the government of India, and it was scarcely possible to recede after the reports of the (Secret and Select) Committees."[12]

During the Fox-North Ministry it was Dundas, then a member of the opposition, who first came forward with an Indian reform plan which, says Sutherland,

> brought together all the major propositions of the "men of business" of the past, added to them some points, which had impressed themselves upon Dundas' mind from his experience on the Secret Committee, and most important of all . . . it was the blueprint of Pitt's East India Act of the next year.[13]

In the tradition of Chatham, Robinson, and Jenkinson, Dundas proposed a Secretary for Indian Affairs on the assumption that an honest and capable governor given great powers was the best hope for checking the evils in India.

Fox opposed the Dundas plan, promising to bring forward one of his own. On November 18 he kept his promise by presenting what Sutherland has termed the most "sweeping attack on the independence of the East India Company" of any proposal since 1767.[14] Fox wanted to transfer the power of the Directors and Proprietors to a Commission appointed by government.

The passage of Fox's bill was by no means a certainty, but Fox emerged a victor in the Commons.[15] But it was Burke, not Fox, who played the central part in the rhetorical triumph. It remains now to identify that essential contribution and fit it into the reform movement which was to be concluded by Pitt and not by Fox.[16]

Burke's Rhetorical Contribution

The debate on the Fox bill began on November 18 and continued on the twentieth and on the twenty-fourth through the twenty-seventh. Though Fox had had moments of brilliance, by December 1, when Burke delivered his famous three-hour address, Fox and his colleagues had mishandled the "charter issue," which had long been a principal object to reform.

Dundas, like the traditional reformers, had proposed a separation of the company's politics and commerce and advocated that the government claim only Indian politics. By this stipulated separation, Dundas had hoped to avoid the troublesome question of "chartered rights" and capitalize on the popular premise that "politics should be for politicians and commerce for merchants."[17] Fox tried to skirt that linguistic truism as well as the question of political sovereignty. Posing the old and perplexing question, Fox asked: "To whom belong the territorial acquisitions in India? To the Crown, or to the Company?" The answer, he continued, depended not only upon a question of "rights," but also upon whether the company's affairs could be divided into economic and political segments. Plowing once more the old unfertile ground, Fox stated that "merchants" could not manage great territories and enter into "all the mazes and refinements of modern politics." Conversely, "mere statesmen were unqualified to enter into and conduct complicated branches of a remote and difficult trade."[18] Such was the dilemma which had been baffling England for more than eighteen years, and now Fox had an answer, or so he said. He would establish a commission for politics and another for commerce and, said he, this "mixed system" was well adapted "to the mixed complexion of our interests in India."[19] So as politics was for politicians and as commerce was for merchants, it stood to reason that a mixed system was best for mixed interests.

Naturally, the Pitt and company factions refused to let Fox duck a central issue. Pitt branded Fox's bill as "an entire abrogation of all the ancient charters and priviledges by which the Company had been first established, and had since existed."[20] After it was agreed generally, however, that some reform was in order and that any reform would affect the charter, the question turned to the kind of justification which would be necessary to override chartered rights. On that point, Thomas Erskine was most helpful.

Operating within the admissions of Pitt and the company (Pitt had said simply that a charter should not be violated without reasons)[21] Erskine stated that a charter could be revoked legally when its continuance became detrimental to the public because of an unforeseen change of circumstances or because of misuse. Clearly, circumstances had changed since the time the charter was first instituted, but the company's increased political involvement merely raised the dilemma again. What right had the government to take commerce with politics, and could the two indeed be separated? In short, the very point Fox had tried to avoid again became central to the debate and unresolvable for the government unless "misuse" could be demonstrated.

In his opening address, Fox had relentlessly attacked the power structure of the company and the proprietors, but he gave no reason why the personnel of the Court of Directors should be fired. In reply, Jenkinson remarked that the "new system would punish the masters for the faults of the servants,"[22] and Pitt restated, "Before men were proceeded against in so violent a manner, they ought to be proved to have merited such vengeance."[23] Company Chairman Sir Henry Fletcher pointed out:

> The directors were legally elected and could not be removed unless there was misconduct. If misconduct was charged, acts of a criminal nature must be stated specifically, and time must be given for a defence to be prepared.[24]

Indeed it seemed necessary for someone to defend what Fox had omitted. Burke did so in a manner adding philosophy and a significant rhetorical dimension to the long-continuing debate over Indian reform.

In his review of Burke's December 1 speech, James Boulton remarked that he had the feeling that "Burke was not playing factious politics, but that he meant profoundly and intensely what he said."[25] Burke, for example, quickly liberated himself from the circular nonsense about merchants and politicians by saying,

> My experience in life teaches me nothing clear upon the subject. I have known merchants with the sentiments and abilities of great statesmen; and I have seen persons in the rank of statesmen, with the conceptions and character of peddlers.[26]

Thus, implied Burke, let us examine the actual company personnel and decide what it is that they are fit to do.

Burke began this examination by asserting the premise that a government was obligated to benefit the governed. He then contested the popular notion that "all charters were sacred." There was a difference, explained Burke, between the kind of *natural* rights protected by a Magna Carta and the *legal* rights sanctioned through the company's charter. The former restrained power and restored monopoly whereas the latter did the opposite. "Political power and commercial monopoly are not the rights of men ... (but) are liable to fall into a direct violation (of them)," declared Burke.[27] Stating the basis whereupon he would measure the company's use of their charter, Burke proclaimed that legal charters ought to be exercised for the benefits of natural rights. Denying that a charter was by definition a "right," Burke declared a charter to be a "trust" for a "privileged" power *never* to be used in opposition to a right. If the company had a trust, it became automatically accountable to Parliament.[28] Therefore, concluded Burke:

> The very charter which is held out to exclude parliament from correcting malversion with regard to the high trust vested in the Company, is the very thing which at once gives a title, and imposes a duty on us to interfere with effect, wherever power and authority originating from ourselves, are perverted from their purposes and become instruments of wrong and violence.[29]

By Burke's reasoning the government could not violate a right, but the company could violate a trust. Hence, the question became, had the company infringed upon the natural rights of men? If so, the contract between the government and the company could be rightfully broken.

After establishing his moral and metaphysical framework, Burke declared that a reform had to be founded on claims that the object of the company's abuse was significant, the impairment of the object great, the abuse habitual, and the abuse incurable in the given constituted body. In creating a sense of demonstration for these four claims, Burke presupposed that his House of Commons audience was ignorant of the nature of India and presumed consequently the Indians to be primitive and inferior creatures who did not share a common humanity with Britishers and who, therefore, had no claim to equal and fair treatment.

In assessing the contribution of Burke's rhetoric, Sutherland correctly states that "the feeling of humanitarianism was finally harnassed . . . by the sentiments he aroused in himself as well as in the hearts of others, by the idealized picture he created of an ancient, ordered, and distinguished civilization borne down by the superior force and ruthlessness of a new and cruder one."[30] Similarly, Boulton says that throughout Burke's speech runs the theme, in Burke's words, "thirty millions of my fellow-creatures and fellow-subjects."[31] Such people, explains Boulton, had qualities of humanness, requiring "the exercise of feeling, sensibility, sympathetic understanding, and imaginative participation in human distress."[32] It was thus Burke's rhetorical task to relate the natural and praiseworthy emotions of his audience to the moral principle and logical criteria he had established to measure the company's exercise of its trust.

Interwoven throughout Burke's logical structure is a contrast between India and the East India Company designed to make his audience feel about the situation as he himself did.[33] He presented a selective description of Indian society which served as a contradiction to the misconception of the Indian as a barbarian. He said that the Indian population—four times that of Great Britain—was varied and included those who had been "for ages civilized and cultivated . . . by all the arts of polished life, whilst we were yet in the woods."[34] Comparing Indian princes to German sovereigns, Burke explained:

> I have compared to Germany . . . not for an exact resemblance, but as a sort of middle term, by which India might be approximated to our understandings, and, if possible to our feelings, in order to awaken something of sympathy for the unfortunate natives, of which I am afraid we are not perfectly susceptible, whilst we look at this very remote object through a false and cloudy medium.[35]

Was the impairment of the object great? Yes, claimed Burke, for the company personnel had failed first as politicians and then as merchants. After promising to be temperate in his language, Burke declared that the company had cheated *every* Indian prince, had broken *every* treaty, and, as a consequence, had ruined every prince or state which had *ever* trusted the company. In support of these distributed generalizations, Burke employed rhetorical proof, for he said he could produce enough evidence in a half an hour to induce belief—or to create a sense of demonstration for generalizations the function of which was to create the impression that the abuse in India had been *great*.[36] Burke concluded by inviting his audience to give an example of an Indian prince who had not been cheated. One example from an audience which included company representatives would have refuted the generalization.

Turning to the conditions of the Indian provinces, Burke made the claim that the barbaric conquerers of the past—the Arabs, Tartars, and Persians —had more justification to govern India than did the company, for they at least had been interested in India's productivity. In contrast, the company's "protection" of India was destroying India. Said Burke to his predominantly English audience:

> England has erected no churches, no hospitals, no palaces, no schools; England has built no bridges, made no high roads, cut no navigations, dug out

no reservoirs. Every other conquerer of every other description has left some monument, either of state or beneficence, behind him. Were we to be driven out of India this day, nothing would remain to tell that it had been possessed, during the inglorious period of our dominion by anything better than the ourangoutang [sic] or the tiger.[37]

Burke's discussion of the barbarians and the English concluded the essential praise-and-blame enthymeme that he had been constructing since he had redefined a charter as a "trust."[38] If he had said enough to create the suspicion that Indians were more civilized than barbaric and if his audience maintained their feelings about the barbaric conquerors of India, the company stood embarrassingly accused. If the company, a presumably civilized organization, had treated the Indians barbarically—more so than had barbarians—then the company was either barbaric or more blameworthy than were the barbarians. If barbarians were blamable for their actions in India, the company was more blamable; for they had treated India worse than had barbarians and hence had lost title to their trust or charter. "In effect, Sir," said Burke,

every legal regular authority in matters of revenue, of political administration, of criminal law, of civil law, in many of the most essential parts of military discipline, is laid level with the ground; and an oppressive, irregular, capricious, unsteady, rapacious, and peculating despotism, with a direct disavowal of obedience to any authority at home, and without any fixed maxim in India, is at present the state of your charter-government over great kingdoms.[39]

Burke skipped quickly over an examination of the company personnel as "merchants"; granting that if the company had managed its "business" properly, he would "pass by the whole mass of their enormities as statesmen."[40] Burke stipulated six attributes of the "ideal merchant" and showed mainly through the implications of rhetorical questions that company practice in commerce had been seriously wanting.

Believing that he had said enough to show that the company's abuse had been habitual, Burke argued, in a manner which answered the question Fox had ignored, that the company was incurable. Why? Because the proprietors, employees, and especially the directors suffered from the incurable vice of hypocrisy. The directors had wondered why they had been condemned for faults of the proprietors and employees. Burke charged that the directors' professed awareness of the abuses in India was positive proof of their guilt. Because they had privately supported what they had condemned publicly, Burke was convinced that their knowledge of wrongdoing would not result in correction. The directors, Burke continued, had sought to ruin every employee who had tried to reveal the true state of India. How could reform be trusted to those who had destroyed India, when "every attempt to correct an abuse would be a satire on their former administration"? "Take away, say they, the court of proprietors, and the court of directors will do their duty," mused Burke.

> Yes; as they have done it hitherto. That the evils in India have solely arisen from the court of proprietors is grossly false. In many of them, the directors were heartily concurring; in all, they were conniving.[41]

Indeed! The abolition of the key personnel of the company was to Burke an essential step to a meaningful Indian reform.

Apart from the eloquence he lent to all his causes, Burke's essential contribution to the rhetoric of the Indian reform movement was in the manner he handled the troublesome "charter issue" in relation to the personnel of the company. Burke substituted for the traditional jargon about "politics" and "merchants" a concept of a charter as a "trust". Implicit in that concept was a distinction between a legal and a natural right and a distinctly antimercantilistic principle that a government ought to improve and nurture the object of its trust. Burke's examination of the company's political and commercial activities, carefully related to audience feelings and preconceptions, injected a humanitarian concern and a personal moral commitment into reform rhetoric and by both logic and feeling made the company personnel blamable for the unhappy state of India. Thus, the charter which had been a shield against reform was transformed by Burke's rhetoric into a warrant for significant reform even if it did not constitute a warrant for the Fox Bill itself.

Reaction to Burke

The reaction to Burke in the Commons was varied. Aside from scattered murmurings about the sanctity of charters and a counterdefinition of a charter as "compact" dissolvable only by the consent of all parties, Burke's detailed and bold address met with general silence. The company interest withdrew and Pitt desperately vowed to propose a reform plan which would withstand his objections to the Fox Bill.[42]

Fox himself triumphantly cast aside the cautious deference which had characterized his November 18 speech. He no longer professed a concern for the company and a reluctance to reform, but said instead that "the subversion of that infamous government is the main object of the Bill in question." Fox also reiterated that if a "trust" had been abused or a benefit not obtained, a charter could be revoked without violating a right; and he repeated that the "misfortune of the Company resulted not more from what the servants did than from what the masters did not."[43] All these points were originated by Burke, and Fox's willingness to employ them meant that the company could no longer defend itself against the government in the long struggle for control of India. But as the Fox Bill failed in the Crown-controlled House of Lords, the significance of Burke's rhetoric was in creating the climate wherein Pitt could pass the kind of reform that the rhetoric of Robinson, Dundas, and Jenkinson historically had been unable to justify.

With conditions in India and in the company being what they were, with reformers on both sides of the House, with the Fox Bill failing only because of the king's fear of Fox's political power, and with their historic shield being shattered by Burke, the company became so desperate as to take whatever the government left them. In such a climate and urged by George III to become head of the Ministry, Pitt was able to obtain the company's consent to his reform bill and that meant that the irrational public fears which had been generated against Fox's bill were put to rest.[44] Operating apart from the climate created in part by the rhetoric of Burke, the company, in all likelihood, would have rejected the reform of Pitt as they had rejected the significant reforms of Pitt's forebears.

When Pitt first presented his reform to the Commons, he used some of the humanitarian aspects of the Burke rationale, made a major point of "the Company's consent," reintroduced the old jargon about merchants and politicians, and then dealt with enduring and only rhetorically meaningful questions concerning the separability of commerce and politics. He declared:

> The political concerns of this country in India . . . ought to be placed under other control than that of the company of merchants in Leadenhall-street.[45]

And, he continued, "The commerce of the Company should be left, as much as possible to their own supervision." The idea that "merchants" should be responsible for "commerce" was, he said, "an idea which must strike every thinking man."[46]

After admitting, however, that in practicality it would be difficult to separate politics from commerce, Pitt thought it proper to allow the king to be the final arbiter in respect to what was what. In essence, without opposition, Pitt had declared the king's sovereignty over India, and the company had thus finally been taken over. Realizing that Pitt's plan was as mild a reform as would be made, the company knew that to continue to argue the inseparability of politics and commerce meant the risk of losing not just dominance, but everything. Thanks to Fox's Bill coupled with Burke's rhetoric, the presumption of sovereignty had been shifted back to the government so that if the inseparability claim was true, commerce as well as politics would go to the government. Thus, the company was forced to accept the fiction of the separability of commerce and politics which the traditional reformers had perpetrated to get a foothold in Indian affairs and at the same time shift the responsibility for mistakes made in India. That fiction had not worked for the traditional reformers. Thanks to Burke, it worked for Pitt.

Burke's rhetorical contribution to the Indian reform movement should now be clear. Yet it is difficult to know if his contribution was more than rhetorical. It appears that he had little effect either on the provisions of the Pitt Act or on British action in India.

Sutherland says that the purpose of the Pitt Act was to carry out the methods of government supervision and infiltration which North and Robinson had been seeking to employ since 1773.[47] Philips called Pitt's Bill "a clever" and "dishonest" means of "subordinating the Court of Directors as a political power."[48] In effect, the Pitt Act left the directors with only "face." As Marriott says,

> All the trappings of greatness, their grand house, their magnificent banquets, their vast patronage: they were still the grandest Corporation in the greatest city in the world, but there was still the checkstring behind the machinery which controlled all its movements.[49]

In Russell's words:

The cloak of an independent authority was still worn, but beneath that cloak was the dictatorial power of which the reality belonged to Mr. Pitt, and of which the odium still clung to Mr. Fox.[50]

The success of the Pitt Act, however, did not mean that the purposes of Burke were fulfilled. Burke wanted to dismiss and punish wayward servants and officials of the company, but Pitt's Bill was prospective and not punitive and as such had a special appeal to the company personnel. Burke would have established a new company structure which would have been account-able to Parliament, whereas Pitt gave the government direct control over Indian politics and indirect control over commerce. Burke proposed a clear chain of responsibility, whereas the chain in the scheme of the traditional reformers was left strategically vague. Most important, however, Burke saw the problem in the relationship between the company and the people of India, whereas Chatham and the reformers who followed him saw the problem in the relations between the company and the government, with the government being unable to tap the rich resources of India.

During the debate on Pitt's Bill, Phillip Francis and Burke argued that the Pitt Bill would not check the corruption in India and be of benefit to the Indian people. Burke, in fact, felt that Pitt's measure was positive proof that the facts contained in his reports and speeches were not believed.[51] But regardless of Burke's feelings, the question remained: did India prosper after coming under the direct auspices of the British government in 1784?

Nineteenth century British historians seem to agree that corruption in India disappeared after 1784 and after the trial of Warren Hastings which followed. Russell wrote that "the spirit of the British Constitution has pervaded India, and the most absolute despotism has been qualified and tempered by the genius of representative government."[52] Morley, likewise, reflecting the essential praise-and-blame enthymeme of Burke's speech, says,

Burke's action was taken, and enlightened modern opinion rests upon the pardonable hypothesis that Europeans ought not only to have been less tyrannical, perfidious, and destructive than barbarous rajahs, but not to have been tyrannical and perfidious at all.[53]

By such judgments we are led to believe that the thought of Burke became the philosophy for an enlightened form of nineteenth century "white man's burden" British imperialism. If such a situation existed, it would have come as a surprise to Burke, who failed to see any progress during his own time.

On May 17, 1784, Burke expressed in a letter to William Eden that he had made no headway in convincing Britishers about the "humanity" of Indians. "You are certainly right," he wrote,

> the havock and destruction of the species made in the East Indies does by no means touch the humanity of our countrymen, who, if the whole Gentoo's race had but one neck, would see it out with the most perfect indifference.[54]

Eight years later Burke wrote to Lord Fitzwilliam that the state of India was worse than it had been,[55] and, in 1785, he had said,

> I confess, I wish that some more feeling than I have yet observed for the suffering of our fellow-creatures and fellow-subjects in that oppressed part of the world had manifested itself in any one quarter of the kingdom, or in any one large description of men.[56]

Between the accounts of Burke and those of later historians, it is not clear when the thoughts of Burke took hold or, indeed, if they ever did. What is clear is that Burke's contribution to Indian reform was substantially rhetorical. The question remains, however, as to whether Burke's philosophy rationalized British imperialism as his rhetoric assisted a government take-over of the private East India Company. If so, then Burke's rhetoric, while effective, may have been counterproductive to his philosophic as well as his political aims.

NOTES AND REFERENCES

1. Edmund Burke, *Reflections on the Revolution in France,* edited by William B. Todd. (New York: Rinehart and Co., 1959), p. 209.

2. L. S. Sutherland, *The East India Company in Eighteenth-Century Politics* (Oxford: Clarendon Press, 1952), p. 369.

3. By the term "Burke's rhetoric," I do not refer in this article to general characteristics of Burke's speech or persuasion such as his powers of imagery and amplifi-

cation or delivery, which had their particular impact upon whatever issue he chose to speak. I refer instead to his choice of topics and arguments or to that part of rhetoric traditionally called *inventio* as it pertained to the "East India question" as it was debated in the House of Commons between 1766 and 1784.

4. The first British East India Company was chartered by Queen Elizabeth in 1600. In 1696 a second company was established by an Act of Parliament. Twelve years later, by another Act of Parliament, the two companies were united and given commercial monopolistic privileges over trade with the provinces of India.

5. Until 1784 the "home government" of the company consisted of "proprietors" and twenty-four "directors". Any owner of the capital stock of the company was a "proprietor" and was permitted to attend the meetings of the General Court of Proprietors. Before 1784 the Court of Proprietors had the power to reverse the decisions of the Court of Directors, but in practice their most important task was electing the directors. The legislature and executive privileges of the proprietors were seldom used because the directors usually could control the proprietors. Thus, the directors were the real managers of the company. To become a director one's stock had to be worth at least two thousand pounds and one had to be elected by the proprietors on the second Wednesday of April when the annual election was held. Voting strength in the Court of Proprietors was built and maintained by patronage. The friends and relatives of those favored by a director were expected to support measures advanced by the directors in general and by their own patron in particular. C H. Philips, *The East India Company, 1784–1834* [Manchester: Manchester University Press, 1961], p. 4.

6. Burke was directly opposed to the scheme of the traditional reformers. He wrote to the Marquis of Rockingham on November 23, 1772, that it was the duty of Parliament to see that the company neither abused its charter nor misgoverned India. At the same time he thought "it abominable to declare their dividends in the House of Commons; and to seize their Revenues into the hands of the Crown". (*The Correspondence of Edmund Burke* [Cambridge: At the University Press, 1963], vol. 2, p. 385.)

7. Philips, *The East India Company, 1784–1834*, p. 4.

8. Sutherland, *The East India Company*, p. 339.

9. Ibid., p. 366.

10. Lord North resigned on March 20, 1782. Seven days later George III appointed Rockingham to replace North. On July 1, 1782, Rockingham died.

11. With Fox refusing to serve with Shelburne, there was no majority in the House of Commons. Shelburne controlled about 140 votes. North controlled about

twenty less than Shelburne, and Fox controlled about ninety. (Donald Grove Barnes, *George III and William Pitt, 1783–1806* [Stanford University Press, 1939], p. 20.) Some political coalition or realignment was obviously necessary if the Commons was to transact business.

12. W. E. H. Lecky, *A History of England in the Eighteenth Century* (New York: D. Appleton and Company, 1893), vol. 5, pp. 230–31.

13. Sutherland, *The East India Company*, p. 391.

14. Ibid., p. 399.

15. On December 8, 1783, James Martin, a consistent opponent of North begrudgingly congratulated the Coalition for winning the independents of the House. (*Great Britain, The Parliamentary History of England from the Earliest Period to the Year, 1803*, edited by William Cobbett [London: T. C. Hansard, 1819], vol. 24, p. 31.) John Luttrell, who had suspended judgment until the last day of debate, announced his support for Fox. (Ibid., pp. 25–26.) William Eden, moreover, in a letter to Lord Northington said, "I will only say that by all accounts, nothing has ever been known equal to the animation of the house, and the triumph of the ministry". (*The Windham Papers*, edited by Earl Rosebery [London: Herbert Jenkins, Ltd., 1912], 1: 54–55.)

16. George III passed the word to the House of Lords that he would not look favorably upon anyone who voted for the Fox Bill. (J. Holland Rose, *William Pitt and the National Revival* [London: G. Bell and Sons, 1911], p. 148.) The bill was thus defeated in the Lords, and George III used that fact to remove Fox from office and replace him with Pitt.

17. The "politics for politicians" and "commerce for merchants" rationale is based on a "conceptual incongruity", which associates the concepts of "merchant" and "politician." The implication is that a merchant cannot be a politician and vice versa, because the attributes of the concept "merchant" include nothing to indicate why a merchant would be qualified to be a politician. This popular rationale of the debate on Indian reform was a sophisticated form of question-begging, which draws a factual conclusion from a definition. Because the definitions of merchant and politician were not congruous, it was asserted implicitly that a given set of men were qualified for what they did because of their name. And it was asserted that any given set of men could not be competent both as merchants and politicians.

18. *PH*, vol. 23, col. 1200.

19. Ibid. Fox proposed that one commission, while dealing essentially with politics, would have power over the "commerce commission," which would have a subordinate power.

20. Ibid., col. 1209.

21. Pitt did not uphold the principle that a charter was sacred. He simply presumed that Fox had not given sufficient reason for his proposed changes in the Company's structure. Pitt's stance allowed him the room both to oppose Fox's bill on its own merits and to propose a countermeasure. (Ibid.)

22. Ibid., col. 1239.

23. Ibid.

24. Ibid., col. 1249

25. James T. Boulton, "The Criticism of Rhetoric and the Act of Communication," *Essays on Rhetorical Criticism*, edited by Thomas R. Nilsen (New York: Random House, 1968), p. 43.

26. PH., vol. 23, col. 1318.

27. Ibid., cols. 1315, 1316.

28. Ibid., col. 1316.

29. Ibid., col. 1317.

30. Sutherland, *The East India Company,* pp. 57–58.

31. Boulton, "The Criticism of Rhetoric," p. 41.

32. Ibid.

33. Boulton says that Burke's often repeated contrast is more than a "debater's trick". It is, he says, "evidence of the civilized, mature humanity of the speaker himself." (Ibid., p. 43.)

34. PH., vol. 23, col. 1320.

35. Ibid., cols. 1321, 1322.

36. According to William J. Brandt, argumentative induction or rhetorical as opposed to logical proof is "an appeal to the experience of the reader. The arguer," says Brandt, "may use one example, or three, or twenty, but they are habitually directed, not to the world of things, but to the reader's experience (or lack of experience) of that world." (*The Rhetoric of Argumentation* [Indianapolis: Bobbs-Merrill, 1970], p. 46.)

37. PH., vol. 23, cols. 1333, 1334.

38. An enthymeme is a deduction which interacts with audience attitudes to create a sense of demonstration or feeling of certainty for matters which do not lend themselves to demonstration or certainty. It is essentially an "argument in the mind" about "contingent" matters which beg for response.

39. *PH.*, vol. 23, col. 1364.

40. Ibid.

41. Ibid., col. 1375.

42. Henry Beaufoy, an "independent" who normally gravitated toward the politics of William Pitt, was in agreement with what Burke had said about the state of India. (Ibid., col. 1397.)

43. Ibid., col. 1408.

44. As long as the concept of charter as "compact" prevailed, it meant that whatever had happened between the government and the company had no relevance to other charters and franchises in England. If the consent of the holders of charters and franchises was required, the holders had a feeling of security which had been threatened by the rhetoric of Pitt and the company against the Fox bill. On the other hand, it was the rhetoric of Burke which upset the company's feeling of security and made them open to Pitt's plan. On January 10, 1784, Pitt conferred with the General Court of the company, and five-sixths of those present agreed to his reform plan. Two days before he had obtained the consent of the directors, although six complained that the chairman and a committee of proprietors had forced the directors "to agree to this Bill, which will annihilate the powers of the Company." (Philips, p. 27.)

45. *PH.*, vol. 24: cols. 322, 323. Fox and Burke made light of the company's consent. Fox said that the concurrence of the Court of Proprietors was not "the deed of a company which at least consists of 1,400." (Ibid., col. 332.) Burke declared that the conditions under which the consent had been obtained meant that company's charter had not been less violated because they had given consent. Knowing that their life was in danger, the company was in a compromising situation. Thus, explained Burke, "they were glad to purchase what the minister was pleased to leave them, by a voluntary surrender, which made men give up what was no longer in their power to keep." (Ibid., col. 358.)

46. Ibid., col. 332.

47. Sutherland, *The East India Company*, p. 7.

48. Philips, *The East India Company, 1784–1834*, p. 34.

49. John A. R. Marriott, *The English in India* (Oxford: Clarendon Press, 1932), p. 75.

50. John Russell, *The Life and Times of Charles James Fox* (London: Richard Bentley, 1866), vol. 2, p. 171.

51. *PH.*, vol. 24: col. 1212. Burke said also that he was ready to defend what he had said about Hastings. In his words, "all he looked for was an opportunity

to maintain them in the face of the House and of the world." (Ibid., col. 1210.)

52. *Fox Correspondence,* vol. 2, pp. 254–55.

53. John Morley, *Edmund Burke* (New York: Alfred A. Knopf, 1924), p. 174.

54. *Burke Correspondence,* vol. 5, p. 151.

55. Ibid., vol. 7, p. 233. Burke wrote, "I was in hope, that the prosecution of Hastings might check and control the Spirit of Rapine and Tyranny there (in India)."

56. "Speech on the Nabob of Arcot's Debts," *The Works of Edmund Burke* (Boston: Little, Brown, and Co., 1894), vol. 3, p. 108.

Edmund Burke and the Regency Crisis of 1788–89

Bruce E. Gronbeck

I feel no desire whatsoever of interfering; especially as too great an infusion of various and heterogeneous opinions may embarrass that decision, which it seems to me so necessary that you should come to; and for which I do not think a great time is allowed you.

—Edmund Burke to Charles Fox,
24 November 1788

Given this quotation from his own hand and similar remarks by contemporaries, historians of the Regency Crisis of 1788–89 have argued for a view which isolates Edmund Burke from party councils on one hand and which also explains his apparent anxious, indiscreet speech patterns on the other. Even admirers of Burke are shocked by his crude, grotesque imagery in oral discourse, and see him as a brooding hermit, rashly thrashing in the darkness of his spirit just before the high noon of his career—the French Revolution. Indeed, some biographers find him so out of favor, out of touch, and (perhaps) out of mind that they completely ignore his work during the Regency Crisis.

Such critical reaction, perhaps, stems from remarks by both his friends and foes of 1788–89. Henry Addington called him "violent almost to madness"; George Selwyn cried "Burke walking at large and him [the king] in a strait waistcoat!"[1] Even two of Burke's staunchest friends, Gilbert Elliot and William Windham, questioned his invective. The moderately pro-Pitt papers such as *The Times* laughed at the spectacle of Burke:

A Correspondent observes, the *Sublime* and *Beautiful* was certainly lost in the vapours of an Irish fog, . . . even his warmest partizans could not but observe the mist before his eyes, though, poor man, he could not even with his *magnifying teliscopes* [*sic*], perceive, he was wandering in the dark.[2]

And if government papers lampooned his performances in Parliament, the pamphleteers' prose bordered on cruelty, as witness a quotation from one entitled *Letters from Simpkin to his Dear Brother:*

> You remember, perhaps, that I formerly said,/ 'Twas suspected that EDMUND was *touch'd in the Head;/* Some thought my assertion was matter of sport,/ But now all the PAPERS confirm the report;/ They describe him one day full of spirits and gladness,/ The next like a *Spectre,* dejected with sadness,/ In the BOOKSELLERS' SHOPS, seeking *Books* upon MADNESS:/ At ST. LUKE'S and in BEDLAM inspect the Cells,/ To see in what comfort INSANITY *dwells* ... / To the TOWER some whisper'd a motion to send him,/ But others more tender, lamenting his case,/ Thought BEDLAM by far a more suitable place.[3]

To be sure, by Burke's own admissions he was "little consulted" and had "grown anxious" during the period of November 1788 to mid-February 1789. The diatribes aimed at him in diaries, letters, and newspapers would seem to circumscribe a mentally disturbed recluse.

Biographers and historians of the Regency Crisis, however, have far from exhausted the sources available for properly describing and evaluating Burke's roles in what was probably the Foxites' last chance to secure office in the eighteenth century. Closer examination of newspaper accounts of the Opposition's activity, letters with casual references to those attending party councils, Burke's private notes relating to the Regency Crisis, actual speeches recorded in Cobbett, documents contained in the recently published *Correspondence of George Prince of Wales,*[4] and accounts of the reception of his parliamentary speaking in less jaundiced memoirs provide us with another Burke. The theses of this essay will be that: Burke was an active, driving force during the Regency Crisis; as a Foxite, he was consulted frequently, at least when compared with other members of Parliament; as a party philosopher and pamphleteer, he was busier than any other member of this party; and as a constitutional theoretician and conscience of Parliament, Burke met Pitt's solution for the Regency Crisis point by point, driven first to his study and then to the floor of Commons by Pitt's analysis and plan. My purpose is to demonstrate that the Burke of the American, Indian, Irish and French *causae* was operating (though nearly sixty) with characteristic depth and breadth during the "Royal Malady" of 1788–89. He may be considered—for reasons to be developed in this study —a rhetorical failure; nevertheless, his rhetorical progression through the Regency Crisis makes his performance worthy of attention.

The "Royal Malady"

In the summer of 1788, George III suffered a dementing attack of porphyria.[5] By mid-October, the king's physician, Sir George Baker, reported that he was "sorry to acquaint Mr. Pitt that he left his Majesty in an agitation of spirits bordering upon delirium."[6] The king's appearance at a levee on October 24 publicly confirmed rumors of insanity,[7] and by November 4, George III was giving out scores of contradictory orders.[8] The effort of governmental papers such as the *Morning Chronicle* to quell open discussion was of no avail—the king was losing his mind.[9]

First, the Prince of Wales's doctor, Richard Warren, was called in to help Baker. By December 5, a specialist, Dr. Francis Willis, was summoned (by the queen or Privy Council) from Lincolnshire to attend.[10] The fact that Warren saw little hope for recovery, while Willis with more than modest assurances promised a cure, added nothing but speed to public rumors.[11] Pitt realized that he had to make preparations for proposing a regency until the king either recovered or died.

Parliament was faced with both a constitutional and a political crisis of the first order. Constitutionally, the situation was unprecedented. England had never beheld an insane king *and* an heir apparent (the Prince of Wales) of full age; previously disturbed kings had no heir ready to rule. Further, no one really knew if the regent should be given full or only partial powers, as the situation was assumed temporary. Finally, while George III had prorogued Parliament that spring with orders to meet November 20, how could it assemble with no king to open it or to put the Great Seal upon bills?

But if the constitutional questions were problematic, Pitt as leading minister had an almost overwhelming political job. The inevitable regent— the Prince of Wales—had aligned himself with the old Fox-North Opposition, with those parliamentarians whom Pitt had unseated in 1783. Pitt faced a political organization led by such talented men as Fox, North, Burke, Sheridan, William Windham, Thomas Powys, Sir Grey Cooper, the young Charles Grey in the Commons, and Loughborough (Wedderburne), the old Northite Lord Stormont, the Duke of Portland, the bright young Lord Rawdon in the Lords. Opposition had tightened its organization since the Foxite martyrdom of 1784,[12] and they still blamed Pitt for the palace plot hatched during the East India Bill debates of 1783. This Opposition, according to a 1788 estimate, commanded some 155 votes, and if they captured a substantial portion of the independent vote and a few "rats" (i.e., defectors from government), they could oust Pitt easily.[13] And, finally, they were fresh off two successful challenges of Pitt: in the spring of 1788 they had forced him to take several amendments to save one of his India bills and in the summer of 1788 they had beaten one of his candidates (Lord Hood) in a vicious bi-election in Westminister.[14] As the Regency Crisis dawned, even Pitt's most ardent supporters made ready for a change in ministry.[15]

Despite this strength, Opposition was not without its problems. At the onset of the Crisis, Opposition was scattered from northern England (where 1688 celebrations were being held) to France (Loughborough) to Italy (Fox himself); they did not assemble as a group until November 24—four days after Parliament's first meeting. And even as they gathered, their ranks were riddled with discord: both Fox and the Duke of Portland still felt badly treated by the prince over his rumored marriage to a Catholic (Mrs. Fitzherbert); Sheridan and Burke were at odds over policy questions concerning the trial of Warren Hastings; and Fox and Sheridan seemed in constant conflict, perhaps because as the prince's favorite, Sheridan, was maneuvering independent of his party chieftain.[16] And, Opposition's third major problem lay in their approach to the Crisis; they apparently fought through three possible strategies—with Loughborough, Fox, and Burke each proposing a different course—and the one they chose emerged only a few days before the opening of debate on December 10. This delay in singling out their general rhetorical strategy meant they had comparatively little time to prepare their actual case.[17]

With such problems besieging them, Opposition spent much of late November and early December repairing interpersonal relations and, as one might expect, seeking converts—both rats from government and uncommitted votes from the independents.[18] As the debate commenced on December 10, the Foxites had at least the outline of a regency doctrine, greatly improved intraparty spirit, and some successes in fattening their votes.

On December 10 the House resolved itself into a Committee of the Whole to consider the nation's predicament.[19] Pitt first proposed three resolutions, after a question was raised by Fox casting doubt on Parliament's right to revitalize the Crown (i.e., appoint a regent). After a debate which filled the rest of December, both Houses agreed to the Three Resolutions. In January, after the physicians for a second time had been called to report progress, Parliament (again as a committee) met to debate Pitt's Five Resolutions (Regency Plan)—resolutions which asked the Prince of Wales to assume the throne with limited powers during his father's incapacity. This debate continued until January 27, at which time the Regency Plan passed both Houses. After both the prince as prospective regent and the queen as prospective caretaker of the king and his household agreed to the Five Resolutions, and after a one-day argument (February 2) on how to open Parliament, the Houses assembled for the first time as a regular "Parliament," as the sixth session of the sixteenth Parliament of Great Britain.

On February 5, Pitt brought in his actual Regency Bill, providing for: the Prince of Wales as sole regent, subject to certain limitations of power; the queen as governess of the king, his private purse, his lands and the household; and a council of advice to aid Her Majesty. The bill passed its third reading in Commons on February 12, and was about to finish its course through Lords when, on February 19, the Lord Chancellor (Thurlow) reported the king's recovery. In less than a month (March 17), Commons was discussing Navy and Army Estimates and repeal of the Shop Tax; by April, the Hastings affair was renewed with the vigor of 1787. As for the Regency Bill itself, it gathered dust until 1812, when George III suffered a relapse so severe that he never returned. The bill was revived and passed, putting the Prince of Wales on the throne as regent until 1820, when George III died and the prince was crowned George IV (1820–27).

Thus Pitt steered his way through a parliamentary crisis, relying upon procedural delays and expert rhetoric to keep Parliament talking until His Majesty recovered.[20] Opposition proved ineffectual in this, probably its last chance for office in the eighteenth century. Among them, as Derry has argued, only one man—Edmund Burke—put up a fight which might have won for them the seals of government.[21]

Burke's Range of Activities

Before we attempt to examine the structure and force of Burke's rhetorical efforts, we should isolate as precisely as possible all facets of Burke's activities, given the charges set out by various biographers and historians. The first three tables summarize those activities.

In Table 1 we find recorded everything (as far as I know) that Burke did during the crucial months. The activities are divided into five categories: (1) *letters,* both sent and received, as found at Sheffield; (2) *speeches,* recorded in Cobbett's *Parliamentary History;* (3) *known meetings,* as recorded in *The Times,* in the Duchess of Devonshire's diary, and in the correspondence of Sir Gilbert Elliot and of Lady Elizabeth Foster; (4) *probable meetings,* as recorded in *The Times;* and (5) *material drafted,* as found in the Wentworth Woodhouse Muniments and the papers of the Prince of Wales.[22]

In all, Burke wrote thirteen letters, received three; he delivered thirty-two speeches in sixty-six calendar days; he is known to have attended five meetings, and I assume he attended another fourteen; and, he drafted forty-eight items of material relating to the regency. About twenty-two of those items were drafted before Burke's first major speech of December 22, and another fifteen probably were written from mid-January to early February.

Next, we should examine Burke's work in party councils. Table 2 indicates that Burke attended fewer of the famous "Carlton House" meetings than did either Sheridan or Fox. But, the numbers found in Table 2 are misleading in one respect: they include many visits of friends. Thus, for example, they include both the Prince's and Sheridan's journeys to Devonshire House for late-evening get-togethers with the Duchess. When we remove such meetings as well as others in which the prince as the central power figure was *not* present, the picture changes. In Table 3 Burke—in comparison with other Commoners—comes off well, for he attended almost as many of these "official" strategy conferences as Sheridan and Fox. Indeed, his record perhaps is remarkable, given his late November arrival in London, his December trip home at Christmas, and his January absences for research on "madhouses." The most frequent visitors of the prince were his brothers and some combination of Lords. The regular appearance of Lothian and Queensbury, prominent "rats" from George III's retinue, and of Northumberland, a leader of the "Armed Neutrality," would seem to indicate that Opposition was using the prince principally as a lure for the votes of their lordships.[23] Commoners were meeting with him only when strategy sessions were necessary; and at most of those meetings, we assume Burke was to be found.

A look at his correspondence reinforces this picture of an energetic

Table 1
SUMMARY OF BURKE'S ACTIVITIES DURING
THE REGENCY CRISIS

Letters	Speeches	Known Meetings*	Possible Meetings*	Material Drafted
Nov. 7				Material before Dec. 22:
Nov. 24			Nov. 27	Items 8–20, 21, 22, 23, 24, 25,
Nov. 24			Nov. 28	29, 35; possible P of W Address
			Nov. 30	to Commons; draft of note from
Dec. 1				P of W to Pitt; draft of possible
			Dec. 2	note from P of W to Pitt on terms
Dec. 5†		Dec. 5	Dec. 4	for regency.
	Dec. 8		Dec. 6	
	Dec. 10		Dec. 8	
Dec. 11				
	Dec. 19		Dec. 14	
	Dec. 22			Draft of Lords' Protest (Dec. 29);
Dec. 25				draft of P of W's answer to
Dec. 29†			Dec. 29	Pitt on restrictions (Dec. 30–
			Jan. 1	Jan. 1).
Jan. 6	Jan. 6	Jan. 10		
	Jan. 13	Jan. 19		Material probably drafted through
Jan. 24				Jan. and early Feb.: Items 1, 2,
	Jan. 26			3–7, 27, 31, 32, 33, 36, 37;
	Jan. 27			"The Present Question, in Its
		Jan. 28	Jan. 28	Constitutional Point of View"
Jan. 29			Jan. 29	[?]; Burke's "Memorandum"; "The
		Jan. 30		Voice of Reason" [later?].
	Feb. 2			P of W's acceptance speech.
	Feb. 5			
	Feb. 6			
	Feb. 7			[Items 26 and 28 are impossible
Feb. 8†			Feb. 8	to date; the content is much
	Feb. 9			too general.] Item 38.
	Feb. 10		Feb. 10	
Feb. 11	Feb. 11			
Feb. 24				
Feb. 25				Draft of P of W's speech to
Mar. 12				the Irish delegates [?].

*These meetings include not only the so-called "Carlton House" assemblies but also visits with Sir Gilbert Elliot, Fox, and other members of Opposition. One should also note that not all "Carlton House" meetings in fact were held in the prince's lodgings; some were held at Loughborough's, at Portland's London abode, at Fox's, and at Sheridan's Burlington House.

†Indicates when Burke received letters—from Portland, Adam (Portland's secretary), and the Prince of Wales respectively.

Table 2*
ATTENDANCE AT THE OPPOSITION MEETINGS, ACCORDING TO *THE TIMES* AND
THE DUCHESS OF DEVONSHIRE

Name	Times		Name	Times	
Prince of Wales†	64	(8)	Dr. Warren	12	
Duke of York	35	(9)	Dr. Baker	6	
Duke of Cumberland	24	(9)	Dr. Gisbourne	2	
Duke of Portland	13	(18)	R. B. Sheridan‡	36	(10)
Earl of Lothian	6	(13)	C. J. Fox	15	(10)
Viscount Stormont	8	(14)	Edmund Burke	5	(14)
Lord Loughborough	9	(10)	Thomas Dundas	3	(11)
Duke of Queensbury	4	(14)	Lord North	3	(13)
Duke of Northumberland	7	(16)	John Payne	2	(10)
Earl of Sandwich	5	(13)			

*Represents the period Nov. 5, 1788, to Feb. 17, 1789; the terminal date was chosen on the basis of when even Dr. Warren admitted that the king was convalescing.

†In several accounts of the meetings, *The Times* did not list the attendants but only indicated that "several nobility" were at Carlton House. The numbers in parentheses indicate such references to "nobility" after the presence of each individual had been noted in a previous account.

‡Similarly, *The Times* often says that "the Opposition" or "friends" or "various MPs" were at a meeting. Sheridan, Fox, Burke, etc., I assume, were at such meetings when they were in town.

Table 3
POLITICAL MEETINGS AT WHICH THE PRINCE WAS PRESENT

Name	Nov.	Dec.	Jan.	Feb.	Total
Prince	6	19	20	12	57
York	3	13	15	7	38
Cumberland	0	10	13	9	32
Portland	4	10	9	1	24
Lothian	1	8	8	2	19
Stormont	2	9	10	1	22
Loughborough	2	9	9	1	21
Queensbury	1	9	8	0	18
Northumberland	1	8	9	1	19
Sandwich	1	8	7	1	17
Sheridan	5	7	6	1	19
Fox	3	9	5	0	17
Burke	2	6	6	1	15
Dundas	1	6	6	1	14
North	2	6	4	1	13
Payne	1	6	3	1	11

Burke. To be sure, some of his letters were written to personal friends—the Duchess of Devonshire, O'Hara, Windham, Philip Francis, Malone, and his family (Richard Burke, Jr., and Sr.). But he also wrote to Portland, Fox, Sheridan, and "Capt. Jack" Payne (the prince's private secretary), and received notes from Portland, William Adam (Portland's secretary), and the Prince of Wales himself. The letter from the Prince of Wales is especially illuminating, for it indicates that his party did not want Burke to feel like an outsider:

> My dear Burke,
>   We are to meet at Lord Loughborough's a little before two, pray come there, as there is no man's whose advice is so necessary to us, at all times, and particularly at this singular and dangerous Chrysis, as Yours.
>
> Ever sincerely Yours
G P [8 February 1789][24]

In summary, there can be little question that Edmund Burke was anything but an isolated, unconsulted political has-been during the Regency Crisis. While his party perhaps did not trust to him major office in their proposed cabinet,[25] nevertheless they received—and often asked for—his advice and his services as orator-pamphleteer.

Phases in Burke's Argument

The central thrust of Burke's thinking toward a regency in general and toward that proposed by Pitt in particular has been articulated most fully by John Derry. Derry, however, concentrated his efforts on outlining Burke's *final* political philosophy.[26] A careful examination of available documents and speech texts will reveal Burke arrived at that position step by step; the dialectic in which he and Pitt (principally) engaged constantly reshaped his argument, outdated his evidence, and deepened his thought. The parliamentary process—Three Resolutions declaring Parliament's right to act, Five Resolutions outlining the principles of a regency bill, and three readings of an actual bill—allowed Burke and Pitt to approach the major questions from various angles and at various depths. I will not argue that Burke changed his position radically as the controversy proceeded through time—only that he made key adaptations in a search for effective rhetorical argument.

As can be seen on Table 4, I divide Burke's speeches, pamphlets, and study notes into five phases, in this process rearranging the Burke Mss. to meet the content of speeches and pamphlets which we can date. These phases correspond generally to the five approaches I see Burke taking to the regency question.

Phase I: Historical Precedent/Constitutional Analogy. While it was Fox who first set forth the doctrine of the prince's right to assume the throne in his father's disability, it was Burke who made the first serious attempt to counter Pitt's stand on parliamentary right, *viz.,* that "the Prince of Wales had no more right (speaking of strict right) to assume the government, than any other individual subject of the country" (*PH,* 27:709). Burke's answer first was advanced on December 10, the day Pitt made that assertion. The speech appears to have been an extemporaneous affair, in that the principles upon which he argued are not clear. In it, however, Burke did advance the first plank of his platform—that the Constitution has provided "for every possible exigency" and that "the exercise of the sovereign power could never be vacant" (*PH,* 27:715). He argued that even if the Constitution does not provide precisely for a case in which a king is sick, by analogy to the doctrine of royal succession the prince is entitled to the throne. This idea receives relatively full treatment in Items 8–14 of Burke's notes; they form what was probably an early draft of a pamphlet and in them the analogy is expanded.

> That he [the prince] would have succeeded to the Government if the King was actually dead, must likewise succeed to it when he is dead to the purpose of existence for all the ends of government. *If there is any force in analogy* the provisions made by the constitution for the K's natural death must apply. . . . If therefore nothing else could be urged that single proposition would be sufficient to maintain that powers which the Constitution has vested in the Crown must during either a temporary or a permanent disability devolve on the undoubted succession to that Crown & the natural guardian of its rights . . . [Item 10; italics mine.]

As noted, however, Burke did not exploit this constitutional position fully on the first day, probably because Fox was attempting to show that actually no major differences of opinion existed between Opposition and Pitt (cf. *PH,* 27:711–13), and because Pitt's blatant, indeed extreme, assertion caught Opposition off-guard.[27] Once Pitt brought in his Three Resolu-

Table 4

SUBJECTS COVERED BY BURKE DURING THE REGENCY CRISIS

Date	Speech Topics	Phase	MS. Topics
12/10	Pitt is ambitious Constitution covers "every exigency" Elective Crown?		*Item 1:* expanded Item 31 (although discussion of lunacy here parallels his 2/11 speech).
12/19	Country gentlemen Pitt has a step-by-step scheme		*Item 21:* Pitt as "competitor"; elective Crown; not a party issue.
12/22	Spirit of the Constitution Necessity no grounds Hereditary vs. elective monarchy Weak government Use of Great Seal	HISTORICAL PRECEDENT/ CONSTITUTIONAL ANALOGY	**Item 22:* 3rd-person references to proceedings, stressing election and precedents. **Item 23:* draft of formal declaration, hitting republicanism. *Item 24:* a summary of topics Burke returns to often— necessity, Constitution, Brunswick, Pitt. *Item 25:* "King never dies" doctrine expanded. *Item 29:* "spirit of Constitution" expanded; references to trust of prince. *Item 31:* perhaps an early outline of 12/22 speech. *Item 35:* introduction to 12/22 speech. *Burke drafts of a possible Commons' address to the prince (in Aspinall); of P of W's possible note to Pitt (dated in Aspinall as c. Dec. 11); of prince's terms to Pitt; of Lords' Protest (dated Dec. 27); of possible prince's answer to Pitt on restrictions (Aspinall has full draft, while Burke Mss. has part; Dec. 29–Jan. 1); of prince's letter to Pitt (c. Jan. 1–2). See Items 30, 44, 45, 48–51.

*References in these items indicate that they are not material for speeches; in these, references are made to parliamentary actions in the third person, to the "public" as an audience, etc.

Table 4—Cont.

Date	Speech Topics	Phase	MS. Topics
1/6	Need new exam of doctors —information old —Warren's testimony in Lords important —possible treachery		*Items 3–7:* 3 an introduction, 4–7 expansion; full statement of all issues, including medical position taken here.
1/13	Exam improperly narrowed Dr. Willis	MEDICAL ARGUMENT	*Items 8–20:* pamphlet draft on "public crisis" and apathy, major constitutional issues (here or earlier).
1/26	Pitt refuses information Pitt violates house rules Pitt destroys deliberative capacity of Commons Pitt forced debate on rights		*Item 27:* expanded treatment of Great Seal issue. *Item 32–33:* the bulk of this is on civil disorder and hence belongs in next section; but Ireland receives
1/27	Pitt disrespectful of prince Pitt too slow Lords too slow Fox is virtuous Republic is being created by our procedures Use of Great Seal	PROCEDURAL ARGUMENT	its treatment here, too. *Item 37:* more vitriolic treatment of Great Seal. *Draft of pamphlet, "The Voice of Reason" (in Aspinall); most constitutional questions covered.
2/2	Definition of "rights" —Parliament's right —prince's right Example: Catholicism Example: resignation Public being confused Ireland's position Use of Great Seal Proper procedure is to address the prince now		*Draft of pamphlet, "The Present Question, in its Constitutional Point of View" (in Aspinall); constitutional arguments plus discussion of ministers —it rings of Items 8–20.
2/5	Pitt's Bill is unclear		TRANSITION
2/6	Review of proceedings —illegal —king's illness —Dr. Willis Separation of powers Degradation of royalty Effects of Pitt's Bill: —retinue taken from prince —king's purse uncontrolled —prince/king separation Step-by-step treason	SUMMARY POSITION	*Item 36:* may belong here, because it attacks the Glorious Revolution as a precedent, which Burke does briefly here. *Items 2–7:* it is a pamphlet draft, but ideas from it appear here. Draft of "Memorandum" (in Aspinall), on the powers of the prince and queen.

2/7	Examination these three		No material apparently
2/9	days of the machinery		drafted for such habitual
2/10	of Pitt's Bill		attacks upon a bill.

2/11	Parliament, not a council,		Item 1: material on
	should determine when	PICTORI-ALIZATION	"delicacy" of subject matter
	king is healthy		comes from here.
	French experience with		Item 34: reference to the king
	insanity		as a "recovered Lunatick."
	Insanity and treatment		*Item 38: a possible
	What if king relapses?		declaration for prince.

tions declaring Parliament's rights in this case, however, Burke had to flesh
out his position—which he did on December 22.

After a preplanned exordium (Item 35) expounding his nonfactiousness,
Burke advanced a three-stage analysis: (1) Their deliberation must be
guided "by the genuine spirit of our constitution" and not a mere consideration of necessities. (2) "To argue upon principle," the English system is
based on an "hereditary monarchy," and not some sort of "republican"
compact among the king and the two Houses of Parliament. (3) And, any
attempt by Commons to determine royal authority would result necessarily
in a "weak government" and thus a threat to "national security and welfare" (*PH*, 27:810–25). Interspersed through the speech were allusions to
Pitt's ambition, analyses of certain alleged precedents—notably the reign of
Henry VI (which Burke considered outdated) and the Restoration (which
he said was a "precedent of a delinquent monarch")—and a short digression
on the problem of getting bills signed into law through a commission's use
of the Great Seal:

> He did not approve of any robbery, whether it was housebreaking, highway-
> robbery, or any other felony; yet each of them, in his opinion, was more
> excusable than law forgery. The Great Seal was to be affixed to a commission
> robbing the executive power of its due function; a certain composition of wax
> and copper was to represent the monarch: this was a species of absurd
> metaphysics. [*PH,* 27:821–22]

His apostrophe reiterated figuratively his reliance upon the analogy with
hereditary rule:

> I disclaim all allegiance, I renounce all obedience and loyalty to a King so
> chose, and a crown so formed. I have given my allegiance to the House of

Hanover. I worship the gods of our glorious constitution, but I will not worship Priapus. [*PH*, 27:822]

Hence, while Pitt argued that crises called for extraordinary actions, that the Houses had passed previous regency bills, that the Houses in the form of convention parliaments had chosen kings, and that actions taken during minority regencies (e.g., Henry VI) were analogous to the present situation, Burke countered with other analogies and with a balanced-constitution proposition. In Cobbett, these analogies and arguments from principle are not particularly lucid, but are somewhat more fully rounded in Burke's study notes. In Item 31, Burke stated that the Constitution knows of "hereditary Monarchy, *described in persons & defined in powers,*" and as for an elective crown "the wisdom of the Constitution knows nothing. It knows of succession, it knows of descents." And in Item 1:

> Was there ever a question of more importance than whether the Sovereign dies in that which is sovereign in man *when the animal is alive and the man dead.* What is the ruling principle. Why reason to be sure. If this does not not exist the King cannot exist the man cannot exist. . . . What is the reason why the Law will not suffer the Royal Function be a moment vacant[?] It is the meaning of the King never dies.

By December 22, therefore, Burke had advanced two sorts of arguments. He relied principally upon a constitutional analogy; by analogy to the actual death of a king, the Prince of Wales had an undeniable right to the throne. He depended secondarily upon an interpretation of the balanced-constitution principle; any attempt to limit George III's successor—as in Pitt's Three Resolutions, which gave Parliament the right to have government administered as it saw fit—would destroy the balance of the governmental powers, vitiate the principle of heredity, and transform England into a virtual parliamentary republic. By December 22, Burke had met Pitt's analogies with an analogy, Pitt's analysis of precedents with a brief (and generally weaker) analysis of precedents.

One must remember, however, that we have gone to Burke's private notes to clarify his thinking. Unless Cobbett has deleted not just words but major portions of Burke's ideational structure, his presentations in Commons were thin. No one replied fully the first few days in Commons; Pitt referred only to his own analyses in answering Burke. And, certainly the public press made little of his ideas. The dominant note was struck as early as November 25, with *The Times* quoting a relatively unjaundiced remark:

> Mr. Burke's abilities are of a very different cast; he was never formed for a Statesman; but in disclosing a most exuberant fancy in any other department of life, he would have stood upon the pinnacle of perfection without a competitor: As a *Poet,* he would have demanded the applauses of the world. He would have viewed a discerning country *gratified* and edified by his Labours, and without even meddling in the *vortices* of public employment: Having seen himself the rival of a *Virgil,* an *Horace* or a *Theocritus.*

Further, on December 11, *The Times* did not even comment on the content of the exchange among Pitt, Fox, and Burke on the question of right; it remarked only that the debate was "unusually violent, and was the smartest and most pointed of any we ever heard in Parliament." And, the first mention of Burke himself came on December 16, when he was scolded for calling Pitt a "competitor" to the prince. *The Times* received the December 22 speech in a similar manner: "Mr. Burke's speech, although eloquent, in point of language, yet was devoid of what is called sound argument. It was, by some, called a Legislative abuse."[28]

If Burke was understood by anyone, he was not answered. He apparently failed rhetorically to make his ideas worth answering.

Phase II: Medical Argument. Pitt's Three Resolutions declaring Parliament's right to fill the throne passed both Houses (the Commons on December 22, and the Lords on December 29). Opposition lost the first round of constitutional argument handily; a new strategy was called for. On January 6, therefore, Burke called for another examination of the king's physicians to ascertain any changes in his condition. One might think Burke was seeking a delay in bringing up something presumably settled a month earlier. In Burke's private notes (Items 3–7), however, we find his logic. First of all, he notes that "The provision of Limitation must have reference to the continuance of the King's incapacity—Necessary to state what the King's illness is—because the Nature of the illness—gives light into the Nature of a Recovery" (Item 3). And, in Item 4, we see him wanting to counter Pitt's analysis of it; government is treating the illness "as if it were a slight cold—sometimes a disorder—sometimes an indisposition, a slight cold an Influenca [*sic*] a feverish delirium of a fortnight." He even wonders if there is a plot: "This Scheme evidently on the face of it, is this, they are to have a King incapacitated by Nature, & a Regent incapacited [*sic*] by art; & in the debility & contempt attending such a government to force either to throw this miserable unballasted Country" (Item 7).

In January, then, we find a new purpose: if Pitt cannot be beaten on philosophical/constitutional questions, perhaps he can be pinioned on pragmatic/medical arguments. If the king's illness can be shown to be serious, then limitations should not be placed on the regent, Pitt will not be able to treat it flippantly, and perhaps a cabal suppressing evidence can be discovered. Beginning on January 6, therefore, Opposition pushed for another examination of the physicians.

Burke built major portions of that case. First, he sought to demonstrate that the king was not improving; this he did by quoting from portions of physicians' testimony before the Lords. The quoted portions indicated that the king was not recovering and that "the probability of cure diminishes as the time of the disorder lengthens" (*PH*, 27:918). He then tied this testimony to the question of limitations, saying that "it was their duty to pay it [the testimony] due attention before they cut and carved the government, as they would cut out morsels for hounds, rather than immolate it as a sacrifice to the gods" (*PH*, 27:918).

Burke in his first speech of January 6 therefore advanced two of the lines of analysis foreshadowed in his private notes. Shortly thereafter, when questioned about the testimony he had read, he opened the third line. After indicating that he was quoting Dr. Warren (at which point a cry of "Hear! Hear!" went up), he exclaimed:

> Were their schemes ripe, that they ventured thus early to betray their sentiments? Were they going to build a weak and miserable machine of government on that foundation of fraud and falsehood and calumny? . . . Mr. Burke concluded with remarking, that a sudden cry was more eloquent than any composition of words, because the genuine sentiment of the soul betrayed itself in involuntary exclamations, while words were frequently used for the purpose of concealing men's feelings, and of exhibiting a false colour for their conduct to the eyes of mankind. [*PH*, 27:919–20]

And, Burke rose a third time this day to defend himself against Pitt's remark about his warmth in debate. He first said that Pitt "not being able to carry any point by reasoning, had fallen upon his motives, instead of his argument, well knowing that it was a safer mode of attack, because every man could judge of the justice of the one, though no one could possibly guess at the truth of the other" (*PH,* 27:923). Then he suggested that the differences in opinion between Drs. Willis and Warren be mitigated by bringing in a third expert—Dr. Munro, keeper of Bedlam (*PH,* 27:924). And finally, he defended himself against the charge of overzealousness in debate:

> The right hon. gentleman [Pitt] was fond of throwing about his treasons and his ill wishes; but, for his [Burke's] own part, he would never tamely submit to either. With regard to any warmth which he had betrayed, he should not hesitate to affirm, that he had not let a word escape him, that he should be ashamed to have recorded. His voice was weak, and therefore he was forced to raise and exert it; but it did not follow that he was in a passion; he might say, with one of the ancients, who had been charged with being in a passion, "Feel my pulse, and say if it does not beat temperately." . . . When he fled from inquiry, then let the right hon. gentleman aim his envenomed shafts at him. [*PH,* 27:924–25].

These three speeches of January 6 were met with Burke's only successes of the Regency Crisis. Pitt submitted to another inquiry of the physicians, and allowed Burke to sit on the Select Committee. Burke's use of Dr. Warren's testimony, his cry of being unduly misrepresented, and his allusion to a possible junto forced Pitt to open the medical issue again.

Unfortunately for Burke and the rest of the Opposition, the re-examination did not settle anything. Pitt steadfastly refused to have any but the attending physicians examined; therefore, Burke was able to get little new evidence, and of course he was not permitted to have a third expert brought in. Consequently, on January 13 he struck out at Pitt once more for narrowing the inquiry and for not allowing a referee expert to compare Warren's and Willis's prognoses. Without such an expert, Burke's only strategy could be one of villifying Dr. Willis; this he did, charging Willis with nearly killing the king (*PH,* 27:931).[29] Later that day, he accused Pitt of refusing to let him ask "substantial" questions during the examination and moved to have the report of the Select Committee recommitted (*PH,* 27:934). He lost.

Hence, Phase II, the medical argument, gave Burke but a hollow victory. He did succeed in getting the physicians re-examined, but the resulting testimony proved nothing. The state of the king still was indeterminate— thereby offering Opposition no help in urging that limitations-of-the-regent be ignored—and Burke did not discredit Pitt to the extent that large blocs of votes swung to Opposition. In any general analysis, Burke had failed in his second major strategy, and Opposition again was thwarted. Another tack would have to be taken.

Phase III: Procedural Argument. Burke spent most of the rest of January pursuing his medical analysis in private. Indeed, his journeys to "madhouses" generated much of the doggerel quoted in the introduction of this essay. What he learned about insanity will be examined under Phase V. For now, let us look at what he had to say after Pitt's Five Resolutions (Regency Plan), which offered the regency to the Prince of Wales with severe limitations on his power, had been passed by both Houses. Once the Five Resolutions were passed and once the prince as regent-elect and the queen as guardian-of-the-king-elect had replied to their respective invitations, the Houses of Parliament had to open themselves officially. Thus far they had functioned only as committees. Before they actually could pass a regency *act,* however, they had to meet *qua* Parliament.

Pitt proposed that a commission put the Great Seal on letters patent in George III's stead to open Parliament; such an action was unusual, and gave Burke a handhold. An attack on Pitt's parliamentary procedures, of course, complemented a general denigration of his competence and motives; while Burke had referred obliquely to Pitt's ambition earlier in the debate, these procedural arguments were accompanied by some of his sharpest *ad personam* shafts of the controversy.

Having returned from his studies of insanity and with Fox bedridden, Burke was Opposition's floor leader; in that capacity he opened the questioning of Pitt on January 26. Pitt announced that Commons would join the Lords in conference that morning. Burke asked why. Pitt said simply that the two Houses would meet concerning the Five Resolutions (Regency Plan). Burke insisted that they should know more about the conference, because "every step they proceeded, was an attempt [by Pitt] to introduce some new principle in the constitution" (*PH,* 27:1095). Pitt insisted the procedure was not novel. Burke replied that the Regency Plan, because it in its initial form committed both Houses to the Plan before they had considered it independent of one another, "mutually pledged" them to each other and therefore "tended to undermine the deliberative capacity of both" (*PH,* 27:1096). His meaning was not perfectly clear, and no one bothered to reply. The conference was held.

After they returned from the conference, Commons was actually ready to move the addresses to the prince and the queen. This, of course, gave Opposition a chance to condemn Pitt's mode of proceeding in general. After Charles Grey and the old Northite William Jolliffe[30] opened the attack, Burke joined. He blamed Pitt for forcing the Commons to debate the question of right:

> The right hon. gentleman had forced the House into the discussion and in his haughty style, had said to the House, "Slaves, do you presume to hesitate, or hint a doubt upon the matter? I will put an end to your scruples. The question shall be debated; it shall be decided." They all knew the nature of the dominion, which the right hon. gentleman meant to exercise over the Regent's government. It was as absolute a tyranny, as any exercised by Julius Caesar, Augustus, or Oliver Cromwell. . . . The right hon. gentleman had stooped from the dignity of the supreme sovereignty which he had assumed to combat a right which had not been claimed. He disliked this union of the fox's tail and the lion's skin. It was an unnatural junction of low cunning and supreme authority. [*PH*, 27:1098]

Pitt did not reply to this stinging indictment of his methods of procedure until the next day, when he actually moved that the Regency Plan be forwarded to the prince and queen for acceptance. The issues of the delay, of proper modes of address, and of the use of the Great Seal to open Parliament were contested viciously, and late in the day, after Pitt's second justification, Burke rose. He (1) chastised Pitt for not consulting the prince more often in these proceedings, (2) reiterated his accusation that Pitt had forced debate on the question of right, (3) accused Pitt of showing too little dignity in his communication with the princes of the blood, (4) demanded that Pitt accelerate his timetable for communicating with the queen and the prince, (5) assaulted the Lords for taking too long to act, (6) defended Fox's virtues, (7) decried the "republic" he believed they were creating (*PH*, 27:1115–19), and (8) again reprobated the idea of having a commission employ the Great Seal:

> So far from being a representative of the forms of the constitution, it was a masquerade, a mummery, a peace [*sic*] of buffoonery, used to burlesque the constitution, and to ridicule every form of government. A phantom conjured up to affright propriety, and drive it from our isle. An hideous spectre, to which, in the language of Macbeth to Banquo's ghost, it might be said,

> "Avaunt and quit my sight! Let the earth hide thee!
> Thy bones are marrowless, thy blood is cold;
> Thou hast no speculation in those eyes
> Which thou doest glare with."

And, so in fact it was with this political spectre; its bones were marrow-less, its blood was cold, and it had no speculation in its eyes. He repro-bated it therefore as a chimera—a monster taken out of the depths of hell. [*PH*, 27:1119].

As can be gathered from this brief outline and quotation, Burke delivered a near-violent speech on this day, through his procedural arguments heaping upon Pitt charges of gracelessness, procrastination, impropriety, republicanism, and mockery (sacrilege). Still, however, the Commons was unmoved; it supported Pitt's motion to address the royal personages.

Burke had but one more chance to use his procedural arguments. On February 2 Pitt moved that the commission to place the Great Seal be set up. Again, the by-play was rough, and again Burke waited until late in the debate to speak. He used Pitt's reference to Fox's statement of December 10 as an excuse to return to the constitutional questions of right. He then offered his fullest analysis of that question!

He opened with what by now was Opposition's constitutional position—that indeed the Houses of Parliament *could* call upon the prince to take up the regency, but that they *could not* make any declaration of rights in the situation because the prince had the rights of succession. The Houses had "a right of action," but not "a right to take possession of a thing" (*PH*, 27:1149). He urged two constitutional analogies in support of his position. First, if a king or a prince converted to Catholicism, he would forfeit his right to the throne, and it would devolve to the next-in-line. In such a case, Parliament would have to act to declare the one ineligible and the next rightful heir—even though the right itself already had transferred. Second, if a king resigned, again "the Crown would descend just as if the King was actually dead; but still the Prince of Wales could not take upon him the government of the country, until the two Houses should have accepted the resignation, and determined that it was voluntary" (*PH*, 27:1150).

Burke concluded this speech with a near-repeat of his Great Seal argument:

They were going to create Milton's monster of sin and death, death to the constitution, and sin to the feelings of the country. They were going to steal the Great Seal, to commit a forgery and fraud, and to support violence. . . . He contended that the House had no right to authorize the Lord Chancellor to put the Great Seal to forgery, fraud and violence, and that giving them the form of the royal authority, instead of the substance, was to give them the sweepings of the cobwebs in Westminster-hall; and the smoke of the dish. . . . Necessity, he observed, had been generally termed the tyrant's plea; but, strange to tell, it was now considered as the guardian of our liberties. [*PH*, 27:1152–53]

This speech thus united a reanalysis of December's questions—through an analogic inspection of royal rights and a circumstantial prediction of what *could* happen in Ireland and the future—with another metaphorical interpretation of the Great Seal question. It was strong enough to call for a high answer, which it got from Pitt's Solicitor-General, Lord John Eldon (later prime minister).[31] In a weighty legal analysis, Eldon returned to the general justification for their actions, and offered long lists of precedents for the use of commissioners in certain extraordinary times. By the end of the day, Pitt's motion for letters patent, issued under the Great Seal wielded by commissioners, passed (although we do not know the vote).

Burke's performance on these days of procedural discussion is noteworthy for several reasons: (1) As we noted, he returned to the December question of right. One might ask, why now? Perhaps the only answer is that he simply was not ready before. Burke has a reputation for slow, methodical analysis; his private papers demonstrate that he drafted an important message several times before accepting it.[32] This speech perhaps represents two months of preparation—hardly a long time for considering a knotty constitutional question. (2) His use of procedural arguments is in itself an important sign of Burke's rhetorical adaptation. Having been beaten on the constitutional (theoretical) issues, and having suffered no gains on the medical (real) grounds, he had to search elsewhere for a rhetorical opening, and the procedural questions were enough different in kind to be thought of as a "new" approach. Of course, Opposition had little chance for success in using them, for once they had been beaten on the rights question, they had nothing constructive to offer in place of Pitt's admittedly cumbersome Great Seal procedure. But even without a viable alternative, the procedural arguments did represent an issue capable of converting parliamentarians to

Opposition's camp, and converts were important with debate on an actual regency bill next on the docket. The procedural questions, then, stood as significant means to a future end. That they had some effect might be attested to by the fact that Pitt's majorities in the next month were the smallest he had in the entire Regency Debate. (3) Of perhaps most interest is Burke's generally intemperate language. As we have seen, it earned him suspicion of lunacy. Maybe he was emotionally disturbed, but I doubt it. Our best evidence—Burke's own testimony—indicates that he was taking a calculated chance in increasing his intensity. In a letter of about January 24 to William Windham, Burke said:

> In the first place we ought to change that tone of calm reasoning which certainly does not belong to great and affecting interests, and which has no effect, but to chill and discourage those upon whose active exertions we must depend much more than on their cold judgment. Our style of argument, so very different from that by which Lord North was run down [in 1782], has another ill effect. I know it encreases [sic] the boldness of some of those who are thus bold less from the courage of their original temperament than from the air of inferiority, debasement, and dejection under which we have appeared for some years past. In daring every thing, they see they risque nothing. . . . I suppose a more excellent speech than Foxes last [January 22?], has never been delivered in any House of Parliament, full of weighty argument eloquently enforced, and richly though soberly decorated. But we must all be sensible that it was a speech which might be spoken upon an important difference between the best friends, and where the parties had the very best opinion of each other's general intentions for the publick good.[33]

Burke, from his concern that the Foxites strike with "boldness" so as to capture those who do not make decisions from "cold judgment" (the country gentlemen?), to scare off men of lesser talent (the back-benchers?), and to show their differences with Pitt, apparently chose the harsh and intemperate language for rhetorical effect. He thus could appear as the conscience of Parliament—the man projecting awful consequences for the Constitution and the country. The reputation Burke had achieved in his thirty-odd years in politics was such that his audience perhaps even expected his fervor.

At any rate, in Phase III Burke had changed his approach, although he made no significant, immediate gains.

Phase IV: Summary Arguments. Parliament officially opened amid contradictory reports on the condition of the king.[34] Nevertheless, on February

5, Pitt's Regency Bill was read for the first time. Some few questions were raised by Powys and Grey for Opposition, but little happened. On February 6, however, the bill was read for a second time, which procedure enraged Burke, pushing him to deliver his longest speech of the controversy:

> He expressed his extreme surprise that the bill should be proposed to be read a second time, without the House having heard a syllable as to what were the principles of the bill, when opened, and its clauses and provisions. He had often known the principles upon which a bill had been ordered to be brought in, either totally lost sight of in the bill itself, or so violently strained and departed from in the various clauses, that scarcely a single principle upon which the House had resolved to legislate, was to be found in the bill, or to be found entire. [*PH*, 27:1167.]

With that expression as a context, Burke proceeded "before they read the bill a second time," to point out "the extent of its provisions, and the extraordinary manner in which the resolutions that the two Houses had come to, were now attempted to be made use of, and carried into effect" (*PH*, 27:1167). Burke: (1) reviewed the course of their actions, in particular blasting "that bold promiser, Dr. Willis," who "could not fix a probable time for the chance of his Majesty's being capable of recovering sufficiently well to be fit and able to resume the exercise of his royal functions" (*PH*, 27:1168); (2) deprecated the "partition of power" occasioned by giving the household to the queen, saying "all that was graceful, all that was honourable, all that was calculated to hold up a character as great, virtuous, and meritorious, was given where an opposition was set up to oppose and counteract the executive government [of the prince]" (*PH*, 27:1169); and (3) chastised Pitt, first by ridiculing the Duke of Chondos's epithet for Pitt as "an heaven-born minister"[35] and second by insisting that the Chancellor of the Exchequer "meant not only to degrade the Prince of Wales, but the whole House of Brunswick, who were to be outlawed, excommunicated, and attainted, as having forfeited all claim to the confidence of the country" (*PH*, 27:1171). With that remark, Burke was called to order and rebuffed by Pitt for his "extraordinary style, and the peculiarly violent tone of warmth and of passion with which they [Burke's sentiments] were generally delivered" (*PH*, 27:1171).

After insisting that none of his words was incendiary and that his passion originated "from a deep consideration of the great importance of the subject, and not from any censurable imbecility of temper" (*PH*, 27:1171), Burke continued: (1) "the splendour of the Crown" was to be separated from the executive government and then given "to other and unknown persons" (*PH*, 27:1172); (2) the queen would be given tremendous power with the king's purse "for distributing money to no person knew whom" (*PH*, 27:1173); and (3) the prince was to be excluded from his father, while "the queen's council [would be given] the power to pronounce his Majesty recovered" (*PH*, 27:1174). Again Burke was called to order.

Undeterred, Burke then referred to the four examinations of the physicians (two by Commons and two by Lords), insisting that if Parliament were so careful to determine the nature of the illness, it should likewise investigate any rumored recovery, for: "A person who had been insane, might, he contended, be so subdued by coercion and severity, as to be capable of being prevailed on to act the farce appointed him, of appearing for a short period to have recovered his intellects" (*PH*, 27:1175–76). After this attack upon Dr. Willis, Burke finished with a general assault upon Parliament:

> The House, he said, had proceeded step after step, and been led on to do that, which, if proposed altogether, would, he was persuaded, have been rejected by every man of honour. Like Macbeth, who, after having murdered Duncan and Banquo, exclaimed,
> > "———I am in blood
> > Stept in so far, that should I wade no more,
> > Returning were as tedious as to go o'er———"
> they found themselves inclined to proceed, from not daring to trace back their steps. [*PH*, 27:1176–77.]

In other words, on February 6 Burke delivered a full summary speech, examining the Regency Bill from three points of view—its purpose, its constitutional basis, and its effects. Outside of his personal attacks upon Pitt and Willis, the core of his argument rested on the doctrine of "limited power" or weakness. All of the ills he summarized in a single sentence: "All limited power was, from its nature, feeble; and the circumstance of its being only temporary and uncertain, rendered it still more deficient in vigour and in efficacy" (*PH*, 27:1169). Burke is most eloquent on the weakness principle in what was probably a pamphlet written in late January or early February. We read in Item 8:

Substituted government is precarious exercise since as depending from derives a radical & incurable weakness. The proximity & hope of change gives courage to resistance strength to flatter resistance with the cabal prospect of impunity; & *rends & thus confounds the order of things* by putting the assertion & denial of authority. . . . The real evils of the present is this: that one of the main springs that government is weakened in its most essential principle, that hold which it has upon the *opinions of mankind.* That is as it were split & divided. [Italics mine.]

In the italicized phrases we see Burke's position on weakness taking a significant bent. Whereas he first had argued simply that the new government would be weak because the Houses of Parliament would be strong, and whereas he argued secondly that the proposal yielded a weak government because an ambitious cabal could subsume it, he has been driven—perhaps through reworking his position, certainly through frustration—to a ground imbedded in the social fabric itself. *The disorder and chaos he has predicted through the controversy finds its ultimate lodging place in general society.* Thus, in Item 32, after insisting that Pitt's bill will "breed endless disorder," Burke chided those "who lay down doctrines tending to set those eternal principles aside, to make the executive power elective disunited what every honest man should wish & pray & labour to the End of his Life hold together for ever as the desperate & Enemies to their Country." In Burke's mind, therefore, Pitt's philosophical/constitutional basis was more than merely factious, personally ambitious, or even illegal—it was perceived as wholly negative and destructive, universal in its havoc and societal in its ramifications.

Burke did not quit his attacks upon Pitt's ambitions; indeed, they increased in venom and frequency. Burke's wrath became that of a man possessed. In his papers we find minutely documented analyses of Pitt as the demon of 1784, and as a nepotist whose friends and relatives ran the Secretariats, the Treasury, the Exchequer, the Church, India, and Ireland (Items 13, 14, 16). In Item 16, in particular, Burke meticulously calculated how many major and minor officers Pitt would fill in the following twenty years if he continued at the rate set 1784–88. He would have "varied all the judges more than once over—all the Bishops—fill'd all the regiments. He would have made 144 peers for more than a majority of the present house of peers, made every admiral, captain & army Lieutenant. So that there would not be considerable station in any service military or civil, ecclesiastic or lay, that was not did owe preferment to Mr. Pitt." Yet, with such inflammatory evidence at his disposal, Burke focused upon Pitt's "treasons" or public faults; the picayune depreciations of Pitt were discarded in favor of a kind of proposition-centered, sociological analysis.

Hence, we see that even though Burke had at least semiscandalous material at his disposal, he deigned not to use it. He kept his abusive material on a general, public, even impersonal level; while called to order, he did not counter with hack, smear evidence. His mode of argument in this phase of his rhetorical progression is perhaps best summarized in Burke's own words of February 10:

> The framers of it [the Regency Bill] had first proceeded to a violation of precedents, next to a violation of law, then to a violation of the constitution, and now they had arrived to a climax of violence: a violence of the laws of nature.[*PH*, 27:1224.]

From Burke's point of view, this was an accurate picture of Pitt's journey through the Regency Crisis; from our point of view, it represents Burke's tracking of Pitt, strategy by strategy.

Phase V: Pictorialization. Burke's final speech of the Regency Crisis is interesting in that it borrowed his earlier descriptive techniques, but with one important difference. All semblance of first principles and societal considerations were suppressed, and rather he launched unmitigated fear appeals. The speech began calmly enough, with two procedural arguments concerning how power would revert to the king upon his recovery (*PH*, 27:1246-47). He then advanced to the subject of insanity.

He opened with a brief review of Charles VI of France, who, when losing his sanity, delegated all of his power to his prime minister and his wife, to the ruin of France (*PH*, 27:1247). From this example, he exclaimed:

> The perusal of the history of foreign states, [offers] a fund of knowledge, infinitely more serviceable than birthday odes or addresses. The disorder with which the sovereign was afflicted, was, he said, like a vast sea which rolled in, and at a low tide rolled back, and left a bold and barren shore. [*PH*, 27:1247.]

Burke then turned to unnamed English authorities on insanity, quoting from a book on the subject:

An author of great authority, in mentioning the uncertainty of the symptoms of sanity, had declared, that after having been kept of month (and the rule was, he said, at all the houses he had visited, though anxious to discharge the patients speedily, to keep them a month after their recovery before they turned them out of the house) they would sometimes dread the day of their departure, and relapse on the very last day, and the consequences which had followed, were of the most fatal kind. Mr. Burke read an extract from the volume to which he alluded, which stated, that some of these unfortunate individuals after a supposed recovery, had committed parricides, others had butchered their sons, others had done violence to themselves by hanging, shooting, drowning, throwing themselves out of windows, and by a variety of other ways. [*PH*, 27:1247–48.]

Cries of "Oh! Oh!" and "Order!" went up in the House. Burke charged that such cries resulted from an overconcern for delicacy, pointing out that the Houses had dealt with other delicate cases of divorce, that ecclesiastical courts heard delicate cases of rape, that in Naples a similar case was discussed publicly in newspapers "because the feelings of the world superseded delicacy," and that London had "burnt to the ground through an idle and over-scrupulous regard to delicacy" (*PH*, 27:1248). Burke then concluded:

He drew a picture of the King's supposed return, which he described as most happy, if really cured, but as horrible in the extreme, in its consequences if a sudden relapse took place. [*PH*, 27:1248.]

Even though Cobbett offers us a bare outline of what Burke said in this, his last speech of the debate, we need little imagination and but passing knowledge of Burke's characteristic discourse to supply what is missing. It is clear, I think, that Burke abandoned his previous argumentative structures in favor of gory description. *This speech can be viewed as the dialectical culmination of his exchanges with Pitt:* he had tried the robes of the lawyer, the public defender, and the political-sociologist. He had run into both counterpropositions and indifference while playing each role. He perhaps had but one mask left—that of the revivalist describing civil hell. He had used *Macbeth,* he had worried about bringing back the king too early, and he had predicted social chaos in his previous speeches; but he had not belabored the illness in terms so gross and vivid. Not even his private notes contain material of such vision.

This was Burke's last speech. Perhaps it had to be. He could proceed no further rhetorically. Only silence and absence could follow.

Conclusions

Generally, the conclusions of this study have been made as we have progressed through it: first, it should be abundantly clear that during the Regency Crisis of 1788–89 Burke was neither inactive nor isolated from party. As tables should, those included here speak for themselves and for his energy. Even if Burke's pamphlets never were published (and we do not know why), they demonstrate his service to his party; when the pamphlets and his thirty-two speeches are added to the meetings he attended, his role in party councils and planning is impressive.

Second, Burke's rhetorical development can be partitioned into five phases, with each phase representing a strategic adjustment to circumstances in Parliament and to his own thoughts. He moved from precedential/analogical analyses to medical/factual argument to procedural inquiry to a quasi-sociological prediction to distasteful descriptions probably deserving their reception. The operating procedures of Commons—a progression from the resolutions on rights in December, through the Regency Plan of January, to the Regency Bill of February—in part determined his argumentative sequence. The progression also seems the result of his own development; if one rearranges the Burke manuscripts according to topics covered in the speeches and if one uses those notes as explanatory aids for certain points made sketchily in Parliament, one finds in Burke's philosophy a growing clarity and wholeness being developed as a result of parliamentary combat with Pitt. As has been intimated (though certainly not developed fully here), Pitt's program and support for that program satisfactorily met Burke's arguments at the first three stages or phases. Only after such tests in disputation did Burke's full theory of constitution coalesce. His most weighty speech was delivered on February 6—over two months into the question. Perhaps he could have generated his theory of government in his study; had George III grown ill, say, in June, perhaps Burke's theory would have been fleshed out by December. But one can argue, more convincingly I think, that it evolved only in interparty warfare, in a kind of parliamentary dialectic.

These have been the two principal conclusions advanced in this study. We are left with the last, knotty question which opened this essay: Was Burke insane, and if not, why was his reception so negative?

I would argue that he certainly was not mentally disturbed in any pathological sense of that term. We have seen several arguments from signs supporting this judgment—the fact that he was sought out as a source of advice by his party, his own testimony that he was taking a calculated chance in appearing violent, the kind of logic we have discovered to his philosophical/argumentative development through the three months, and the fact that his harshest *ad personam* material was left in his library along with drafts of unpublished pamphlets.

Why, then, was he received with puzzled retorts, laughter, and calls-to-order? The first reason is obvious: he was slow in developing a full-fleshed constitutional position. Not until February 2 and 6 did it emerge complete. Not until the Commons committed itself to Pitt was the interpretation a philosophical whole, parallel to the finely stitched cases he produced in the American, French, and Indian questions. Perhaps February was too late for fine constitutional distinctions; perhaps, in Burke's own words, "they found themselves inclined to proceed, from not daring to trace back their steps" (*PH,* 27:1177).

And, what apparently worked even more to Burke's disadvantage than the slowness of his thinking was the language in which he chose to clothe those ideas. We have noted many of the incendiary metaphors and images, and have seen him called to order four times. Although the language apparently was preplanned and although his passion perhaps could be expected, Burke did go too far.

Hence, while Burke in fact performed useful services for the Foxites, playing the propagandist, offering advice on their constitutional position, and preparing himself for another stint as Paymaster of the Forces, nevertheless his inability to argue clearly (and thus create the feeling of constitutional certainty) at the opening of the debate in combination with his overlush language made him a *rhetorical failure.* Thus, an historian such as Derry can see merit in his final position on the Regency, and an observer of individual speeches such as Wraxall can heap plaudits[36] on his February 6 address; but *the Member of Parliament looking for immediate guidance to a perplexing constitutional and political problem in December 1788 could not find it in Burke.*

Burke was without doubt a rhetorical failure in 1788–89. This performance, however, had no long-term negative effects on his reputation. Indeed, if the Regency Crisis did anything for him, it prepared him—as Sarason argues convincingly[37]—for the French Revolution, for a time when these same ideas of government were welcomed even by George III. For all of the apparent bitterness with which he attacked Pitt and government, Burke was devoted enough to a theory of constitution to join in 1794 the very men he vilified in 1788–89. The Regency Crisis apparently crystallized a set of principles to which Edmund Burke would pledge the rest of his life.

NOTES AND REFERENCES

1. George Selwyn to Lady Carlisle, 5 December 1788, *Carlisle MSS.* (H.M.C.), p. 660. Quoted in John W. Derry, *The Regency Crisis and the Whigs; 1788–9* (Cambridge: At the University Press, 1963), p. 154. The Addington remark is quoted in George Pellew, *The Life and Correspondence of the Right Honourable Henry Addington, First Viscount Sidmouth* (London: John Murray, 1847), vol. 1, p. 60, quoted in Derry, p. 154.

2. *The* (London) *Times,* 21 January 1789.

3. Quoted in Carl B. Cone, *Burke and the Nature of Politics; The Age of the French Revolution* (Louisville: University of Kentucky Press, 1964), vol. 2, p. 274.

4. Arthur Aspinall (ed.), *The Correspondence of George, Prince of Wales 1770–1812* (London: Cassell, 1963), vol. I. This volume devotes some 170 pages to correspondence during the Regency Crisis.

5. The standard diagnosis of George III's illness indicated some form of manic depression. Since then, however, medical historians have demonstrated that the king—unbeknown even to his attending physicians—was suffering from an hereditary disease of the nervous and blood systems, porphyria. See British Medical Association, *Porphyria—A Royal Malady* (London: B.M.A., 1968), especially the articles by Ida Macalpine and by Ida Macalpine, Richard Hunter, and C. Rimington. The very fact that the physicians were treating the *wrong* disease perhaps explains much of the confusion that surrounded George III.

6. In Charles Chenevix-Trench, "The Royal Malady: Some Aspects of the Regency Crisis, 1788–9," *History Today* 12 (1962):385.

7. After Baker noted the delirium, he aroused the press by selling stock, precipitating a ten percent fall in the market. The king immediately told Pitt he would

attend a levee "to stop further lies and any fall in the stocks." His appearance at St. James did anything but calm the budding rumors: Sir Gilbert Elliot told his wife that the king was "certainly in a bad state of health," and Wraxall noted that his clothes "exhibited strong proofs of absence or oblivion." See Chenevix-Trench, "Royal Malady," p. 386; Derry, *Regency Crisis*, p. 6; and Henry Wheatley (ed.), *Historical and Posthumous Memoirs of Sir Nathaniel Wraxall* (London: Bickers & Sons, 1884), vol. 5, p. 188.

8. Chenevix-Trench, "Royal Malady," p. 386.

9. *Morning Chronicle,* 8 November 1788. Simultaneously, however, this paper also entered into the political arena, denying that the prince had a right to his father's throne in the event of a regency.

10. Aspinall, *Correspondence of George, Prince of Wales,* in a footnote (1:405 n. 2), accepts the *General Advertizer's* statement that Thurlow recommended Willis. Chenevix-Trench in his book, however, says that the wife of an equerry advised the queen to send for him, because Willis had cured her mother; Derry concurs (p. 61). Lecky intimates that the Privy Council actually issued the call, while Fanny Burney says simply that the queen allowed Willis to be called. Piecing all of these opinions together, we might guess that the equerry's wife told the queen about Willis, and she in turn checked out the recommendation with Thurlow and then allowed the Privy Council to send out the call. See Charles Chenevix-Trench, *The Royal Malady* (orig. 1964; New York: Harcourt, Brace & World, 1965), p. 93; William E. H. Lecky, *A History of England in the Eighteenth Century* (orig. 1879–90; New York: D. Appleton, 1893), vol. 5, p. 385; and Fanny Burney [Madame D'Arblay], *Diary and Letters . . .* (London: Colburn, 1842–6), vol. 4, p. 204.

11. Dr. Richard Warren was the Prince of Wales's personal physician and a general practitioner who spent most of his ministering in the great Whig households. Indeed, considering not only his visits to Carlton House but also his journeys to the Duchess of Devonshire's abode, he was an integral part of the Foxites. See Walter Sichel, *Sheridan From New and Original Material; Including a Manuscript Diary by Georgiana Duchess of Devonshire* (London: Constable & Co., 1909), vol. 2, Appendix III.

While Warren was a general practitioner, Dr. Francis Willis was a specialist who had run a mental hospital in Lincolnshire for thirty years. He achieved extraordinary success (for the eighteenth century) by working on the mind, not the body, through a series of alternating sessions of coercion and reward. Opposition knew of his success, but yet (of course) attacked his favorable prognostications. See the Prince of Wales' *Correspondence,* vol. 2, pp. 405–6, for Opposition's fact sheet on him.

12. Pitt had been given the seals of government after Fox's East India Bill had been quashed by the Lords (17 December 1783), on the king's orders. Pitt became

first Lord of the Treasury on the following day. The Fox-North Coalition defeated Pitt on no less than fourteen divisions, until 10 March 1784, when Pitt was able to pass his Mutiny Bill. With a one-vote majority, he called for general elections. In probably the most spectacular election of the century, Pitt gathered a comfortable 150-vote majority, with at least that number of Foxites "martyred." For a fuller discussion of the "palace plot" to overthrow Fox-North and the subsequent election, see Dorothy George, "Fox's Martyrs: The General Election of 1784," *Transactions of the Royal Historical Society* (Society Series 4, vol. 21; London: R.H.S., 1939), pp. 133–68; and J. Steven Watson, *The Reign of George III 1760–1815*, "Oxford History of England" Series, No. 12 (Oxford: Clarendon, 1960), esp. pp. 266–72.

13. The estimate, in a circular headed "Proposals," is in the Braybrooke papers, Essex Record Office, Chelmsford (D/DByC9/44), and is reprinted in Sir Lewis Namier, "Monarchy and the Party System," *Personalities and Powers; Selected Essays* (London: Harper's, 1955), pp. 31–32. The list apparently was drawn up by one P. V. Smith, an MP trying to organize a "third party" in Commons and Lords. The organizational effort in the spring of 1788 produced the so-called "Armed Neutrality," a group of some twenty Lords and thirty Commoners ready to vote en masse. See John Eden to William Eden, 15 December 1788, in The Bishop of Bath and Wells (ed.), *The Journal and Correspondence of William, Lord Auckland* (London: Richard Bentley, 1861), vol. 2, pp. 258–59.

    The estimate showed Pitt and "place-men" with 237 votes, his supporters (Lonsdale, Landsdowne, Dundas, and the East Indians) with fifty-two votes, Opposition with 155 votes, and the Independents with 122 votes. If, then, Opposition could capture most of the Independents and a few key rats, it could turn out the minister.

14. For full details on the two events, see: C. H. Philips, *The East India Company, 1784–1834* (Manchester: Manchester University Press, 1940), pp. 57–61; Keith G. Feiling, *The Second Tory Party 1714–1832* (London: Macmillan, 1938), esp. p. 176; Wraxall, 5:85; Donald E. Ginter, *Whig Organization in the General Election of 1790; Selections From the Blair Adams Papers* (Berkeley: University of California Press, 1967), p. xxxvi; and *Auckland Papers,* 2:223.

15. E.g., Lord Sheffield to William Eden, 12 November 1788; John Storer to William Eden, 28 November 1788; Duke of Dorset to William Eden, 29 November 1788; and Sir John Eden to William Eden, 12 December 1788, in *Auckland Papers,* vol. 2. Indeed, Pitt was making preparations to return to his legal practice— hardly a sign of great expectations.

16. Fox had discredited himself two sessions previous by vigorously denying the prince's marriage to Mrs. Fitzherbert when in fact the secret marriage had been consummated; both Fox and Portland were put off for not being knowledgeable parties (see Christopher Hobhouse, *Fox* [New York: Houghton-Mifflin, 1935], pp. 173–76). Sheridan, meanwhile, knew of the marriage and delivered a speech

for which he received the overwhelming thanks of the prince (see Loren D. Reid, "Sheridan's Speech on Mrs. Fitzherbert," *QJS* 33 [1947]:15–22). On the Burke-Sheridan squabble, see Sir Lewis Namier and John Brooke (eds.), *The History of Parliament; The House of Commons 1754–1790* 3 vols. (London: H.M.S.O., 1964), 3:433, and Ginter, p. xxv. And, for some opinions on the Fox-Sheridan disagreements, see Derry, p. 77, and Lucyle Werkmeister, *The London Daily Press; 1772–1792* (Lincoln: University of Nebraska Press, 1963), esp. p. 6.

17. Loughborough drew up a paper proposing the so-called "right-" or "devolution-principle." He argued that as the king was "one and the same" with the heir, when the king was disabled officially the heir apparent should assume the throne. Burke proposed that because any debate over a prince's right would consume time, the prince rather should more simply assume command of Parliament, asking its counsel; such a move "would put him forward and with advantage in the Eyes of the people, it would teach them to look on him with respect, as a person possessed of the Spirit of Command, and it would, . . . stiffle [*sic*] an hundred Cabals, both in Parliament, and elsewhere, in their very Cradle." Fox offered the third strategy: simply sit back and accept whatever bill Pitt proposed. That way, even if they went into office with limited powers (as everyone knew Pitt would propose limitations), they nevertheless would be in office—and then could work to remove incumbrances. Loughborough's paper may be found in the Prince of Wales's *Correspondence,* vol. 1, p. 381. Burke wrote directly to Fox in late November proposing his idea; see Holden Furber and P. J. Marshall (eds.), *The Correspondence of Edmund Burke* (Chicago: University of Chicago Press, 1965), vol. 5, pp. 428–29. Fox in turn wrote to the prince, c. 26 November 1788; see Prince of Wales's *Correspondence,* 1:383–84. Of the three positions, Loughborough's finally was adopted.

18. Opposition sought rats in high places: they went after Lord Chancellor Thurlow (unsuccessfully), but did manage to garner the support of the Duke of Queensbury (Lord of the Bedchamber), Lord Lothian (commander of the First Life Guards), James Harris (Lord Malmesbury, ambassador-without-portfolio), Lord Rawdon (aide-de-campe to the king), the Duke of Northumberland, the Bishop of Llandaff, and Lonsdale (James Lowther, a "King's Friend" with nine votes in Commons). Sheridan in particular worked hard also at gathering in the Independents, concentrating his efforts on the "Armed Neutrality" and the so-called St. Albans Tavern group—a group of generally conservative Tory-type country gentlemen who had tried unsuccessfully in 1784 to reconcile Pitt and Fox. Opposition managed to capture almost all of the Armed Neutrality, and by January almost half of the St. Albans Tavern Group.

19. Because they had not been opened officially by a king, both Houses met as Committees of the Whole. Thus, a procedural question would be created in the debates: How could they meet *qua* Parliament to pass a bill for remedying the

situation if there was no king to open them? Pitt's answer—a special commission to place the Great Seal in the king's place—received the universal condemnation of Opposition in general and of Burke in particular.

20. For a discussion of Pitt's apparent tactics in maneuvering his government through the Crisis, see Bruce E. Gronbeck, "Government's Stance in Crisis: A Case Study of Pitt the Younger," *Western Speech* 34 (1970):250–61.

21. Derry's basic thesis (p. 155) on Burke is parallel to my own: "Although in one aspect his speeches were the frantic denunciations of a desperate man, in another sense they were the only coherent interpretation of the predicament on the part of an Opposition spokesman in the Commons."

22. For his letters, see especially volume 5 of his *Correspondence*. His speeches may be found in William Cobbett, *The Parliamentary History of England*, . . . (London: T. C. Hansard, 1816), vol. 27, and in Anon., *An Impartial Report of all the Proceedings in Parliament on the Late Important Subject of a Regency* (London: Printed and sold by J. Bew, 1789). The meetings he attended are described in the sources mentioned in the text, and the material he drafted may be found in the Burke Mss., Bk. 15, and the Prince of Wales's *Correspondence*, vol. 1.

   I graciously acknowledge the permission of Earl Fitzwilliam, his Trustees, and the City Librarian of Sheffield City Libraries for allowing me to photoduplicate and quote from the Wentworth Woodhouse Muniments, Burke Mss., Bk. 15. I also thank the Horace H. Rackham School of Graduate Studies for the fellowship and grant (FRR-961), which provided for my trip to Sheffield in the summer of 1971; the support allowed me to finish this project begun under Donald C. Bryant at the University of Iowa in 1967.

23. The list of names in n. 18 would seem to bear this statement out—all the prominent rats sat in Lords.

24. The Prince of Wales's *Correspondence*, 1:486.

25. Morley offers several reasons why Burke was not awarded an office more important than Paymaster of the Forces. Morley thinks the prince did not care for Burke's constant moralizing, and that even his friends thought him in imperfect control of his faculties; and, too, the Irish prejudice and the reputation as an "adventurer" with n'er-do-well relatives might have still clung to his image. See Lord John Morley, *Burke* ("English Men of Letters" series; New York: Harper, n.d.), pp. 135–40. Another, more simple reason might be this: Burke never pushed for major office. Even upon retirement, when many were willing to give him public reward, he was most reluctant to accept.

26. In attempting to capture Burke's constitutional theory, Derry draws his first quotation from Burke's 6 February 1789 speech—from one of the last he delivered. Derry makes no attempt to treat his subject's development chrono-

logically. As a result, much of Burke's adaptation—of particular rhetorical interest—is lost.

27. Opposition was more than surprised. Sheridan is reported to have said sourly after the day's debate, "I suppose he [the prince] has some little right, has he not?" See the Duchess of Devonshire's diary for December 10 in Sichel, *Sheridan From New and Original Material,* 2:414.

28. *The Times,* 26 December 1788.

29. Burke was referring to an incident where Dr. Willis gave the king a straight-edge razor to shave himself. Willis presumably was demonstrating his trust in the by-now domesticated king, but Burke seized upon the action, of course, as a dangerous one, supposedly demonstrating Willis's foolhardiness.

30. For readable short biographical sketches of all Members referred to in this essay, see Namier and Brooke, vols. 2 and 3. One should only note here that the Grey mentioned is the same Charles Grey who became prime minister in the nineteenth century. He was in his first Parliament at this time.

31. Later to become Lord Chancellor, Eldon the previous summer had received this, his first major office. Pitt's confidence in him was borne out during the Regency Crisis, as Eldon delivered two generally well-received speeches. See Horace Twiss (ed.), *The Public and Private Life of Chancellor Eldon, With Selections From His Correspondence* (London: John Murray, 1844), vol. 1.

32. An examination of Table 4, for example, indicates that several items show Burke first striking the heads of ideas and then later filling out such with developmental material. See especially Items 2–7 and 8–20. The last group is of particular interest, for we find many strike-outs and additions, some of which are in Richard Burke, Jr.'s hand. The long revising process apparently included critiques.

33. Burke's *Correspondence,* 5:440.

34. On January 30 Dr. Willis was forced to confine George III by tying him down in the Coronation Chair. Yet, after this last violent day, His Majesty forewent any coercion, progressing rapidly. By February 1 he was conversing sensibly with Fanny Burney about her father's *History of Music;* by the third, both the queen and the princesses were visiting him without incident. See Chenevix-Trench, *Royal Malady,* pp. 166–70.

   Opposition, therefore, was confused. While Elliot admitted that "the King has been really considerably better the last two days" and that "Warren also . . . found him considerably better," yet he clung to the idea that "he [Warren] does not seem to think the hope of a perfect recovery even now a probable one." See Elliot's *Life and Letters,* 1:271.

35. The Duke of Chondos, as a member of the king's household, was speaking on January 23 against the idea that householders would fall prey to the political influence of the queen. To quote the appropriate section from Cobbett: "He had supported the present administration from principle, and he knew them to be an administration which had rendered the greatest services to their country. The duke, parodying what Mr. Pitt's father had said of general Wolfe, pronounced the present Chancellor of the Exchequer a heaven-born minister" (*PH,* 27: 1080). It is no wonder that the Foxites reacted.

36. Said Wraxall: "No fact can more forcibly prove the degree of unpopularity to which Burke had sunk at this period, than the circumstance of a speech containing matter so impressive, and so much calculated to awaken deep reflections in the minds of his hearers, eliciting no reply. Not a word of answer was made to it, either by Pitt or by any member of Administration" (Wraxall, 5:298). Wraxall certainly heard in the February 6 address the qualities of constitutional argument I have attributed to it.

    The Times, however, did not. Rather, its February 7 reaction ran as follows: "In what respectability might this man have been, had he spoke but *once* or *twice* in a Session. The *Cacoethes Loquendi* has been his ruin. . . . Mr. Burke was let loose, and became fanatick." Perhaps Burke thus undercut his own effectiveness through overexposure; perhaps, however, he could not help himself in view of the late emergence of his constitutional theory.

37. Bertram D. Sarason, "Burke and the Crisis Before the Reflections," *Connecticut Review* 1 (1967):31–50. Sarason's argument is that Burke's thinking on hereditary succession in all of its manifestations solidified during the Regency Crisis, preparing him to write on that subject in his *Reflections on the Revolution in France* (1790).

Rhetoric and the Humane Tradition

Marie H. Nichols

In a letter to me in which he described his expectations for a program he was planning on Rhetoric, a colleague suggested that my part should somehow be related to the recently published *Prospect of Rhetoric,*[1] and that I might speculate a bit. I was to share the program with John Wilkinson of the Center for the Study of Democratic Institutions, talking on the subject, "Rhetoric, History, and Systems."[2] Well, I did speculate. I speculated about why I should be on a program with a former physicist and historian of science. Then, knowing that Mr. Wilkinson had taken work in philosophy, I speculated about whether, as a student at the University of Chicago, he might have sat in on semiotician Charles Morris's seminar in philosophy in which, in 1937, Ludwig von Bertalanffy, in fear and trembling, presented his first paper outlining General Systems theory.[3] Then, I speculated about what he might draw upon from his part in the translation of Chaim Perelman's and Olbrechts-Tyteca's *The New Rhetoric.*[4] And finally, I speculated on Wilkinson's interview in *Center Magazine* on "Retrospective Futurology,"[5] which suggests that one might project 6,000 years of history by way of computer printouts on a chart right in front of one's eyes; and I wondered all the while if that German historiographer Von Ranke, who believed that history should be written exactly as it was, could, if he were alive, now do the job. The subtitle of Mr. Wilkinson's interview intrigued me. It was: "Idea for a Project that Would Prepare for What Is to Come by Studying What Has Been." The more I thought about the subtitle the more clear it became to me that what I wanted to do also involved a retrospective look, not in the "heady" way of computer analysis, but in a much less sophisticated way.

I speculated about Mr. Wilkinson, the rhetorician, in his opening statement to the *Center Magazine* interviewer: "You always need a catchy title even when it is not particularly accurate simply in order to get people interested."[6] In partial defiance I chose a title, "Rhetoric and the Humane Tradition." In the context of our times, with computer analysis everywhere in evidence and the dominion of science generally taken for granted, I suspect my title violates Wilkinson's principle rather unmercifully, and his methodology quite as much. I might add that Wilkinson never completely satisfied my curiosity because of indisposition at the time of the program, but I must credit him with prompting me to re-examine a subject that has interested me for a very long time.

In 1967, at a convention of the Speech Association of America, Samuel Becker, a contributor to the recent *Prospect of Rhetoric,* made the observation, ". . . if the research which has been done in the past three years in . . . the field of communications were wiped out, I cannot conceive that it would make the slightest difference in our lives."[7] And recently, in *Speech Monographs,* David H. Smith has added five years to that statement, by remarking that Becker's statement "is as true today as it was in 1967." "Part of the reason," says Smith, "for our continued failure is the heavy commitment of this field to behavioristic methodology."[8]

I do not call attention to these statements to attack empirical research and quantification because I believe that science of a rigorous sort is absolutely indispensable. A society which believes that knowledge and truth need no more seeking, by any means available to it, is authoritarian. I call attention to the statements to ask some questions. What have rhetoricians done? What do they do? What can they do that will "make the slightest difference in our lives"? I take it that education at any level has something to do with those questions.

On a page of the *New York Times* of November 21, 1972, announcing the opening of the London season at Covent Garden and Broadway's production of *Two Gentlemen of Verona* and *Much Ado About Nothing,* there also appeared a news item announcing Grossman's publication of a book entitled *That Pestilent Cosmetic Rhetoric;* ". . . just in time for the 1976 campaign," the story ran. Done by a sociologist, Dr. Sol Chaneles, it defines and illustrates about a hundred figures of speech employed knowingly or unknowingly by political candidates and other speakers and writers. He keeps the Greek labels to avoid the ambiguities of either English or Latin. Israel Shenker had a good time reporting litanies of abuse such as that of

Michael J. Quill against John Lindsay: "You are nothing but a juvenile, a lightweight and a pipsqueak" and calling it by the Greek label; and another allegation in a lawsuit against Bertrand Russell, describing Russell as "lecherous, salacious, libidinous, lustful, venerous, erotomaniac, aphrodisiac, atheistic, irreverent, narrow-minded, untruthful and bereft of moral fibre." This is illustative of Aeschrologia, says Shenker, winking over his own shoulder, "A figure of derogation whose explicit terms offend public taste or the listener's ear." Henry Kissinger was there, too, using a figure designed to avoid needless acerbity with reference to Hanoi's radio draft-agreement on a cease fire and calling it a "very fair account," but adding, "I don't refer to the last two pages of rhetoric."[9]

Both the author of *That Pestilent Cosmetic Rhetoric* and the reviewer then advanced the sobering statement: "To imply that public utterance is rhetoric and therefore something derogatory is to defame thought and its expression."[10]

Thus, by a roundabout route, I want to imply that rhetoric is public utterance, with a gloss on utterance which makes it either spoken or written, and designed to produce an effect of some kind.

"The construction of a coherent theory—a set of connected ideas about some whole subject—," says Susanne Langer, ". . . begins with the solution of a central problem; that is, with the establishing of a key concept."[11] My key concept is that rhetoric is an act of adapting discourse to an end outside of itself. And, as anyone can recognize, this is an adaptation of concepts deriving from George Campbell's eighteenth century *Philosophy of Rhetoric* and Kenneth Burke's writings. Rhetoric is a verbal art. It serves many ends, from promoting decision to giving pleasure. It does not include ships, guns, an alluring sun, the dance, or the Cathedral of Chartres. It does not include rolling drums or the sound of marching feet; it does not include extralinguistic symbols of peace or the clenched fist of power. It does not deny that there are other symbolic forms for altering behavior, which often accompany or reinforce it. It is a handmaid of politics, but also of culture generally. In fine, it is a verbal act of a subject trying to relate himself to another subject or subjects who are endowed with a capacity to understand and respond to language. As an instrument, it has cohesive, transcending, and alienating possibilities and resources. It can befuddle or move to feelings of beauty or ecstasy; it can clarify thought and direct judgment; it can give energy to truth, or make truth to seem a lie. In the words of Chaim

Perelman, in one of its functions, it ". . . reveals the evils from which the city suffers and calls forth remedies, or presents the image of an ideal city which men should strive to bring into being."[12]

I ask no one to accept my version of rhetoric, my key concepts. I state them in order to do as H. J. Muller has recommended in *Science and Criticism*—lay one's cards on the table in order that someone else might understand the starting point.[13]

I do not know all the things that went through the minds of Cornell University faculty and students during the second decade of this century when they began to look into ancient treatises on rhetoric in earnest. The pages of the speech journals in the second decade and thereafter reveal that a whole cluster of men, including Alex Drummond, Lane Cooper, Harry Caplan, Herbert Wichelns, James A. Winans, Hoyt Hudson, Everett Hunt, and others did, indeed, seriously examine the theory of rhetoric and its practice. Some of the treatises, of course, were known and used as guides in the colleges of the times almost from the beginning of the nation. From the men I know who gave impetus to the study of rhetoric, I do not believe they shared the "residual impression" that Gerald Else, professor of Classics at the University of Michigan, claims still to be widespread in the United States, namely, that the "classical humanities," including rhetoric, were exclusively a verbal study "dominated by an imperious but now obsolete kind of grammar." I believe they knew that "language was not the be-all and end-all of the old humanities, at least in their best periods." I believe they knew, in the words of Else, that rhetoric and other humane studies, had "three modes or points of impact, each with its own educational purpose: First, they worked in and through *language,* aiming to develop educated taste; second, they worked with and on the *mind,* aiming to develop educated judgment and persuasiveness; and third, they operated in and upon *the whole man,* aiming to make him a moral person and a responsible citizen or political leader—in other words, a free man." As Else points out, "The old humanistic training in logic and argument was not given in a vacuum . . . the center of gravity was . . . in moral-political issues."[14] And if one goes to the Italian Renaissance, as Paul Kristeller and John Herman Randall have done, they will find that although language forms were borrowed from classical models, the humanists "tried and managed to express the concrete circumstances of their own life and their personal thoughts and feelings . . ."[15]

In Classical times, in the Renaissance, in the early and later life of this country the authors studied were men who "provided the best definition of the duties of man in society, man guiding the destinies of his society."[16]

That function of rhetoric, namely, man's preparation of himself for his duties in a society, man guiding the destiny of a society, is not out of date today; it is probably merely out of the curriculum, or, if not out of it, so subordinated that it is all but forgotten. It is what I think I mean when I refer to the humane tradition in rhetoric.

"To be conscious is both to know and to imagine," says J. Bronowski, Deputy Director and Fellow of the Salk Institute for Biological Studies, "and our humanity flows from this deep spring. When we imagine nature outside ourselves into the future, we create the mode of knowledge which is science. And when we imagine ourselves alive into the future, we create another mode: knowledge of the self. They are the inseparable halves of the identity of man."[17] A humane rhetoric has something to do with the possibilities of the self in helping to shape that future which one imagines himself alive in. It has something to do with knowing the successes and failures of the past in choosing its objects, articulating beliefs and values, both rational and irrational, remembering what one has articulated, prejudging the results of one's articulations designed for the shaping of the future, and ultimately post-judging the consequences.

Sam Adams knew its functions during the Revolution; Franklin knew it at Philadelphia in 1787; Channing knew it at Baltimore in 1819; Emerson knew it in 1838, when he defied the authorities at Harvard in the Divinity School Address; Webster, Clay, and Calhoun knew it in 1850; Whittier knew it in "Ichabod"; Lincoln knew it in 1861, Wilson knew it in 1917; Kennedy, Stevenson, and Churchill knew it; and so have many men, great and small, in all times, even unto the present.

A humane rhetoric has purpose. And its practical purpose is to bridge the differences among men, that separateness from one another that all of us experience. On its theoretical side, it investigates and explains alienation and union. "Academic rhetorics," says one of our colleagues, "have been for the most part instruments of established society." This sounds to me like the politically motivated talk, considerably left of center, of Louis Kampf who argued in 1971 that "Initiating the underprivileged to the cultural treasures of the West could be a form of oppression—a weapon in the hands of those who rule . . ."[18] Political ideology has been no part of a theory and philosophy of a humane rhetoric; and its practitioners have not recognized

it as being ideological. They have used it to pursue ideological ends, sometimes ends which do not serve the common good, but that is not to say that
rhetoric was intended as an instrument of established society. The opposing
proposition is probably easier to defend. Were the proposition true, how
would one account for Luther fed on Aristotle, Wendell Phillips and Channing fed on Plato and Cicero, and scores of others nurtured on academic
rhetorics familiar to most of us who turned out to be heretics?

Lawrence Rosenfield laments the demise of the humane tradition in
rhetoric,[19] but even as he does so, political scientists are pursuing rhetorical
studies. I call your attention to James D. Barber's research on presidential
leadership. Notice the title, for instance, of his study of Andrew Johnson,
"Adult Identity and Presidential Style: The Rhetorical Emphasis."[20] Or,
notice Robert Tucker, Professor of Politics and Director of the Program of
Russian Studies at Princeton, on "The Theory of Charismatic Leadership";[21] or Stanley and Inge Hoffman, Harvard professors of government,
"The Will to Grandeur: de Gaulle as Political Artist,"[22]—humanistic rhetorical studies all. Or, think of Joseph Gusfield's *Symbolic Crusade.*[23] And
if that is not enough, what of John Maddox, one of England's leading
scientists, writing *The Doomsday Syndrome,* a study of the rhetoric of
hyperbole and overkill in our time.[24]

So it has often been; while we lament, someone else does the work. So
it is in studies of the medium of language which we claim to be the medium
with which we are concerned, since, in its potentialities it differentiates us
from other members of the animal kingdom and makes the fulfillment of
our purposes possible. Noam Chomsky, Thomas Sebeok, Roman Jakobson,
and others pay no attention to the wails of the frustrated, each in his own
way trying to understand more fully the foundation and dimensions of the
instrument by which we are made human, creative, and persuasive.

The humane tradition in rhetoric has had continuous existence, whether
some of us know it or not. What is one to make of Kenneth Burke, doubtless
the best exemplar of the humane tradition in rhetoric of the century, and
possibly of a good many previous centuries? To what has he dedicated his
voluminous writings, which continue even though he is in his seventies, if
it is not to improving the lot of the human condition through an understanding of the possibilities of language to bridge differences among men
and unite them in the pursuit of peace and justice, and point out the pitfalls
to obtaining those ends?

There is a notion around that a humane rhetoric is merely a concern with the past for its own sake. There is nothing about a humane rhetoric which says that either its theory or the practices must be used as recordings or invariant examples and models. Doubtless a syncretic approach has sometimes done that. But as G. Jon Roush has pointed out, in this antihistorical age, a dialectical approach by which one interrogates the past, is also part of the tradition. "I do not teach, I relate," said Montaigne, ". . . as, with tennis players, the man who takes the service shifts his position and makes ready according to the movements of the striker and to the nature of the stroke."[25] George Campbell did it in the eighteenth century when he was taking a "service" from Bacon and Locke with reference to inductive method which contrasted with an authoritarian deductive method and a system of *topoi*. And, although Richard Whately thought him "ignorant of the nature and object of logic,"[26] so much the worse for Whately's readiness to "relate." John Stuart Mill did it. A. E. Phillips and James A. Winans did it in the early part of this century, as have a score of others since.

Great and good men have lived in all times, and what they have left us is that which contributes to what Michael Polanyi has called "tacit"[27] knowledge and understanding, a store of which all of us need in order to understand much about the human condition.

Under the impact of the existentialists from Dostoevsky to Sartre, many young persons shout "I am freedom," "truth is subjective," and it is "here and now," but the shout is hollow without that knowledge of options of what to be free about and what to be subjective about. What distinguishes the humanities, says James Ackerman, is that they are devoted to the "study of things that men have made and thought, and on this account they cannot be adequately studied or taught without reference to value systems."[28] Despite the slogan, "We are the new men come aboard," the new men face many of the old problems and decisions that men in all times have had to make and have made either wisely or foolishly, rationally or irrationally. The rhetoric of all times gives the student a "sense of the immediacy of human problems, an open door into the minds and passions of men, within which he finds himself to be both singular and universal."[29] To articulate the new understanding and depths of feeling requires craft and skill, something woefully lacking in the new man come aboard. A vocabulary of "Wow" and "You know" tells me little about the new truths discovered.

All around us we hear calls for a "new rhetoric." There is nothing inconsistent with such calls and a humane tradition in rhetoric. Notker

Labeo, a monk of St. Gall did it in the tenth century, and produced a *New Rhetoric,* aiming, as Otto A. Dieter has pointed out, to "re-associate rhetoric with life in the living present."[30]

It seems to me that there is a little of William Blake's *Jerusalem* in many of our calls for new theories of rhetoric and new theories of criticism: "I must Create a System or be enslav'd by another Man's." It is doubtless true that no art is ever ordered for long. "Even as the critic sets his hand to the last note of his composition, painting, music, and poetry are changing around him," notes Lawrence Lipking.[31] But whereas this is true, new theories are not made to order. They are responses to altered conditions, increased knowledge, and outworn practices, pinpointed and specified, rather than vaguely and sometimes romantically asserted opinions.

Psychology went through a period in which it tried to make new theories to order, says Sigmund Koch, psychologist at Duke University—during a period in the thirties and forties which he labels the "Age of Theory." It produced, in his words, the "imagery of hypothetice-deduction, the subculture surrounding operational definition, the lore concerning the intervening variable, the belief in the imminence . . . of precisely quantitative behavioral theory of comprehensive scope . . . the fixed vocabulary for the comparative dissection and analysis of theory." The production of such theories "could be scheduled by educating the work-force into the presumptive dictates of the 'new view' of science."[32] Becker, to whom I alluded earlier, is something of an inheritor of that tradition when he remarks that "A major concern for every contemporary rhetorical theorist or public address scholar is to be confident that his work is contributing to the development of systems and theories." Becker goes on to say, "No physicist worries about whether Isaac Newton's apple was red, rotten, tasty—or even whether it was, in fact, an apple. The essential fact for the physicist is that it was a body of a certain mass moving with a certain acceleration relative to other bodies." Becker then calls for a message-audience centered rhetoric, as opposed to a source-message centered rhetoric.[33] As someone has recently pointed out, it was not merely the apple that fell with Newton. "An apple ready to fall is presumably ripe, shapely, colored, textured, and potentially tasty. But these 'secondary' traits are precisely those the legend ignores. . . . Also lowered was man's capacity for understanding this fruit of the earth not merely as an example of mass descending, but also as an item of sustenance and of sensory enjoyment."[34]

A humane tradition in rhetoric is not reductionist. It is mightily concerned with source, purpose, values, and sustenance; it knows that a theory which omits consideration of purpose, value, and sustenance can be nothing but reductionist.

Both Abraham Kaplan[35] and Noam Chomsky are right when they warn of the danger in our narrowly empirical studies, when we let the technology determine our values, rather than the other way around. As Chomsky puts it, "There are strong pressures to make use of new educational technology and to design curriculum and teaching methods in the light of the latest scientific advances. In itself, this is not objectionable. It is important, nevertheless, to remain alert to a very real danger: that new knowledge and technique will define the nature of what is taught and how it is taught, rather than contributing to the realization of educational goals that are set on other grounds and in other terms."[36]

Many of the behavioral studies that I encounter reveal little compass and little knowledge of the larger nature of things, and how either scientist or humanist can have much to tell us without compass and depth of knowledge remains a mystery.

A humane tradition in rhetoric asks: does your new theory explain man's purposes, his methods for achieving them, and what are the consequences of those purposes? Does your new critical method illuminate man's behavior in such a way as to make us more aware of his purposes, his methods, his decisions, his good will or the lack of it?

Science "destroys" its past,[37] says Thomas Kuhn, author of *The Structure of Scientific Revolutions*. A humane tradition in rhetoric destroys neither its past theory nor its past critical practices. Aristotle lives on at the same time as does Donald Bryant; Plato's dialogues at the same time as Henry Kissinger's. The Mona Lisa has not been outmoded by the art of the present, even as modern art departs from it. The riddle of man has not been solved.

Just about anybody around who has lived through the last quarter century, or even the last five years, knows that any humane discipline is in deep trouble. Oscar Handlin has called attention to the plight of the historian;[38] Abraham Kaplan has called attention to the plight of philosophy;[39] and now René Wellek has called attention to the plight of literary study.[40]

There is little doubt that questions should be raised. There is little doubt that in the past many persons could study the finest German literature and at the same time support Hitler; that philosophy students and professors saw nothing inconsistent with that study and with keeping the Blacks subordinate; that students and teachers of rhetorical studies should turn their backs on the slums.

But neither is there any doubt that a former college president has said that the single greatest influence on his college career was his work in debate at Penn State, and that Marshall McLuhan has argued that the single greatest influence on his work was his study of classical rhetoric from the Greeks through the Renaissance.

What does all this show? Very likely it shows the need for improvement, not the need for elimination. It may also show that a considerable amount of abdication has taken place with reference to the humanities, under the impact of science. What humane scholar these days dares to use the word "model" simply to mean something exemplary?

"Rhetoric's survival is menaced by such Manichaean competitors as attitude change research and psycholinguistics,"[41] says Rosenfield in *Prospect of Rhetoric*. Rhetoric's survival is menaced by nothing of the sort, except by humanists who have lost their way. Someone's theory may be, or someone's method of teaching may be—but this is not to say that rhetoric will not survive. There is a fitting rejoinder to this attitude in Amos Wilder's *Early Christian Rhetoric:* "Jesus was a voice not a penman, a herald not a scribe, a watchman with his call in the market-place and the Temple, and not a cry of alarm in the wilderness like John the Baptist."[42]

What is the prospect for rhetoric? This depends on whether or not we want to take the tawdry aspects of rhetoric revealed in *Rudy's Red Wagon* as our model or restore as quickly as possible rhetoric as a truly humane study to the curriculum. It depends on whether or not the humanist refuses to let the behavioralist with his reductionist model of human behavior dictate the goals, the curriculum, and the methods of rhetorical education. It depends on whether or not we are willing to hand over to the sociologist and political scientist, concerned chiefly with the present, the work of the humanist.

We forget, I think, that the humane tradition in rhetoric has always been a voice, proclaiming, judging, warning, pleading—always to somebody. And I would suppose that structure of relationship will continue to exist into a future whose end is not foreseeable, despite the cries of alarm. We are dealing with a cultural instrument, conditioned by the needs of the times, whether that be in litigous Athens, the courtly Renaissance, or the urgent present. Addison saw the need for a change in the eighteenth century; George Bernard Shaw saw it in the nineteenth century; and McLuhan has seen it in the twentieth century. All these men adjusted their modes of discourse to what they thought to be the needs of the times. If Addison used homely grace, and Shaw used biting humor to knock the indifferent off their perch, and McLuhan uses the shocking pun, their reasons are to be understood before they are either praised or condemned. They recognized there is a public out there to be reached, sometimes a boisterous public, sometimes an apathetic public, sometimes a barbaric public, sometimes a public turning in upon itself.

It occurs to me that more of our time should be spent as Father Walter J. Ong has spent his time in *Rhetoric, Romance, and Technology*, revealing the responsiveness of rhetoric to changing cultural phenomena. Just as Greek and Latin are no longer "puberty rites," to use Ong's phrase,[43] so rhetoric can no longer parade its formulas for producing a call, a judgment, a warning, a plea, a hope. It is nonetheless in the humane tradition to make the adjustment, not to abdicate.

I believe that the humane tradition in rhetoric means that we must in our muddled times use our effort to train men and women who can make an authentic statement, an honest judgment, and display a contagious allegiance to truth, justice, tolerance, courage, and hope, all parts of man's work as citizen and statesman.

In a moving essay on "The Hope of Man," Loren Eiseley, Benjamin Franklin Professor of Anthropology at the University of Pennsylvania, recalled the words of Bacon, uttered more than three hundred years ago: "Nature is most violent in the return." "We are a free nation," he said, "seeking our own way beyond and above our great machines. . . . There confronts . . . [us] now, hope for earth's frail web of life, or that choice of cold indifference which leads to the pathway of no return."[44]

NOTES AND REFERENCES

1. Lloyd F. Bitzer and Edwin Black (eds.), *The Prospect of Rhetoric* (Englewood Cliffs, N.J.: Prentice-Hall, 1971).

2. *Convention Program,* Speech Communication Association, 58th Annual Meeting, Chicago, Ill., Dec. 27–30, 1971, p. 61.

3. Ludwig von Bertalanffy, "General Systems Theory—A Critical Review," *General Systems* 7 (1962):1–20.

4. Chaim Perelman and L. Olbrechts-Tyteca, *The New Rhetoric,* translated by John Wilkinson and Purcell Weaver (Notre Dame and London: University of Notre Dame Press, 1969).

5. John Wilkinson, "Retrospective Futurology: Interview," *Center Magazine* 5 (Nov./Dec. 1972):59.

6. Ibid., p. 59.

7. Samuel L. Becker, "Approaches to Inquiry in Communication," a paper presented to the Speech Association of America Convention, Los Angeles, California, December, 1967, cited by David H. Smith, "Communication Research and the Idea of Process," *Speech Monographs* 39 (August 1972):182.

8. David H. Smith, p. 182.

9. *New York Times,* Nov. 21, 1972, p. 52.

10. Ibid., p. 52.

11. Susanne K. Langer, *Problems of Art* (New York: Charles Scribner's Sons, 1957), p. 3.

12. Chaim Perelman, "The New Rhetoric," in *The Prospect of Rhetoric,* p. 116.

13. Herbert J. Muller, *Science and Criticism* (New Haven: Yale University Press, 1964), Chap. 2.

14. Gerald F. Else, "The Old and the New Humanities," *Daedalus* (Summer 1969), pp. 803–8 passim.

15. Paul Oskar Kristeller and John Herman Randall, Jr., "General Introduction," *The Renaissance Philosophy of Man* (Chicago, Ill.: University of Chicago Press, Phoenix Books, 1948), pp. 3, 4.

16. Gerald F. Else, op. cit., pp. 803–8 passim.

17. J. Bronowski, *The Identity of Man* (Garden City, N.Y.: Natural History Press, 1965), p. 80.

18. Cited in René Wellek, "The Attack on Literature," *American Scholar* 42 (Winter 1972–73):27.

19. Lawrence W. Rosenfield, "An Autopsy of the Rhetorical Tradition," *Prospect of Rhetoric,* pp. 64–77.

20. *Daedalus* (Summer 1968), pp. 938–68.

21. *Daedalus* (Summer 1968), pp. 731–56.

22. *Daedalus* (Summer 1968), pp. 829–87.

23. Joseph Gusfield, *Symbolic Crusade* (Urbana, Ill.: University of Illinois Press, 1966).

24. Benjamin DeMott, "Attacking Ecological Overkill," Rev. of John Maddox, *The Doomsday Syndrome, Saturday Review: Science* (Nov. 1972), pp. 77–80.

25. G. Jon Roush, "What Will Become of the Past?" *Daedalus* (Summer 1969), p. 647. Cf. Michel de Montaigne, *Essays,* translated by J. M. Cohen (Baltimore: Penguin Books, 1958), p. 237.

26. Wilbur Samuel Howell, *Eighteenth-Century British Logic and Rhetoric* (Princeton, N. J.: Princeton University Press, 1971), pp. 406, 708.

27. Michael Polanyi, *The Study of Man* (Chicago: University of Chicago Press, 1959), p. 28.

28. James S. Ackerman, "Two Styles: A Challenge to Higher Education," *Daedalus* (Summer 1969), p. 865.

29. J. Bronowski, "Protest—Past and Present," *American Scholar* 38 (Autumn 1969):546.

30. Otto Alvin Dieter, "The Rhetoric of Notker Labeo," *Papers in Rhetoric,* edited by Donald C. Bryant (St. Louis, Missouri: Printed by subscription, copyright by Donald C. Bryant, 1940), p. 27.

31. Lawrence Lipking, *The Ordering of the Arts in Eighteenth-Century England* (Princeton, N. J.: Princeton University Press, 1970), p. 463.

32. Sigmund Koch, "Psychology and Emerging Conceptions of Knowledge as Unitary," in *Behaviorism and Phenomenology,* edited by T. W. Wann (Chicago, Ill.: University of Chicago Press, Phoenix Books, 1965), pp. 11, 12.

33. Samuel L. Becker, "Rhetorical Studies for the Contemporary World," in *Prospects of Rhetoric,* pp. 21–43 passim.

34. Reuel Denney and Frances Sydow, "Isaac Newton's Unfortunate Fall," *Change* (Winter 1972/73), p. 55.

35. Abraham Kaplan, "The Life of Dialogue," *Communication,* edited by John D. Roslansky (Amsterdam: North-Holland Publishing Co., 1969), p. 92.

36. Noam Chomsky, "Form and Meaning in Natural Language," *Communication,* p. 66.

37. Thomas S. Kuhn, "Comment," *Comparative Studies in Philosophy and History,* 11 (1969), 407.

38. Oscar Handlin, "History: A Discipline in Crisis?" *American Scholar* 40 (Summer 1971):447–65.

39. Abraham Kaplan, "The Travesty of the Philosophers," *Change* (Jan.-Feb. 1970), p. 14.

40. René Wellek, "The Attack on Literature," *American Scholar* 42 (Winter 1972–73):27–42.

41. Lawrence W. Rosenfield, "An Autopsy of the Rhetorical Tradition," *Prospect of Rhetoric,* p. 64.

42. Amos N. Wilder, *Early Christian Rhetoric* (Cambridge, Mass.: Harvard University Press, 1971), p. 13.

43. Walter J. Ong, S. J., *Rhetoric, Romance, and Technology* (Ithaca, N. Y. and London: Cornell University Press, 1971), p. 113.

44. Loren Eiseley, "The Hope of Man," *New York Times,* Nov. 6, 1972, p. 41.

STUDIES IN TRANSITION

Rhetoric: Its Functions and Its Scope*

Donald C. Bryant

When a certain not always ingenuous radio spokesman for one of our large industrial concerns some years ago sought to reassure his audience on the troublesome matter of propaganda, his comfort ran thus: Propaganda, after all, is only a word for anything one says for or against anything. Either everything, therefore, is propaganda, or nothing is propaganda; so why worry?

The more seriously I take this assignment from the editor to re-explore for the *Quarterly Journal of Speech* (1953), the ground surveyed by Hudson and Wichelns thirty years ago, and since crossed and recrossed by many another, including myself,[1] the nearer I come to a position like our friend's conclusion on propaganda. When I remember Quintilian's *Institutes* at one extreme of time, and Kenneth Burke's "new rhetoric" at the other, I am almost forced to the position that whatever we do or say or write, or even think, in explanation of anything, or in support, or in extenuation, or in despite of anything, evinces rhetorical symptoms. Hence, either everything worth mentioning is rhetorical, or nothing is; so let's talk about something encompassable—say logic, or semantics, or persuasion, or linguistics, or scientific method, or poetics, or social psychology, or advertising, or salesmanship, or public relations, or pedagogy, or politics, or psychiatry, or symbolics—or propaganda.

But that is not the assignment. Others have dealt with those subjects, and have given us such illuminating definitive essays as "Speech as a Science"

*Reprinted by permission of the Speech Communication Association from *The Quarterly Journal of Speech* 39 (December 1953):401–24.

by Clarence Simon,[2] "The Spoken Word and the Great Unsaid" by Wendell Johnson,[3] "General Semantics[1952]" by Irving Lee,[4] and many other interpretive essays and *apologiae* for the various branches of our curricula and for the multiform captions in our departmental catalogues and organization charts. Among these, "Rhetoric and Public Address" can hardly be thought neglected over the years, at least in the *QJS* and *SM*. But perhaps we have assumed too quickly that rhetoric is now at last well understood. On the other hand, Hudson's "The Field of Rhetoric" may be inaccessible or out of date, and Burke's "new rhetoric" too cumbersome or recondite in statement, even after Marie Hochmuth's admirable exposition of it.[5] Even if all this be true, however, one can hardly hope to clarify here what may remain obscure in the work of thirty years—or twenty centuries; but in proper humility, no doubt one can try. At least, common practice seems to presume a restatement of most complex ideas about once in a generation.

I shall not undertake to summarize Hudson's or Wichelns' pioneer essays, relevant as they are to the central problem. They and certain others like Hunt's "Plato and Aristotle on Rhetoric"[6] are by now woven into the fabric of our scholarship. Nor shall I try to duplicate the coverage of my two papers on "Aspects of the Rhetorical Tradition." They can be easily reread by anyone interested.

One further limitation upon the scope of this essay seems necessary: I shall not try to present a digest of rhetoric or even an explanation of the main principles of rhetorical method. Those are also easily available, from Aristotle's *Rhetoric* to the newest textbook in persuasion. Furthermore, I intend to discuss no particular system of rhetoric, but the functions and scope which any system will embrace.

Confusion in Meaning of "Rhetoric"

Very bothersome problems arise as soon as one attempts to define rhetoric, problems that lead so quickly to hairsplitting on the one hand or cosmic inclusiveness on the other, and to ethical or moral controversy, that the attempt usually ends in trifling with logomachies, gloss on Aristotle, or flat frustration. *Rhetoric* is a word in common parlance, as well as in technical use in the SAA and the Chicago school of literary critics. Hence, we may presume it to have meanings which must be reckoned with, however vague, various, and disparate; for a word means what responsible users make it mean. Various as the meanings are, however, one occasionally encounters uses which seem little short of perverse, in persons who ought to know better. Not long since, a doctoral candidate in the classics, who had written as his dissertation a "rhetorical" analysis of one of St. Paul's sermons, was asked how Aristotle had defined rhetoric. Though the question, it would appear, was relevant, the candidate was unable to answer satisfactorily. Whereupon the questioner was taken firmly to task by one of his fellow examiners and was told that after all rhetoric could be adequately defined as a *way of saying something.* Now of course rhetoric may be so defined, as poetic may be defined as a way of making something; but there is little intellectual profit in either definition.

Rhetoric also enjoys several other meanings which, though more common and less perverse, serve to make analysis of it difficult. In general these are the same meanings which Hudson reviewed thirty years ago: bombast; high-sounding words without content; oratorical falsification to hide meaning; sophistry; ornamentation and the study of figures of speech; most commonly among academic folk, Freshman English; and finally, least commonly of all, the whole art of spoken discourse, especially persuasive discourse. This last meaning has gained somewhat in currency in thirty years, especially among scholars in speech and Renaissance literature.[7] During the same period the use of the term *rhetoric* (or the combinations *composition and rhetoric* and *grammar and rhetoric*) to label courses and textbooks in Freshman English has somewhat declined, and simultaneously the "rhetorical" content of them has declined also. The tendency now is to prefer just *Composition* or *English Composition,* or to resort to such loaded names as *Basic Writing, Effective Writing, Problems in Writing, Writing with a Purpose,* or *Communication and Analysis.*

In one of his early speeches, President Eisenhower declared that we want action from the Russians, not rhetoric, as evidence of their desire for peaceful settlement. Here is the common use of *rhetoric* to mean empty language, or language used to deceive, without honest intention behind it. Without question this use is in harmony with the current climate of meaning where what our opponents say is rhetoric, and what we say is something else. Hence our attempt to define rhetoric leads almost at once into questions of morals and ethics.

Rhetoric as figures of speech or artificial elegance of language is also a healthy perennial, nurtured in literary scholarship and criticism as well as lay comment. Hence the second of the two meanings of *rhetorical* in *Webster's New Collegiate Dictionary* is "emphasizing style, often at the expense of thought." Here we encounter a second obscuring or limiting factor in our attempt at definition. We are to describe rhetoric in terms of those *elements* of a verbal composition for which it is to be held responsible. This mode of procedure has always been attractive. It can produce interesting and plausible conclusions, and it can be defended as schematically satisfying and pedagogically convenient. Thus, it proved in the *trivium* of the Middle Ages and Renaissance. If grammar has charge of the correctness of discourse, and if logic has charge of the intellectual content, then it is natural to assign to rhetoric the management of the language of discourse (or the *elocutio*), and if we do not include poetic in our system, the imaginative and emotional content also.

Another definition in the *New Collegiate Dictionary* points to the identification of rhetoric not with the elements of verbal composition but with the *forms* or *genres:* "The art of expressive speech or of discourse, orig. of oratory, now esp. of literary composition; esp., the art of writing well in prose, as disting. from versification and elocution." This approach is promising and on the whole the most popular through the ages. "Originally of oratory, now especially the art of writing well in prose—" this phrase does well enough as a general description of the scope of rhetoric in ancient Greece, as Baldwin has pointed out, when prose itself was virtually defined as oratory and history, and when even history was composed largely in the spirit of oratory. That is, rhetoric could be the art of prose when prose was predominantly concerned with the intentional, directional energizing of truth, of finding in any given situation all the available means of persuasion, and of using as many of them as good sense dictated.

Even then, however, the weakness of genres as the basis for constructing theories or writing handbooks was evident. What is the art of Plato's dialogues, which are in prose? or of Sappho's compositions, which are poems? Neither poetic nor rhetoric is adequate to either. The difficulty multiplies as variety in the kinds of compositions increases in Roman, Renaissance, and modern times, and as print supplements—and often supplants—speech as the medium of verbal communication. As *poetic,* the art of imitation in language, became crystallized in Roman and Renaissance learning as the theory and practice of the drama (especially tragedy) and the epic, so *rhetoric,* in Quintilian's and Cicero's theory the whole operative philosophy of civil leadership, showed in practice as the art of making winning speeches in the law courts, or later in public exhibitions. The very doctrine in rhetoric of the epideictic or ceremonial speech, as I shall show later, is excellent evidence of the weakness of the types or *genres* as the basis for definition.

All these meanings of rhetoric, in spite of their limitations, contribute something to the exposition of our subject, and the pursuit of each has yielded lucrative insights into the subject, or at least into the problem. Some of them, especially rhetoric as bombast, as excessive ornamentation, and as deceit, are evidence of the falling off of rhetoricians from time to time from the broad philosophy of the art which they inherited from the founders. For a redefinition, therefore, I know no better way of beginning than to return to that broad philosophy.

Working Definition of Rhetoric

First of all and primarily, therefore, I take rhetoric to be the *rationale of informative and suasory discourse.* All its other meanings are partial or morally-colored derivatives from that primary meaning. This rhetoric has been, at least since Aristotle; and at least since Aristotle there has existed a comprehensive, fundamental codification of its principles. It would be idolatrous to suggest that Aristotle uttered the first and last authentic words on rhetoric, or that his system is still adequate, or that it was completely satisfactory even for the Greeks of his day. Like his poetic theory, however, it enjoys unequalled scientific eminence in its field though it has sustained many additions and modifications through the centuries. Its limitations are historical rather than philosophical. Like the limitations of his poetic, the limitations of his rhetoric derive mainly from his failure to consider phenomena which had not yet occurred and to make use of learnings which had not yet been developed.

Now as then, therefore, what Aristotle said of the nature and principles of public address, of the discovery of all the available means of persuasion in any given case, must stand as the broad background for any sensible rhetorical system. Much of Aristotle's formulation, even in detail, survives ungainsaid and can only be rearranged and paraphrased by subsequent writers. Again to cite a parallel with his poetic: though the relative impor- tance of plot in drama has shifted radically since Aristotle, when good plots are made their excellences will still be best discovered by the application of Aristotle's criteria. Similarly, though modern psychology is very different from that of the Greeks, and doubtless more scientific, modern enlightenment has produced no new method of analyzing an audience which can replace Aristotle's.

Aristotle, however, identified rhetoric with persuasion. His chief interests lay in the speaking to popular audiences in the law court and in the legislative assembly, and his system of classification and analysis obviously was framed with those types of speaking as its principal object. Some means of persuasion, however, in spite of Aristotle's comprehensive definition, are not within the scope of rhetoric. Gold and guns, for example, are certainly persuasive, and the basic motives which make them persuasive, profit and self-preservation, may enter the field of rhetoric; but applied directly to the persons to be persuaded, guns and gold belong to commerce or coercion, not to rhetoric.

No more shall we admit the persuasive use of all symbols as belonging to rhetoric. Undoubtedly the persuasive force of pictures, colors, designs, nonlanguage sounds such as foghorns and fire alarms, and all such devices of symbolic significance is great and useful. Traffic lights, however, are not normally agents of rhetorical influence. No more, in themselves, are elephants, donkeys, lions, illuminated bottles of whiskey, or animated packs of cigarettes. Their use has a kinship to rhetoric, and when they are organized in a matrix of verbal discourse, they become what Aristotle called the extrinsic or nonartistic means of persuasion. They are instruments of the wielder of public opinion, and they are staples of two techniques which must be recognized as strongly rhetorical—advertising and propaganda. Unless we are to claim practically all interhuman activity as the field of rhetoric, however, some limits must be admitted, even within the field of persuasion. True, in the "new rhetoric" of Kenneth Burke, where the utmost extension rather than practical limit-setting is the aim, any manifestation of "identification," conscious or unconscious, is within rhetoric. Though the classic limitations of rhetoric are too narrow, others are too broad. Therefore I am assuming the traditional limitation to discourse.

Let us look now at Aristotle's apparent failure to include exposition as well as persuasion within rhetoric. Ancillary to persuasion, of course, exposition is clearly included. The idea of *demonstration,* the characteristic result of the logical mode, implies the most perfect exposition for audiences susceptible of reasoned instruction. Furthermore, another aspect of Aristotle's system admits exposition to independent status. At the expense of a slight venture into heresy (though I believe only a benign heresy) I suggest that any systematic construction of human phenomena, even Aristotle's, will either leave out something important and significant, or will include a category, however named, which is, in effect, "miscellaneous." That I think Aristotle did in discussing the rhetoric of the ceremonial or epideictic speech. The success of his categories, even so, is remarkable. The extension and effective application to the ceremonial speech in general of the principles of the persuasive speech whose end is active decision, provide very plausible coverage of that somewhat anomalous form. The threefold, tripartite classification of speeches was too nearly perfect to abandon:

Forensic (time, past; ends, justice and injustice; means, accusation and defense.)

Epideictic (time, present; ends, honor and dishonor; means, praise and blame.)

Deliberative (time, future; ends, the expedient and inexpedient; means, exhortation and dehortation.)

When the problems of what to do with time-present in the system, and with Pericles' funeral oration among the observed phenomena had to be solved, the coincidence was too attractive to be resisted. It provided for a piece of practical realism which no system should be allowed to defeat. Through that adjustment Aristotle admitted within the scope of rhetoric the predominantly literary performance on the one hand and gave an opening on the other for the primarily informative and instructional as well as the demonstrative and exhibitionistic. Through this third category, rhetoric embraces, in a persuasion-centered system, the *docere* and *delectare*, the teach and delight, of the Roman and Renaissance rhetoric-poetic and permits them an independent status outside their strictly ancillary or instrumental functions in persuasion.

Aristotle's system, therefore, and his rationale of effective speaking comprehend with very little violence the art of the good man skilled in speaking of Cicero and Quintilian, or Baldwin's equation of rhetoric to the art of prose whose end is giving effectiveness to truth[8]—effectiveness considered in terms of what happens to an audience, usually a popular or lay audience as distinguished from the specialized or technical audience of the scientific or dialectical demonstration. This distinction, strictly speaking, is a practical rather than a logical limitation, a limitation of degree rather than kind. No matter what the audience, when the speaker evinces skill in getting into their minds, he evinces rhetorical skill.

If the breadth of scope which I have assigned to rhetoric is implicit in Aristotle's system, the basic delimitation of that scope finds early and explicit statement there. Rhetoric is not confined in application to any specific subjects which are exclusively its own. Rhetoric is method, not subject. But if it has no special subjects, neither are all subjects within its province. In its suasory phase, at least, rhetoric is concerned, said Aristotle, only with those questions about which men dispute, that is, with the contingent—that which is dependent in part upon factors which cannot be known for certain, that which can be otherwise. Men do not dispute about what is known or certainly knowable by them. Hence the characteristic concern of rhetoric is broadly with questions of justice and injustice, of the expedient and the inexpedient (of the desirable and undesirable, of the good and the bad), of praise and blame, or honor and dishonor.

To questions such as these and their almost infinite subsidiary questions, vital and perennial as they are in the practical operation of human society, the best answers can never be certain but only more or less probable. In reasoning about them, men at best must usually proceed from probable premise to probable conclusion, seldom from universal to universal. Hence Aristotle described the basic instrument of rhetoric, the enthymeme, as a kind of syllogism based on probabilities and signs.

Rhetoric, therefore, is distinguished from the other instrumental studies in its preoccupation with informed opinion rather than with scientific demonstration. It is the counterpart, said Aristotle, of dialectic. Strictly speaking, dialectic also may be said to attain only probability, not scientific certainty, like physics (and, perhaps, theology). The methodology, however, is the methodology of formal logic and it deals in universals. Hence it arrives at a very high degree of probability, for it admits the debatable only in the assumption of its premises. Rhetoric, however, because it normally deals with matters of uncertainty for the benefit of popular audiences, must admit probability not only in its premises but in its method also. This is the ground upon which Plato first, and hundreds of critics since, have attacked rhetoric —that it deals with opinion rather than knowledge. This is the ground also from which certain scholars have argued,[9] after some of the medieval fathers, that rhetoric really deals, characteristically, not with genuine probability but only with adumbration and suggestion. It is, they say, distinguished from dialectic in *degree* of probability—dialectic very high, and rhetoric very low.

The epistemological question is interesting and, in a world of philosophers where only certain knowledge was ever called upon to decide questions of human behavior, it would be the central question. Rhetoric exists, however, because a world of certainty is not the world of human affairs. It exists because the world of human affairs is a world where there must be an alternative to certain knowledge on the one hand and pure chance or whimsey on the other. The alternative is informed opinion, the nearest approach to knowledge which the circumstances of decision in any given case will permit. The art, or science, or method whose realm this is, is rhetoric. Rhetoric, therefore, is the method, the strategy, the organon of the principles for deciding best the undecidable questions, for arriving at solutions of the unsolvable problems, for instituting method in those vital phases of human activity where no method is inherent in the total subject matter of decision. The resolving of such problems is the province of the "Good man skilled in speaking." It always has been, and it is still. Of that there can be little question. And the comprehensive rationale of the functioning of that good man so far as he is skilled in speaking, so far as he is a wielder of public opinion, is rhetoric.

The Problems of Vocabulary in This Essay

Traditionally *rhetoric* and *oratory* have been the standard terms for the theory and the product. The *rhetor* was the speaker, the addresser of the public, or the teacher of speaking; the *rhetorician,* the teacher of rhetoric or the formulator of the principles of rhetoric. Hence, the special bias of the terms as I use them has been and probably still is oral. That is a practical bias and is not carelessly to be thrown away. From the beginning of publication in writing, however, essentially rhetorical performances, whether already spoken or to be spoken, have been committed to paper and circulated to be read rather than heard—from Isocrates' *Panathenaicus* or Christ's *Sermon on the Mount* to Eisenhower's message on the state of the nation. Furthermore, for centuries now, especially since the invention and cheapening of the art of printing, the agitator, the teacher, the preacher, the wielder of public opinion has used the press quite independently of the platform. Hence, obviously, rhetoric must be understood to be the rationale of informative and suasory discourse both spoken and written: of Milton's *Aeropagitica* as well as Cromwell's Address to the Rump Parliament; of John Wilkes' *North Briton* as well as Chatham's speech on the repeal of the Stamp Act; of Tom Paine's *Common Sense* as much as Patrick Henry's Address to the Virginia Assembly; of Swift's pamphlet on the *Conduct of the Allies* as well as Dr. Sacheverell's sermon on Passive Obedience; of George Sokolsky's syndicated columns in the press equally with Edward R. Murrow's radio commentaries or Kenneth McFarland's appearances before conventions of the Chambers of Commerce. I will use *rhetoric* and *rhetorical* with that breadth of scope.

Furthermore, the terms *orator* and *oratory* have taken on, like *rhetoric* itself, rather limited or distorted meanings, not entirely undeserved perhaps, which make them no longer suitable for the designation of even the normal *oral* rhetorical performance. *Practitioner of public address,* or some such hyphenated monstrosity as *speaker-writer,* might be used as a generic term for the user of rhetoric, but the disadvantages of such manipulations of vocabulary are obvious. I am using the terms *speech* and *speaker* for both written and oral performance and written and oral performer, unless the particular circumstances obviously imply one or the other. Likewise, in place of such a formula as *listener-reader,* I shall use *audience,* a usage not uncommon anyway.

One must face still another problem of vocabulary, that of the term *rhetoric* in the three distinguishable senses in which I use it: (1) as the rationale of informative and suasory discourse, a body of principle and precept for the creation and analysis of speeches; (2) as a quality which characterizes that kind of discourse and distinguishes it from other kinds; (3) as a study of the phenomenon of informative and suasory discourse in the social context. Similarly, I fear, the term *rhetorician* will sometimes mean the formulator and philosopher of rhetorical theory; sometimes the teacher of the technique of discourse; sometimes the speaker with rhetorical intention; and finally the student or scholar whose concern is the literary or social or behavioral study of rhetoric. I have been tempted to invent terms to avoid certain of these ambiguities, such as *logology,* or even *rhetoristic* (parallel with *sophistic*), but the game would probably not be worth the candle.

In summary, rhetoric is the rationale of informative and suasory discourse, it operates chiefly in the areas of the contingent, its aim is the attainment of maximum probability as a basis for public decision, it is the organizing and animating principle of all subject matters which have a relevant bearing on that decision. Now let us turn to the question of the subject matters in which rhetoric most characteristically functions and of the relations it bears to special subject matters.

Subjects of Rhetorical Discourse

Wrote Aristotle, "The most important subjects of general deliberation . . . are practically five, viz. finance, war and peace, the defense of the country, imports and exports, and legislation." This is still the basic list, though legislation now would be far more generally inclusive than it was to the Athenian assembly. In addition, within the scope of rhetorical discourse fall the subjects of forensic address—crime and its punishment and all the concerns of justice and injustice. Furthermore, the concerns of teaching, preaching—moral, intellectual, practical, and spiritual instruction and exhortation—and commercial exploitation, wherever the problems of adaptation of idea and information to the group mind are concerned, depend upon rhetorical skill for their fruition. Thus, we are brought again to the position that the rhetorical factor is pervasive in the operative aspects of society.

Does this mean that the speaker must be a specialist in all subjects, as well as in rhetorical method? Cicero seemed willing to carry the demands thus far, at least in establishing his ideal orator; and this implication has been ridiculed from Plato onwards for the purpose of discrediting first the claims of the sophists and then all men "skilled in speaking." Plainly, in practice and in plausible human situations, the suggestion is absurd. Does the public speaker or the columnist or the agitator have to be a military specialist in order rightly to urge peace or war? Does the citizen have to be a dentist and a chemist and a pathologist intelligently to advocate the use of fluorine in the municipal water supply? He does not become a specialist in these fields, of course, any more than the head of an industrial plant is the technical master of the specialties of all the men who serve under him. "He attempts to learn the authorities and sources of information in each, and to develop a method which he can apply to specific problems as they arise. He learns, in any given situation, what questions to ask and to answer.

The peculiar contribution of the rhetorician is the discovery and use, to the common good, of those things which move men to [understanding and] action."[10] Looked at another way, the relation of rhetoric to the subject-matters of economics, or public health, or theology, or chemistry, or agriculture is like the relation of hydraulic engineering to water, under the specific circumstances in which the engineer is to construct his dam or his pumping station or his sewage system, and in view of the specific results he is to obtain. He develops a method for determining what questions to ask and answer from all that which can be known about water. If he is a good hydraulics engineer, he will see to it that his relevant knowledge is sound, as the good speaker will see to it that his relevant knowledge of hydraulic engineering is the best obtainable if he is to urge or oppose the building of a dam in the St. Lawrence River. If either is ignorant, or careless, or dishonest, he is culpable as a man and as a rhetorician or hydraulics engineer.

It was not the scientific chronologist, the astronomer Lord Macclesfield, who secured the adoption in England of the Gregorian calendar, thoroughly as he understood the subject in all its mathematical, astronomical, and chronometrical aspects. It was the Earl of Chesterfield, learning from the chronologist all that was essential to the particular situation, and knowing rhetoric and the British Parliament, who was able to impress upon his fellows not necessarily the validity of the calculations but the desirability and the feasibility of making a change. If the truth of scientific knowledge had been left to its own inherent force with Parliament, we would doubtless be many more days out of phase with the sun than England was in 1751. As Aristotle observed in his brief and basic justification of rhetoric, truth itself has a tendency to prevail over error; but in competition with error, where skillful men have an interest in making error prevail, truth needs the help of as attractive and revealing a setting as possible. In the Kingdom of Heaven, truth may be its own sole advocate, but it needs mighty help if it is to survive in health among the nations on earth. As Fielding wrote of prudence in *Tom Jones:* "It is not enough that your designs, nay, that your actions, are intrinsically good; you must take care that they shall appear so. If your inside be never so beautiful, you must preserve a fair outside also. This must be constantly looked to."[11]

In this sense even honest rhetoric is fundamentally concerned with appearances, not to the disregard of realities as Plato and his successors have industriously charged, but to the enforcement of realities. Rhetoric at the command of honest men strives that what is desirable shall appear desirable, that what is vicious shall appear vicious. It intends that the true or probably true shall seem so, that the false or doubtful shall be vividly realized for what it is. A bridge or an automobile or a clothes-line must not only *be* strong but must *appear* to be so. This fact has been an obstacle to the use of many new structural materials. Accustomed to an older kind, we have been reluctant to accept the adequacy of a new, more fragile-seeming substance. Hence, one important reason for surrounding steel columns with stone pillars is the necessity of making them seem as strong as their predecessors. Appearances, then, must be the concern of the wielder of public opinion, the rhetorician. Through ignorance or malice, to be sure, skill in establishing appearances may be applied to deceive. This is a grave peril which must be the concern of all men of good will. Knowledge of the devices of sophistry will always be acquired by those whose purposes are bad; ignorance of them will provide no defense for the rest. No great force can be used without hazard, or ignored without hazard. The force understood, rather than the force not understood, is likely to be the force controlled. That understanding is provided by rhetoric, the technique of discourse addressed to the enlightenment and persuasion of the generality of mankind —the basic instrument for the creation of informed public opinion and the consequent expedient public action.

Occasions of Rhetorical Discourse

Whether we will or no, we cannot escape rhetoric, either the doing or the being done to. We require it. As Edmund Burke wrote, "Men want reasons to reconcile their minds to what is done, as well as motives originally to act right."[12] Whether we seek advice or give it, the nature of our talk, as being "addressed," and of the talk of which we are the audience, as being addressed to us, necessitates speaking the language of the audience or we had as well not speak at all. That process is the core of rhetoric. It goes on as genuinely, and is often managed as skillfully, over the frozen-meats counter of the local supermarket as in the halls of Congress; on the benches in front of the Boone County Court House on Saturday afternoon before election as below the benches of the Supreme Court the next Wednesday morning; around the table where a new labor contract is being negotiated as in the pulpit of Sainte-Marie de Chaillot where Bossuet is pronouncing the funeral oration upon Henriette d'Angleterre; in the Petition from Yorkshire to King George III for redress of grievances as in the Communist Manifesto or the Declaration of Independence.

As we are teachers, and as we are taught, we are involved with rhetoric. The success of the venture depends on a deliberate or instinctive adjustment of idea-through-speaker-to-audience-in-a-particular-situation. Pedagogy is the rhetoric of teaching, whether formally in the classroom or the book, or informally in the many incidental situations of our days and nights. The psychological principle, for example, that we learn through association becomes a rhetorical principle when we use it to connect one day's lesson with what has gone before. It is the same principle by which Burke attempted to establish in the minds of the House of Commons the rights of American colonists when he identified the colonists with Englishmen, whose rights were known.

As we are readers of newspapers and magazines and all such information-giving and opinion-forming publications, and as we write for them, we are receiving or initiating rhetorical discourse, bad or good, effective or ineffective. The obligations of the journalist as investigator of the facts, as thinker about the facts, as discoverer of ideas and analyst and critic of ideas, are fundamental. They demand all the knowledge and skill that the political, scientific, and technical studies can provide. The journalist's distinctive job, however, is writing for his audience the highest grade of informative and suasory discourse that the conditions of his medium will permit. Whether editorial writer, commentator, or plain newswriter, reaching into his audience's mind is his problem. If the people who buy the paper miss the import, the paper might as well not be published. Call it *journalism* if you choose; it is the rhetoric of the press: "it is always public opinion that the press seeks to change, one way or another, directly or indirectly."[13] Seldom can the journalist wait for the solution of a problem before getting into the fray, whether the question be a more efficient way of handling municipal finances or independence for India. He must know the right questions to ask and the bases for answering them with greatest probability for his audience now. That is his rhetorical knowledge.

The same is true of the radio and television news reporter, news analyst, and commentator. He must have rhetorical skill to survive in his occupation, and he must have knowledge and integrity if his effect is to be beneficial rather than destructive to informed public opinion. His staple, also, whether good or bad, is rhetoric. His efforts are aimed at the public mind and are significant only as they affect the public mind. If he is an honest rhetorician, he does not imply of most things, "It is so because," but only "I believe so because"; or "I recommend so because it seems probable where I cannot be sure." If he is tempted into exploiting the force of extravagant and authoritative assertion, his morals rather than his rhetoric have gone awry. Whether the use be honest or dishonest, the instrument is rhetoric.

It is obvious and commonplace that the agitator, the political speaker, the pamphleteer, the advocate, the preacher, the polemicist and apologist, the adviser of kings and princes, the teacher of statesmen, the reformer and counter-reformer, the fanatic in religion, diet, or economics, the mountebank and messiah, have enhanced the stature of a noble discourse or have exploited a degraded, shallow, and dishonest discourse. It matters not that we resort to exalted names for the one—eloquence, genius, philosophy, logic, discourse of reason; and for the other, labels of reproach and contempt—sophistry, glibness, demagoguery, chicanery, "rhetoric." That naming process itself is one of the most familiar techniques of rhetoric. The fact is that in their characteristic preoccupation with manipulating the public mind, they are one. They must not all be approved or emulated, but they must all be studied as highly significant social phenomena, lest we be ignorant of them, and hence powerless before them, for good or for ill.

Similarly, though perhaps not so easily acceptable into rhetoric, we must recognize most of what we know as advertising, salesmanship, propaganda, "public relations," and commercial, political, and national "information" services. I shall have some special consideration to give to these later. At present I merely cite them as great users of rhetoric. In this day of press, radio, and television perhaps their rhetoric is that most continuously and ubiquitously at work on the public.

Relations of Rhetoric to Other Learnings

These, then, are fundamental rhetorical situations. In them, human beings are so organizing language as to effect a change in the knowledge, the understanding, the ideas, the attitudes, or the behavior of other human beings. Furthermore, they are so organizing that language as to make the change as agreeable, as easy, as active, and as secure as possible—as the

Roman rhetoric had it, to teach, to delight, and to move (or to bend). What makes a situation rhetorical is the focus upon accomplishing something predetermined and directional with an audience. To that end many knowledges and sciences, concerning both what is external to audiences and what applies to audiences themselves, may be involved, many of which I have discussed in a previous essay.[14] These knowledges, however, have to be organized, managed, given places in strategy and tactics, set into coordinated and harmonious movement toward the listener as the end, toward what happens to him and in him. In short, they have to be *put to use,* for, as Bacon said, studies themselves "teach not their own use; but that is a wisdom without them, and above them, won by observation." "Studies themselves do give forth directions too much at large, except they be bounded in by experience."[15] Rhetoric teaches their use toward a particular end. It is that "observation," that "experience" codified, given a rationale. Other learnings are chiefly concerned with the discovery of ideas and phenomena and of their relations to each other within more or less homogeneous and closed systems. Rhetoric is primarily concerned with the relations of ideas to the thoughts, feelings, motives, and behavior of men. Rhetoric as distinct from the learnings which it uses is dynamic; it is concerned with movement. It *does* rather than *is*. It is method rather than matter. It is chiefly involved with bringing about a condition, rather than discovering or testing a condition. Even psychology, which is more nearly the special province of rhetoric than is any other study, is descriptive of conditions, but not of the uses of those conditions.

So far as it is method, rhetoric is like the established procedures of experimental science and like logic. As the method for solving problems of human action in the areas of the contingent and the probable, however, it does not enjoy a privilege which is at the same time the great virtue and the great limitation of science and logic—it cannot choose its problems in accordance with the current capacities of its method, or defer them until method is equal to the task. Rhetoric will postpone decision as long as feasible; indeed one of its most valuable uses in the hands of good men, is to prevent hasty and premature formulation of lines of conduct and decision. In this it is one with science—and good sense. But in human affairs, where the whole is usually greater than the most complete collection of the parts, decisions—makings up of the mind—cannot always wait until all the contingencies have been removed and solutions to problems have been tested in advance. Rhetoric, therefore, must take undemonstrable problems and do its best with them when decision is required. We must decide when the blockade is imposed whether to withdraw from Berlin or to undertake the air lift, not some time later when perhaps some of the contingencies may have been removed. And the making of the choice forever precludes trying out and testing the other possibilities under the circumstances which would have prevailed had we chosen differently at first. Likewise, we must make a choice on the first Tuesday in November, whether we are scientifically sure or not. In each case, rhetoric, good or bad, must be the strategy of enlightening opinion for that choice.

To restate our central idea still another way: rhetoric, or the rhetorical, is the function in human affairs which governs and gives direction to that creative activity, that process of critical analysis, that branch of learning, which address themselves to the whole phenomenon of the designed use of language for the promulgation of information, ideas, and attitudes. Though it is instrumental in the discovery of ideas and information, its characteristic function is the publication, the publicizing, the humanizing, the animating of them for a realized and usually specific audience. At its best it seeks the "energizing of truth," in order to make "reason and the will of God prevail." But except in science, and no doubt theology, the promulgation of *truth*, sure or demonstrable, is out of the question. Normally the rhetorical function serves as high a degree of probability as the combination of subject, audience, speaker, and occasion admits. Rhetoric may or may not be involved (though the speaker-writer must be) in the determination of the validity of the ideas being promulgated. Such determination will be the province in any given situation of philosophy, ethics, physics, economics, politics, eugenics, medicine, hydraulics, or bucolics. To rhetoric, however, and to no other rationale, belongs the efficiency—the validity if you will—of the relations in the idea-audience-speaker situation.

Functioning of Rhetoric

We are ready now, perhaps, if we have not been ready much sooner, to proceed to the question of how rhetoric works, what it accomplishes in an audience. Speaking generally, we may say that the rhetorical function is the *function of adjusting ideas to people and people to ideas*. This process may be thought of as a continuum from the complete modification or accommodation of ideas to audiences (as is sometimes said, "telling people only what they want to hear") at the one extreme, to complete regeneration at the other (such perfect illumination that the "facts speak for themselves"). This continuum may, therefore, be said to have complete flattery (to use Plato's unflattering epithet) at one end and the Kingdom of Heaven at the other! Good rhetoric usually functions somewhere well in from the extremes. There, difficult and strange ideas have to be modified without being distorted or invalidated; and audiences have to be prepared through the mitigation of their prejudices, ignorance, and irrelevant sets of mind without being dispossessed of their judgments. The adjustment of ideas to people, for example, was being undertaken by the Earl of Chatham in his speech for the repeal of the Stamp Act, when he agreed that Parliament had legislative supremacy over the Colonies but that legislative supremacy did not include the right to tax without representation. And when Booker T. Washington assured the southern white folk that they and the Negroes could be as separate as the fingers in social affairs and as united as the hand in economic, he was adjusting people to the idea of real freedom for his race.

The moral disturbances which rhetoric and rhetorical activity seem to breed do not usually result from this process of mutual accommodation itself. Most of them arise when the speaker tries so to adjust ideas to people that the ideas are basically falsified, or when he attempts so to adjust people to ideas as to deform or anesthetize the people. Report has it that after Senator Hiram Johnson had campaigned through rural New England charging that England would have three votes to one for the United States in the League of Nations, he was taxed by a critic with misrepresenting the nature of the British Empire. One could not assume, so Johnson's critic declared, that Canada and South Africa would vote with England as a single bloc. "That may be," Johnson is said to have replied, "but New England farmers do not know the nature of the British Empire, and they do know common arithmetic." That is adjusting ideas to people so far as to falsify the basic idea. In the other direction, stimulating the "Red-menace-in-the-air-we-breathe" terror in order to adjust people to the idea of giving up their right of dissent is an effort to dispossess people of their judgments.

In terms of the old, but still convenient, faculty psychology, the terms in which rhetoric is most frequently attacked—reason, imagination, passions (emotions), judgment, will—rhetoric may still be described as the method of applying "reason to imagination for the better moving of the will." To complete our broad idea of the scope of rhetoric we should add "and the better clarification of the understanding." That is Francis Bacon's succinct statement of how rhetoric functions in the audience,[16] and it is still a good one. It establishes rhetoric squarely as an instrumental learning which manages the creative powers of the whole logical-psychological man toward a single dynamic end.

Rhetoric, therefore, has the greatest possible involvement with the logical and psychological studies. These learnings must be the core of the speaker's equipment. They are the *sine qua non* in the knowledge through which rhetoric must function. In the good rhetoric which Plato described in the *Phaedrus,* after knowledge of the truth, he saw the equipment of the rhetorically skilled man to consist in knowledge of the various possible kinds of arguments, knowledge of the various kinds of souls, and knowledge of which kinds of souls will be affected by which kinds of arguments—that is, knowledge of the rational processes and knowledge of the mutual adaptation of these processes to audiences. Furthermore, in the great counter-Platonic *Rhetoric* of Aristotle, the first Book is devoted chiefly to the rational processes of rhetoric, and the next Book is the first extant comprehensive treatise on individual and group psychology. Likewise, in one of the best of the recent books on liberal education, which is, therefore, something like a basic statement on rhetoric, Hoyt Hudson sees the fundamental equipment of the liberally educated man to require three parts: the Arm of Information, the Arm of Operative Logic, and the Arm of Imagination.[17] Of these, in practical affairs, rhetoric is based on the second and third, and the first must be the starting place of the speaker in each particular situation.

Where in this pattern, then, does emotion come in, that famous roughneck who is said to spoil the rational life and vitiate the logic of behavior? As Hudson and many others have observed, and as Bacon knew well, emotion is a derivative of both reason and imagination. Love of truth and of the good life must be the results of any genuinely rational functioning, that is, of operative logic; and vivid realization of experience, which is imagination, can hardly occur without those strong emotional accompaniments which, in practice, have given rise to the identifying of emotion with imagination. This point seems hardly to need laboring over again. Hudson's book gives it adequate coverage, and I have summarized the traditional position of rhetoric and rhetoricians on it in the essay already mentioned.[18]

The position is that a complete rhetoric, and that is the kind of rhetoric which we are discussing, knows the whole man and seeks to bring to bear the whole man in achieving its ends—what he is and what he thinks he is, what he believes and what he thinks he believes, what he wants and what he tells himself he wants. Toward its special ends, rhetoric recognizes the primacy of rational processes, their primacy in time as well as in importance, as Bacon's definition implies—applying reason to the imagination. Just so poetry recognizes the primacy for its purposes of the imagination. But rhetoric has always been akin to poetry—for long periods of history it has in fact annexed poetry—in its recognition of the honest and highly important power of imagination and of that emotion which does not supplant but supports reason, and sometimes even transcends it. Thus, Sir Philip Sidney and most literary theorists of the Renaissance attributed to poetry the distinctly rhetorical function of using imagination to create what might be called historical fictions to give power and life to ideas. Rhetoric recognizes the strength of the fictions men live by, as well as those they live under;[19] and it aims to fortify the one and explode the other. Rhetoric aims at what is *worth* doing, what is *worth* trying. It is concerned with *values,* and values are established with the aid of imaginative realization, not through rational determination alone; and they gain their force through emotional animation.

We have observed that psychology, human nature, has been a staple of rhetorical learning through the ages. No doubt, therefore, scientific psychology will have more and more to contribute to modern rhetoric. The first notable attempt to ground rhetoric in a systematic modern psychology was made by George Campbell in his *Philosophy of Rhetoric* (1776), in which he stated as his purpose

> to exhibit . . . a tolerable sketch of the human mind; and, aided by the lights which the poet and the orator so amply furnish, to disclose its secret movements, tracing its principal channels of perception and action, as near as possible, to their source: and, on the other hand, from the science of human nature, to ascertain with greater precision, the radical principles of that art, whose object it is, by the use of language, to operate on the soul of the hearer, in the way of informing, convincing, pleasing, moving, or persuading.[20]

That same purpose governs our contemporary writers of treatises and textbooks on public speaking, argumentation, and persuasion, and most of them include as up-to-date a statement as possible of the psychological and the rational bases of rhetoric. It is a commonplace that of the studies recently come to new and promising maturity, psychology, especially social psychology, and cultural anthropology have much to teach modern rhetoric and to correct or reinterpret in traditional rhetoric. The same may be said of the various new ventures into the study of meaning, under the general head of semantics. How language *means* is obviously important to the rationale of informative and suasory discourse. Nevertheless, in spite of I. A. Richards' book,[21] the theory of meaning is not *the* philosophy of rhetoric, any more than is the psychology of perception. Rhetoric is the organizer of all such for the wielding of public opinion.

Advertising, Salesmanship, and Propaganda

Now that we have sketched the rhetorical process functioning at its best for the exposition and dissemination of ideas in the wielding of public opinion, with the ethical and pathetic modes of proof in ancillary relation to the logical, with the imagination aiding and reinforcing the rational, let us turn to some of the partial, incomplete, perhaps misused, rhetorics which I have already mentioned briefly.

It is axiomatic that men do not live by reason alone or even predominantly, though reason is such a highly prized commodity and stands in so high a repute even among the unreasoning and unreasonable, that men prefer to tell themselves and to be told that they make up their minds and determine their choices from reason and the facts. Intellectual activity, both learning and thinking, is so difficult that man tends to avoid it wherever possible. Hence, education has almost always put its first efforts into cultivating the reasonable portion of the mind rather than the imaginative or emotional. Furthermore, the strength and accessibility of imaginative and emotional responses is so great in spite of education that though men seldom make effective reasonable decisions without the help of emotion, they often make, or appear to make, effective emotional decisions without the help of rational processes or the modification of reasonable consideration. Inevitably, therefore, the available reason in rhetorical situations will vary tremendously, and the assistance which imagination must provide toward the moving of the will must vary accordingly. Except in Swift's unexciting land of the Houyhnhnms, however, imagination will always be there.

Ever since men first began to weave the web of words to charm their fellows, they have known that some men can impose their wills on others through language in despite of reason. Almost as long, other men have deplored and feared this talent. If the talent were wholly a matter of divine gift and were wholly unexplainable, the only alternative to succumbing to the orator would be to kill him. In time it appeared, however, that this skill could be learned, in part at least, and could be analyzed. Thus, if it were good, men could learn to develop it further; and if it were bad, they could be armed in some measure against it. Hence rhetoric, and hence the partial rhetoric of anti-reason and pseudo-reason. And hence the appeal of such rhetorical eruptions as Aldous Huxley's total condemnation of oratory in *The Devils of Loudon.* [22] His indictment of public speakers is indeed skillful, and ought to be taken seriously. If the talent of his golden-voiced Grandiers be indeed magic, then we will have to agree that the fate of man before such wizards is hopeless. Rhetoric teaches, however, that the method and the power of this kind of discourse can be analyzed, at least in large part, and if its subtleties cannot be wholly *learned* by every ambitious speaker, the characteristics of its operation can be understood, and if understood, then controlled, for better or for worse. [23]

The oratory which Huxley would extirpate presents a rewarding approach to the rhetoric of advertising and propaganda, of which it is the historic prototype. In them, the techniques of suggestion, reiteration, imaginative substitution, verbal irrelevance and indirection, and emotional and pseudological bullying have been developed beyond, one might hazard a guess, the fondest dreams of the sophists and the historic demagogues. This development does not represent a change in intention from them to our contemporaries, but an advance in knowledge and opportunity and media.

If you have a soap or a cigarette or a social order for quick, profitable sale, you do not neglect any method within your ethical system of making that sale. That is the paramount problem of the advertiser and the propagandist, and their solutions are very much alike. They are rhetorical solutions, at their best very carefully gauged to the mass audience, adapted to special audiences, and varying basically only as the initial sale or the permanent customer is the principal object. What advertising is in commerce, propaganda is in politics, especially international politics. Neither scorns reason or the likeness of reason, the rhetoric of information and logical argument, if the message and the audience seem to make that the best or only means to the sale. Neither, on the other hand, prefers that method to the shorter, quicker ways to unconsidered action. They concentrate—forcibly where possible, rhetorically where necessary—on the exclusion of competing ideas, on the short-circuiting or by-passing of informed judgment. By preference they do not seek to balance or overbalance alternative ideas or courses of action; they seek to obliterate them, to circumvent or subvert the rational processes which tend to make men weigh and consider. As Adlai Stevenson said, slogans, the common staple of advertising and propaganda, "are normally designed to get action without reflection."

That advertising should enjoy a happier reputation than propaganda in a competitive, commercial-industrial nation such as the United States, which is only just now learning the term *psychological warfare,* is not to be wondered at. We do not have a public service institution for the defensive analysis of advertising, like the Institute of Propaganda Analysis, which assumed that propaganda is something from which we must learn to protect ourselves. The ethical superiority of our advertising is no doubt a compliment to our dominant business code—and to our laws. Still, if one wishes to know what the ungoverned rhetoric of advertising can be, he may get a suggestion by listening to some of what is beamed to us from certain radio stations south of the border.

The kinship of advertising and salesmanship, and their somewhat denatured relatives "public relations" and "promotion," to conventional public address, the established vehicle of rhetoric, may be embarrassing at times, but it must be acknowledged. The family resemblance is too strong to be ignored and too important to be denied. The omnipresence of the rhetoric of advertising, as I have suggested, gives it a standing which must be reckoned with, no matter what opinion the student of public address may hold of it. The rhetoric of public address, in this country at least, must function, whether or no, in a public mind which is steeped in the rhetoric of advertising, a rhetoric whose dominating principles must be recognized as adaptations of a portion of the fundamentals of any rhetoric. One need only compare a textbook or handbook of advertising methods with standard, conventional rhetorics—textbooks in public speaking and persuasion —especially in the handling of such topics as interest, suggestion, and motivation, to be convinced of the coincidence of method if not of philosophic outlook. Many times in adult evening classes in public speaking have I heard speeches on the secrets of successful salesmanship, and as often have

I found myself being offered a more or a less competent parody of certain portions of our textbook, which for some reason the student had omitted to read. Not by mere chance, one must confess, does the nonacademic public take great interest in the four "miracle" courses to be found among the offerings of many universities—advertising, salesmanship, psychology, and effective speaking. Nor is it remarkable, though one may think it deplorable, that appearances of the officers of our national government before the mass audience of the citizens are characteristic products of the country's leading advertising agencies.

Likewise propaganda and its brother "information" borrow and refine upon certain portions of rhetoric. No doubt it serves a useful purpose to identify propaganda with the vicious forces in the modern world, with the German government of World War I and with the Nazi and Soviet totalitarianisms of the present time. At the same time, however, it would be the better part of wisdom to recognize that most of the major techniques of this propaganda are long-known rhetorical techniques gone wrong, that propaganda is not a new invention which we have no ready equipment for combatting, let alone fumigating and using for our honorable ends. The understanding of propaganda will be founded in the understanding of rhetoric first of all, whatever else may be necessary.[24] Both Ross Scanlan and Kenneth Burke have demonstrated the enlightenment which can come from the application of rhetorical criticism to both the internal and external propaganda of the Nazis;[25] and two articles by Scanlan and Henry C. Youngerman in the first issue of *Today's Speech* (April 1953) are grounded on the assumption of a close kinship between rhetoric (or its corollary, "public address") and propaganda.[26] In fact, one of Scanlan's concluding statements indirectly makes both the identification and the basic distinction: "Today it is to be hoped that America will find means to match enemy propaganda in effectiveness without sacrificing the standards of morality and intellect that distinguish democracy from the totalitarian order."

Rhetoric as a Method of Inquiry

More than once in the preceding pages I have in passing assigned to rhetoric a secondary function of the discovery of ideas, contributory to its prime function of the popularizing of ideas. That is the consequence of the division of *inventio,* the term applied in Roman rhetoric to the systematic investigative procedures by which rhetoric sought to turn up all the relevant arguments or considerations in any given situation. As part of *inventio,* for example, the elaborate doctrine of *status* was developed, through which by the application of analytical criteria it was possible to determine just what was the core, the central issue in any given case, just what had to be proved as a *sine qua non,* and where the lines of argument for proving it would lie if they were available. In general the division of *inventio* constituted a codification of the *topoi* or *places where arguments are to be found;* for instance, in *fact past, fact future, more and less, etc.* Rhetoric, thus, as we have said, provides scientific assistance to the speaker in discovering what questions to ask and how to go about answering them. It serves the speaker as laboratory procedures for analysis serve the chemist—by systematic inventory it enables him to determine with reasonable completeness what is present and what is absent in any given case.

We need not be surprised, therefore, that so useful a method tended to be incorporated into other arts and sciences where its original provenience was often forgotten. Historically, some of the studies to profit greatly from this borrowing from rhetoric have been the law, theology, logic, and poetic.[27] The Polandizing of rhetoric, one of the characteristic phenomena of its history, accounts in large part for the splinter meanings and the distortions which we have seen as typical of its current and historic significance. It has been the fate of rhetoric, the residual term, to be applied to the less intellectual segments of itself, while its central operating division, *inventio,* has been appropriated by the studies and sciences which rhetoric serves.

The functions of a complete rhetoric, however, have usually been operative under whatever temporary auspices as the whole art of discourse, even as they were in the Renaissance tripartite grammar-logic-rhetoric. This splintering may go so far toward specialism, however, that the investigative function of rhetoric, the method of *inventio,* may be diverted from that to which it most properly applies. This diversion may very well be the tendency today, where a complete rhetoric hardly exists as a formal discipline except in those classically oriented courses in public speaking, debate, group discussion, argumentation, and persuasion whose central focus is on *inventio*—the investigation and discovery of lines of argument and basic issues. Mostly rhetoric today survives, as we have seen, under other names and special applications in those specialties which contribute to it or draw upon it or appropriate selectively from its store of method—psychology,

220

advertising, salesmanship, propaganda analysis, public opinion and social control, semantics, and that which is loosely called "research" in common parlance.

May I attempt in summary of this matter to bring rhetoric back to its essential investigative function, its function of discovery, by quoting from Isocrates, the Athenian politico-rhetorical philosopher, and from Edmund Burke, the eighteenth century British statesman-orator? Wrote Isocrates in the *Antidosis*, "With this faculty we both contend against others on matters that are open to dispute and seek light for ourselves on things which are unknown; for the same arguments which we use in persuading others when we speak in public, we employ when we deliberate in our thoughts."[28] Twenty-two centuries later, the young Burke included in his notebook digest of the topics of rhetoric, which he headed "How to Argue," the following succinct, Baconian statement about the functions of *inventio:*

> To invent Arguments without a thorough knowledge of the Subject is clearly impossible. But the Art of Invention does two things—
> 1. It suggests to us more readily those Parts of our actual knowledge which may help towards illustrating the matter before us, &
> 2. It suggests to us heads of Examination which may lead, if pursued with effect, into a knowledge of the Subject. So that the Art of Invention may properly be considered as the method of calling up what we do know, & investigating that of which we are ignorant.[29]

Rhetoric in Education

If the burden of the preceding pages is not misplaced, the importance of rhetoric in the equipment of the well-educated member of society can hardly be in doubt. I am not inclined, therefore, especially in this journal, to offer to demonstrate the desirability of speech as an academic study. Our conventions and our journals have been full of such demonstration for, lo, these thirty years.[30] If enlightened and responsible leaders with rhetorical knowledge and skill are not trained and nurtured, irresponsible demagogues will monopolize the power of rhetoric, will have things to themselves. If talk rather than take is to settle the course of our society, if ballots instead of bullets are to effect our choice of governors, if discourse rather than coercion is to prevail in the conduct of human affairs, it would seem like arrant folly to trust to chance that the right people shall be equipped offensively and defensively with a sound rationale of informative and suasory discourse.

In general education, especially, rhetoric would appear to deserve a place of uncommon importance. That is the burden of a recent article by Dean Hunt of Swarthmore. Rhetoric is the organon of the liberal studies, the formulation of the principles through which the educated man, the possessor of many specialties, attains effectiveness in society.[31] A complete rhetoric is a structure for the wholeness of the effective man, the aim of general education. But, as Dean Hunt concludes, the rhetorician himself must not become a technical specialist:

> He will keep his wholeness if he comes back again and again to Aristotle, but he must supplement those conceptions with what modern scientists have added to the mirror for man; he must illuminate the classical rhetoric with psychology, cultural anthropology, linguistics and semantics, special disciplines, perhaps, but disciplines in which he can lean heavily on interpreters who speak to others than their professional colleagues. Departments of speech which have emphasized training in rhetoric have a new opportunity to establish their place in general education. Their very claim to wholeness has been a source of distrust in an atmosphere of specialism. If now they can relate themselves to newer conceptions in the sciences, social sciences, and humanities, they can show that the ideal of the good man skilled in speaking is like the sea, ever changing and ever the same.[32]

So much for rhetoric in education as a study directed at the creation and at the analysis and criticism of informative and suasory discourse—at the ability, on the one hand, "to summon thought quickly and use it forcibly,"[33] and on the other to listen or read critically with the maximum application of analytical judgment.

Rhetoric would appear thus to be in certain senses a literary study, or as Wichelns wrote, at least "its tools are those of literature." It is a literary study as it is involved in the creative arts of language, of informing ideas. It is a literary study also as it contributes substantially to literary scholarship. Not only have literature and literary theory been persistently rhetorical for long periods—during much of the Renaissance, for example, the seventeenth and eighteenth centuries in England, and for most of the short history of American literature—but writers and readers until fairly recently had been so generally educated in rhetoric that it provided the vocabulary and many of the concepts in terms of which much literature was both written and read. Clark's *Milton at St. Paul's School* may be cited as one conclusive demonstration of the importance of rhetoric in Renaissance education and its importance in Renaissance literature. This importance is now being recognized by literary scholars, and rhetoric is taking on considerable proportions in their studies, especially among those who are studying the Renaissance. Myrick's study of Sir Philip Sidney as a literary craftsman,[34] for example, demonstrates how thoroughly Sidney was schooled in rhetoric and how carefully he constructed his defense of poetry on familiar rhetorical principles. If Myrick has been in error in his construction of the specific genealogy of Sidney's rhetoric, the fact of Sidney's rhetorical system is nevertheless in no doubt.

The plain truth is that whatever the inadequacies in specific cases of the analytical method ingrained in our educated ancestors, they *had* method, the method of formal rhetoric; whereas a general characteristic of our contemporary education is that it inculcates *no* method beyond a rather uncertain grammar and a few rules of paragraphing and bibliography. Rigidity of method is doubtless a grievous obstacle to the greatest fulfillment of genius in either belles-lettres or public address; but the widespread impotence and ineptitude even of our best-educated fellows when faced with the problem of constructing or analyzing any but the most rudimentary expository or argumentative discourse, much less a complicated literary work, are surely worse. Rhetoric supplies the equipment for such practical endeavor in the promulgation of ideas, and twenty centuries have learned to use it to supplement and perfect chance and natural instinct.

That such method has at times become sterile or mechanical, that at other times it has been put to uses for which it was least adapted is amusing, perhaps lamentable, but not surprising. The remote uses to which rhetorical methods of analysis and description have been put, in the absence of a more appropriate method, are well illustrated by the following passage from Sir John Hawkins' *History of Music,* first published in the late eighteenth century:

> The art of invention is made one of the heads among the precepts of rhetoric, to which music in this and sundry instances bears a near resemblance; the end of persuasion, or affecting the passions being common to both. This faculty consists in the enumeration of common places, which are revolved over in the mind, and requires both an ample store of knowledge in the subject upon

which it is exercised, and a power of applying that knowledge as occasion may require. It differs from memory in this respect, that whereas memory does but recall to the mind the images or remembrance of things as they were first perceived, the faculty of invention divides complex ideas into those whereof they are composed, and recommends them again after different fashions, thereby creating variety of new objects and conceptions. Now, the greater the fund of knowledge above spoken of is, the greater is the source from whence the invention of the artist or composer is supplied; and the benefits thereof are seen in new combinations and phrases, capable of variety and permutation without end.[35]

From its lapses and wanderings, however, rhetoric when needed has almost always recovered its vitality and comprehensive scope, by reference to its classic sources. But that it should be ignored seems, as Dean Hunt suggests, hardly a compliment to education.

Rhetoric as a serious scholarly study I have treated in my former essay, and I shall not go over the same ground again. That there is a body of philosophy and principle worth scholarly effort in discovery, enlargement, and reinterpretation is beyond question, and fortunately more competent scholars each year are working at it. Rhetorical criticism and the study of rhetoric as a revealing social and cultural phenomenon are also gaining ground. New and interesting directions for research in these areas are being explored, or at least marked out; they are based on newly developed techniques and hitherto neglected kinds of data. One might mention, for example, those new approaches listed by Maloney:[36] the quantitative content analysis as developed by Lasswell; the qualitative content analysis as used by Lowenthal and Guterman; figurative analysis such as applied to Shakespeare by Caroline Spurgeon; and intonational analysis. Extensive and provocative suggestions are to be found in quantity in the text and bibliography of Brembeck and Howell's *Persuasion: A Means of Social Control*,[37] especially in Part VI. Lucrative also are the new attempts at the analysis of the rhetoric of historical movements, such as Griffin's study of the rhetoric of the anti-Masonic movement and others under way within the Speech Association of America. Elsewhere in this issue [*QJS*] Thonssen's review of recent rhetorical studies illustrates amply both the new and the traditional in rhetorical scholarship; and the section on rhetoric in the annual Haberman bibliography is convincing evidence of the vitality of current enterprise.[38]

Though new avenues, new techniques, new materials such as the forego-

ing are inviting to the increasing numbers of scholars whose interests and
abilities—to say nothing of their necessities—lie in rhetorical research,
especially those new directions which lead to rhetoric as a cultural, a
sociological, a social-psychiatric phenomenon, the older literary-historical-
political studies are still neither too complete nor too good. In any event,
each new generation probably needs to interpret afresh much of the relevant
history of thought, especially the thought of the people as distinguished
from what is commonly considered the history of ideas. For this the scholarship of rhetoric seems particularly adapted. Toward this purpose, I find no
need to relocate the field of rhetorical scholarship as envisioned by Hudson
and Wichelns, nor to recant from the considerations which I outlined in the
QJS in 1937.[39] One may find it reassuring to observe, however, that much
which was asked for in those essays has since then been undertaken and
often accomplished with considerable success. Especially is this true of the
study of public address in its bulk and day-to-day manifestations: in the
movement studies, the "case" studies, the sectional and regional studies, the
studies of "debates" and "campaigns" such as the debates on the League
of Nations and the campaigns for conservation.

There remains much to do, nevertheless, and much to redo in the more
familiar and conventional areas of research and interpretation. The editing
and translation of rhetorical texts is still far from complete or adequate. The
canon of ancient rhetoric is, to be sure, in very good shape, and when
Caplan's translation of the *Ad Herennium* is published in the Loeb Library
there will hardly be a major deficiency. In post-classical, medieval, and
Renaissance rhetoric the situation is not so good, though it is improving.
There are still too few works like Howell's *Rhetoric of Alcuin and Charle-
magne* and Sister Therese Sullivan's commentary on and translation of the
fourth book of St. Augustine's *De Doctrina.* Halm's *Rhetores Minores,* for
example, is substantially unmolested so far.

English and continental rhetoric of the sixteenth, seventeenth, and eighteenth centuries is slowly appearing in modern editions by scholars who
know rhetoric as the theory of public address. Our bibliographies show
increasing numbers of these as doctoral dissertations, most of which, alas,
seem to be abandoned almost as soon as finished. Only a few works of the
sort, like Howell's *Fénelon,* represent mature, published work.

In the history and historical analysis of rhetoric, nothing of adequate
range and scope yet exists. Thonssen and Baird's *Speech Criticism,* ambi-

tious as it is, is only a beginning. The general history of rhetoric, and even most of the special histories, have yet to be written. Works now under way by Donald L. Clark and Wilbur S. Howell will make substantial contributions, but rhetoric from Corax to Whately needs far fuller and better treatment than it gets in the series of histories of criticism by the late J. W. H. Atkins.

Toward the study of the rhetorical principles and practice of individual speakers and writers the major part of our scholarly effort seems to have been directed. The convenience of this kind of study is beyond question and is hard to resist, either in public address or in literature. And this is as it should be. The tendency to write biographies of speakers, however, rather than rhetorico-critical studies of them, must be kept in check, or at least in proportion. Again for reasons of convenience, if not also of scholarly nationalism, the studies of American speakers are proportionately too numerous. British and foreign public address is still far too scantily noticed by competent rhetorical scholars.

Rhetoric and Poetic

This would not be the place, I think, even if Professor Thonssen's review of rhetorical works were not appearing in this same issue of the *QJS*, for a survey of rhetorical scholarship. The preceding paragraphs are intended only as a token of decent respect to accomplishment and progress in a discrete and important branch of humane scholarship. A further area where rhetorical scholarship may be very profitably pursued, however, perhaps deserves some special consideration.

Even if it were not for the contributions of Kenneth Burke, the study of rhetoric in literature and of the relation of the theory of rhetoric to the theory of poetic would be taking on renewed importance at the present time. The lively revival of rhetorical study in Renaissance scholarship which I have mentioned is only one phase of the problem. A renewed or increased interest in satire, deriving in part, perhaps, from the excellent work which of late has been done on Swift, leads directly to rhetoric. The rhetorical mode is obviously at the center of satire, and any fundamental analysis of satire must depend upon the equipment for rhetorical analysis. Likewise, a complete dramatic criticism must draw upon rhetoric, both practically and philosophically. The internal rhetoric of the drama was specifically recognized by Aristotle when he referred readers of the *Poetics* to the *Rhetoric* for coverage of the element of *dianoia,* for the analysis of speeches in which agents try to convince or persuade each other. What, however, is the external rhetoric of the drama? What is the drama intended to do to an audience? Herein lies the question of the province of poetic as opposed to the province of rhetoric. When Antony addresses the Roman citizens in *Julius Caesar,* the existence of an internal rhetoric in the play is clear enough; the relation between Antony and his stage audience is unmistakably rhetorical. But what of the relation between Antony and the audience in the pit, or the Antony-stage-audience combination and the audience in the pit? The more we speculate about the effect of a play or any literary work on an audience, the more we become involved in metaphysical questions in which rhetoric must be involved.

Much contemporary poetry or pseudo-poetry in any generation is rhetorical in the most obvious sense—in the same sense as the epideictic oration. It "pleases" largely by rhetorical means or methods. It "reminds" us of experience instead of "organizing" or "creating" experience. It appeals to our satisfaction with what we are used to; it convinces us that what *was* still may be as it was, that old formulas are pleasantest if not best. It is not so much concerned with pointing up the old elements in the new, even, as establishing the identity of the old and the contemporary. "What oft was thought, but ne'er so well expressed" is a distinctly rhetorical attainment, and it would not have occurred to Pope to suppose that the poetic and the rhetorical were antithetical, if indeed they were separable. Though sporadically the effort of critics and theorists has been to keep *rhetoric* and *poetic* apart, the two rationales have had an irresistible tendency to come together, and their similarities may well be more important than their differences. When the forming of attitude is admitted into the province of rhetoric, then, to Kenneth Burke, rhetoric becomes a method for the analysis of even lyric poetry. Hence, a frequent term in certain kinds of literary analysis now is *poetic-rhetoric,* as for example in the first two sentences in Ruth Wallerstein's analysis of two elegies: "I want this paper to consider two poems, John Donne's elegy on Prince Henry and Milton's *Lycidas,* in the light that is shed on them by seventeenth-century rhetoric-poetic as I understand it. Both the significance of that rhetoric and the test of my view of it will reside in its power to illuminate the poems."[40]

Undoubtedly there are basic differences between *poetic* and *rhetoric,* both practical and philosophical, and probably these differences lie both in the kind of method which is the proper concern of each and the kind of effect on audiences to the study of which each is devoted. The purely poetic seeks the creation or organization of imaginative experience, probably providing for reader or audience some kind of satisfying spiritual or emotional therapy. The rhetorical seeks a predetermined channeling of the audience's understanding or attitude. Poetry works by representation; rhetoric by instigation. The poetic is fulfilled in creation, the rhetorical in illumination. "An image," wrote Longinus, "has one purpose with the orators and another with the poets; . . . the design of the poetic image is enthralment, of the rhetorical, vivid description. Both, however, seek to stir the passions and the emotions. . . . In oratorical imagery its best feature is always its reality and truth."[41] Poetry, declared Sir Philip Sidney, cannot lie because it affirms nothing; it merely presents. Rhetoric not only presents but affirms. That is its characteristic. Both poetic and rhetoric attain their effects through language. If the poet's highest skill lies in his power to make language do what it has never done before, to force from words and the conjunction of words meanings which are new and unique, perhaps it is the highest skill of the speaker to use words in their accepted senses in such a way as to make them carry their traditional meanings with a vividness and effectiveness which they have never known before.

Summary

In brief, we may assign to rhetoric a fourfold status. So far as it is concerned with the management of discourse in specific situations for practical purposes, it is an instrumental discipline. It is a literary study, involving linguistics, critical theory, and semantics as it touches the art of informing ideas, and the functioning of language. It is a philosophical study so far as it is concerned with a method of investigation or inquiry. And finally, as it is akin to politics, drawing upon psychology and sociology, rhetoric is a social study, the study of a major force in the behavior of men in society.

NOTES AND REFERENCES

1. Hoyt H. Hudson, "The Field of Rhetoric," *Quarterly Journal of Speech Education* 9 (April 1923):167–80; Herbert A. Wichelns, "The Literary Criticism of Oratory," *Studies in Rhetoric and Public Speaking in Honor of James Albert Winans* (New York: Century Co., 1925), pp. 181–216; Donald C. Bryant, "Some Problems of Scope and Method in Rhetorical Scholarship," *Quarterly Journal of Speech* 23 (April 1937):182–88, and "Aspects of the Rhetorical Tradition," *Quarterly Journal of Speech* 36 (April and Oct. 1950):169–76, 326–32.

2. *Quarterly Journal of Speech* 37 (Oct. 1951): 281–98.

3. Ibid. (Dec. 1951), pp. 419–29.

4. *Quarterly Journal of Speech* 38 (Feb. 1952):1–12.

5. Ibid. (April 1952), pp. 133–44.

6. *Studies . . . in Honor of James Albert Winans,* pp. 3–60.

7. In his *The Ethics of Rhetoric* (Chicago: Henry Regnery, 1953), Richard M. Weaver, of the College at the University of Chicago, makes an interesting and useful effort to restore rhetoric to a central and respectable position among the arts of language and to assign it the function of giving effectiveness to truth.

8. Charles Sears Baldwin, *Ancient Rhetoric and Poetic* (New York: Macmillan Co., 1924), p. 5.

9. For example, Craig La Drière, "Rhetoric as 'Merely Verbal' Art," *English Institute Essays—1948,* edited by D. A. Robertson, Jr. (New York: Columbia University Press, 1949), pp. 123–52.

10. Hudson, "Field of Rhetoric," p. 177; see note 1.

11. Book III, Chapter 7, Modern Library Edition, p. 97.

12. *Correspondence* (1844), 1:217.

13. *The Press and Society: A Book of Readings,* edited by George L. Bird and Frederic E. Merwin (New York: Prentice-Hall, 1951), p. iv.

14. Bryant, "Aspects of the Rhetorical Tradition"; see note 1.

15. Francis Bacon, "Of Studies."

16. From *The Advancement of Learning.* See Karl R. Wallace, *Francis Bacon on Communication and Rhetoric* (Chapel Hill, N.C.: University of North Carolina Press, 1943), p. 27.

17. *Educating Liberally* (Stanford, Calif.: Stanford University Press, 1945), pp. 10 ff.

18. See note 14.

19. See the very relevant analysis of some of the fictions in the ideology of American business in C. Wright Mills, *White Collar* (New York: Oxford University Press, 1951), chap. 3, "The Rhetoric of Competition."

20. George Campbell, *Philosophy of Rhetoric,* 7th ed. (London: William Baynes & Son, 1823), pp. vii–viii.

21. I. A. Richards, *The Philosophy of Rhetoric* (New York: Oxford University Press, 1936).

22. Aldous Huxley, *The Devils of Loudon* (New York: Harper, 1952), pp. 18–19.

23. Observe the tradition of rhetoric as a systematic study, summarized in my "Aspects of Rhetorical Tradition," pp. 169–72; see note 1.

24. See for example, Everett L. Hunt, "Ancient Rhetoric and Modern Propaganda," *Quarterly Journal of Speech* 37 (April 1951):157–60.

25. Kenneth Burke, *The Philosophy of Literary Form* (Baton Rouge: Louisiana State University Press, 1941), pp. 191–220; Ross Scanlan, "The Nazi Party Speaker System, I & II," *Speech Monographs* 16 (Aug. 1949):82–97; 17 (June 1950):- 134–48; "The Nazi Rhetorician," *Quarterly Journal of Speech* 27 (Dec. 1951):- 430–40.

26. Ross Scanlon, "Two Views of Propaganda," *Today's Speech* (April 1953), pp. 13–14; Henry C. Youngerman, "Propaganda and Public Address," ibid., pp. 15–17.

27. See Richard McKeon, "Rhetoric in the Middle Ages," *Critics and Criticism, Ancient and Modern,* edited by R. S. Crane (Chicago: University of Chicago Press, 1952), pp. 260–96, reprinted from *Speculum* (Jan. 1942); and Marvin T. Herrick, "The Place of Rhetoric in Poetic Theory," *Quarterly Journal of Speech* 34 (Feb. 1948):1–22.

28. *Isocrates,* translated by George Norlin (New York: Loeb Classical Library, 1929), 2:327.

29. From an original manuscript among the Wentworth-Fitzwilliam papers in the Sheffield City Library, used with the kind permission of Earl Fitzwilliam and the trustees of the Fitzwilliam settled estates. [Later published in *A Notebook of Edmund Burke,* edited by H. V. F. Somerset (Cambridge: At the University Press, 1957), p. 47.]

30. See, for example, one of the latest, W. N. Brigance, "General Education in an

Industrial Free Society," *Quarterly Journal of Speech* 38 (April 1952), esp. p. 181.

31. Everett L. Hunt, "Rhetoric and General Education," *Quarterly Journal of Speech* 35 (Oct. 1949):275, 277

32. Ibid., p. 279

33. Herbert A. Wichelns, "Public Speaking and Dramatic Arts," in *On Going to College: A Symposium* (New York: Oxford University Press, 1938), p. 240.

34. Kenneth O. Myrick, *Sir Philip Sidney as a Literary Craftsman* (Cambridge, Mass.: Harvard University Press, 1935).

35. Sir John Hawkins, *History of Music,* 2 vols. (London: Novello, Ewer & Co., 1875), 1:xxv.

36. Martin Maloney, "Some New Directions in Rhetorical Criticism," *Central States Speech Journal* 4 (Feb. 1953):1–5.

37. W. L. Brembeck and W. S. Howell, *Persuasion: A Means of Social Control* (New York: Prentice-Hall, 1952).

38. "A Bibliography of Rhetoric and Public Address," edited by F. W. Haberman, formerly appearing annually in the *Quarterly Journal of Speech,* latterly in *Speech Monographs.*

39. Bryant, "Some Problems of Scope and Method in Rhetorical Scholarship"; see note 1.

40. Ruth Wallerstein, "Rhetoric in the English Renaissance: Two Elegies," *English Institute Essays, 1948,* p. 153; see note 9.

41. Translated by Rhys Roberts, sec. 15.

Rhetoric: Its Functions and
Its Scope *Rediviva**

Donald C. Bryant

To discuss the concepts, and especially to use the terms, *rhetoric* and *rhetorical* before a general audience (though learned) is potentially to step off into a pretty soggy morass—there to conjure with confusion, amble in ambiguity, manipulate misconception, fumble with fatuities, and flounder in fluctuation and fluidity. Somewhere in the rosy semantic mist is "Rhetoric, the Harlot of the Arts," selling herself to him who can pay; but somewhere nearby is pretty Dame Rhetoric in her medieval gown, open palm extended, and festooned with the gay flowers of language. And ever and everywhere is Samuel Butler's pedagogue-rhetorician who "could not ope/ His mouth but out there flew a trope," and all of whose rules "Teach nothing but to name his tools."[1]

Over the centuries one great trouble with the term *rhetoric* has been that it is used loosely for the art, the artifact, and a quality of discourse; and often the reference of the designation is quite unclear. That problem is less troublesome in the realm of poetry, for there we have a full complement of useful differentiating terms for artist, art, and output:

poet poetic[s] poetry

With rhetoric we are in something of a mess. I do not know how to get clear of it; but I shall suggest a parallel triplet for our present purposes of distinction:

rhetor *rhetoric* *rhetory*

I do not expect it to become very popular; but make what you can of it—

*From Donald C. Bryant, *Rhetorical Dimensions in Criticism* (Baton Rouge, La.: Louisiana State University Press, 1973).

at least for the time being. The situation with *criticism* is hardly better; but I shall try to do something with it in due course.

I should like to be understood, nevertheless; so without trying to disenfranchise any of the meanings of *rhetoric* and *rhetorical* which may be current in learned and popular usage, I claim the prerogative of the famous Humpty Dumpty in *Alice Through the Looking Glass* and declare that for these lectures and for our common purposes, *rhetoric* means what I say it means—no more and no less.

And so—when I say "Rhetoric is" or "Rhetorical signifies," please understand me to mean, "I am using the word *rhetoric* as a name for . . ." or "I am using the adjective *rhetorical* to characterize. . . ." By *rhetoric* I shall not usually mean the output of speakers, writers, songsters, revolutionary guitarists, or mass chanters of "Right on" and "We shall overcome," though all of that output, I should readily agree, may be rhetorical. It may be rhetory in the new triplet. I shall admit that in its most unrestricted sense rhetoric may signify those principles, theories, laws, hypotheses, and other statable propositions which govern and explain the making and the functioning of symbolic communicative efforts through which men direct and control each other's beliefs, convictions, and behavior. That will be the most comprehensive meaning within which I shall move. I shall wish to confine that meaning, however, in certain traditional ways—for this present context, at least.

Consequential changes are abroad in the means and phenomena of instrumental communication in our society, and in the needs and resources for understanding them. Impressive new efforts are being made to refine and strengthen old methods and to develop new ones for achieving enlarged understanding and consequent measures of control. I shall direct attention to some of them as we proceed. First, however, I would review certain elements of the relevant past in order to interpret the title I have given this lecture: "Rhetoric: Its Functions and Its Scope, *Rediviva.*"

Two decades ago, Bower Aly, then the editor of the *Quarterly Journal of Speech,* invited me to write for that journal a piece which should delineate for the general academic reader essential characteristics, extent, functions, and limits for rhetoric as a field of study as it had been redeveloped in the first half of this century. No comprehensive, characterizing statement had been published for thirty years—that is, since Hoyt H. Hudson's "The Field of Rhetoric" of 1923,[2] early in the new era. The appreciable maturing of the study during the intervening three decades seemed to call for a fresh view.

Nine years before the appearance of Hudson's essay a small group, identifying itself as Academic Teachers of Public Speaking, had separated from the organized teachers of English and from the "elocutionists," in order, the secessionists thought, more freely and profitably to pursue, revive, and redevelop in Academia Americana the principles, teaching, practice, and theory of oral discourse, especially public address.

Soon, around the original seventeen "academic teachers of public speaking" who founded a national association and created a professional organ, the *Quarterly Journal of Public Speaking*, clustered more and more dissidents of similar or associated interests—teachers of argumentation from departments of English, debate coaches, sponsors of dramatic clubs and directors of academic theater, speech correctionists of clinical and scientific bent, phoneticians and those successors of the late elocutionists, the professors of oratory and of the oral interpretation of literature. By the time of the publication of Hudson's essay, a broader term than public speaking was required for this enlarged academic tent. The organization had become the National Association of Teachers of Speech and the official publication, the *Quarterly Journal of Speech Education.* The principal pedagogical and scholarly preoccupation of most of the members, however, remained public address—the teaching of speechmaking for use in the contemporary public context, and the revival and remastery of the Western inheritance of rhetorical theory and principles from Corax and Tisias, Plato and Aristotle, Cicero and Quintilian, Wilson and Blair, to Whately, J. Q. Adams, and their successors (in the forefront of whom was James A. Winans).

This tradition, long a staple of Western culture—with ups and downs to be sure—had gone into one of its downs in the nineteenth century. The Boylston Professorship of Rhetoric and Oratory at Harvard had gradually been reformed into the professorship of English literature, and the teaching of public address for public life had become the teaching of English composition for the writing of essays, mainly literary in their mode and matter. To this transformation may be credited the building of departments of English preoccupied with the teaching of composition in the schools and colleges and establishment of a literacy of the pen in the educated population of America.

That was a fitting and salutary development, for which we of this century should have no regrets. With it, however, came a reduction of the field of rhetoric—on the one hand to the techniques of sentence and paragraph, of word and figure, in the service chiefly of written composition, and on the other hand to the art of delivery, "elocution," mainly for purposes of literary interpretation and the oratory of scholastic competition and exhibition.

Hence, when the professors of public address of Hudson's day sought once again to retrieve the whole art of discourse—the inventional and argumentative rhetoric of Aristotle and Cicero—they found it necessary to reassert the province of their study and their teaching. They needed to reestablish it as the theory and principles of useful public discourse. They needed, also, to redistinguish it from poetics and the fine art of imaginative writing. That distinction and that definition constituted the burden of Hudson's essay and of the other and perhaps more influential contribution two years later by Herbert A. Wichelns, "The Literary Criticism of Oratory."[3]

In the thirty years between Hudson's essay and mine, much happened to rhetoric and to the scope of the field of speech. Not only did public speaking develop a new and prolific pedagogy and a healthy scholarship—first, perhaps, at Cornell and then in the state universities of the Middle West—but other denizens of the tent flourished like the farms and groves of the Imperial Valley: students and teachers of drama and theater, of phonetics and pronunciation, of speech correction and speech science, of the oral interpretation of literature, of group discussion and group methods, of general semantics and the sciences of communication, of the pedagogy of classroom and curriculum. With the growth of diverse interests grew diverse scholarship and a search for separate identities; and the National Association of Teachers of Speech became the Speech Association of America; the journal, the *Quarterly Journal of Speech,* to be joined by *Speech Monographs* (a journal of research) and *The Speech Teacher* (a journal directed primarily to the schools).

By then, of necessity, attempts were being made to redescribe the confederated field of speech, to find a satisfactory statement of the common ground of a province where residents of the several parishes, though mutually sympathetic (usually), were coming more and more to bear the relationship of laymen to each other. In this atmosphere the editor of the *Quarterly Journal of Speech* undertook to commission a series of longish articles on some of the principal substantive areas of instruction, theory, and scholarship served by the journal. These articles were to be acceptable to specialists within the several areas, to be sure; but primarily they were to present to specialists in other areas, or generalists (in effect, laymen), as comprehensive and contemporary expositions as possible of the hallmarks and basic characteristics of the several provinces as they appeared to the professionals within them. At least four such articles appeared, of which mine was the last—"Rhetoric: Its Functions and Its Scope."[4]

I offer this extended tale of the generation of that article in order to account for the particular bias and idiom of it and to show why it is what it is and is not other things which one coming to it afresh might expect . . . [A reader may trace it for himself in the preceding article in this collection.]

Of course I would moderate and modify portions of that statement if I might. I would mitigate the special pleading which was a function of the time, I might damp a tendency to pontification and self-assurance, and perhaps I would obscure some visible touches of neo-Aristotelian myopia. For what it is and for what it was intended to be, however, I still think it a fair, defensible, and serviceable statement.

Apparently I read pretty well the mind and temper of our disciplines at the time. The essay, so to speak, hit the teachers and doctrinaries in speech and English "between wind and water." Perhaps, as Burke said of Charles Townshend, it seemed to lead because it was so sure to follow.[5] At any rate, it has been anthologized six or eight times in the two decades and seems destined for another appearance or two. In the burgeoning field of graduate study in rhetoric, "Functions and Scope" joined the orthodox canon as a "classic" essay; and later it came to serve as a staple, conservative explication of rhetoric for the makers of anthologies and writers of articles among those new rediscoverers of rhetorical concepts, the students of English composition. I cannot feel displeased—for myself or for the study and teaching of discourse.

Though I would not recall that statement of 1953 even if I might, or recant any of its major tenets, I welcome this opportunity to review it publicly in the light of the education I have enjoyed for the past two decades, especially from my associates, both students and colleagues, at the University of Iowa. Those have been the decades of rapid acceleration of "new" rhetorics—Kenneth Burke's and I. A. Richards' of course (already mellowed into subjects of doctoral dissertations) and Richard Weaver's; but especially the explosive concepts of Marshall McLuhan on the one hand, and on the other the philosophical explorations into rhetoric and the rhetorical explorations into philosophy led by Chaim Perelman, Henry Johnstone, and the journal *Philosophy and Rhetoric*. During those same decades behavioral-quantitative studies in communication have achieved a certain maturity which reinforces the impossibility of ever viewing things rhetorical again, either substantively or methodologically, precisely as we could in 1953. So it is; but not to all eyes are prominent features of the rhetorical world of 1973 invisible in that of 1953, or the principal propositions of 1953 irrelevant to 1973.

Perhaps it is presumptuous, or at least premature, to refurbish and in a sense to relaunch my notions of the function and scope of rhetoric until the essays and commentaries deriving from the recent National Developmental Project in Rhetoric and published in its report have had time to infiltrate the classrooms, the seminars, the dissertations, and the learned studies of the rhetorical scholars of the seventies. If so, perhaps I may meliorate the presumption or haste by confessing at once that with many of the prominent concepts promulgated by the conferees I find it congenial to associate mine. Their "ruling objective," for example, is stated in terms with which I am altogether comfortable:

> to develop an outlined conception of rhetoric applicable to our own time. We conceived of rhetoric in the classical, and richest, sense—as the theory of investigation, decision, and communication concerned particularly with practical, especially civic, affairs. Our central aims, then, were to revitalize a humanistic discipline whose theory and literature are exceptionally rich, and to attempt redefinition and perfection of that discipline as a modern method of problem-solving and decision-making.[6]

The sources and forces for discovery and redevelopment are many and vigorous. So far as they are humanistic and humane their results will be salutary. So far as they are focused and embodied in the yield from the National Developmental Project, they may be uncertain; but they are striving, as I see it, in the proper arena.

Let us turn, then, to some important features of the doctrine of two decades ago to see how it should be different, and how the same, were I now proposing it for the first time.

No doubt it would now be well to alter, or at least to qualify, the working definition of rhetoric as it then appeared. "First of all and primarily," I wrote, "I take rhetoric to be *the rationale of informative and suasory discourse*. All its other meanings are partial or morally-colored derivatives from that primary meaning." I still find that definition defensible and operationally viable. At the same time, I recognize that it may be interpreted as setting arbitrary limits to the scope in one respect and opening it up too much in another. That definition has been questioned on two grounds: first, for the inclusion of "informative" with "suasory" and second for the limitation to "discourse."

Edwin Black, for example, found the coupling of informative and suasory "open to question" because "informative discourse is not usually associated with rhetoric, either historically or at present. . . . In the tradition that can be traced from Plato and Aristotle through Campbell in the eighteenth century and Whately in the nineteenth to Kenneth Burke in our own time, only two major writers on rhetoric have involved informative as well as persuasive discourse in their definitions of rhetoric: Quintilian and Campbell."[7] And, Black argues, neither really meant to include the informative as a clearly separate genre. As a matter of fact, I think, neither did I. At least, now I do not; and now I modify the wording of the definition accordingly in order to put the focus on the functions or dimensions of discourse rather than the genres.

Black's historical argument serves his immediate purposes well enough, no doubt, but it would seem to require for validity a special definition of *informative* which somehow excludes the instructional or illuminative. Such a limitation has certainly been obsolete at least since the eighteenth century.[8] If, however, one wished to counter Black's argument historically, one might cite the three ends of oratory reiterated in Roman rhetoric— *docere, delectare, movere* (teach, please, and move)—and the strong implication, at least in principle if not in operational doctrine, that any of the three could be the dominant purpose in a particular rhetorical work. When *docere* is the dominant purpose, the genre informative is potential. It is not necessarily created, of course, unless we have some analytic use for it; and genre criticism at best has limited usefulness. Even if we apply to the ancient ends of discourse the linear adjunct interpretation, as Black does to Campbell's "enlighten the understanding, please the imagination, move the passions, and influence the will," the case against informative discourse within the province of rhetoric is far from conclusive. Let us suppose that Campbell did consider rhetorical discourse generically persuasive, and that the first three ends were rhetorical only as cumulatively they serve to influence the will. Still Campbell cannot have held so unrealistic a notion of individual discourses as not to admit that a particular discourse may serve primarily the end of enlightening the understanding.

Historically biased as I may be, however, and as neo-Aristotelian as Black and my essay may label me, I cannot accept as conclusive the argument from silence—I cannot agree that the absence of explicit recognition of the informative as a kind in the rhetorical tradition is permanently confining. Prevailing and developing uses of discourse invite the discovery or formulation of adequate rationales appropriate to them. If for reasons of tradition those rationales may not be conceived as rhetorics, they must be developed nevertheless. James L. Kinneavy, for example, has recently undertaken to develop comprehensive rationales of discourse.[9] Deriving his model from the now-hackneyed communication triangle, Kinneavy arrives at four categories discriminated according to aim: reference discourse, persuasive discourse, literary discourse, and expressive discourse. For each he delineates defining concepts and operational features in massive detail. For persuasive discourse the rhetorical inheritance furnishes the chief substance, and the literary draws upon poetics and criticism from Aristotle to M. H. Abrams —as one might expect. Reference discourse (trifurcated into scientific, informative, and exploratory) and expressive discourse do not emerge sharply or, to me, convincingly. Kinneavy's effort, however, may serve at least to remind some of us that our concepts of rhetoric and poetic may not be altogether adequate to account for all discourse that we are likely to encounter in our time. Whether we adapt to changing modes by making rhetoric more capacious as Kenneth Burke does, or by assigning new names and new concepts to subrationales, may be matters of convenience or of the capacities of our instruments. I cannot now see it as involving theoretic imperatives.

Considering rhetoric, as I do, to comprehend the theory, principles, and technology of instrumental, "advisory" communication, functioning first of all but by no means exclusively in practical, public discourse, perhaps it would be well to avoid, without denying, the operationally doubtful difference between informative discourse and suasory discourse. The informative and the suasory as kinds are hard to disentangle with firm assurance except in the textbooks and classrooms of English composition and speechmaking.

Earlier it had seemed important to counteract and correct the common assumption that discourse whose principal service is enlightenment—and which is, therefore, not explicitly either persuasive or fictive—is outside the bounds of any systematic theory or rationale of critical analysis except the logical, the grammatical, or the syntactical. That corrective is now, perhaps, hardly necessary. If so, I should be content with the stipulation that the principles of informative discourse (at least so far as the discourse is addressed to the lay audience) are subsumed under the suasory, as they appear to have been in antiquity. Or I might settle for the concept of informative-suasory as all-one-word, or for the double concept sublimated into the term *communicative*. That term, however, popular though it now is through academic associations and departments, and comprehensive and capacious enough to encompass most social activity, comes pretty close, I think, to defeating valid discriminations.

For the foregoing considerations, and for others which I shall develop a little later, I would now define rhetoric as *the rationale of the informative and suasory in discourse*. That wording implies two distinguishable but closely entangled dimensions of discourse as rhetorical, and it implies others which are not. Perhaps it dodges or circumvents the problems of genre, but I think rather that it recognizes pure genres as fictions and implies that most artifacts of discourse exhibit various dimensions, the informative-suasory of which comprise the province of rhetoric. The new wording also removes the obstacle, which I never intended, to admitting the rhetorical into literary analysis.

A second major difficulty critics have found with my original definition is not removed or mitigated by the revision just presented. It is the objection not to enlarging the scope of rhetoric but to confining it to discourse. . . . For what I think adequate reasons I still choose to treat rhetoric as concerned primarily with discourse—with the web of words. I would not, however, be finicky or arbitrary about how many words in what form qualify as discourse, as long as there are informative or suasory dimensions to their use. Hence, I would have no significant trouble with Kenneth Burke's idea of the basic function of rhetoric as "the use of words by human agents to form attitudes or to induce actions in other agents."[10]

When the concept of rhetoric is enlarged, as it now tends to be, to include all symbolic behavior, the enlargement certainly brings out significant kinships among principles operating in the various symbolic systems. Recognition of those kinships, to be sure, may convince us that the primary genus we seek to account for is larger than we had permitted ourselves to suppose. To deny the kinships, remote though some of them may seem, and to ignore the enlarged genus, is blindness. To assign *rhetoric* as the most fitting term or concept for the comprehensive genus seems to me to commit an unnecessary offense against useful terminology. It is to force and distort relationships by detaching the designation from a major species and making it serve for a genus which it has not characterized except, perhaps, metaphorically —the "silent rhetoric of thine eye," for example. Bowers and Ochs' definition in *The Rhetoric of Agitation and Control* enlarges the genus about as far as it can go: "the rationale of instrumental symbolic behavior."[11] That definition permits the authors, under the rubric "the Rhetoric of," to combine generically the "symbolic behavior" of pelting policemen with feces, lying down in front of army buses, editorializing in the Chicago *Tribune,* and toasting the Chinese hosts in the Great Hall of the People. There may be theoretic or operational gain from joining together such diverse phenomena and seeking comprehensive principles to illuminate them. Those principles, however, may need to be stated so broadly and vaguely as to be unserviceable for the illumination or generation of constructive distinctions. Bowers and Ochs succeed well in composing a rationale for the basically nonverbal (certainly nondiscourse) behavior which their definitions of agitation and control characterize. The analogical relationships of that rationale to rationales of suasory discourse may be illuminating in both directions; and I would have them and others like them pursued with all the enterprise and ingenuity that may be brought to bear. If it requires the special sanction of the label *rhetoric,* therefore, to make that pursuit viable, or to channel it effectively, the gains, I suppose, could be worth the terminological blur.

The scope assigned to rhetorical studies by the Committee on the Scope of Rhetoric at the Pheasant Run conference of the National Developmental Project, too, is expansive but not reckless: "Rhetorical studies are properly concerned with the process by which symbols and systems of symbols have [*i.e.,* exert] influence upon beliefs, values, attitudes, and actions, and they embrace all forms of human communication, not exclusively public address nor communication within any one class or cultural group."[12] The Committee on the Advancement and Refinement of Rhetorical Criticism, at the same conference, enlarged the scope of rhetoric even more explicitly, and to my mind recklessly. They declared: "We shall no longer assume that the subject of rhetorical criticism is only discourse or that any critic studying discourse is *ipso facto* a rhetorical critic. The critic becomes rhetorical to the extent that he studies his subject in terms of its suasory potential or persuasive effect." Hence, they declare, rhetoric as a rationale may profitably serve as an important basis for explaining "any human act, process, product, or artifact which . . . may formulate, sustain, or modify attention, perceptions, attitudes, or behavior."[13]

The liberation of the rhetorician from the shackles of inherited concepts and doctrine so that he may view his role in the 1970s with concepts adequate to the 1970s was the assigned mission of the Pheasant Run conferees and their predecessors in the prior phase of the National Developmental Project, the scholars of Wingspread. The mission was to free the rhetorician from the shackles of his inheritance, not, I think, to forbid him access to it. That is a good mission—one to be accepted and pursued. It requires, I think, the adoption of what Wayne Booth calls a "rhetorical stance"[14] in the redevelopment of theory and doctrine for the study and explanation of human interaction and human behavior, and for the improvement of that behavior. That rhetorical stance, however, it seems to me, must be founded in the assumption—none the worse because traditional and conformable to the experience of the centuries—that discourse has been and will be the primary vehicle of instrumental, symbolic behavior and that the central rationale, the mother lode, is the rationale of the informative and suasory—in the web of words. Reconceiving the concept of discourse as vehicles and users of it change has gone on historically and will continue. Hence, Karl Wallace can declare that "Rhetoric is . . . primarily an art of discourse" and then find every rhetorician "directly concerned with what goes on when men adjust to one another through their communications." He concludes, "The ultimate data of the rhetorician are the speech and language men use when they believe they are communicating with one another."[15]

And so, with no impulse to confine the understanding and the exploration of how men communicate, for what, according to what principles, through what languages, what symbols, what signs, and what extrasensory vibrations, I confirm and to some degree extend the concept of the earlier essay —that discourse is the most characteristically rhetorical vehicle. All the more do I feel warranted in such limitation in the present context, because, like Wallace, I am considering rhetoric as the foundation of a productive art whose artifacts are formed in a matrix of words.[16]

Further, for 1973 I would add a modest gloss rather than reinterpretation to the most frequently quoted and paraphrased statement of 1953: that, speaking generally, the central rhetorical function is the *"function of adjusting ideas to people and people to ideas."* I understand that some important exception has been taken to that concept, but I do not know what. I would remark, however, the enhanced importance of the concepts and idiom of behavioral science in the study of communication in twenty years, and the permeation of those concepts and that idiom through rhetorical studies. It would be well, therefore, to recognize more explicitly than I did formerly the obvious involvement of rhetorical discourse in affecting action (BEHAVIOR) as well as ideas—involvement with ideas in action. We must think of rhetorical transactions as functioning to modify the features of desired changes of idea and behavior so that the changes seem feasible and attractive in the available circumstances. We must think of them as functioning at the same time to modify the attitudes of people toward change. Implicit in this concept is the assumption, of course, that the rhetorical function includes the reverse of adjustment to change—reinforcement of the acceptability of no change, that is, intensification of acceptance.

For 1973 I should reassert and reinforce my view of 1953, that rhetoric and poetic are and must be closely and complementarily related. That is the view of enlightened neo-Aristotelians, those of us in the now disestablished Cornell tradition, salted and savored, of course, by the Chicago critics and the Bairdians of Iowa. It is the view I reasserted in our little Iowa collection of papers on rhetoric and poetic of 1965:[17] the view of the parallel and interactive operation of rhetorical and poetic processes in many sorts of communicative artifacts and situations. . . . They are among the relations recognized in the modification I have made in my definition of rhetoric: that rhetoric is a contributory rationale, as Aristotle and most major theorists since have known it is, for the explanation of imaginative, fictive literature.

It may be unnecessary to reiterate the concept of rhetoric as a rationale of discourse both written and oral—for reader and listener; but in a context where English and speech are distinct and often competing disciplines and departments, and in a society in which orality through the electronic media has regained and secured its place as a prime mode of public discourse, there is profit in the re-emphasis. Like dramatic discourse, rhetorical discourse throughout the ages has been oral but has functioned and does function in writing and print as well. Orality, with its particular and distinctive features, is historically, and also genetically, the prime potential dimension of the rhetorical. The surrogate orality of print, with its built-in limitations, is with us, is necessary, and will continue to be. Sometimes among students of literature, and even of rhetoric, there seems to have been the tacit assumption that speaking should be treated, artistically at least, as a kind of lively but loose and undisciplined stage of writing. Serious, responsible students of language, however, have returned firmly (if they ever really departed) to the position that writing is primarily recorded speech with, of course, its special dimensions. Whether oral utterance precedes writing or writing is preparation for potential speaking has functional but not generic significance.

Let the discourse be spoken or written, however, the rhetorical function was and is central to the preacher, the teacher, the courtroom lawyer, the labor leader, the politician, the critic. It is central also to the advertiser, the propagandist, the journalist, the salesman, the demagogue (and to the writer or lecturer on the rhetorical art)—not only to the individual saint or fanatic, but to the institutionalized, anonymous agencies for engineering consent. Furthermore, the rhetorical in discourse spans the spectrum from the most commonplace harangue to the greatest literature—that is, to the highest eloquence.

In approaching the close of this supplement or codicil to the statement of my rhetorical views of twenty years ago, let me clear up a minor confusion—whether mine or my critics'—which has arisen from a too neat contrast in too crisp a sentence in "Functions and Scope." There I wrote, "Rhetoric is method, not subject." Out of its context, that is certainly an unfortunate statement. Karl Wallace, in one of his often mentioned articles, has demonstrated that rhetoric has substantive, not methodological content only, that it has its characteristic subject matter, even its special subject matter.[18] That subject matter is the values, the prevailing ethical tenets and moral foundations on the basis of which, and in the context of which, men make decisions in their public or social transactions. This is the sort of subject matter which Aristotle atomizes in perhaps tedious detail in specifying the "goods" in the first book of the *Rhetoric*. With that kind of definition of subject matter one can but agree without protest. I can see that the passage to which my controversial sentence contributes has a sort of double face. The one looks upon something like Wallace's foundation of "good reasons." That is the face of the substance of the art of rhetoric. The other looks upon the subject matter of rhetorical discourse. The sentence in question should serve to distinguish the two. Apparently it does not.

At the conclusion of my former essay I identified four distinct but closely related roles for rhetoric. (1) As the systematic formulation and organization of principles for the management of discourse with informative-suasory potential, it is an instrumental discipline. (2) So far as it furnishes theory, principles, and methods for describing and accounting for the informing of ideas and the functioning of language in discourse, it is a critical discipline. (3) As it may furnish method for investigation looking to the nature of meaning and the validity and interrelations of ideas, it is philosophical. (4) And as it identifies and treats significant forces governing the behavior of men in society, it is a social discipline. Of those four, stated somewhat differently, I then devoted most space and attention to the first—the instrumental—as I have done in this retrospect. That, no doubt, is why the new friends of rhetoric in the teaching of English composition have been attracted to the essay. Of the philosophy of rhetoric or rhetoric as philosophy, and of rhetorics as rationales for analysis and criticism of discourse, I said very little explicitly. In fact, that essay, because of its limitations, served in part to prompt one of the early pieces in the new philosophical examination of rhetoric, Maurice Natanson's "The Limits of Rhetoric."[19] That is an important kind of enterprise for which I have only the most modest of equipment and no inclination.

If I were literally presenting my rhetoric *rediviva* in the Latin sense as I understand it—that is, if I were now rebuilding with old materials renewed —it should be evident from what I have said that I should utterly reject little that had formed the old building. I should reshape a good many of the old stones, sandblast them to clear the grime of antiquity, and rearrange here and there to harmonize the architecture with the new construction arising nearby. To escape from the metaphor: So far as I understand the movement of rhetorical studies over the past two decades—and my continuing education has been in the very good hands of younger rhetoricians and older, of behavioral scientists and philosophers—the basic concepts may need to be adapted and supplemented, but not abandoned. Improvements there surely would be, even within the confines of the purpose of the earlier essay; but those improvements would affect the complexity and sophistication of theories, methods, and doctrines rather than concepts of function and scope.

NOTES AND REFERENCES

1. *Hudibras,* Part 1, Canto I, 11. 81–82, 89–90.

2. Hoyt H. Hudson, "The Field of Rhetoric," *Quarterly Journal of Speech Education* 9 (1923):167–80; reprinted in Raymond F. Howes (ed.), *Historical Studies of Rhetoric and Rhetoricians* (Ithaca, N.Y.: Cornell University Press, 1961), pp. 3–15.

3. Herbert A. Wichelns, "The Literary Criticism of Oratory," in *Studies in Rhetoric and Public Speaking in Honor of James Albert Winans,* edited by Alexander M. Drummond (New York: Century Co., 1925), pp. 181–216; reprinted in *The Rhetorical Idiom,* edited by Donald C. Bryant (Ithaca, N.Y.: Cornell University Press, 1958), pp. 5–42.

4. Donald C. Bryant, "Rhetoric: Its Functions and Its Scope," pp. 195–230.

5. Edmund Burke, "Speech on American Taxation," in *The Works of the Right Honorable Edmund Burke,* 12 vols. (Boston: Little, Brown, 1894), 2:64–65.

6. Lloyd F. Bitzer and Edwin Black (eds.), *The Prospect of Rhetoric: Report of the National Developmental Project* (Englewood Cliffs, N.J.: Prentice-Hall, 1971), p. 237.

7. Edwin Black, *Rhetorical Criticism: A Study in Method* (New York: Macmillan Co., 1965), pp. 11–12.

8. See, for example, Wilbur Samuel Howell, *Eighteenth-Century British Logic and Rhetoric* (Princeton, N.J.: Princeton University Press, 1971), pp. 496–97, 510–11; or Gerard A. Hauser, "Empiricism, Description, and the New Rhetoric," *Philosophy and Rhetoric* 5 (Winter 1972):24–44. As a contemporary witness, may I cite Douglas Ehninger: "A rhetoric I define as an organized, consistent, coherent way of talking about practical discourse in any of its forms or modes. By practical discourse I mean discourse, written or oral, that seeks to inform, evaluate, or persuade, and therefore is to be distinguished from discourse that seeks to please, elevate, or depict." [Ehninger, "On Systems of Rhetoric," *Philosophy and Rhetoric* 1 (1968):131.]

9. James L. Kinneavy, *A Theory of Discourse: The Aims of Discourse* (Englewood Cliffs, N.J.: Prentice-Hall, 1971).

10. Kenneth Burke, *A Rhetoric of Motives* (New York: Prentice-Hall, 1950), p. 41.

11. John Waite Bowers and Donovan J. Ochs, *The Rhetoric of Agitation and Control* (Reading, Mass.: Addison-Wesley, 1971), p. 2.

12. Bitzer and Black (eds.) *The Prospect of Rhetoric,* p. 208.

13. Ibid., p. 220.

14. Wayne Booth, "The Rhetorical Stance," *College Composition and Communication* 14 (Oct. 1963):139–45.

15. Karl Wallace, "The Fundamentals of Rhetoric," in Bitzer and Black (eds.), *The Prospect of Rhetoric,* pp. 3–4.

16. There might arise some resolution of the difficulties I have been treating if, knowing that no one universal system is possible, we spoke as Douglas Ehninger recommends ("On Systems of Rhetoric," Part V), of rhetoric-*s* and rationale-*s*. We might then, if we wished, extend rhetorics beyond discourse and treat of a rhetoric of the film, a rhetoric of the dance, and so forth, without implying that they are all basically one. With respect to the rhetoric of discourse, I have understood and I do understand the plurality of particular systems as implicit in my definition.

17. Donald C. Bryant, "Uses of Rhetoric in Criticism," in Donald C. Bryant (ed.), *Papers in Rhetoric and Poetic* (Iowa City: University of Iowa Press, 1965), pp. 1–14.

18. Karl Wallace, "The Substance of Rhetoric: Good Reasons," *Quarterly Journal of Speech* 59 (1963):239–49.

19. Maurice Natanson, "The Limits of Rhetoric," *Quarterly Journal of Speech* 41 (1955):133–39

The Rhetorical Situation*

Lloyd F. Bitzer

If someone says, "That is a dangerous situation," his words suggest the presence of events, persons, or objects which threaten him, someone else, or something of value. If someone remarks, "I find myself in an embarrassing situation," again the statement implies certain situational characteristics. If someone remarks that he found himself in an ethical situation, we understand that he probably either contemplated or made some choice or action from a sense of duty or obligation or with a view to the Good. In other words, there are circumstances of this or that kind or structure which are recognized as ethical, dangerous, or embarrassing.

What characteristics, then, are implied when one refers to "the rhetorical situation"—the context in which speakers or writers create rhetorical discourse? Perhaps this question is puzzling because "situation" is not a standard term in the vocabulary of rhetorical theory. "Audience" is standard; so also are "speaker," "subject," "occasion," and "speech." If I were to ask, "What is a rhetorical audience?" or "What is a rhetorical subject?"—the reader would catch the meaning of my question.

When I ask, "What is a rhetorical situation?," I want to know the nature of those contexts in which speakers or writers create rhetorical discourse: How should they be described? What are their characteristics? Why and how do they result in the creation of rhetoric? By analogy, a theorist of science might well ask, "What are the characteristics of situations which

*Reprinted with permission of the author and the editors of *Philosophy and Rhetoric,* where the essay was first published, 1 (1968):1–14. Other versions of the essay were presented at Cornell University (1966), University of Washington (1967), and the Central States Speech Association Convention (1967).

inspire scientific thought?" A philosopher might ask, "What is the nature of the situation in which a philosopher 'does philosophy'?" And a theorist of poetry might ask, "How shall we describe the context in which poetry comes into existence?"

The presence of rhetorical discourse obviously indicates the presence of a rhetorical situation. The Declaration of Independence, Lincoln's Gettysburg Address, Churchill's Address on Dunkirk, John F. Kennedy's Inaugural Address—each is a clear instance of rhetoric and each indicates the presence of a situation. While the existence of a rhetorical address is a reliable sign of the existence of situation, it does not follow that a situation exists only when the discourse exists. Each reader probably can recall a specific time and place when there was opportunity to speak on some urgent matter, and after the opportunity was gone he created in private thought the speech he should have uttered earlier in the situation. It is clear that situations are not always accompanied by discourse. Nor should we assume that a rhetorical address gives existence to the situation; on the contrary, it is the situation which calls the discourse into existence. Clement Attlee once said that Winston Churchill went around looking for "finest hours." The point to observe is that Churchill found them—the crisis situations— and spoke in response to them.

No major theorist has treated rhetorical situation thoroughly as a distinct subject in rhetorical theory; many ignore it. Those rhetoricians who discuss situation do so indirectly—as does Aristotle, for example, who is led to consider situation when he treats types of discourse. None, to my knowledge, has asked the nature of rhetorical situation. Instead rhetoricians have asked: What is the process by which the orator creates and presents discourse? What is the nature of rhetorical discourse? What sorts of interaction occur between speaker, audience, subject, and occasion? Typically the questions which trigger theories of rhetoric focus upon the orator's method or upon the discourse itself, rather than upon the situation which invites the orator's application of his method and the creation of discourse. Thus, rhetoricians distinguish among and characterize the types of speeches (forensic, deliberative, epideictic); they treat issues, types of proof, lines of argument, strategies of ethical and emotional persuasion, the parts of a discourse and the functions of these parts, qualities of styles, figures of speech. They cover approximately the same materials, the formal aspects of rhetorical method and discourse, whether focusing upon method, product or process; while conceptions of situation are implicit in some theories of rhetoric, none explicitly treat the formal aspects of situation.

I hope that enough has been said to show that the question—What is a rhetorical situation?—is not an idle one. I propose in what follows to set forth part of a theory of situation. This essay, therefore, should be understood as an attempt to revive the notion of rhetorical situation, to provide at least the outline of an adequate conception of it, and to establish it as a controlling and fundamental concern of rhetorical theory.

I

It seems clear that rhetoric is situational. In saying this, I do not mean merely that understanding a speech hinges upon understanding the context of meaning in which the speech is located. Virtually no utterance is fully intelligible unless meaning-context and utterance are understood; this is true of rhetorical and nonrhetorical discourse. Meaning-context is a general condition of human communication and is not synonymous with rhetorical situation. Nor do I mean merely that rhetoric occurs in a setting which involves interaction of speaker, audience, subject, and communicative purpose. This is too general, since many types of utterances—philosophical, scientific, poetic, and rhetorical—occur in such settings. Nor would I equate rhetorical situation with persuasive situation, which exists whenever an audience can be changed in belief or action by means of speech. Every audience at any moment is capable of being changed in some way by speech; persuasive situation is altogether general.

Finally, I do not mean that a rhetorical discourse must be embedded in historic context in the sense that a living tree must be rooted in soil. A tree does not obtain its character-as-tree from the soil, but rhetorical discourse, I shall argue, does obtain its character-as-rhetorical from the situation which generates it. Rhetorical works belong to the class of things which obtain their character from the circumstances of the historic context in which they occur. A rhetorical work is analogous to a moral action rather than to a tree. An act is moral because it is an act performed in a situation of a certain kind; similarly, a work is rhetorical because it is a response to a situation of a certain kind.

In order to clarify rhetoric-as-essentially-related-to-situation, we should acknowledge a viewpoint that is commonplace but fundamental: a work of rhetoric is pragmatic; it comes into existence for the sake of something beyond itself; it functions ultimately to produce action or change in the world; it performs some task. In short, rhetoric is a mode of altering reality, not by the direct application of energy to objects, but by the creation of discourse which changes reality through the mediation of thought and action. The rhetor alters reality by bringing into existence a discourse of such a character that the audience, in thought and action, is so engaged that it becomes mediator of change. In this sense rhetoric is always persuasive.

To say that rhetorical discourse comes into being in order to effect change is altogether general. We need to understand that a particular discourse comes into existence because of some specific condition or situation which invites utterance. Bronislaw Malinowski refers to just this sort of situation in his discussion of primitive language, which he finds to be essentially pragmatic and "embedded in situation." He describes a party of fishermen in the Trobriand Islands whose functional speech occurs in a "context of situation."

> The canoes glide slowly and noiselessly, punted by men especially good at this task and always used for it. Other experts who know the bottom of the lagoon . . . are on the look-out for fish. . . . Customary signs, or sounds or words are uttered. Sometimes a sentence full of technical references to the channels or patches on the lagoon has to be spoken; sometimes . . . a conventional cry is uttered. . . . Again, a word of command is passed here and there, a technical expression or explanation which serves to harmonize their behavior towards other men. . . . An animated scene, full of movement, follows, and now that the fish are in their power the fishermen speak loudly, and give vent to their feelings. Short, telling exclamations fly about, which might be rendered by such words as: "Pull in," "Let go," "Shift further," "Lift the net."

In this whole scene, "each utterance is essentially bound up with the context of situation and with the aim of the pursuit. . . . The structure of all this linguistic material is inextricably mixed up with, and dependent upon, the course of the activity in which the utterances are embedded." Later the observer remarks: "In its primitive uses, language functions as a link in concerted human activity, as a piece of human behaviour. It is a mode of action and not an instrument of reflection."[1]

These statements about primitive language and the "context of situation" provide for us a preliminary model of rhetorical situation. Let us regard rhetorical situation as a natural context of persons, events, objects, relations, and an exigency which strongly invites utterance; this invited utterance participates naturally in the situation, is in many instances necessary to the completion of situational activity, and by means of its participation with situation obtains its meaning and its rhetorical character. In Malinowski's example, the situation is the fishing expedition—consisting of objects, persons, events, and relations—and the ruling exigency, the success of the hunt. The situation dictates the sorts of observations to be made; it dictates the significant physical and verbal responses; and, we must admit, it constrains the words which are uttered in the same sense that it constrains the physical acts of paddling the canoes and throwing the nets. The verbal responses to the demands imposed by this situation are clearly as functional and necessary as the physical responses.

Traditional theories of rhetoric have dealt, of course, not with the sorts of primitive utterances described by Malinowski—"stop here," "throw the nets," "move closer"—but with larger units of speech which come more readily under the guidance of artistic principle and method. The difference between oratory and primitive utterance, however, is not a difference in function; the clear instances of rhetorical discourse and the fishermen's utterances are similarly functional and similarly situational. Observing both the traditions of the expedition and the facts before him, the leader of the fishermen finds himself *obliged* to speak at a given moment—to command, to supply information, to praise or blame—to respond appropriately to the situation. Clear instances of artistic rhetoric exhibit the same character: Cicero's speeches against Cataline were called forth by a specific union of persons, events, objects, and relations, and by an exigency which amounted to an imperative stimulus; the speeches in the Senate rotunda three days after the assassination of the President of the United States were actually required by the situation. So controlling is situation that we should consider it the very ground of rhetorical activity, whether that activity is primitive and productive of a simple utterance or artistic and productive of the Gettysburg Address.

Hence, to say that rhetoric is situational means: (1) rhetorical discourse comes into existence as a response to situation, in the same sense that an answer comes into existence in response to a question, or a solution in response to a problem; (2) a speech is given *rhetorical* significance by the situation, just as a unit of discourse is given significance *as* answer or *as* solution by the question or problem; (3) a rhetorical situation must exist as a necessary condition of rhetorical discourse, just as a question must exist as a necessary condition of an answer; (4) many questions go unanswered and many problems remain unsolved; similarly, many rhetorical situations mature and decay without giving birth to rhetorical utterance; (5) a situation is rhetorical insofar as it needs and invites discourse capable of participating with situation and thereby altering its reality; (6) discourse is rhetorical insofar as it functions (or seeks to function) as a fitting response to a situation which needs and invites it; (7) finally, the situation controls the rhetorical response in the same sense that the question controls the answer and the problem controls the solution. Not the rhetor and not persuasive intent, but the situation is the source and ground of rhetorical activity—and, I should add, of rhetorical criticism.

II

Let us now amplify the nature of situation by providing a formal definition and examining constituents. Rhetorical situation may be defined as a complex of persons, events, objects, and relations presenting an actual or potential exigency which can be completely or partially removed if discourse, introduced into the situation, can so constrain human decision or action as to bring about the significant modification of the exigency. Prior to the creation and presentation of discourse, there are three constituents of any rhetorical situation: the first is the *exigency;* the second and third are elements of the complex, namely the *audience* to be constrained in decision and action, and the *constraints* which influence the rhetor and can be brought to bear upon the audience.

Any *exigency* is an imperfection marked by urgency; it is a defect, an obstacle, something waiting to be done, a thing which is other than it should be. In almost any sort of context, there will be numerous exigencies, but not all are elements of a rhetorical situation—not all are rhetorical. An exigency which cannot be modified is not rhetorical; thus, whatever comes about of necessity and cannot be changed—death, winter, and some natural disasters, for instance—are exigencies to be sure, but they are not rhetorical. Further, an exigency which can be modified only by means other than discourse is not rhetorical; thus, an exigency is not rhetorical when its modification requires merely one's own action or the application of a tool, but neither requires nor invites the assistance of discourse. An exigency is rhetorical when it is capable of positive modification and when positive modification requires discourse or can be assisted by discourse. For example, suppose that a man's acts are injurious to others and that the quality of his acts can be changed only if discourse is addressed to him; the exigency —his injurious acts—is then unmistakably rhetorical. The pollution of our air is also a rhetorical exigency because its positive modification—reduction of pollution—strongly invites the assistance of discourse producing public awareness, indignation, and action of the right kind. Frequently rhetors encounter exigencies which defy easy classification because of the absence of information enabling precise analysis and certain judgment—they may or may not be rhetorical. An attorney whose client has been convicted may strongly believe that a higher court would reject his appeal to have the verdict overturned, but because the matter is uncertain—because the exigency *might* be rhetorical—he elects to appeal. In this and similar instances of indeterminate exigencies the rhetor's decision to speak is based mainly upon the urgency of the exigency and the probability that the exigency is rhetorical.

In any rhetorical situation there will be at least one controlling exigency which functions as the organizing principle: it specifies the audience to be addressed and the change to be effected. It may or may not be perceived clearly by the rhetor or other persons in the situation; it may be strong or weak depending upon the clarity of their perception and the degree of their interest in it; it may be real or unreal depending on the facts of the case; it may be important or trivial; it may be such that discourse can completely remove it, or it may persist in spite of repeated modifications; it may be completely familiar—one of a type of exigencies occurring frequently in our experience—or it may be totally new. When it is perceived and when it is strong and important, then it constrains the thought and action of the perceiver who may respond rhetorically if he is in a position to do so.

The second constituent is the *audience*. Since rhetorical discourse produces change by influencing the decision and action of persons who function as mediators of change, it follows that rhetoric always requires an audience —even in those cases when a person engages himself or ideal mind as audience. It is clear also that a rhetorical audience must be distinguished from a body of mere hearers or readers: properly speaking, a rhetorical audience consists only of those persons who are capable of being influenced by discourse and of being mediators of change.

Neither scientific nor poetic discourse requires an audience in the same sense. Indeed, neither requires an audience in order to produce its end; the scientist can produce a discourse expressive or generative of knowledge without engaging another mind, and the poet's creative purpose is accomplished when the work is composed. It is true, of course, that scientists and poets present their works to audiences, but their audiences are not necessarily rhetorical. The scientific audience consists of persons capable of receiving knowledge, and the poetic audience, of persons capable of participating in aesthetic experiences induced by the poetry. But the rhetorical audience must be capable of serving as mediator of the change which the discourse functions to produce.

Besides exigency and audience, every rhetorical situation contains a set of *constraints* made up of persons, events, objects, and relations which are parts of the situation because they have the power to constrain decision and action needed to modify the exigency. Standard sources of constraint include beliefs, attitudes, documents, facts, traditions, images, interests, motives and the like; and when the orator enters the situation, his discourse not only harnesses constraints given by situation but provides additional important constraints—for example, his personal character, his logical proofs, and his style. There are two main classes of constraints: (1) those originated or managed by the rhetor and his method (Aristotle called these "artistic proofs"), and (2) those other constraints, in the situation, which may be operative (Aristotle's "inartistic proofs"). Both classes must be divided so as to separate those constraints that are proper from those that are improper.

These three constituents—exigency, audience, constraints—comprise everything relevant in a rhetorical situation. When the orator, invited by situation, enters it and creates and presents discourse, then both he and his speech are additional constituents.

III

I have broadly sketched a conception of rhetorical situation and discussed constituents. The following are general characteristics or features.

1. Rhetorical discourse is called into existence by situation; the situation which the rhetor perceives amounts to an invitation to create and present discourse. The clearest instances of rhetorical speaking and writing are strongly invited—often required. The situation generated by the assassina-

tion of President Kennedy was so highly structured and compelling that one could predict with near certainty the types and themes of forthcoming discourse. With the first reports of the assassination, there immediately developed a most urgent need for information; in response, reporters created hundreds of messages. Later as the situation altered, other exigencies arose: the fantastic events in Dallas had to be explained; it was necessary to eulogize the dead president; the public needed to be assured that the transfer of government to new hands would be orderly. These messages were not idle performances. The historic situation was so compelling and clear that the responses were created almost out of necessity. The responses —news reports, explanations, eulogies—participated with the situation and positively modified the several exigencies. Surely the power of situation is evident when one can predict that such discourse will be uttered. How else explain the phenomenon? One cannot say that the situation is the function of the speaker's intention, for in this case the speakers' intentions were determined by the situation. One cannot say that the rhetorical transaction is simply a response of the speaker to the demands or expectations of an audience, for the expectations of the audience were themselves keyed to a tragic historic fact. Also, we must recognize that there came into existence countless eulogies to John F. Kennedy that never reached a public; they were filed, entered in diaries, or created in thought.

In contrast, imagine a person spending his time writing eulogies of men and women who never existed: his speeches meet no rhetorical situations; they are summoned into existence not by real events, but by his own imagination. They may exhibit formal features which we consider rhetorical —such as ethical and emotional appeals, and stylistic patterns; conceivably one of these fictive eulogies is even persuasive to someone; yet all remain unrhetorical unless, through the oddest of circumstances, one of them by chance should fit a situation. Neither the presence of formal features in the discourse nor persuasive effect in a reader or hearer can be regarded as reliable marks of rhetorical discourse: a speech will be rhetorical when it is a response to the kind of situation that is rhetorical.

2. Although rhetorical situation invites response, it obviously does not invite just any response. Thus, the second characteristic of rhetorical situation is that it invites a *fitting* response, a response that fits the situation. Lincoln's Gettysburg Address was a most fitting response to the relevant features of the historic context which invited its existence and gave it

rhetorical significance. Imagine for a moment the Gettysburg Address entirely separated from its situation and existing for us independent of any rhetorical context: as a discourse which does not "fit" any rhetorical situation, it becomes either poetry or declamation, without rhetorical significance. In reality, however, the address continues to have profound rhetorical value precisely because some features of the Gettysburg situation persist; and the Gettysburg Address continues to participate with situation and to alter it.

Consider another instance. During one week of the 1964 presidential campaign, three events of national and international significance all but obscured the campaign: Khrushchev was suddenly deposed, China exploded an atomic bomb, and in England the Conservative Party was defeated by Labour. Any student of rhetoric could have given odds that President Johnson, in a major address, would speak to the significance of these events, and he did; his response to the situation generated by the events was fitting. Suppose that Johnson had treated not these events and their significance but the national budget, or imagine that he had reminisced about his childhood on a Texas farm. The critic of rhetoric would have said rightly, "He missed the mark; his speech did not fit; he did not speak to the pressing issues—the rhetorical situation shaped by the three crucial events of the week demanded a response, and he failed to provide the proper one."

3. If it makes sense to say that situation invites a "fitting" response, then situation must somehow prescribe the response which fits. To say that a rhetorical response fits a situation is to say that it meets the requirements established by the situation. A situation which is strong and clear dictates the purpose, theme, matter, and style of the response. Normally, the inauguration of a president of the United States demands an address which speaks to the nation's purposes, the central national and international problems, the unity of contesting parties; it demands a speech style marked by dignity. What is evidenced on this occasion is the power of situation to constrain a fitting response. One might say metaphorically that every situation prescribes its fitting response; the rhetor may or may not read the prescription accurately.

4. The exigency and the complex of persons, objects, events, and relations which generate rhetorical discourse are located in reality, are objective and publicly observable historic facts in the world we experience, are therefore available for scrutiny by an observer or critic who attends to them. To say

the situation is objective, publicly observable, and historic means that it is real or genuine,—that our critical examination will certify its existence. Real situations are to be distinguished from sophistic ones in which, for example, a contrived exigency is asserted to be real; from spurious situations in which the existence or alleged existence of constituents is the result of error or ignorance; and from fantasy in which exigency, audience, and constraints may all be the imaginary objects of a mind at play.

The rhetorical situation as real is to be distinguished also from a fictive rhetorical situation. The speech of a character in a novel or play may be clearly required by a fictive rhetorical situation—a situation established by the story itself; but the speech is not genuinely rhetorical, even though, considered in itself, it looks exactly like a courtroom address or a Senate speech. It is realistic, made so by fictive context. But the situation is not real, not grounded in history; neither the fictive situation nor the discourse generated by it is rhetorical. We should note, however, that the fictive rhetorical discourse within a play or novel may become genuinely rhetorical outside fictive context—if there is a real situation for which the discourse is a rhetorical response. Also, of course, the play or novel itself may be understood as a rhetorical response having poetic form.

5. Rhetorical situations exhibit structures which are simple or complex, and more or less organized. A situation's structure is simple when there are relatively few elements which must be made to interact; the fishing expedition is a case in point—there is a clear and easy relationship among utterances, the audiences, constraints, and exigency. Franklin D. Roosevelt's brief Declaration of War speech is another example: the message exists as a response to one clear exigency easily perceived by one major audience, and the one overpowering constraint is the necessity of war. On the other hand, the structure of a situation is complex when many elements must be made to interact: practically any presidential political campaign provides numerous complex rhetorical situations.

A situation, whether simple or complex, will be highly or loosely structured. It is highly structured when all its elements are located and readied for the task to be performed. Malinowski's example, the fishing expedition, is a situation which is relatively simple and highly structured; everything is ordered to the task to be performed. The usual courtroom case is a good example of situation which is complex and highly structured. The jury is not a random and scattered audience but a selected and concentrated one;

it knows its relation to judge, law, defendant, counsels; it is instructed in what to observe and what to disregard. The judge is located and prepared; he knows exactly his relation to jury, law, counsels, defendant. The counsels know the ultimate object of their case; they know what they must prove; they know the audience and can easily reach it. This situation will be even more highly structured if the issue of the case is sharp, the evidence decisive, and the law clear. On the other hand, consider a complex but loosely structured situation, William Lloyd Garrison preaching abolition from town to town. He is actually looking for an audience and for constraints; even when he finds an audience, he does not know that it is a genuinely rhetorical audience—one able to be mediator of change. Or consider the plight of many contemporary civil rights advocates who, failing to locate compelling constraints and rhetorical audiences, abandon rhetorical discourse in favor of physical action.

Situations may become weakened in structure due to complexity or disconnectedness. A list of causes includes these: (1) a single situation may involve numerous exigencies; (2) exigencies in the same situation may be incompatible; (3) two or more simultaneous rhetorical situations may compete for our attention, as in some parliamentary debates; (4) at a given moment, persons comprising the audience of situation A may also be the audience of situations B, C, and D; (5) the rhetorical audience may be scattered, uneducated regarding its duties and powers, or it may dissipate; (6) constraints may be limited in number and force, and they may be incompatible. This is enough to suggest the sorts of things which weaken the structure of situations.

6. Finally, rhetorical situations come into existence, then either mature or decay or mature and persist—conceivably some persist indefinitely. In any case, situations grow and come to maturity; they evolve to just the time when a rhetorical discourse would be most fitting. In Malinowski's example, there comes a time in the situation when the leader of the fishermen should say, "Throw the nets." In the situation generated by the assassination of President Kennedy, there was a time for giving descriptive accounts of the scene in Dallas, later a time for giving eulogies. In a political campaign, there is a time for generating an issue and a time for answering a charge. Every rhetorical situation in principle evolves to a propitious moment for the fitting rhetorical response. After this moment, most situations decay; we all have the experience of creating a rhetorical response when it is too late to make it public.

Some situations, on the other hand, persist; this is why it is possible to have a body of truly *rhetorical* literature. The Gettysburg Address, Burke's Speech to the Electors of Bristol, Socrates' Apology—these are more than historical documents, more than specimens for stylistic or logical analysis. They exist as rhetorical responses *for us* precisely because they speak to situations which persist—which are in some measure universal.

Due to either the nature of things or convention, or both, some situations recur. The courtroom is the locus for several kinds of situations generating the speech of accusation, the speech of defense, the charge to the jury. From day to day, year to year, comparable situations occur, prompting comparable responses; hence rhetorical forms are born and a special vocabulary, grammar, and style are established. This is true also of the situation which invites the inaugural address of a president. The situation recurs and, because we experience situations and the rhetorical responses to them, a form of discourse is not only established but comes to have a power of its own—the tradition itself tends to function as a constraint upon any new response in the form.

IV

In the best of all possible worlds, there would be communication perhaps, but no rhetoric—since exigencies would not arise. In our real world, however, rhetorical exigencies abound; the world really invites change—change conceived and effected by human agents who quite properly address a mediating audience. The practical justification of rhetoric is analogous to that of scientific inquiry: the world presents objects to be known, puzzles to be resolved, complexities to be understood—hence the practical need for scientific inquiry and discourse; similarly, the world presents imperfections to be modified by means of discourse—hence the practical need for rhetorical investigation and discourse. As a discipline, scientific method is justified philosophically insofar as it provides principles, concepts, and procedures by which we come to know reality; similarly, rhetoric as a discipline is justified philosophically insofar as it provides principles, concepts, and procedures by which we effect valuable changes in reality. Thus, rhetoric is distinguished from the mere craft of persuasion which, although it is a legitimate object of scientific investigation, lacks philosophical warrant as a practical discipline.

NOTE

1. "The Problem of Meaning in Primitive Languages," sections III and IV. This essay appears as a supplement in Ogden and Richards' *The Meaning of Meaning.* (New York: Harcourt, Brace and Company, 1923).

Rhetoric, Communication, and Psycho-epistemology

Gary Cronkhite

The charge against Dame Rhetoric has been variously stated by those who would malign her honor, but it has usually been some form of this: *Rhetoric creates a verbal elite capable of manipulating the masses, putting the masses at the mercy of such ethics as that elite may deem appropriate for its purposes.*

Such a notion was extant at least as early as Plato's time, and it has been a recurring theme throughout the history of human dialogue. "Rhetoric" appears in the modern public press almost exclusively as a pejorative term. One of the more forceful examples I have encountered was the statement by California State Superintendent of Public Instruction Wilson Riles in a speech in Fresno on August 17, 1972, to the effect that "Rhetoric is of no use to anyone." Of course, Riles is being quoted out of context, and, of course, if one could probe beneath the semantics, the myriad popular writers and speakers who do violence to the term "rhetoric" may not have reference to the sort of rhetoric we profess to teach. But the fact of the matter is that the banner under which we march is defamed at one point or another in practically every issue of every popular magazine and newspaper.

Why? One reason is that the rhetorician is in a poor position to defend himself, a position akin to that of a witch on trial in colonial Salem. If he says nothing, it can be assumed he has no defense. If he defends himself with the tools of his trade, his detractor can say, in essence: "Methinks the lady doth protest not only too much but too well; if the sophistic devil were not in her she could not be so eloquent in defense of her honor."

A second, and far more disturbing, reason, plainly put, is that the circumstantial evidence in favor of the charge is overwhelming. It is, after all, difficult to deny the accusation of manipulation in view of the inordinate and almost compulsive attention rhetoricians have lavished upon the means of persuasion contrasted with their near neglect of the criteria for rational response to persuasion.

The purpose of this article is, then, to respond to the charge that rhetoric produces cunning verbal manipulators capable of seducing the minds of their listeners by arguing that, while the accusation has been true too often in the past, it is not inherent in the nature of rhetoric: a rhetoric which includes the study of the rational bases for belief in a society which nurtures and reciprocally depends upon individual freedom of choice is necessarily ethical. Put succinctly, the thesis of this article is that *the best antidote for a sophistic rhetor is a sophisticated rhetoree, and we had best get at the business of producing such an antidote.* What is advanced here is not so much an attempt to refute the charge as a proposal for corrective action involving a different view of the role of rhetoric and a different approach to its teaching.

The Place of Rhetoric in Academe

It appears to have been Douglas Ehninger who coined the term "psychoepistemology" to describe the rhetorical theory of Campbell.[1] I believe that the concept Ehninger suggests, and hence the term, is appropriate in my definition of rhetoric, viz.: *Rhetoric is the study of the function of communication in psychoepistemology.*

That definition is obviously unclear without additional definitions of "psychoepistemology" and "communication." "Epistemology," grossly defined, is the study of how men know what they know, and is generally considered to be a branch of philosophy. For the agnostic, who is not certain men "know" *anything,* the term "psychoepistemology" should be much more comfortable and might be defined as the study of why men believe what they believe.

If we approach the definitions of "communication" and "rhetoric" from this frame of reference, we must adopt a different perspective from that maintained by most theorists. The new perspective is that of an individual who begins life with no knowledge of his environment and, in order to survive, must immediately set about the task of gathering information, sorting the reliable from the unreliable. The information arrives through various sense modalities at different times; to determine its reliability, the individual searches for consistencies in the incoming data. Some information is not accessible to immediate sense verification, so a person learns to make inferences from present sensory input regarding events remote in time and space. Some of the sensory input from which he makes inferences originates with other persons in the form of "reports," and in these cases he learns to use copersonal or social validation as well.

This is the role communication plays in psychoepistemology. *Communication, from this perspective, occurs whenever the sensory and/or cognitive apparatus of another person is interposed between oneself and the object, event, or idea under consideration.*

The study of communication, then, becomes a subset of psychoepistemology. Communication operates very much as a sixth sense. The five senses are sometimes distinguished into two groups: those involving receptors which must contact the object perceived (touch and taste), and those involving distance receptors (smell, sight, hearing). Communication, as defined here, is a sixth sense involving a distance receptor par excellence, the highly elaborated human cortex. It is a distant early warning system which allows man to deal with his environment at a distance and before the fact, to experience it vicariously, and to develop alternative contingency plans and make preparations to deal with it firsthand.

Part of the price paid for the distance-eroding ability of this sixth sense is its lack of reliability. When one interposes the sensory and cognitive apparatus of another between himself and an object, event, or idea, one exposes himself to all the errors which may be introduced by the frailties of that apparatus. These include not only errors of perception and inference on the part of the other, but also errors introduced by the fact that the other is not bound to serve a strictly reporting function, so that his reports may deviate considerably from what he perceives and infers. Consequently, the inferences one makes from data reported by others are fraught with the possibility of error. Rhetoricians have spent thousands of years studying this process of inference and its bases, but often from a peculiar vantage point: they have studied how the "other" can cause the individual to whom he is reporting to infer that his reports are accurate. Is it any wonder that the world has suspected rhetoricians of motives somewhat closer to malignancy than altruism?

Rhetoric is the study of how people come to believe that which they believe, not through immediate sense verification, but by inference from the opinion of others. Rhetoric is the study of communication as defined here, and is thus a part of the field of psychoepistemology. Such a study, the application of disciplined scholarly inquiry to a process absolutely essential to human survival, must be inherently ethical by almost anyone's definition.

Relation to Other Definitions

There is no pretense that the perspective or definitions advanced here constitute a synthesis of other definitions of rhetoric and communication. I have argued that there is a need for a study of the role played by inferences from communication which provide the individual with information about his environment, information necessary to his survival and to the survival of the species. I have argued that the traditional role of rhetoric places that discipline in a natural position to assume such a study.

While a survey of other views and definitions of rhetoric does not suggest that the present definition even approaches a synthesis, it does suggest a trend toward this perspective.[2] One cannot avoid noting that trend if one begins by considering the classical treatises which dealt primarily with oral persuasion, through Campbell's analysis[3] of the reasons people come to believe (albeit for the benefit of the persuader), through Richards' position[4] that the function of rhetoric is to eliminate misunderstanding for the benefit of speaker and listener as well, through Simons' view[5] of rhetoric as a search for discursive means of handling social problems to the benefit of all those involved, and ends with Becker,[6] who seems to view rhetoric as the study of the ways people seek information, or with Perelman[7] who, as Dearin[8] puts it, assigns "to rhetoric a fundamental role in epistemology." Neither Becker nor Perelman departs so radically from traditional definitions of rhetoric as does the present proposal. However, drawing a line of sight from Aristotle through Becker and Perelman, the present definition is an almost necessary extrapolation.

Ethics and Social Utility

This approach to rhetoric and communication is ethical in the sense that it is *useful:* first, to the individual in his quest for knowledge about the universe into which he is so unceremoniously dropped; second, to a society based, theoretically at least, upon freedom of individual choice in economic and sociopolitical matters; and, third, to the survival of rationality in what is essentially a social evolution of ideas.

Utility for the Individual

The premise underlying this approach is that communication behavior developed and is maintained because of its survival value. That premise cannot pretend to be anything more than an assumption, since the origins of communication are locked rather securely in prehistorical and preverbal antiquity. It does seem rather reasonable. As Spence has so succinctly put it, any organism which persists in nonadaptive behavior is likely to come from a long line of extinct ancestors.

Communication seems to perform two functions having clear survival value: the function of information—gathering and the function of social control. I have already covered the information-gathering function to some extent. That certainly should not overshadow the importance of the control function, for it does exist and has considerable apparent utility as a survival device.

The sending of control-communication by others is, however, to some degree inimical to the use of incoming communication as a means of information-gathering, since control-communication may or may not be accurate and may or may not be perceived by the listener to be control-communication. On the other hand, we would receive much less information from others if they were not motivated by the desire to control; otherwise, we would have to depend entirely on cooperative information-sharing arrangements. If everyone perceived the human situation as Kenneth Burke does, as a race "huddled together, nervously loquacious, on the edge of an abyss," then such cooperative arrangements might suffice. The fact of the matter is, however, that they do *not* suffice.

Thus, the central task of an individual operating as a receiver seems to be to evaluate the accuracy of incoming messages, reserving special skepticism for those behind which he detects a high degree of control-intent.

The task of the individual operating as a message source is to decide on the balance he wishes to maintain between cooperative information-sharing and self-serving control, and to manage that balance successfully. The choice of balance is governed by a variety of factors:

(1) If the receiver does not perceive a high proportion of useful information in the message, he will not attend to it, and it will fail to serve its control function.

(2) If the receiver perceives too much control-intent behind the message, he will cease to reciprocate with messages of high information-value.

(3) The source may consider a message with too much control-intent to be selfish, unethical, and thus unfair to the receiver.

Complicating this somewhat simplistic view is the fact that communication serves many additional needs for both sender and receiver. Some of these, for example, are the need for stimulation in general and for a variety of stimulation in particular, the need for pattern-recognition or the imposition of order on experience, the need for ego-gratification, and the need for social interaction in and of itself. Some of these appear to be biologically based, some appear to be learned secondary needs, and most are a mixture of the two. There is no assumption here that the satisfaction of certain needs is inherently more or less "rational" than satisfaction of others; the assumption is that all participants in a communication exchange should share maximal awareness of the function that exchange is serving for themselves and others. The more basic assumption, eliminating the troublesome word "should," is that a group of individuals will have a higher probability of survival if their decisions in response to communication are made in an atmosphere of need-awareness or, if you must, "rationality."

The problem is that the basic conflict between the listener's desire for accurate information and the sender's desire to control militates against such need-awareness; it tempts both parties to engage in deception. The sender deceives in that he attempts to disguise his control intent, to disguise inaccurate information, and to disguise the fact that the alternative he is proposing may satisfy his own needs more than those of the listener. The listener deceives in that he leads the sender to believe he (the listener) is being controlled in order to induce the sender to send those messages which satisfy those needs which are most salient, even though such messages may be inaccurate and/or inimical to the best interests of both sender and listener.

The function of the rhetorical or communication theorist, researcher, or critic then becomes clear; it is to identify communication deception and its causes. The practical, utilitarian value of rhetorical theory for the individual is that it ought to tell him something about the conditions under which the sensory and cognitive system of another functions as a reliable instrument, providing data from which he can make useful inferences about "reality" or his environment. That value has yet to be realized.

Utility in a Free Society

Secondly, this critical ability to discriminate between sense and nonsense lies at the very heart of our democratic political system and our economic system of free enterprise. A critical assumption for democracy is that voters are capable of listening to political oratory and making rational decisions; a critical assumption for free enterprise is that the consumer is capable of critically evaluating the incredible barrage of sophistry perpetrated every day by the advertising industry. Neither of these assumptions seems very well founded at the moment. Yet rhetoricians have characteristically worked in the midst of this economic and political arena, armed with supposedly expert knowledge of the ways in which decisions are made in response to communication and have offered their services almost invariably to the persuader.

It must appear strange to those outside the field that we devote our efforts almost exclusively to improving the offensive arsenal of the persuader and have so little to say about the means by which the listener can defend himself against such weapons. Our offensive capabilities are over two thousand years ahead of our defensive capabilities, and only a tremendous crash program will close that gap. These offensive capabilities have transformed our world into a gigantic replica of a Tijuana used car lot instead of a marketplace of ideas.

Sociocultural Utility

But important as it may be to the individual and to a society based on democracy and free enterprise, the epistemological approach to rhetoric and communication is even more important in sociocultural evolution, the evolution of ideas. Donald T. Campbell, the psychologist-philosopher from Northwestern University, has been the leading contemporary proponent of the evolutionary analysis of social behavior. He described his theory at the 1965 Nebraska Symposium on Motivation:

> For the evolutionary process to take place there need to be variations (as by mutation, trial, etc.), stable aspects of the environment differentially selecting among such variations and a retention-propagation system rigidly holding on to the selected variations. The variation and the retention aspects are inherently at odds.[9]

Among other things, Campbell thus provides an interesting potential distinction between the overused terms "liberal" and "conservative," and a different framework for considering the social crisis we observe today on all fronts. By this analysis, liberalism is the force acting to provide variation or mutation, while conservatism is merely a term for the force acting to retain ideas already selected, inhibiting variation and mutation. The current epidemic of social crisis can be viewed as the result of a sudden drastic increase in the rate of ideological mutation, opposed at every turn by the retention-propagation system. This puts tremendous stress on the selector mechanism which must choose those ideological mutations worth retaining, recommending them for care and feeding by the retention-propagation system. *The functioning of this selector mechanism depends upon the use of communication as an epistemological device.*

Of course, communication is involved in all three processes: mutant ideas are carried like seeds on the winds of communication; the retention-propagation system uses communication as a selective herbicide to destroy the ideological mutations and as a fertilizer to maintain the health of the ideological strains that have been chosen for preservation. But at the heart of the entire process is the selector mechanism and the discipline which ministers to its health: epistemological communication.

Consider for a moment the nature of that selector mechanism. The selection mechanism in the process of biological evolution is biological death (or failure to reproduce). The selection mechanism for ideological evolution is not death or failure to reproduce in a biological sense, for language and communication have freed ideas from dependence on life-span units and biological reproduction. Ideas do not survive because of the survival of their proponents; if they did, the idea of preferring death to dishonor would have passed from the scene long ago. Instead, in order to survive, an idea must gain enough acceptance during the life of its originator to be perpetuated by others after his death.

For most of us this is a rather unwelcome thought: that public opinion is the selector mechanism for ideological evolution. Fortunately, the situation is not so bleak. First, an idea can be nurtured in the smallest enclaves from generation to generation until its time comes. Second, this selector mechanism has the unique property of being itself susceptible to an evolutionary process, though that does not mean it is inherently self-corrective. The process of ideological selection by public acceptance does change, but the direction of change is yet to be decided in open contest. We must act so as to assure the survival of reason as the basis of public acceptance because we are rational. You would not ask a boa constrictor why he reproduces boa constrictors; he does so because he is one. The touchstone of rational man is not "I think, therefore I am"; it is, rather, "I think, therefore I am advocating the survival of thinking." "Man is a rational animal" becomes less of a definition than a rallying cry.

Implications for Research

Most of the research that has been done in the name of rhetoric and communication is applicable to the study of communication as a psycho-epistemological device. However, too many researchers have been trained to view communication from the same occluded view which has infected the field in general. The glaucoma which has resulted has produced in a number of cases the illusion of a dilemma, especially when experimental results have been translated into what "should" be taught. Consider a few instances.

Organization

Early experimental research in message organization suggested that random rearrangement of message segments had only a mild effect on information recall and essentially no detectable effect on attitude change on the part of the listener.[10] This was rather difficult to reconcile with the emphasis on message organization which has characterized teaching in our field for most of its existence. Part of the problem with the research lay in the fact that "organization" covers such a hodgepodge of variables that "disorganization" is bound to have both negative and positive effects on attitude change. When those confounded variables have been sorted out and considered separately in more recent research, the effects have been clearer.[11]

However, even more of the problem lies in the fact that researchers have almost invariably maintained a posture crouched behind the speaker, peering over his shoulder to observe the effects of his message. The author certainly has been guilty of that cramped, awkward posture. I once made the statement, for example, that "most audiences respond most favorably to a message in which the persuader does not state his purpose in the introduction."[12] The statement has adequate research support, but it was a response to the wrong question. An analysis in the terms of this paper would produce this question: "Can audiences more reliably evaluate messages in which the purpose, thesis, and major arguments are clearly stated in the introduction?" My guess is that they can, but I know of no research in communication that has dealt with the question. The reason is simple: researchers consistently show more interest in whether such introductions increase or decrease *favorable attitude change*. Reliable evaluations of an irrational message will produce a decrement in attitude change, and reliable evaluation of a rational message will produce the opposite. But who would argue that purveyors of irrational messages "should" conceal their purposes, theses, and major arguments in the hope that the audience will be deceived?

My guess may be wrong. It may be that an initial statement of purpose decreases the listener's ability to evaluate a message reliably when he is initially biased against that message and the message is rational. But the prediction is not important; the point is that we should be dealing with *that* question rather than with the more confounded question of attitude change in general. Our failure to do so is symptomatic of our concern for the persuader and his purpose, and a lack of concern for the listener's interest in rational response to the message.

Evidence

The research dealing with the effects of evidence is another case in point. Again, the early research seemed to point to the conclusion that evidence made little difference in audience attitude change.[13] More recently, McCroskey concluded that the presence or absence of evidence in a message interacts with the ethos or credibility of the message source,[14] while others have found that the effect depends upon whether the source of the evidence is cited before or after the evidence is presented.[15] Once again, however, all these researchers have used audience attitude change as the criterion variable. Again, one might ask more pertinent questions. Under what conditions, for example, does the presentation of evidence improve the ability of the listener to make a valid evaluation of the message, or to make a rational decision in response to the message? Can audiences evaluate evidence more reliably when the source is cited before the evidence is presented? What kinds of evidence improve the validity and rationality of audience response, and what kinds of evidence are detrimental? Regarding the interaction of evidence and ethos, under what circumstances does the presentation of evidence improve the listener's ability to evaluate the credibility of the message source? Certainly the citation of evidence can mislead a listener under some conditions: I believe an extensive analysis of *None Dare Call It Treason* would confirm that judgment. Even more certainly our field could profit from less attention to the simple question whether any evidence improves the effectiveness of any message, especially when "effectiveness" is defined merely as the compliance of the listener.

Ethos and/or Credibility

Studies of source credibility have been basically of two types: those which have varied something about the speaker or the way he was introduced and observed the resulting attitude change,[16] and those which have attempted to determine by factor analysis the dimensions on which the listener judges the speaker.[17] Studies of the first type have been handicapped in that they have either failed to consider the intervening audience perceptions of the speaker, or have treated them as if they were unidimensional. The second type has been handicapped in that they have generally failed to determine whether the dimensions of the listener's perception produce his response to the message, or the reverse, added to the fact that various studies have produced anywhere from two to as many as eleven dimensions, with different factor structures seldom bearing any detectable relationships to one another. More important to the present analysis is that neither type of study has considered this question: what clues can a listener rely upon when he is trying to decide whether a speaker is trustworthy and knowledgeable? Happily, recent research regarding the means by which deception can be detected from nonverbal cues is being introduced into our field. However, there is much more to be done to decipher this peculiar nonverbal code, and there are many cues besides the nonverbal: those that lie in the verbal message and in the circumstances surrounding the speaker and his message. Further, perceived trustworthiness, expertness, and dynamism on the part of the speaker may under certain circumstances distract the listener from an objective evaluation of the message. We need to identify those circumstances. Again, we need to be more concerned with the variables which contribute to reliable message evaluation and less concerned with listener compliance per se.

Refutation and Inoculation

The research in the area of refutation and inoculation has dwelt on the question of how a speaker can best reduce the persuasive effect of preceding or subsequent messages which are opposed to his own.[18] The present analysis would suggest, instead, that we study the situation in which a listener encounters a sequence of contradictory messages in order to determine what factors in the messages or their sequences tend to distort the listener's comparative evaluation of those messages. The basic question would be how the listener can assure himself that he is judging the messages on their merits without being influenced by irrelevant factors involved in their sequencing or their references to one another.

Fear Appeals and Language Intensity

The last research area from which I would like to draw an example is encompassed by the labels "fear appeals" and "language intensity." The labels are not synonymous by any means, but the studies conducted under the two rubrics exhibit some striking similarities. Basically, research of both types has indicated that messages which could be expected to be emotionally arousing for the listener produce, *under certain circumstances,* less listener compliance than do messages of less intensity.[19] The analysis used throughout this series of examples applies once again. The studies in question have always used some form of listener *compliance* rather than listener *objectivity* as the criterion variable. We can reasonably assume that messages of intense emotionality, especially in times of emotional crises, are especially destructive of objectivity. The listener needs to be able to recognize both an intensely emotional message and his own emotional arousal, and needs to learn how to deal with them in order to preserve his objectivity.

He cannot afford to suppress all activity whenever the message is intensely emotional or whenever he is emotionally aroused, for that will often lead to inaction in a real crisis. On the other hand, he can no better afford to respond with knee-jerk reflexes to any highly intense message he encounters. We will not have much useful to tell the listener; indeed, we will not know much in this area, until we stop worrying about whether highly intense messages produce more or less compliance and begin to ask what effect message intensity has upon the listener's ability to respond decisively and objectively. Once again the question, as we have asked it, has produced research that is inherently confounded and which has contributed to our reputations as manipulators.

These few examples have not begun to detail the research problems created by our inordinate fascination with the persuader. The examples only serve to illustrate the point. Consider now what implications for teaching are contained in the psychoepistemological definition of rhetoric.

Implications for Teaching

The public image of our discipline is probably determined more by our courses in the public high schools and in the first course at the college level than by any other endeavor. Even if the approach to rhetoric that I am suggesting in this article were to be accepted immediately as academically and theoretically viable, cultural lag being what it is, it would probably be twenty years before it had any significant impact at the level of public education. Yet this appears to be the direction in which the field is moving, it seems ethically more defensible than influence-oriented rhetorics, it provides a new and less confounded analysis on which to base communication research, and it will probably make a considerable improvement in the public image of the field of rhetoric if it is seriously pursued. Certainly, we cannot expect the public to view us as altruistically motivated as long as we continue to stockpile offensive weapons and train our cadets in their use.

Fortunately, the change in teaching methods would not be so drastic as might at first appear. We simply need to inject a great deal of training in defensive listening and reading into our curriculum. Training in defensive listening and reading is not far removed from what many fundamental courses already contain. The evaluation of evidence and recognition of specious reasoning already appear there. What appear too infrequently are consideration of the psychological and social bases of decision and actual practice in critical response to propaganda. These should not be too difficult to provide, if we can overcome the mental glaucoma, cerebrosclerosis, and rigor mentis that tend to infect teachers who have too many years invested in their lecture notes.

I have written a book in the area of persuasion which has been occasionally (and ill-advisedly) adopted as a textbook.[20] Were I to write such a book from the present perspective, I would probably cover much the same theory and research, but the recommendations and examples for application of that theory and research would be directed toward teaching the student to critically evaluate persuasive attempts. Most other textbooks in our field could profit from similar rewriting. In the interim, it should not be too difficult for inventive teachers to use the existing fundamental textbooks in a different way, and to supplement those textbooks with others such as the excellent *Thinking Straight* by Beardsley.[21] At least two books written from this point of view have recently appeared, both of which are to be commended. These are *Logic and Contemporary Rhetoric* by Kahane[22] and, at a very different level, *Rudy's Red Wagon* by Rein.[23]

Consider some of the information that could be gleaned from the theory and research in persuasion and put to use to protect the interests of the consumer. The consumer of communication could better defend himself if he knew, for example, that when he is unusually defensive or aggressive, he is especially susceptible to certain types of argument; that when he has made an irrevocable choice, he is especially susceptible to arguments which seem to justify those choices; that he is especially likely to agree with people who serve the functions of identification, ego-satisfaction, and reward; that he is likely to maintain those beliefs to which he is publicly committed, even if they are useless or even harmful; and that he is likely to try to maintain various types of consistency among his beliefs, attitudes, values, and behaviors.

Some discipline is going to fill this void if we do not, yet at this time we are clearly in the most advantageous position. We have much of the necessary information at hand, and we occupy a place in most curricula very close to that described here. The obstacle which we must overcome is our chauvinistic worship of the persuader.

Conclusion

Dame Rhetoric has been characterized as the Whore of the Arts, but she
need not be so. It is only that she can be all things to all men: used by an
unethical businessman, she can be the Prostitute of Prosperity; in the hands
of a political demagogue she can be the Lay of the Land; under the influence
of a religious fanatic she can be Our Lady of the Immaculate Deception or
Our Lady of the Wholly Assumption. We can rant against these forms of
white slavery, but harangues will never rid the world of unethical business-
men, political demagogues, and religious fanatics, or of their capacities for
successful seduction. We can introduce her into holy matrimony with
causes which we deem just and place our *imprimatur* on the offspring of
such wedlock, hoping they will be more numerous and robust than the issue
of illegitimacy. Still, we can never hope to chaperone all her liaisons. Our
ultimate hope lies in ordaining the population, training them to recognize
and to deal with her potentially salacious nature. We must demonstrate to
the world that the principles of persuasion are equally useful as tools of
critical deliberation, absolutely essential elements in the education of men
who function in a society devoted to freedom of economic, political, and
moral choice.

NOTES AND REFERENCES

1. Douglas Ehninger, "Campbell, Blair, and Whately Revisited," *Southern Speech Journal* 28 (1963):169–182.

2. The writer does not propose to review all the definitions and perspectives
   advanced by rhetorical theorists in the past 2.6 millenia. The perspectives of
   pre-twentieth century theorists, however, were almost exclusively from the
   point of view of a speaker interested in influencing his listeners, and the rhetorical works generated from that viewpoint were designed primarily to aid the
   speaker in achieving that objective. Twentieth century theorists have generally
   followed the same line, with some important exceptions which certainly include
   I. A. Richards, Kenneth Burke, Stephen Toulmin, Herbert Simons, Samuel
   Becker, and Chaim Perelman, and may include a number of others in which
   the perspective is not so clear but is not strictly influence-oriented. The theories
   of Richards, Simons, Becker, and Perelman are cited in footnotes 4, 5, 6, and

7. The others are as follows: Kenneth Burke, "The Range of Rhetoric," in *A Rhetoric of Motives* (Berkeley and Los Angeles: University of California, 1969); Stephen Toulmin, *The Uses of Argument* (Cambridge: At the University Press, 1959).

3. George Campbell, *The Philosophy of Rhetoric*, reprint, edited by Lloyd Bitzer (Carbondale: Southern Illinois University, 1963). Originally published in London and Edinburgh, 1776.

4. I. A. Richards, *The Philosophy of Rhetoric* (New York: Oxford University Press, 1936).

5. Herbert W. Simons, "Toward a New Rhetoric," *Pennsylvania Speech Annual* 24 (1967):7–20.

6. Samuel Becker, "Rhetorical Studies for the Contemporary World," in *The Prospect of Rhetoric*, edited by Lloyd Bitzer and Edwin Black (Englewood Cliffs, N. J.: Prentice-Hall, 1971), pp. 21–43.

7. Chaim Perelman, "The New Rhetoric," in Bitzer and Black, op. cit., pp. 115–22; Chaim Perelman and L. Olbrechts Tyteca, *The New Rhetoric*, translated by John Wilkinson and Purcell Weaver (South Bend, Ind.: University of Notre Dame Press, 1969), especially the introduction, pp. 1–26.

8. Ray Dearin, "The Philosophical Basis of Chaim Perelman's Theory of Rhetoric," *Quarterly Journal of Speech* 55 (1969):213–24.

9. Donald T. Campbell, "Ethnocentric and Other Altruistic Motives," in *Nebraska Symposium on Motivation*, edited by D. Levine (Lincoln: University of Nebraska Press, 1965), pp. 306–7.

10. Raymond G. Smith, "An Experimental Study of the Effects of Speech Organization upon Attitudes of College Students," *Speech Monographs* 18 (1951):292–301; E. Thompson, "An Experimental Investigation of the Relative Effectiveness of Organization Structure in Oral Communication," *Southern Speech Journal* 26 (1960):59–69; Kenneth C. Beighley, "An Experimental Study of the Effect of Four Speech Variables on Listener Comprehension," *Speech Monographs* 19 (1952):249–58; Donald K. Darnell, "The Relation between Sentence Order and Comprehension," *Speech Monographs* 30 (1963):97–100; Harry Sharp, Jr., and Thomas McClung, "Effects of Organization on the Speaker's Ethos," *Speech Monographs* 33 (1966):182–83. While the results are mixed, no consistent deficit in attitude change appears in studies of disorganization above the sentence level.

11. These studies are too numerous to be cited here. The interested reader might refer to the discussion in Gary Cronkhite, *Persuasion: Speech and Behavioral Change* (Indianapolis: Bobbs-Merrill, 1969), pp. 192–202.

12. Ibid., p. 195.

13. Ibid., p. 187; also see next footnote.

14. James C. McCroskey, "A Summary of Experimental Research on the Effects of Evidence in Persuasive Communication," *Quarterly Journal of Speech* 55 (1969):169–76.

15. T. R. Husek, "Persuasive Impacts of Early, Late, or No Mention of a Negative Source," *Journal of Personality and Social Psychology* 2 (1965):125–28; P. Tannenbaum, J. Macauley, and E. Norris, "Principle of Congruity and Reduction of Persuasion," *Journal of Personality and Social Psychology* 3 (1966):233–38; Bradley S. Greenberg and Gerald R. Miller, "The Effects of Low-Credible Sources on Message Acceptance," *Speech Monographs* 33 (1966):127–36.

16. Much of the research of both types has been surveyed in Kenneth Anderson and Theodore Clevenger, Jr., "A Summary of Experimental Research in Ethos," *Speech Monographs* 30 (1963):59–78. While the survey certainly needs to be updated, it presents examples of both types of research to which I refer.

17. Probably the most often-cited example is David K. Berlo, James B. Lemert, and Robert J. Mertz, *Dimensions for Evaluating the Acceptability of Message Sources* (East Lansing: Department of Communication, Michigan State University, 1966).

18. A good survey of the literature appears in the discussion of inoculation theory in Chester A. Insko, *Theories of Attitude Change* (New York: Appleton-Century-Crofts, 1967).

19. A brief survey of the "fear appeal" literature appears in Cronkhite, op. cit., pp. 179–85. Studies of language "intensity," "potency," and the like include: John Bowers, "Language Intensity, Social Introversion, and Attitude Change," *Speech Monographs* 30 (1963):345–52; Bowers, "Some Correlates of Language Intensity," *Quarterly Journal of Speech* 50 (1964):415–20; Bowers and Michael Osborn, "Attitudinal Effects of Selected Types of Concluding Metaphors in Persuasive Speeches," *Speech Monographs* 33 (1966):147–55; Carl Carmichael and Gary Cronkhite, "Frustration and Language Intensity," *Speech Monographs* 32 (1965):107–11; Helen Franzwa, "Psychological Factors Influencing Use of 'Evaluation-Dynamic' Language," *Speech Monographs* 36 (1969):103–9; and Michael Burgoon and Gerald Miller, "Prior Attitude and Language Intensity as Predictors of Message Style and Attitude Change Following Counterattitudinal Advocacy," paper presented at the Speech Communication Association Convention in New Orleans in December, 1970.

20. Cronkhite, op. cit.

21. Monroe C. Beardsley, *Thinking Straight* (Englewood Cliffs, N.J.: Prentice-Hall, 1966).

22. Howard Kahane, *Logic and Contemporary Rhetoric: The Use of Reason in Everyday Life* (Belmont, Calif.: Wadsworth Publishing Co., 1971).

23. Irving J. Rein, *Rudy's Red Wagon: Communication Strategies in Contemporary Society* (Glenview, Ill.: Scott, Foresman, 1972).

Toward a Rhetoric of Counterattitudinal Advocacy

Gerald R. Miller

Among rhetorical scholars, one's *ethos* is not likely to be bruised by harkening yet again to *the* pre-eminent definition of *rhetoric:* "Rhetoric may be defined as the faculty of observing in any given case the available means of persuasion."[1] Although this definition has numerous implications for the student of rhetoric, its catholicity best explains its role as initial signpost for this essay. For while one may agree with Bryant's assertion that "guns and gold belong to commerce or coercion, not to rhetoric,"[2] such assent still preserves a vast sphere of human activities as fair game for rhetorical scrutiny, activities best characterized in the contemporary idiom by the antiseptic label, *communication phenomena.*

Rhetorical theorists, past and present, have certainly used the broad scope of Aristotle's definition to scholarly advantage. The preferred "available means of persuasion" have depended not only upon, in Duhamel's words, "The prevailing epistemology, psychology, and metaphysic of the age,"[3] but in a few cases, upon the whim and quirk of the theorist himself. Still, there is a thread linking the immortal works of ancient Greece; the Roman rhetorics, with their emphasis upon the union of moral men and eloquent discourse; the ornamental preoccupations of Ramus and his disciples; the treatises of Campbell and Whately, which signaled a rhetorical reawakening in England in the late eighteenth and early nineteenth century; and the new rhetorics of Richards and Burke. Indeed, this unifying force might intellectually be better likened to a fabric than a thread, for its roots are found in the viewpoint these theorists share concerning the fundamental nature of the rhetorical paradigm.

In its simplest terms, this paradigm takes the following form: an active speaker strives to do something to a relatively passive audience—to change its attitudes or alter its behavior by skillful use of linguistic and paralinguistic codes. Central to this view of the rhetorical paradigm are the terms *active speaker* and *relatively passive audience;* for even after one pays the customary, contemporary homage to the importance of audience feedback there still remains no doubt about the major locus of activity, involvement, and energy. It is, of course, by design rather than by accident that the only kind of question not requiring an overt answer is a rhetorical question. Nor is it a coincidence that one often hears references to dynamic speakers, but seldom to dynamic audiences. In the traditional rhetorical paradigm, the persuader *acts,* while the "persuadee" is *acted upon.*

Skeptical readers may point to recent trends in rhetorical theory to refute my preceding claim; they may argue that many contemporary theorists take pains to stress the dynamic nature of audiences. While this point has some merit, it does not warrant a lengthy digression. Sufficient to say that these developments do not signal a change in the traditional paradigm's basic structure; instead, they reflect changing scholarly assessments of the importance of particular dimensions of the paradigmatic framework. Persuasion still occurs as a result of a speaker acting upon an audience; all that has changed are the priorities assigned by the speaker to the various "available means of persuasion." To say that a speaker's analysis should be audience-centered, rather than message-centered, is not to deny his primacy as the active agent in the influence process.

Just as McLuhan has argued that linear type subtly dictated our entire pre-electronic world view,[4] I would contend that the unquestioned hegemony of the traditional rhetorical paradigm has determined the questions with which rhetorical scholars have dealt. The primary purpose of this essay is to sketch the outlines of a different rhetorical paradigm: one that recognizes certain "available means of persuasion" not formerly treated by rhetorical theorists. This new paradigm involves a drastic change in the roles taken by both the persuader and the persuadee. No longer is the persuader the active agent; rather, once the influence attempt has been triggered, he plays a relatively minor, passive role. By contrast, the persuadee is highly involved throughout the influence attempt: *rather than being acted upon, persuasion occurs only if he acts upon himself.* In order to compare and contrast this new paradigm, called *counterattitudinal ad-*

vocacy, with the traditional rhetorical paradigm, let us next consider several typical persuasive situations.

The Counterattitudinal Advocacy Paradigm: Some Salient Characteristics

A college professor extols the virtues of grading on the curve to members of an undergraduate communication class. A union steward stresses the benefits of a proposed contract to a group of fellow employees. A television announcer praises a particular brand of soap in a one-minute network commercial. Situations such as these are commonplace in our society; moreover, all three can be analyzed using the traditional rhetorical paradigm. Here, the analysis would presume that the intended persuadees are undergraduate students, company employees, and network viewers. One would then attempt to determine what speaker characteristics and message strategies are likely to be most persuasive for the particular target audience.

But let us stipulate two additional dimensions common to these three situations. First, assume that none of the three sources initially believes the argument he is advocating. Actually, the professor is opposed to all grading; the union steward feels that he is party to a sweetheart contract, and the television announcer despises the brand of soap he is plugging. Thus, all three speakers are engaged in counterattitudinal advocacy; they are publicly espousing positions that are at odds with their prior beliefs.

If this disparity between public behavior and private beliefs were the only additional dimension, all three situations could still be treated within the context of the traditional rhetorical paradigm. But let us add a second dimension: assume that the actual, intended persuadees are not the college students, fellow employees, or network viewers—the ostensible target audiences of these messages—but rather the college professor, the union steward, and the television announcer—the ostensible persuaders. In reality, the actual persuaders are the professor's department chairman, who is only minimally interested in student grading attitudes but who is quite concerned that the professor supports the departmental line on grading; the union steward's immediate superiors, who know that the rank-and-file will fall into line if the steward himself consistently champions the contract; and the announcer's work supervisor, who has an idiosyncratic dislike for any employee who does not manifest brand loyalty. Rather than encoding arguments aimed at persuading the actual, intended target audiences, these three actual persuaders have, through some set of circumstances, induced the persuadees to encode the arguments themselves. The persuaders assume that, indeed, "saying is believing," that in the process of publicly advocating these belief-discrepant arguments, the persuadees will become more favorable toward them. When a persuader consciously employs counterattitudinal advocacy to change the attitudes or behaviors of another—when counterattitudinal advocacy is viewed as an "available means of persuasion"—the resultant process constitutes a rhetorical paradigm differing substantially from the one traditionally studied by rhetorical theorists.

Central to counterattitudinal advocacy is the active involvement of the intended persuadee. Unlike the traditional rhetorical paradigm, which places the persuadee in a relatively passive position, counterattitudinal advocacy requires that he publicly role-play the position the persuader wishes him to adopt. The efficacy of such a role-playing approach was first revealed in a study by Janis and King.[5] These researchers had one group of students deliver speeches as sincerely as possible. In all cases, the position taken was at odds with the speakers' prior beliefs; thus, the speakers engaged in counterattitudinal advocacy. A second group of students listened to a belief-discrepant speech presented by a fellow student, a role consistent with that of the persuadee in the traditional rhetorical paradigm. Immediately after speaking or listening, all students filled out an attitude-change measure. The results indicated that students who engaged in counterattitudinal advocacy were significantly more favorable toward the position taken in the message than students who passively listened to speeches.

In a second study, King and Janis sought to determine why considerable attitude change followed active role-playing by the students.[6] Two conceivable explanations were tested: first, improvisation of belief-discrepant arguments may have produced conditions conducive to attitude change; and second, speakers may have changed because of the satisfaction associated with their public performances. King and Janis conclude that the first explanation is more tenable; furthermore, they suggest that the crucial dimension of improvisation is invention. "Arguments invented by the individual are more likely to convince him, and, in addition, the individual inventing arguments is less likely to have interfering responses."[7]

The publication of Festinger's theory of cognitive dissonance provided another possible explanation for the persuasive efficacy of counterattitudinal advocacy.[8] The theory originally held that attitude change takes place because of dissonance produced by two conflicting cognitions: the cognition, on the one hand, that one does not believe x; and on the another hand, the cognition that one is publicly professing belief in x. Given these dissonance-producing circumstances, one way for the counterattitudinal encoder to restore consonance is to change the nature of the first cognition—i.e., to persuade himself that he does, in fact, believe x more than he originally thought.

The explanations of both Janis and King and of Festinger underscore another crucial difference between the traditional rhetorical and counterattitudinal advocacy paradigms. Traditionally, the persuadee has been persuaded *by someone;* counterattitudinal advocacy rests on the assumption that if certain conditions exist, the persuadee will *persuade himself.* This reliance on the self-persuasion process is one of the potential strengths of the paradigm; for, in the words of Pascal, "We are more easily persuaded, in general, by the reasons we ourselves discover than by those which are given to us by others."[9] The staple rhetorical commodity of counterattitudinal advocacy is discovery, rather than exchange.

While counterattitudinal advocacy differs markedly from the traditional rhetorical paradigm, the two models share certain similarities. For instance, as indicated above, the persuader who employs counterattitudinal advocacy must first entice the persuadee to espouse publicly a belief-discrepant position. During this initial stage of the process, the persuader strives to act upon the persuadee, to influence him to perform a behavior that will likely be perceived as repugnant. This initial influence attempt fits the traditional rhetorical paradigm nicely. Moreover, as we shall see later, the strategies employed by the persuader are of considerable importance, for the magnitude of subsequent persuadee attitude change depends upon the conditions under which the counterattitudinal message is encoded.

A second similarity between the two paradigms results from the fact that the persuadee must perceive that he has *publicly* assumed a counterattitudinal stance. Since public commitment implies the existence of some audience, the counterattitudinal message may itself modify the attitudes of that audience, a possibility clearly falling within the province of traditional rhetorical concerns. Here, however, two reservations must be noted. First, a genuine audience is not a necessity; the paradigm requires only that the persuadee perceive that other persons are privy to his remarks. Thus, a clever persuader may create the illusion of an audience where none actually exists. Second, even if an audience is present, its attitudes are of little or no concern to the persuader, for his success or failure hinges not on the audience, but on the attitudes expressed by the persuadee following public endorsement of the belief-discrepant position. While the traditional rhetorical paradigm assesses persuasive effectiveness in terms of audience effect, counterattitudinal advocacy looks to the speaker to evaluate the success of an influence attempt.

Thus far, this essay has established the status of counterattitudinal advocacy as an "available means of persuasion" and has argued that when consciously used by a persuader, counterattitudinal advocacy constitutes a rhetorical paradigm differing significantly from the one traditionally studied by rhetorical theorists. Obviously, however, each instance of counterattitudinal advocacy will not culminate in a substantial amount of self-persuasion. It is likely that the reader can point to instances when public behavior was not accompanied by subsequent private acceptance. What is needed, then, are the beginnings of a rhetoric of counterattitudinal advocacy; i.e., we must enunciate a set of principles or a rationale that will bear upon the probable success of an influence attempt based on counterattitudinal advocacy.

Justification and the Rhetorical Efficacy of Counterattitudinal Advocacy

The traditional rhetorical paradigm suggests the following as a defensible generalization: the greater the justification provided for audience attitude change, the greater the likelihood of a successful influence attempt. When this generalization is translated to fit the counterattitudinal advocacy paradigm, it implies that the greater the justification for engaging in counterattitudinal encoding, the greater the subsequent self-persuasion. Interestingly enough, the situation is not this simple. For while one school of thought does argue for a direct relationship between justification and self-persuasion, a second position holds that the two are negatively related; i.e., the less the justification, the greater the self-persuasion. Thus, one view opts for rewarding a man extravagantly for lying, while the other argues that he should be paid a bare minimum.

A study by Festinger and Carlsmith gave initial support to the view that justification for engaging in counterattitudinal advocacy is negatively related to subsequent self-persuasion.[10] After performing a dull task which they rated unfavorably, subjects were asked to engage in the counterattitudinal assignment of telling the next "subject" (actually an experimental confederate) that the task was an attractive, enjoyable undertaking. Half of the subjects were told that they would receive one dollar for their work, while the other half were promised twenty dollars—the justification manipulation used in the study. Following counterattitudinal encoding, all subjects rated the task a second time. Subsequent analysis of these ratings revealed that, as predicted, subjects paid one dollar for engaging in counterattitudinal advocacy rated the task significantly more attractive than subjects paid twenty dollars. Low justification thus produced greater attitude change than high justification.

Festinger and Carlsmith predicted this outcome on the basis of certain implications of cognitive dissonance theory. If, as discussed above, commitment to engage in counterattitudinal advocacy creates cognitive dissonance, self-persuasion is only one possible mode of dissonance reduction. Given highly rewarding circumstances, the person may reduce dissonance by reasoning that his belief-discrepant behavior is justified. This mode of dissonance reduction eliminates the need for changing one's attitude toward the issue. Consequently, Festinger and Carlsmith's twenty dollar subjects could easily rationalize their behavior by emphasizing the handsome wage they received. By contrast, the one dollar subjects did not have the benefit of this substantial payment; hence, they were forced to reduce dissonance by reevaluating the dull task, by reasoning that the task was really not as banal as they had originally thought.

Thus, the findings of Festinger and Carlsmith—as well as those of a later study by Cohen—suggest that the persuasive efficacy of counterattitudinal advocacy rests upon establishment of the minimal justifying conditions to induce belief-discrepant behavior.[11] Not surprisingly, however, the dissonance position has come under attack. For certain aspects of reinforcement learning theories imply that belief-discrepant arguments are more likely to be accepted if the reward for encoding them is substantial. Moreover, studies by Scott; Bostrom, Vlandis, and Rosenbaum; Janis and Gilmore; and Elms and Janis indicate that after counterattitudinal advocacy, more self-persuasion occurs under conditions of high, rather than low, justification.[12] These researchers hold that if self-persuasion is the desired end, persons should be given positive incentives for encoding counterattitudinal messages.

Given these conflicting findings, how is one to assess the status of justification in a rhetoric of counterattitudinal advocacy? While it is tempting to seek a means for asserting the universal sovereignty of one viewpoint, debates along these lines have not proved fruitful.[13] Rather, it is probable that under certain conditions of counterattitudinal advocacy, low justification will enhance opportunities for self-persuasion; while under other conditions, high justification will be more effective. For example, Carlsmith, Collins, and Helmreich have shown that when counterattitudinal encoding occurs in a face-to-face situation, low justification produces more attitude change; when encoding occurs anonymously, high justification is more effective.[14] In a similar vein, Linder, Cooper, and Jones report that low justification results in greater self-persuasion if the person perceives he is relatively free to refuse to engage in counterattitudinal encoding; if perceived decision freedom is low, high justification yields greater attitude change.[15]

Further complications arise from Miller and McGraw's finding that dissonance effects may occur apart from actual message encoding.[16] In their study, low justification subjects evidenced a dramatic amount of self-persuasion after agreeing to argue counterattitudinally but before engaging in message encoding. Finally, while the issue remains open, the relative efficacy of high and low justification may depend upon the time at which justification is extended to the counterattitudinal advocate. It is interesting to note that in studies supporting the dissonance position, subjects have been appraised of the justifying circumstances before encoding counterattitudinal messages. By contrast, in at least two of the studies favoring the reinforcement position, subjects did not know the extent of justification until after message encoding.[17] Carlsmith has argued that if a dissonance effect is desired, subjects should know the extent of justification before engaging in belief-discrepant behavior.[18]

Obviously, the task of specifying the place of justification in counterattitudinal advocacy has just begun. While most of the unanswered questions about this variable can best be answered by behavioral scientists, there is no reason why the answers cannot be employed by the rhetorical theorist to develop a more refined rhetoric of counterattitudinal advocacy. Moreover, skeptics who decry our sparse stock of knowledge about justification would do well to remember that the traditional rhetorical paradigm has benefited from over 2,000 years of scholarship, while systematic study of counterattitudinal advocacy has been confined to the past quarter-century.

Effort and the Rhetorical Efficacy of Counterattitudinal Advocacy

Effort is a second variable of potential relevance to counterattitudinal advocacy. As pointed out above, counterattitudinal advocacy, unlike the traditional rhetorical paradigm, requires active role-playing by the persuadee. But, obviously, because of either differing environments in which role-playing occurs or differing levels of motivation on the part of persuadees, performance of counterattitudinal tasks involves varying amounts of effort. What is the relationship between differences in required effort and the magnitude of subsequent self-persuasion?

Dissonance theory posits that the two variables are positively related: the more the effort the more the self-persuasion. For if dissonance arises from public commitment to a position that is privately unacceptable, expenditure of considerable effort when taking the position should result in heightened dissonance. Conversely, if belief-discrepant behavior requires little effort, dissonance can readily be reduced by underscoring the trivial cost of the undertaking.[19]

At least two studies support the dissonance prediction.[20] Cohen asked subjects to work on counterattitudinal communications, a procedure that involved reading rather than presenting the messages. Half the subjects were told the arguments would be easily understood, while the other subjects were warned they would be difficult. Consistent with expectations, subjects who believed the arguments would be difficult reported significantly greater attitude change in the belief-discrepant direction. Even though all subjects read the same arguments, induction of an effortful set facilitated self-persuasion.

Zimbardo asked student advocates of a numerical grading system to read aloud a series of arguments opposing the system. Effort was manipulated by having subjects read under varying conditions of delayed auditory feedback. In the high effort condition, the delay interval (.3 seconds) produced speech disruption and made comprehension difficult; in the low effort condition, the delay (.01 seconds) did not create severe problems. The post-encoding attitude change measures revealed that high effort subjects had a significantly less favorable attitude toward the previously endorsed numerical grading system. Interestingly, the two groups did not differ in comprehension of message content; hence, the findings cannot be attributed to differential learning.

While the reinforcement view does not speak directly to the effort variable, its theoretical posture suggests a positive relationship between effort and self-persuasion. Janis and Gilmore provide this summary of the reinforcement, or incentive position:

> when a person accepts the task of improvising arguments in favor of a point of view at variance with his own personal convictions, he becomes temporarily motivated to think up all the good positive arguments he can, and at the same time suppresses thoughts about the negative arguments which are supposedly irrelevant to the assigned task. This "biased scanning" increases the salience of the positive arguments and therefore increases the chances of acceptance of the new attitude position.[21]

Obviously, the harder one works to improvise new belief-discrepant arguments and to suppress old belief-congruent ones—i.e., the more effort he expends—the more likely it is that the new attitude position will be accepted. Moreover, implicit in the argument that high incentives facilitate self-persuasion is the assumption that people will work harder if rewards are substantial. On the whole, then, dissonance and reinforcement theories are in concert about the status of effort in counterattitudinal advocacy.

Despite this theoretical harmony, application of the effort variable to a rhetoric of counterattitudinal advocacy is not without operational problems. While such devices as delayed auditory feedback are useful in generating neat laboratory manipulations of effort, their practical utility in "real world" persuasive situations is limited. In previous studies, several of us have sought to manipulate effort by asking subjects to devise varying numbers of arguments or to plan messages of differing lengths—operations more in keeping with the characteristics of any rhetorical situation.[22] Unfortunately, we have not had good luck with this approach. Not only has it failed to produce reliable differences in self-persuasion; but in addition, subjects in the various conditions have not reported differing perceptions of the amount of effort required to encode counterattitudinally. We attribute this failure to the generally minimal effort expended by student subjects in all the conditions, plus the cognitive unavailability of any substantial number of belief-discrepant arguments. Obviously, people cannot encode that which is mentally unavailable; if a person is aware of only two arguments opposing his position, he cannot articulate six.

Recently, we have sought to deal with effort by varying the type of communication environment in which the counterattitudinal advocate is placed.[23] Since our experiences with written messages revealed a lack of encoding effort, the advocate has been asked to engage in counterattitudinal encoding while face-to-face with an uncooperative confederate, a procedure similar to Festinger and Carlsmith's. By resisting influence, the confederate forces the counterattitudinal advocate to improvise new arguments, to re-state points, to call up new information—in short, to expend more effort communicating. This procedure also capitalizes on the typical tendency to become more interested, involved, and energetic when an actual argument starts to take shape. Thus, the approach focuses upon factors intrinsic to the persuasive act, a dimension of effort not examined in prior studies. While our research is still in the preliminary stages, the technique shows promise.

At first glance, present limitations in the extent to which effort can be effectively manipulated would seem to cast doubt on its utility to a rhetoric of counterattitudinal advocacy. Still, the situation does not differ greatly from the present state of affairs regarding certain factors central to an understanding of the traditional rhetorical paradigm. For instance, although rhetorical theorists have long acknowledged that *ethos,* or credibility, is vital to persuasive effectiveness, researchers have only recently commenced the search for ways that a speaker may communicate to enhance his initial credibility or to foster favorable perceptions of *ethos.*[24] The quest for ways to insure substantial speaker effort in the encoding of counterattitudinal messages must proceed along similar lines. As our understanding of the effort variable increases, the elements of a viable rhetoric of counterattitudinal advocacy will emerge.

Aversive Audience Consequences and the Rhetorical Efficacy of Counterattitudinal Advocacy

As stated above, initial analyses of the place of cognitive dissonance in counterattitudinal advocacy underscored the probable inconsistency resulting from one's perception that he is publicly advocating a position at odds with his private beliefs. Recently, however, writers such as Aronson, Carlsmith, and Collins have propounded an alternative interpretation of the dissonance producing dynamics of counterattitudinal advocacy.[25] Their position holds that the mere act of encoding a belief-discrepant communication is not itself dissonance producing—that under certain conditions one can publicly endorse a counterattitudinal viewpoint without experiencing dissonance. What does produce dissonance is the advocate's perception of possible aversive consequences of his behavior—his perception that audience members may accept the belief-discrepant position and his awareness that he is unable to warn them not to succumb to his persuasive wiles. As Aronson puts it, dissonance is aroused by the cognitions: (1) "I am a decent, truthful human being," and (2) "I have misled a person; I have conned him into believing something which just isn't true; he thinks that I really believe it and I cannot set him straight because I probably won't see him again."[26] In much the same vein, Carlsmith contends that "anytime a person makes some statement counter to his attitudes, and a listener (whose opinion is important to the speaker) is unaware of both the speaker's attitudes and his motivation for speaking against these attitudes, dissonance will be aroused."[27] Thus, according to this view, cognitive dissonance is not generated by the discrepancy between public behavior and private belief per se, but rather from the negative implications that such public behavior has for the individual's self-concept. In these situations, the counterattitudinal advocate is faced, to use Baron's terms, with a moral dilemma.[28]

Several recent studies have supported the position that perceived aversive consequences, rather than public-private discrepancy, constitute the most likely cause for dissonance in situations requiring counterattitudinal encoding.[29] Helmreich and Collins asked subjects to present videotaped or audiotaped counterattitudinal speeches under one of three conditions: a condition which neither allowed subjects to tell the audience their reasons for giving the speeches nor their real attitudes about the issue (No Takeback), a condition in which the audience would be debriefed and the subjects would be allowed to make second speeches explaining their real attitudes (Takeback), and a condition in which subjects made anonymous audiotaped speeches (Anonymous Audio). In addition, justification was varied for all three types of presentation. Consistent with predictions, there was a significant dissonance effect in the No Takeback condition; i.e., subjects given low justification demonstrated significantly greater self-persuasion than those given high justification. The two Takeback conditions did not differ. Finally, there was a significant reinforcement effect for the Anonymous Audio conditions; i.e., high justification subjects manifested more self-persuasion than low justification subjects. Thus, the decisive factor leading to dissonance seems to be the No Takeback subjects' knowledge that they were not only publicly espousing a counterattitudinal stance, but that, in addition, their speeches would be used to persuade others to adopt the belief-discrepant viewpoint.

Nel, Helmreich, and Aronson varied both justification and prior audience attitude: the audience was represented as being in favor of, opposed to, or uncommitted toward the counterattitudinal position. The investigators hypothesized a dissonance effect for the uncommitted audience, since this group would be perceived by the counterattitudinal advocates as potentially the most persuasible. While none of the comparisons were statistically significant, the results were in the predicted direction.

Using only low justification conditions, Bodaken and Miller varied decision freedom (Choice-No Choice) and prior audience attitude (Favorable-Uncommitted). They predicted that the most self-persuasion would occur in the Choice:Uncommitted Audience treatment and the least in the No Choice:Favorable Audience group. Although an ineffective manipulation prevented a successful test of the effects of the choice variable, Bodaken and Miller obtained a significant main effect for the prior audience attitude variable: subjects encoding counterattitudinal messages to uncommitted audiences demonstrated significantly more self-persuasion than subjects who encoded for audiences already predisposed toward the belief-discrepant position. Thus, the public-private discrepancy does not seem to be a primary determinant of dissonance; rather it appears that, as Bodaken and Miller conclude, "an individual's overriding concern in the performance of counterattitudinal tasks is the effect, or potential effect, that such messages have on others."[30] Apparently, harmless lying is one thing, lying with a purpose is another.

Taken together, the preceding findings have obvious implications for a rhetoric of counterattitudinal advocacy. Earlier in this essay, it was emphasized that the persuader who relies on belief-discrepant communication for persuasive effects must convince the persuadee he is encoding arguments for some audience—at a minimum, the persuader must succeed in creating the illusion of an audience. But, obviously, not just any audience will suffice. Instead, if the persuasive impact of counterattitudinal advocacy hinges upon dissonance arousal, the persuadee must perceive that his arguments may actually affect the audience, that he may convince them to say or do something which he himself does not believe. This is not to say that self-persuasion is impossible when the audience is committed or when the persuadee has a later chance to recant his position. But the studies suggest that if it is to happen, counterattitudinal encoding should be accompanied by relatively substantial justifying circumstances and by an opportunity for persuadee anonymity.

Unlike the five classical canons of the traditional rhetorical paradigm, the variables of justification, effort, and prior audience attitude undoubtedly do not comprise an exhaustive list of factors relevant to a rhetoric of counterattitudinal advocacy. Still, they do constitute a good start, and while I am tempted to reflect briefly on such additional variables as choice and commitment, the beginnings of a rhetoric of counterattitudinal advocacy can best be insured by devoting the remainder of this essay to several problems of general import to counterattitudinal encoding situations.

On Inducing Counterattitudinal Message Behavior: A Potential Problem

Even if a persuadee agrees to encode a counterattitudinal message, how can the persuader be assured the actual content of the communication is belief-discrepant? This question is both perplexing and significant, for people may accept counterattitudinal tasks and still devise belief-congruent messages. Such inconsistency between assent and behavior may occur consciously, because of the aversive consequences associated with public endorsement of a counterattitudinal viewpoint, or unconsciously, because of the notorious inaccuracy and capriciousness of human perception.

Until recently, the possibility that the intentions and deeds of counterattitudinal advocates do not correspond has received little research attention. In an attempt to identify reasons for nonsignificant findings, Burgoon asked persons to judge the viewpoint advocated in samples of belief-congruent and belief-discrepant messages drawn from a study by Miller and Bodaken.[31] Belief-congruent communications posed no serious problems; for ninety-six percent of these messages, the judges correctly identified the position taken by the communicator. In sharp contrast, only forty-nine percent of the belief-discrepant messages were correctly identified. Thirty-one percent were perceived as adopting a neutral stance on the issue, while twenty percent were perceived as diametrically opposed to the counterattitudinal posture the communicator had agreed to adopt. Obviously, many of the belief-discrepant subjects did not actually encode clearly identifiable counterattitudinal messages.

Intrigued by this finding, Burgoon and Miller next designed three studies to investigate systematically the relationship between prior attitude and message intensity.[32] Their procedures required subjects to complete partially prepared messages by choosing from words of varied intensity. In the first study, half of the subjects prepared belief-congruent messages, while the other half constructed belief-discrepant communications. Subjects in both conditions chose from word lists of comparable overall intensity. Burgoon and Miller hypothesized that subjects in the belief-congruent condition would encode more intense messages; i.e., that they would choose highly intense words with greater frequency. In the second and third studies, subjects prepared counterattitudinal messages under one of three conditions of language intensity: low, moderate, or high. Here, the researchers predicted that self-persuasion would be directly related to message intensity: that the most self-persuasion would occur in the high-intensity condition and the least in the low-intensity condition, with the moderate-intensity condition falling between.

Results of the studies confirmed both hypotheses. As predicted, belief-congruent subjects did encode more intense messages, a finding that points to the reluctance of individuals to "put their hearts" into counterattitudinal advocacy. In addition, the results of the second and third studies indicated that relatively intense counterattitudinal encoding is a prerequisite to self-persuasion. While both the high and moderate intensity groups reported significantly greater attitude change than a no-message control group, the low intensity and control groups did not differ. The mean attitude change scores conformed to theoretic expectations: high-intensity subjects changed the most, lows the least, and moderates fell in between.

Burgoon and Miller's findings thus reveal that the persuasive success of counterattitudinal advocacy hinges upon the persuader's ability to insure public adoption of a belief-discrepant posture. Although completion of partially prepared messages provides a useful method for studying certain problems in the laboratory setting, its utility is limited in everyday persuasive situations. As in the case of the effort variable, the best solution may lie in creating face-to-face confrontations of the counterattitudinal advocate and his audience. Either indirectly, through argument, or directly, by indicating that the communicator is not arguing the stipulated position, the audience may compel the advocate to encode an intensely counterattitudinal message. In any event, the theorist interested in developing a rhetoric of counterattitudinal advocacy cannot shirk the problems created by potential deviations from the prescribed encoding task.

On the Ethics of Counterattitudinal Advocacy

There is, of course, an ethical dimension to all rhetorical questions. Admittedly, the major thrust of this essay has been to sketch the factual foundation of a rhetoric of counterattitudinal advocacy. Still, some readers may feel that counterattitudinal strategies short-circuit rational processes; for this reason, they may equate counterattitudinal advocacy with evil rhetoric. While I have no intention of arguing for the moral purity of counterattitudinal advocacy, several ethical matters merit at least brief mention.

Certainly, there is much in the cognitive dissonance interpretation of counterattitudinal advocacy that smacks of mindless rationalization. In fact, in its earliest formulation, the dissonance viewpoint paints a rather dismal picture, a picture of man lying and then exerting all his cognitive efforts toward living the lie. By contrast, later dissonance theorizing is more benign; as indicated above, it identifies the source of cognitive inconsistency as man's guilt about deceiving his fellow men. But, in either case, there is no doubt that self-persuasion as a means of dissonance reduction springs from extralogical roots; it does not conform with typical conceptions of a rational rhetoric.

On the other hand, one might make a better ethical case for reinforcement learning theory interpretations of counterattitudinal advocacy. There is a substantial body of psychological opinion which holds that persons insulate their beliefs from attack.[33] If this opinion is correct, it follows that individuals may often ignore or overlook good refutations of certain dimensions of their belief systems. Reinforcement theorists hold that self-persuasion takes place because the counterattitudinal advocate is forced to re-examine and reconsider previously neglected arguments. To force such a re-evaluation is at least partially consistent with much rhetorical writing about the importance of the thorough search for truth, or at least for well-informed opinion. In addition, the reinforcement position stresses the need for strong justifying circumstances if self-persuasion is to occur. Although some sources of justification may be crass and materialistic (e.g., the monetary inducements used in much research), others (e.g., conformity with the request of a highly credible sponsor) may not be entirely incompatible with a rational view of man.

But what of the broader ethical question: is it ever justified to induce a man to utter public falsehood? Here, I suspect that many readers will respond negatively. Given the best of all possible worlds, I might accept this negation; but, unfortunately, the situation is not that simple. People engage in counterattitudinal advocacy every day; probably every reader of this essay, as well as its author, has encoded belief-discrepant messages in the not too distant past. The persuasive situations described earlier in this essay —the college professor defending a disliked grading system, the union steward supporting a questionable contract, the television announcer plugging an undesirable product—may well be the societal rule, rather than the exception. Thus, many people who would sincerely deplore reliance upon a rhetoric of counterattitudinal advocacy might themselves be surprised were they aware of the numerous times they have induced others to utter counterattitudinal statements. Moreover, there is little doubt that counterattitudinal advocacy is central to a number of processes vital to the preservation of our social foundations. Early socialization of children relies heavily on techniques of counterattitudinal role-playing as does the educational system, from nursery school through the doctoral degree. Given these considerations, a blanket indictment of counterattitudinal advocacy seems inappropriate; rather, one must focus attention on the ends for which it is employed.

Because it departs so sharply from the traditional rhetorical paradigm, the ethical status of counterattitudinal advocacy cannot be adequately assessed in this short essay. Personally, I believe that when used discerningly, it provides a legitimate means of persuasion. But even if others disagree with this ethical judgment, they are likely to admit that counterattitudinal advocacy is a frequently used rhetorical strategy; and, as such, it is fair game for rhetorical scholarship.

Counterattitudinal advocacy provides an adjunct to the traditional rhetorical paradigm, not a replacement for it. Recently, Arnold has underscored the importance of extending our rhetorical horizons, stating that "one does not decide what is rhetorical by looking at the *form* of communication; attempted influence with practical goals in view is rhetorical, no matter what the *form.*"[34] Because counterattitudinal advocacy often pursues practical goals of influence, contemporary theorists should heed the words of the paramount rhetorical scholar and not only seek to discover, but to understand "the available means of persuasion" provided by a rhetoric of counterattitudinal advocacy.

NOTES AND REFERENCES

1. Aristotle, *Rhetoric* i. 1355^{b}626. Translated by W. Rhys Roberts.

2. Donald C. Bryant, "Rhetoric: Its Functions and Its Scope," p. 200.

3. P. Albert Duhamel, "The Function of Rhetoric as Effective Expression," *Journal of the History of Ideas* 10 (1949):344–56.

4. Marshall McLuhan, *Understanding Media* (New York: McGraw-Hill, 1964), pp. 3–6.

5. Irving L. Janis and Bert T. King, "The Influence of Role Playing on Opinion Change," *Journal of Abnormal and Social Psychology* 49 (1954):211–18.

6. Bert T. King and Irving L. Janis, "Comparison of the Effectiveness of Improvised vs. Non-Improvised Role-Playing in Producing Opinion Changes," *Human Relations* 9 (1956):177–86.

7. Jack W. Brehm and Arthur R. Cohen, *Explorations in Cognitive Dissonance* (New York: John Wiley & Sons, 1962), p. 251.

8. Leon Festinger, *A Theory of Cognitive Dissonance* (Stanford: Stanford University Press, 1957).

9. Cited in Alan C. Elms (ed.), *Role Playing, Reward, and Attitude Change* (New York: Van Nostrand Reinhold Company, 1969), p. iii.

10. Leon Festinger and J. Merrill Carlsmith, "Cognitive Consequences of Forced Compliance," *Journal of Abnormal and Social Psychology* 58 (1959):203–10.

11. Brehm and Cohen, *Explorations in Cognitive Dissonance,* pp. 73–78.

12. William A. Scott, "Attitude Change Through Reward of Verbal Behavior," *Journal of Abnormal and Social Psychology* 55 (1957):72–75; Robert N. Bostrom, John W. Vlandis, and Milton E. Rosenbaum, "Grades as Reinforcing Contingencies and Attitude Change," *Journal of Educational Psychology* 52 (1961):112–15; Irving L. Janis and J. Barnard Gilmore, "The Influence of Incentive Conditions on the Success of Role Playing in Modifying Attitudes," *Journal of Personality and Social Psychology* 1 (1965):17–27; Alan C. Elms and Irving L. Janis, "Counter-Norm Attitudes Induced by Consonant versus Dissonant Conditions of Role-Playing," *Journal of Experimental Research in Personality* 1 (1965):50–60.

13. See, for example, Elliot Aronson, "The Psychology of Insufficient Justification: An Analysis of Some Conflicting Data," and Milton J. Rosenberg, "Some Limits of Dissonance: Toward a Differentiated View of Counter-Attitudinal Performance," in Shel Feldman (ed.), *Cognitive Consistency: Motivational Antecedents and Behavioral Consequents* (New York: Academic Press, 1966), pp. 109–70. Also, Gerald R. Miller, "Counterattitudinal Advocacy: A Current Appraisal," in C. David Mortensen and Kenneth K. Sereno (eds.), *Advances in Communication Research* (New York: Harper & Row, 1973), pp. 105–52.

14. J. Merrill Carlsmith, Barry E. Collins, and Robert K. Helmreich, "Studies in Forced Compliance: I. The Effect of Pressure for Compliance on Attitude Change Produced by Face-to-Face Role Playing and Anonymous Essay Writing," *Journal of Personality and Social Psychology* 4 (1966):1–13.

15. Darwyn E. Linder, Joel Cooper, and Edward E. Jones, "Decision Freedom as a Determinant of the Role of Incentive Magnitude in Attitude Change," *Journal of Personality and Social Psychology* 6 (1967):245–54.

16. Gerald R. Miller and Richard L. McGraw, "Justification and Self-Persuasion Following Commitment to Encode, and Actual Encoding of Counterattitudinal Communication," *Speech Monographs* 36 (1969):443–51.

17. Scott; also Bostrom et al., op. cit.

18. J. Merrill Carlsmith, "Varieties of Counterattitudinal Behavior," in Robert P. Abelson, Elliot Aronson, William J. McGuire, Theodore M. Newcomb, Milton J. Rosenberg, and Percy H. Tannenbaum (eds.), *Theories of Cognitive Consistency: A Sourcebook* (Chicago: Rand McNally, 1968), p. 804.

19. Undoubtedly, the conceptual status of some of these variables may be confounded. For instance, the *effort* variable could be conceptually viewed as one dimension of the *justification* variable. Future research should aim at untangling such conceptual snarls.

20. Arthur R. Cohen, "Communication Discrepancy and Attitude Change: A Dissonance Theory Approach," *Journal of Personality* 27 (1959):386–96; Philip G.

Zimbardo, "The Effect of Effort and Improvisation on Self-Persuasion Produced by Role-Playing," *Journal of Experimental Social Psychology* 1 (1965):- 103–20.

21. Janis and Gilmore, p. 17.

22. Gerald R. Miller and Bonita L. Perry, "Open- and Closed-Mindedness, Effort, and Tolerance for Inconsistency Following Counterattitudinal Advocacy," manuscript, Department of Communication, Michigan State University, 1969.

23. Gerald R. Miller and Bonita L. Perry, "Some Dimensions of Effort in Counterattitudinal Advocacy," manuscript, Department of Communication, Michigan State University, 1971.

24. See, for example, Gerald R. Miller and Murray A. Hewgill, "The Effects of Variations in Nonfluency on Audience Ratings of Source Credibility," *Quarterly Journal of Speech* 50 (1964):36–44, and Bradley S. Greenberg and Gerald R. Miller, "The Effects of Low-Credible Sources on Message Acceptance," *Speech Monographs* 33 (1966):127–36.

25. Elliot Aronson, "Dissonance Theory: Progress and Problems," in Abelson, Aronson, McGuire, Newcomb, Rosenberg, and Tannenbaum (eds.), pp. 5–27; J. Merrill Carlsmith, "Varieties of Counterattitudinal Behavior," in Abelson et al. (eds.), pp. 803–9; Barry E. Collins, "The Effect of Monetary Inducements on the Amount of Attitude Change Produced by Forced Compliance," in Alan C. Elms (ed.), *Role Playing, Reward, and Attitude Change*, pp. 209–23.

26. Aronson, p. 24.

27. Carlsmith, p. 806.

28. Reuben M. Baron, "Attitude Change through Discrepant Action: A Functional Analysis," in Anthony G. Greenwald, Timothy C. Brock, and Thomas M. Ostrom (eds.), *Psychological Foundations of Attitudes* (New York: Academic Press, 1968), pp. 297–326.

29. Robert K. Helmreich and Barry E. Collins, "Studies in Forced Compliance: Commitment and Magnitude of Inducement to Comply as Determinants of Opinion Change," *Journal of Personality and Social Psychology* 10 (1968):- 75–81; Elizabeth Nel, Robert K. Helmreich, and Elliot Aronson, "Opinion Change in the Advocate as a Function of the Persuasibility of His Audience: A Clarification of the Meaning of Dissonance," *Journal of Personality and Social Psychology* 12 (1969):117–25; Edward M. Bodaken and Gerald R. Miller, "Choice and Prior Audience Attitude as Determinants of Attitude Change Following Counterattitudinal Advocacy," *Speech Monographs,* 38 (1971):109– 12.

30. Bodaken and Miller, p. 112.

31. Michael Burgoon, "Ability of Individuals to Judge the Positions Taken in Belief-Congruent and Belief-Discrepant Messages," manuscript, Department of Communication, Michigan State University, 1969.

32. Michael Burgoon and Gerald R. Miller, "Prior Attitude and Language Intensity as Predictors of Message Style and Attitude Change Following Counterattitudinal Advocacy," *Journal of Personality and Social Psychology*, 20, (1971):246–53.

33. This notion, labeled *selective exposure*, has come under attack in recent years. For a summary of the issues involved, see Jonathan L. Freedman and David O. Sears, "Selective Exposure," in Leonard Berkowitz (ed.), *Advances in Experimental Social Psychology*, vol. 2 (New York: Academic Press, 1965), pp. 57–97.

34. Carroll C. Arnold, "Reflections on the Wingspread Conference," in Lloyd F. Bitzer and Edwin Black (eds.), *The Prospect of Rhetoric* (Englewood Cliffs, N.J.: Prentice-Hall, 1971), p. 195.

Paradox as a Rhetorical Strategy

John Waite Bowers and Robert E. Sanders

Jennifer Cavilleri asks, "What's wrong with doing all the right things?"[1] Ben Marvel refuses to go to the hospital because he is "too sick."[2] Major Major can be seen in his office only when he is out of it.[3] Sophie Portnoy loves her son so much that she threatens him with a knife and locks him out of the apartment.[4] Across the thin line separating fiction from experience, students vie for leadership and ask for votes as representatives of the Apathy Party.[5] National candidates build images to make themselves appear what they are not.[6] The government "winds down" a war by expanding it, protects international trade by restricting it, defends free enterprise by controlling it, and orders its soldiers to destroy villages in order to save them.

Paradox pervades contemporary culture, and it has not escaped the notice of social scientists. Watzlawick, Beavin, and Jackson make it central to their *Pragmatics of Human Communication,*[7] and Giffin and Patton depend heavily on that analysis in their *Fundamentals of Interpersonal Communication.*[8] As far as we can determine, however, no experimental treatment of paradox and its consequences has preceded this one.

A paradox exists when the same message necessarily entails two exclusive states of affairs, and it has behavioral consequences (or is "pragmatic") when it demands mutually exclusive responses. Hence, IGNORE THIS SIGN is a paradox. So is the statement of mother to child or lover to lover, "Whenever you say 'no,' I know you mean 'yes.' "

Various routes can be followed to escape the mutually exclusive implications of paradox. If a paradox has no or only trivial behavioral implications for an individual, he can ignore it. If he cannot ignore it, he can sometimes resolve it by redefining terms, detecting slippery terms, or supplying missing premises. When avoidance or resolution is impossible, however, paradox may have potent behavioral implications. Watzlawick and his associates supply anecdotal and clinical evidence indicating that paradox might induce schizophrenia and interpersonal disability when certain conditions are met: (1) an individual (X) has a sustained dependence on another individual or institution (Y); (2) Y continually sends paradoxical messages requiring mutually exclusive behaviors by X; (3) Y refuses to permit X to evade the paradoxes; (4) Y refuses to cooperate with X in proceeding to a higher conceptual level where the paradoxes may be resolved.

Watzlawick, Beavin, and Jackson have identified three methods of adapting to such paradoxes. The individual may become "obsessed with the need of finding [vital] clues, of giving a meaning to what is going on in and around him, and . . . eventually be forced to extend this scanning for clues and meaning to the most unlikely and unrelated phenomena."[9] Or he may "choose what recruits quickly find to be the best possible reaction to the bewildering logic, or lack of it, in army life: to comply with any and all injunctions with complete literalness and to abstain overtly from any independent thinking."[10] Or he may "withdraw from human involvement."[11] All these patterns of response are "suggestive of the clinical pictures of schizophrenia."[12]

Watzlawick and his associates explicitly draw their conclusions from anecdotal and clinical observation alone; the relationship between paradox and contingent behavior has not been experimentally tested. Furthermore, they assume that paradox will only have the stated consequences when an individual is exposed to a paradoxical "universe" over an extended period of time. But extended exposure to paradox is not typical (though this might be disputed by political iconoclasts), and in a controlled experiment would introduce ethical problems. Hence, the experimental investigation of the effects of limited exposure to paradox is an extension of the work of Watzlawick and his colleagues.

It should be emphasized that while the impetus for this study and for its hypotheses is essentially clinical, the study has rhetorical significance: it tests paradox as a rhetorical strategy, a symbolic means of inducing a previously specified set of attitudes and beliefs.

Method and Hypotheses

Watzlawick, Beavin, and Jackson stipulate three consequences which depend on extended exposure to paradox: (1) obsessive quest for means of resolution; (2) acceptance in a literal sense of all messages regardless of internal consistency and external validity; or (3) withdrawal from human involvement. For practical reasons, none of these outcomes can be used as a criterion when the stimulus is short-term paradox, as in this study. But it is reasonable to suppose that any of the three is mediated by a period of uncertainty and confusion. Uncertainty, at least, can be readily measured by a variety of belief and attitude scales.

In brief, the study tests the effects of short-term paradox by contrasting a "paradox condition" with three others: a control (no message) condition, a "right horn" of the pragmatic dilemma condition where subjects were exposed to one of the two mutually exclusive concepts of the paradox, and a "left horn" condition. The four groups of subjects were told that they were participating in a survey (consisting of attitude and belief tests). With the exception of the control group, subjects were told that earlier respondents to the survey had apparently been unaware of the issues involved and that to clarify the issues some tape-recorded remarks would precede their questionnaire responses.

Messages

The topic chosen for the survey was "the grading system at the University of Iowa," a topic which had behavioral implications for the subjects, freshman students at the university. The texts of the three messages began with the same paragraph:

> The curriculum committee of the Department of Speech and Dramatic Art is conducting a survey to learn the preferences in grading systems among undergraduates. On the basis of this survey and other information, the Department hopes to make a recommendation to the Educational Policies Committee of the College of Liberal Arts. Some of us have studied the problem of grading policies rather thoroughly in the past, even to the point of carrying out pilot surveys, and we have discovered that many undergraduates have not thought about the implications of various grading practices. For that reason, we ask you to listen to this brief statement before you participate in the survey.

The first two sentences of this introduction also headed the booklet of dependent measures so that the control group, which heard no remarks, would have equivalent motivation for taking seriously the tasks required by the booklet. All messages were tape-recorded by the same speaker (Bowers), and all were very nearly equivalent in delivery, organizational pattern, and even syntactic structure.

The *radical* (left horn) message pointed out that the university should have an across-the-board policy of pass-fail grading. (Present university policy permits a student to take a limited number of courses from outside his major department on a pass-fail basis.) It took for granted the proposition, "Everyone now recognizes that the most valuable individuals, both in the university and outside it, are those who have somehow learned to be innovative, original, individualistic." It went on to establish that a pass-fail grading system would be instrumental in producing such individuals. It also argued that the traditional A-B-C-D-F grading system had been used "to enforce conformity, to inhibit innovation." And, finally, it asserted that the change to a pass-fail system was prevented because "administrators and faculty members, like most other people, are reluctant to give up power, and letter grades represent power." The message was 496 words long.

The *reactionary* (right horn) remarks pointed out that the university depends heavily on traditional A-B-C-D-F grades and that it should use a traditional system exclusively. It took for granted the proposition, "Everyone now recognizes that the most valuable individuals, both in the university and outside it, are those who have somehow learned to follow directions, be disciplined and cooperative." It went on to establish that a traditional grading system would be instrumental in producing such individuals. It also argued that the traditional system makes academic achievement "a matter of record, and society's recognition of the student's talents and accomplishments is assured." And, finally, it asserted that a return to the traditional system was prevented because "administrators and faculty members, like most other people, are afraid of the reaction from those who prefer what is pleasant and easy to what is difficult and, in the long run, good." The message was 508 words long.

Where both other speeches identified a "problem," the *paradox* message identified a "paradox." Its theme was that a pass-fail system is instrumental both in producing innovative individuals and in preventing their recognition. This is a form of the classic paradox asserting that a tree makes no sound when it falls in an uninhabited forest. The penultimate paragraph was:

> Paradoxically, however, to the extent that a student is permitted to take courses on a pass-fail basis, and does take them on that basis, the *recognition* of his innovative talent, his skill in exercising freedom, is prevented. . . . The traditional system provides more information to society than the pass-fail system does. But this information is not about the most important thing— the responsible exercise of freedom.

The message was 509 words long.

Dependent Measures and Methods of Analysis[13]

The dependent measures were of three types: a social judgment test, several attitude tests of the semantic differential type, and a series of Likert-type items. As noted earlier, we thought that the unconventional nature of the paradoxical message justified a variety of measures any or all of which might indicate the predicted uncertainty of subjects in that condition.

Social judgment test. Since we think that our method of analyzing the social judgment test is a significant methodological contribution, and since this method would be difficult to describe in the absence of the test, we reproduce it in full:

> Below is a brief description of the present grading policy in the College of Liberal Arts at the University of Iowa. Please read it. Then, for each of the six statements listed under the policy, do the following:
> If you find the statement acceptable, circle the *A* (for *acceptable).*
> If you find the statement unacceptable, circle the *R* (for *reject).*
> If you neither accept nor reject the statement, circle the *N* (for *noncommitment).*
> Under the present system, an undergraduate student must take virtually all courses in his major and closely related to it for a letter grade (A-B-C-D-F). He may not take more than two courses per semester from outside his major for a P-F grade. He may only count 32 semester hours of P-F work toward graduation.
> Remember, *A* = accept, *N* = noncommitment, *R* = reject.
> *A N R* 1. Students should be required to take all courses for a letter grade (A-B-C-D-F).
> *A N R* 2. Students should be permitted to take only one course per semester

from outside their major for a P-F grade.

A N R 3. The present system should be maintained.

A N R 4. Students should be permitted to take as many courses from outside their major field as they wish for a P-F grade.

A N R 5. Students should be permitted to take as many courses as they wish both in their major field and outside it for P-F grades.

A N R 6. Students should be required to take all courses for P-F grades.

A number of scholars have suggested alternative methods of scoring social judgment tests of the type used in this study, but when various methods are used for the same subjects on the same propositions only very low correlations have been found among them.[14] The basic problem is in using all or even most of the information such a test provides about each subject. In responding to our social judgment test, for example, a subject could choose any of 729 possible response patterns. (Six propositions each can be responded to in any one of three ways, or 3^6.) This state of affairs is an analyst's nightmare. Our solutions to the problem, we think, realistically combine the 729 possibilities in ways that might generalize to many other social judgment tests.[15]

The 137 subjects in the study made use of only 51 of the possible response patterns. Arbitrarily assigning a "score" of 3 for rejection, 2 for noncommitment, and 1 for acceptance, we constructed curves for each of these 51 response patterns. The curve for a subject who rejected the first three statements, accepted the fourth and fifth, and rejected the sixth (the most popular response pattern), for example, looked like this:

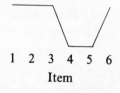

3 (reject)
2 (noncommit)
1 (accept)

1 2 3 4 5 6
Item

We then searched the 51 curves for conceptually respectable ways of combining them. Since we had deliberately constructed the test to fit a scale of positions we envisioned as *reactionary* (item 1), *conservative* (items 2 and 3), *liberal* (items 4 and 5), and *radical* (item 6), we expected to have little difficulty in extracting such combinations. We were not disappointed, and we think that other social judgment tests designed to fit similar conceptual schemes can employ our categories. We labeled and operationally defined nine categories of subjects as shown below. For the sake of economy in expression, we are coining the transitive verb "noncommits."

1. *Reactionary.* Accepts the reactionary proposition, rejects or noncommits the radical proposition. In our sample, 1 subject (.7 percent).

2. *Reactcon.* Accepts one or both conservative propositions but neither liberal proposition and noncommits the reactionary proposition. In our sample, 6 subjects (4.4 percent).

3. *Conservative.* Rejects the radical proposition and the reactionary proposition, accepts one or both conservative propositions, rejects or noncommits both liberal propositions. In our sample, 8 subjects (5.9 percent).

4A. *Skeptic.* Rejects or noncommits all propositions. In our sample, 13 subjects (9.5 percent).

4B. *Ambivalent.* Rejects or noncommits the reactionary proposition and the radical proposition, accepts at least one liberal proposition and at least one conservative proposition. In our sample, 5 subjects (3.7 percent).

4C. *Undecided Extremist.* Accepts both the reactionary proposition and the radical proposition. In our sample, 1 subject (.7 percent).

5. *Liberal.* Rejects the radical proposition and the reactionary proposition, accepts one or both liberal propositions, rejects or noncommits both conservative propositions. The mirror image of all *conservative* curves. In our sample, 65 subjects (47.8 percent).

6. *Radiclib.* Accepts one or both liberal propositions but neither conservative proposition and noncommits the radical proposition. The mirror image of all *reactcon* curves. In our sample, 24 subjects (17.6 percent).

7. *Radical.* Accepts the radical proposition, rejects or noncommits the reactionary proposition. The mirror image of all *reactionary* curves. In our sample, 14 subjects (10.3 percent).

We validated the category system with an independent sample of upper-class students in a group discussion class. All 35 students taking the test fit the category system (3 skeptics, 9 radicals, 10 radiclibs, 13 liberals). We suggest that a subject who does not fall into one of the categories is suspect either on the basis of inattentiveness to the test or of gross abnormality in his judgments. In fact, we suspect our single undecided extremist on one or the other of these bases.

Once subjects are placed in categories, at least two possibilities exist for scoring. One is to devise a scale of "radicalism." Such a score might assign, as we have done (as shown on page 306), a score of 1 to reactionary; 2 to reactcon; 3 to conservative; 4 to the undecided categories (skeptic, ambivalent, undecided extremist); 5 to liberal; 6 to radiclib; and 7 to radical.

We tried to determine whether the radicalism scores are meaningful by correlating them with semantic differential attitudes expressed toward the concepts A SYSTEM IN WHICH ALL GRADES ARE PASS-FAIL and A SYSTEM IN WHICH ALL GRADES ARE A-B-C-D-F. If the radicalism scores signified what we thought they did, then correlation with the first concept should be positive, with the second, negative. As a point of comparison, we also correlated attitudes toward a pass-fail system with attitudes toward an A-B-C-D-F system. Table 5 shows these correlations. Although all three correlations are in the expected direction and statistically significant (.05 level), none is especially high. Still, the radicalism correlation with attitudes toward an A-B-C-D-F system is slightly higher than the correlation of the two attitudes with each other, an encouraging result as far as the radicalism score is concerned.

Table 5
CORRELATIONS AMONG RADICALISM SCORES AND TWO ATTITUDE TESTS

	Attitude Toward P-F	Attitude Toward A-B-C-D-F
Radicalism	.46	−.36
Attitude toward P-F		−.32

Table 6
CORRELATIONS AMONG RADICALISM SCORES AND TWO ATTITUDE TESTS
EXCLUDING LIBERALS AND CONSERVATIVES

	Attitude Toward P-F	Attitude Toward A-B-C-D-F
Radicalism	.72	−.47
Attitude toward P-F		−.42

It occurred to us that the correlations might be low as a function of the demonstrated tendency for those identified as liberals and conservatives on the social judgment test to reject statements in which one system or the other is "required." Since the relevant attitude concepts concerned systems where "all grades" would be one kind or the other, we thought that liberals and conservatives might reject both concepts equally (by expressing negative attitudes), thus attenuating the correlation with the social judgment test. We, therefore, carried out another set of post hoc correlations, this time eliminating from the sample all those identified as liberals or conservatives on the social judgment test. Table 6 shows these correlations. The procedure had the effect of raising all correlations, which again are all significant statistically. The correlation of radicalism with attitude toward a pass-fail system is a most satisfactory .72. Again, correlations involving the radicalism score are higher than the one in which attitudes toward the two concepts are correlated with each other.

We decided that this correlational evidence was strong enough to justify our applying the analysis of variance statistic to radicalism scores. This analysis is reported in a later section.

The second alternative for analysis of the radicalism scores is to collapse categories in such a way that cells are sufficiently populated to apply the chi square statistic. This we did, collapsing the nine categories into three: I (radical, radiclib, liberal); II (skeptic, ambivalent, undecided extremist); and III (conservative, reactcon, reactionary).

Attitude tests. A number of concepts were tested against the semantic differential type seven-level evaluative scales fair/unfair, good/bad, valuable/worthless, and pleasant/unpleasant. A subject's attitude for each concept tested could range from 4 (very negative) to 28 (very positive). The two concepts relevant to the paradox hypothesis were the two already mentioned, A SYSTEM IN WHICH ALL GRADES ARE PASS-FAIL and A SYSTEM IN WHICH ALL GRADES ARE A-B-C-D-F. For general interest value, we also analyzed attitudes toward THE SPEECH YOU JUST HEARD (except for the control group, which did not fill out those scales) and CURRICULUM COMMITTEE—DEPARTMENT OF SPEECH AND DRAMATIC ART, the alleged source of the messages and the questionnaire.

Belief tests. Two Likert-type scales were used on which a subject could score from 1 (strongly disagree) to 7 (strongly agree). The propositions tested were: (1) "A system in which all grades are P-F is preferable to one in which all grades are A-B-C-D-F." (2) "A system in which there are both A-B-C-D-F and P-F grades is preferable to either a system which is only P-F or only A-B-C-D-F."

Separate analyses of variance were executed for each of the four attitude tests and each of the two belief tests.

Subjects

The 137 subjects (less for some analyses because of failure to fill out all tests) comprised eight second-semester classes in the Rhetoric (freshman speech and composition) Program at the University of Iowa. Intact classes were randomly assigned to the four conditions, two classes in each: *radical* message, *reactionary* message, *paradoxical* message, and *control* (no message).

Hypotheses

The general hypothesis was that subjects in the paradox condition would reveal more uncertainty than subjects in any of the other conditions. Operationally:

1. For the social judgment test, subjects in the paradox condition will be more nearly neutral (4) on the radicalism scale and will be more likely to fall into category II (skeptics, ambivalents, undecided extremists) than subjects in any other condition.

2. For the attitude tests, subjects in the paradox condition will be more nearly neutral (16) toward the two relevant concepts (A SYSTEM IN WHICH ALL GRADES ARE PASS-FAIL and A SYSTEM IN WHICH ALL GRADES ARE A-B-C-D-F) than subjects in any other condition.

3. For the belief tests, subjects in the paradox condition will be more nearly neutral (4) toward the two propositions tested than subjects in any other condition.

RESULTS

Social Judgment Test

Neither the analysis of variance of radicalism scores nor the chi square test of categories across conditions was statistically significant. Table 7 shows the means across conditions for radicalism, Table 8 the frequencies in the various cells for the chi square test. Both tables reflect the very high proportion across all conditions of liberals, individuals who reject both extremes, accept one or both liberal propositions, and reject or noncommit both conservative propositions. Since the analyses lack statistical significance, they do not support hypothesis (1), though the apparent pattern among the radicalism means shows the paradox condition slightly closer to neutrality than the other three conditions.

Table 7
MEAN RADICALISM ACROSS CONDITIONS*

Paradox	Radical	Reactionary	Control
4.7	5.1	4.8	5.2

*$F = 1.17$; df $= 3,135$; p $> .05$.

Table 8
FREQUENCIES WITHIN CATEGORIES ACROSS CONDITIONS*

Category	Paradox	Radical	Reactionary	Control
I (radical, radiclib, liberal)	21	33	21	27
II (skeptic, ambivalent, undecided extremist)	5	5	7	3
III (conservative, reactcon, reactionary)	5	4	3	3

*Chi square $= 3.75$; df $= 6$; p $> .05$.

Attitude Tests

The two semantic differential type tests relevant to the hypothesis were for the concepts A SYSTEM IN WHICH ALL GRADES ARE PASS-FAIL and A SYSTEM IN WHICH ALL GRADES ARE A-B-C-D-F. Attitudes toward two other concepts were also analyzed for their general interest value: CURRICULUM COMMITTEE—DEPARTMENT OF SPEECH AND DRAMATIC ART (the alleged source) and THE SPEECH YOU JUST HEARD (for all except the control condition). Table 9 shows means for all concepts across conditions.

Table 9
MEAN ATTITUDES TOWARD VARIOUS CONCEPTS ACROSS CONDITIONS

Concept	Condition			
	Paradox	Radical	Reactionary	Control
System in which all grades are pass-fail	16.13*	20.17**	17.52	17.55
System in which all grades are A-B-C-D-F	12.06	9.12	10.58	10.97
Curriculum Committee— Dept. of Speech and Dramatic Art	16.93	16.15	17.45	16.72
The speech you just heard	18.74*	20.55*	15.00**	

*Means designated by an unequal number of asterisks in the same line differ significantly from each other (.05 level).

The analysis of attitudes toward A SYSTEM IN WHICH ALL GRADES ARE PASS-FAIL revealed significant differences ($F = 2.79$; $df = 3,132$; $p < .05$). Although Scheffé tests showed no significant differences among individual means, it is safe to say that subjects in the radical condition were more favorable toward the concept than subjects in the paradox condition. Subjects who heard the reactionary message and subjects in the control condition are midway between and their means are nearly identical. This analysis supports hypothesis (2), that the mean for subjects in the paradox condition would be more nearly neutral than for subjects in the other conditions, since "ideal" neutrality would be indicated by a score of 16.00.

Mean scores on the concept A SYSTEM IN WHICH ALL GRADES ARE A-B-C-D-F show a pattern which also supports that hypothesis, but the differences among means did not quite reach significance (F = 2.35; df = 3,133; p < .10). For that concept, the paradox mean of 12.06 more nearly approaches ideal neutrality (16.00) than any of the other means.

Attitudes expressed toward the alleged source of the messages, CURRICULUM COMMITTEE—DEPARTMENT OF SPEECH AND DRAMATIC ART, did not differ significantly across conditions (F = .68). Significant differences were found across conditions for the concept THE SPEECH YOU JUST HEARD (F = 14.44; df = 2,101; p < .05). This analysis shows that the reactionary speech was considerably less favorably received than either the paradox or the radical speech. This is not surprising in view of subjects' negative predisposition toward the reactionary position as shown by the control group's performance on all tests.

Belief Tests

The Likert-type belief scales tested agreement or disagreement on a scale of 1–7 (a higher score indicating stronger agreement) with each of the statements "A system in which all grades are pass-fail is preferable to one in which all grades are A-B-C-D-F," and "A system in which there are both A-B-C-D-F and pass-fail grades is preferable to either a system which is only pass-fail or only A-B-C-D-F." Table 10 shows means for all conditions on both propositions.

Table 10
MEAN AGREEMENT WITH BELIEF PROPOSITIONS ACROSS CONDITIONS

	Condition			
Proposition	Paradox	Radical	Reactionary	Control
A system in which all grades are P-F is preferable to one in which all grades are A-B-C-D-F	3.87*	5.34**	4.26	4.33
A system in which there are both A-B-C-D-F and P-F grades is preferable to either a system which is only P-F or only A-B-C-D-F	5.97	5.12	6.23	6.12

*Means designated by an unequal number of asterisks in the same line differ significantly from each other (.05 level).

The analysis of variance for the first proposition showed significant differences across conditions (F = 3.68; df = 3,131; p < .05). Scheffé tests revealed that subjects in the radical condition were significantly more sympathetic to an exclusive pass-fail system than were those in the paradox condition. Subjects in the reactionary and control conditions were midway between and nearly identical. The now familiar pattern places subjects in the paradox condition closest to the ideal neutrality point, 4. This supports hypothesis (3).

The analysis of variance for the proposition supporting a mixed system did not quite reach significance (F = 2.59; df = 3,131; p < .10). In this case, the mean for the paradox condition was not closest to neutrality, that position being occupied by the radical condition. A moment's reflection, however, produces the conviction that the hypothesis was not well conceived for this proposition. The state of confusion we predicted for subjects in the paradox condition could well be indicated by agreement with a statement favoring a mixed system.

Discussion

This experiment tested the effects of a paradoxical message in a rhetorical context of the kind usually employed in studies of persuasion. Although no dramatic effects were found for the paradoxical message (or for either of the others), those analyses which revealed significant differences supported our hypothesis, which was that subjects exposed to paradox express their confusion by being more nearly neutral than subjects in the other conditions. We infer from these findings that the paradoxical message produced some uncertainty, a short-term effect compatible with the long-term effects of paradox observed by Watzlawick, Beavin, and Jackson.

Experimental tests of the long-term effects of paradox are obviously desirable, though difficult to design in a way that avoids the possibility of significant harm to subjects. In our study, paradox had its predicted (though weak) effect in spite of the ease with which subjects could ignore the paradox or escape its implications by resolving it on a higher conceptual level. It seems reasonable to assume in the absence of evidence to the contrary that if these avenues of avoidance were even partially closed (for example, by a manipulation of source credibility), the effects of paradox would be considerably more potent, possibly approaching even in an experimental, short-term exposure the schizophrenic-like reactions observed by the authors of *Pragmatics of Human Communication.*

NOTES AND REFERENCES

1. Erich Segal, *Love Story* (New York: New American Library, 1970), p. 29. The line is from the movie. In the book, Segal helps resolve the paradox by putting "right things" in single quotation marks and labeling the statement an "apparent paradox."

2. Peter DeVries, *Through the Fields of Clover* (Boston-Toronto: Little, Brown, 1959), p. 4.

3. Joseph Heller, *Catch-22* (New York: Dell, 1955), pp. 102–3.

4. Philip Roth, *Portnoy's Complaint* (New York: Bantam Books, 1967), pp. 13–17.

5. Two such parties, the Apathy Party and the Apathetic Party, competed with several others at the University of Iowa in the spring of 1971. Both lost the election but, of course, they could (and did) claim that their loss was a victory.

6. For example, see Joe McGinnis, *The Selling of the President, 1968* (New York: Pocket Books, 1969).

7. Paul Watzlawick, Janet Helmick Beavin, and Don D. Jackson, *Pragmatics of Human Communication* (New York: W. W. Norton and Company, 1967).

8. Kim Giffin and Bobby R. Patton, *Fundamentals of Interpersonal Communication* (New York: Harper and Row, 1971).

9. Watzlawick, Beavin, and Jackson, *Pragmatics,* p. 218.

10. Ibid.

11. Ibid.

12. Ibid., pp. 218–19.

13. We gratefully acknowledge the assistance of James J. Bradac of the University of Iowa in carrying out the statistical analyses.

14. For example, see William W. Wilmot, "A Test of the Construct and Predictive

Validity of Three Measures of Ego Involvement," *Speech Monographs,* 38 (August 1971):217–27.

15. For examples of a few such tests, see Dennis Stephen Gouran, "Variables Related to Consensus in Group Discussions of Questions of Policy," Ph.D. dissertation, University of Iowa, 1968.